A Century of Theological
and Religious Studies in Britain

A Century of Theological and Religious Studies in Britain

edited by
Ernest Nicholson, FBA

Published for THE BRITISH ACADEMY
by OXFORD UNIVERSITY PRESS

Oxford University Press, Great Clarendon Street, Oxford OX2 6DP

Oxford New York
Auckland Bangkok Bogotá Buenos Aires Cape Town Chennai
Dar es Salaam Delhi Hong Kong Istanbul Karachi Kolkata
Kuala Lumpur Madrid Melbourne Mexico City Mumbai Nairobi
São Paulo Shanghai Singapore Taipei Tokyo Toronto

British Library Cataloguing in Publication Data
Data available

ISBN 0–19–726305–4

Typeset in Times by
J & L Composition
Printed in Great Britain
on acid-free paper by
Antony Rowe Limited
Chippenham, Wiltshire

Contents

List of abbreviations

Notes on Contributors

James Barr, FBA held professorships in Old Testament at Princeton and Edinburgh, and was Professor of Semitic Languages at Manchester. He was Oriel Professor of the Interpretation of Holy Scripture at Oxford from 1976 to 1978 and was appointed Regius Professor of Hebrew in 1978. He retired in 1989 but continued teaching as Professor of Hebrew Bible at Vanderbilt University in Tennessee until 1998. Among the many books he has published recently are *Biblical Faith and Natural Theology* (1993), *The Concept of Biblical Theology* (1999) and *History and Ideology in the Old Testament* (2000).

Patrick Collinson, CBE, FBA, FAAH held appointments at Khartoum and King's College London, was professor successively at the University of Sydney, the University of Kent at Canterbury, and Sheffield University. He was Regius Professor of Modern History at Cambridge from 1988 to 1996. He is author of numerous books, articles and essays on aspects of the Reformation and on the religious, social, cultural and political history of England in the later sixteenth and early seventeenth centuries. His books include *The Elizabethan Puritan Movement* (1967, 1990), *The Religion of Protestants: The Church in English Society 1559–1625* (1982) and, most recently, *Elizabethans* (2003), and *The Reformation* (2003).

Martin Goodman, FBA is Professor of Jewish Studies at the University of Oxford, a Fellow of Wolfson College and of the Oxford Centre for Hebrew and Jewish Studies. He has written widely on both Jewish and Roman history including, for example, *Mission and Conversion* (1993), and *The Roman World 44BC–AD180* (1997). He is editor of *Jews in the Graeco-Roman World* (1998) and *The Oxford Handbook of Jewish Studies* (2002).

William Horbury, FBA is Professor of Jewish and Early Christian Studies at the University of Cambridge and a Fellow of Corpus Christi College, Cambridge. He has written on ancient Judaism, the New Testament and early church, the history of biblical study and the history of Jewish–Christian relations. His publications include *Jews and Christians in Contact and*

Controversy (1998), *Jewish Messianism and the Cult of Christ* (1998), *Christianity in Ancient Jewish Tradition* (1999), and, with David Noy, *Jewish Inscriptions of Graeco-Roman Egypt* (1992).

David Luscombe, FBA was Fellow successively of King's College, Cambridge and Churchill College, Cambridge before being appointed Professor of Medieval History at Sheffield University where he was also Pro-Vice-Chancellor from 1990 to 1994. From 1995 to 2000 he held a Leverhulme Personal Research Professorship. He has written extensively on the history of thought and religion in the Middle Ages. Among his recent books are *Medieval Thought* (1997) and *The Twelfth-Century Renaissance: Monks, Scholars and the Shaping of the European Mind* (in Japanese, 2000).

Ernest Nicholson, FBA was Lecturer at Trinity College, Dublin and subsequently at Cambridge before becoming Oriel Professor of the Interpretation of Holy Scripture at Oxford and Fellow of Oriel College in 1979. He became Provost of Oriel in 1990 and has been Pro-Vice-Chancellor of the University since 1993. He is the author of a number of books in Old Testament studies including, most recently, *The Pentateuch in the Twentieth Century: The Legacy of Julius Wellhausen* (1998).

Jane Shaw is Dean of Divinity, Chaplain and Fellow of New College, Oxford. She is a graduate of Oxford, Harvard and the University of California, Berkeley. Her research is in modern ecclesiastical history, especially the eighteenth century, and her book *Miracles in Enlightenment England* will shortly be published by Yale University Press. She co-directs, with Professor Christopher Rowland, The Prophecy Project, a research project based at the University of Oxford that studies modern prophecy movements and their antecedents.

Stewart Sutherland (Lord Sutherland of Houndwood), FBA has been President of the Royal Society of Edinburgh since 2002. Prior to that he was Professor of the History of the Philosophy of Religion at King's College, London from 1977 to 1985. He was appointed Principal of King's College in 1985 and was Vice-Chancellor of London University from 1990 to 1994. He was Principal and Vice-Chancellor of the University of Edinburgh from 1994 to 2002. Among his publications are *Atheism and the Rejection of God* (1977), *The Philosophical Frontiers of Christian Theology* (1983) and *Faith and Ambiguity* (1984).

Keith Ward, FBA taught Philosophy at the Universities of Glasgow, St Andrews and Cambridge, before becoming Professor of the History and Philosophy of Religion at King's College, London. He was Regius Professor of Divinity at the University of Oxford and Canon of Christ Church from 1991 to 2003. He has published extensively in the philosophy of religion and on Christian doctrine, including, most recently, his four-volume comparative theology, *Religion and Revelation* (1994), *Religion and Creation* (1996), *Religion and Human Nature* (1998) and *Religion and Community* (2000).

Maurice Wiles, FBA was Professor of Christian Doctrine at King's College, London from 1967 to 1970 and Regius Professor of Divinity and a Canon of Christ Church, Oxford from 1970 to 1991. He has published extensively on patristic studies and modern doctrine, including, for example, *The Making of Christian Doctrine* (1967) and *Archetypal Heresy: Arianism through the Centuries* (1996). His book on *Faith and the Mystery of God* was awarded the Collins Biennial Religious Book Award in 1983.

Rowan Williams, FBA was University Lecturer in Divinity at Cambridge and Dean of Clare College from 1980 to 1986. He was Lady Margaret Professor of Divinity and Canon of Christ Church, Oxford from 1986 to 1992 when be became Bishop of Monmouth. He was appointed Archbishop of Canterbury in 2002. Among his many publications are *Arius: Heresy and Tradition* (1987) and *Sergii Bulgakov: Towards a Russian Political Theology* (1999). He was joint editor of *The New Dictionary of Pastoral Studies* (2002).

Preface and acknowledgements

This volume of essays was commissioned by the Theology and Religious Studies Section of the British Academy to mark the Academy's centenary in 2002. I am indebted to a number of colleagues for their help and advice throughout the preparation of the volume, and especially to Oliver O'Donovan, Diarmaid MacCulloch, John Barton, Jeremy Catto, Hugh Williamson and John Emerton. I have had the good fortune of a most cooperative band of contributors. The copy-editor of the volume, Susan Milligan, came to my rescue on many matters. I am, as ever, indebted also to the unstinting help of my Personal Assistant, Yvonne Scott, and Secretary, Jenny Savin.

William Horbury's essay when completed was rather longer than either he had intended or the Editor had prescribed! Upon reading it, however, it seemed preferable to publish it unabridged, since in describing developments in New Testament research it narrates a broad background of theological movements and controversy during the twentieth century that is also helpful in reading the other essays in the volume.

Ernest Nicholson
Provost's Lodgings
Oriel College
May 2003

INTRODUCTION

Theological and religious studies at the founding of the British Academy

ERNEST NICHOLSON

The rise of critical methods in British theology in the late nineteenth century

The theological controversies of the second half of the nineteenth century brought about a sea change in theological enquiry and scholarship in Great Britain. By the time the British Academy was founded in 1902 such a change was established, though there were was much turbulence to come. Indeed, the founding of the Academy itself came on a tide of profound change in British intellectual life during the second half of the nineteenth century.

The storm centre of theological controversy had been Oxford, which from the beginnings of the Oxford Movement in the 1830s was the arena of virtually unending division throughout the century. The clash of mentalities and the frequent bitterness of division at Oxford did not carry to Cambridge. Different reasons have been adduced for this, but of special significance and influence was the presence at Cambridge of the 'Triumvirate' of J. B. Lightfoot (1828–89), B. F. Westcott (1825–1901), and F. J. A. Hort (1828–1902) whose 'gentle criticism' combined with deep piety was a major influence in winning ground for the new methods of historical research in the biblical literature.[1] Lightfoot and Hort especially are sometimes accredited by historians with having been amongst the first in England to develop critical methods for the study of history.[2] It was at Cambridge too, again at the hands

[1] For a discussion of this see Peter Hinchliff, *God and History: Aspects of British Theology 1875–1914* (Oxford, 1992), esp. ch. 4, 'The Older the Better: Benson (and Lightfoot and Westcott)'.
[2] See Hinchliff, *God and History*, pp. 74–5.

of Lightfoot and Hort, that German New Testament scholarship was thoroughly discussed, and the radical conclusions of the 'Tübingen School' in particular were effectively challenged and undermined, for Lightfoot's careful study of the Ignatian epistles in his *Apostolic Fathers* (1885) destroyed this 'school's' chronology of second-century Christianity, especially its late dating of the Gospels.

A major difference between Cambridge and Oxford was that irreconcilable opposition between personalities in Oxford contributed significantly to the clash between conservatism and the adoption of new methods and results of historical criticism and theological enquiry. There was the formidable presence until his death in 1882 of E. B. Pusey (1800–82), one of the founders of the Tractarian movement, who, unremittingly conservative, led the opposition to the rising 'liberal' challenge represented by an equally strong-minded Benjamin Jowett (1817–93), fellow of Balliol and subsequently Master of that College and the leader of the 'liberals'. It was Jowett who edited and published the volume *Essays and Reviews* (1860) that so shocked church opinion and gained for its contributors the description the *Septem contra Christum*. The volume signalled the advent of a new age in theological thought, but it took a generation of divisive debate, involving adversity and deprivation for some of the leading figures involved, as well as the concurrent development of other modernising intellectual trends, before the new temper of mind reflected by the authors of this volume took root in British theological and religious studies. Meanwhile the more conservative camp included some who notably advanced historical and biblical scholarship, for example William Stubbs, a founder of modern British medieval studies, and John Wordsworth (1843–1911), famous as editor of the Vulgate New Testament.

Pusey's death in 1882 undoubtedly marked the end of an era, and it has been claimed that with his passing the younger generation of Tractarians felt free to move into the modern age and to open up areas of thought, including the results of historical critical study of the Bible, which would hitherto have seemed a betrayal of the catholic movement within the Church of England. It was this new-found freedom, it is then suggested, that provided the climate in which this later generation of Tractarians published a few years later in 1889, under the editorship of Charles Gore (1853–1932), *Lux Mundi: A series of studies of the Religion of the Incarnation*, which shocked and saddened H. P. Liddon (1829–90), upon whom Pusey's mantle had fallen.

No doubt there would have been some feeling of emancipation among the younger generation of Tractarians released from the overbearing and intimidating persona of Pusey. However, the sophistication of the essays in *Lux Mundi* did not come out of a vacuum, but reflects an engagement with new ideas that began some years before the passing of Pusey. [3] Already in 1884 Liddon, in a letter to Henry Scott Holland (1847–1918), wrote: 'I have feared sometimes that the younger Churchmanship of Oxford was undergoing a silent but very serious change through its eagerness to meet modern difficulties and its facile adoption of new intellectual methods.'[4] Scott Holland himself was to be one of the contributors to *Lux Mundi* the publication of which, it was claimed, broke Liddon's heart and precipitated his death less than a year later. Gore later maintained that his own adoption of modern biblical criticism began as early as 1876 and, indeed, it seems likely that he had already been influenced in this direction by Westcott at Harrow and Jowett at Balliol. In short, *Lux Mundi* is 'better understood as effect rather than cause of a widespread change in attitude'.[5]

Lux Mundi was a prime indication that a new era of doctrinal reconstruction had now begun. It authors shared a common desire to grapple with the intellectual questions that Christians were having to face at the time, and they had the courage to treat contemporary secular thought as an ally rather than as an enemy. Their intention, declared in Gore's Preface to the book, was 'to put the Catholic faith in its right relation to modern intellectual and moral problems', reflecting the manifest fact that

> the epoch in which we live is one of profound transformation, intellectual and social, abounding in new needs, new points of view, new questions; and certain therefore to involve great changes in the outlying departments of theology, where it is linked on to other sciences, and to necessitate some general statement of its claim and meaning.

Indeed, by the 1880s one would have to have been in a state of denial not to acknowledge how far the new ideas were reshaping contemporary intellectual life, and the extent to which a completely new temper of mind was now becoming pervasive and irreversible. There had emerged a scientific and secular society. Historical method, with the inevitable relativism it brought with it, was fully accepted by the 1880s. The anthropological study of religion had entered a new and modern phase with the work of E. B. Tylor (1832–1913) and others,[6] and the 'comparative study of religion' entered a period of extensive research in the work of Friedrich Max Müller (1823–1900), who in 1875

---

[3] For the background to the *Lux Mundi* essays see Hinchliff, *God and History*, ch. 5, 'Separate Spiritual Truth: The Essays in *Lux Mundi*'.

[4] S. Paget (ed.), *H. S. Holland: Memoir and Letters* (London, 1921), p. 112.

[5] Hinchliff, *God and History*, p. 99.

[6] For a convenient survey see Edmund Leach, 'Anthropology of Religion: British and French Schools', in Ninian Smart, John Clayton, Steven Katz and Patrick Sherry (eds.), *Nineteenth Century Religious Thought in the West*, vol. 3, (Cambridge, 1985), pp. 215–62.

began his massive edition of *Sacred Books of the East*; James Frazer (1854–1941) published the first edition of *The Golden Bough* in 1890; William Robertson Smith (1846–94), who had famously fought and effectively won the victory for the liberty of historical criticism of the Bible in Scotland in 1876–81 (see below), delivered his *Lectures on the Religion of the Semites* in 1888–9 partly with the purpose of illuminating religious institutions and practices in the Old Testament in the light of other ancient Near Eastern religions, cults and customs. As a result of the new interest and research in these areas of study, the inherited belief in the absolute uniqueness of Christianity was qualified, whilst the affinities found between institutions, practices, and beliefs in the Bible and those of other religions raised the question whether the biblical description of the origin of cultic institutions and religious beliefs was a wholly God-given revelation.[7] In short, it was as though the momentum of intellectual change gathered more and more pace as the century approached its end.

Philosophical thought during the second part of the century contributed significantly to the new intellectual temper of the time, in this instance, however, as an ally of religious belief, not only in its profound interest in religion but also in its social ethic and in its stance against the growing threat of a purely materialistic interpretation of the world. This was the British Idealist movement, which had its centre in Oxford but with strong representation also in Scotland (see below).[8] In part this movement was stimulated by the growing study of religion itself as a human phenomenon, as something, that is, that was apparently a fundamental and inalienable expression of humanity's spiritual consciousness. It created a frame of mind that sees religion as an interpretation of the world as well as of the church. As a movement it dominated philosophical thinking during the second half of the century. Its beginnings are associated with the teaching and influence of T. H. Green (1836–82), who had been a fellow of Balliol since 1860 and White's Professor of Moral Philosophy from 1878 until his untimely death in 1882. Green believed that modern people could neither do without religion nor do with it as it was. He set himself 'to present Christianity in a form in which what had been supposed to be history was converted into metaphysics, so that the religious ideas of the gospel might thus be protected from the attacks of historical criticism'.[9]

---

[7] See Bernard Reardon, *From Coleridge to Gore: A Century of Religious Thought in Britain* (London, 1971), pp. 8–9.

[8] For a brief history of this movement see H. D. Lewis, 'The British Idealists', in Smart *et al.*, *Nineteenth Century Religious Thought*, vol. 2, pp. 271–314, and Hinchliff, *God and History*, ch. 6, 'Cut Loose from History: British Idealism and the Science of Religion'.

[9] Hinchliff, *God and History*, p. 126.

He believed it possible to construct a Christian faith impervious to the contingencies of history or the uncertainties of historical criticism.

As though to counter the Idealist movement and a potent reminder that the British empiricist tradition in philosophy had by no means been eclipsed, however, there was a vigorous and widely influential agnostic movement in the second half of the century that added further to the sense of a new era of intellectual ferment and change.[10] Its leaders included H. Spencer, Leslie Stephen (1832–1904), and T. H. Huxley, the word 'agnostic' being coined by Huxley himself. Of course in part the surge and growth of agnosticism in the second half of the century was fomented by other intellectual developments of the time, including the assault on the veracity of the biblical creation narratives in the face of new geological evidence of the great age of the world, the impact of Darwin's *Origin of Species*, the rise of biblical criticism itself, and the emerging study of religions, both primitive and advanced, that introduced some element of relativism to the claims of Christianity. In turn, however, agnosticism, which appealed widely among the educated classes and in the universities, contributed to the growing climate of doubt and scepticism concerning the claims of traditional Christian teaching. Such was the influence of the movement that one commentator at the close of the century wrote of the two most characteristic attitudes of the latter half of the century as 'Evolutionism and Agnosticism'.[11] The 'agnostic controversy not only marked an especially important chapter in modern intellectual and religious history, in that the agnostic debates succeeded in posing serious problems for religious belief but also, and more importantly, helped to create a temper of mind antipathetic to *traditional* religious belief . . . This cast of mind was a significantly new social phenomenon.'[12]

The influence of Idealist thought upon the authors of *Lux Mundi* has often been noted, though also qualified.[13] As a volume of essays on the 'Religion of the Incarnation', *Lux Mundi* could scarcely be expected to abandon history for a philosophical 'immanentism'. For all that, however, Idealism, which after the death of Green was influentially led as a movement by Edward Caird (1835–1908; see below), was seen as an ally of Christian apologetic, both in being a fundamentally religious understanding of the world and in equipping

---

[10] For this see J. C. Livingston, 'British Agnosticism', in Smart *et al.*, *Nineteenth Century Religious Thought*, vol. 2, pp. 231–70.

[11] James Seth quoted in Livingston, 'British Agnosticism', p. 231.

[12] Livingston, 'British Agnosticism', p. 233.

[13] See Michael Ramsey, *From Gore to Temple* (London, 1960), pp. 9–10.

it in significant ways to meet the challenge of scientific materialism and naturalism.

In Oxford several appointments made in the 1880s brought change, including acceptance, albeit cautious, of 'Higher Criticism' which Pusey and Liddon had decried as the product of a bankrupt 'rationalism' that would be short-lived.[14] In 1882 S. R. Driver (1846–1914) succeeded Pusey as Regius Professor of Hebrew and soon showed himself to have been already won over by the new critical views, especially those of Julius Wellhausen. Driver was most responsible for introducing the critical methods and their results to British students, especially in his *Introduction to the Old Testament* (1891).[15] Such was his piety and personal appeal, combined with the exacting caution he exercised, that it was said of him that 'he taught the faithful criticism, and the critics faith.' Driver's appointment was followed shortly, in 1883, by that of William Sanday (1843–1920) to the Dean Ireland Professorship of the Exegesis of Holy Scripture in succession to Liddon. Sanday was at this stage of his life conservative in his approach to New Testament criticism—he later embraced a more liberal position—but was of a different temperament and disposition from his predecessor. Though he could not accept the main conclusions of German scholarship, he was none the less a conscientious student of it and his periodic reviews of it made him something of a bridge-builder, where Liddon had been, so to speak, a drawbridge. There followed in 1885 the appointment of T. K. Cheyne (1841–1915) to the Oriel Professorship of the Interpretation of Holy Scripture in succession to the conservative John Wordsworth. There could scarcely have been a more telling sign than this appointment of the changing intellectual climate at that time, for Cheyne was altogether a more radical scholar than either Driver or Sanday, one who was impatiently outspoken in his adoption and advocacy of modern critical views, and who had already in the 1870s declared himself in agreement with Bishop J. W. Colenso's (1814–83) analysis of the Hexateuch which had evoked such condemnation.

Other influential theologians in Oxford at this time who favoured the new methods and an engagement with modern movements of thought were the

---

[14] Of Wellhausen's *Prolegomena to the History of Israel*, Liddon wrote: 'I have read Wellhausen, and have a robust confidence that he will go the way of other Rationalists before him.' See J. O. Johnston, *Life and Letters of Henry Parry Liddon* (London, 1904), p. 361.

[15] See J. A. Emerton, 'Samuel Rolles Driver 1846–1914', in C. E. Bosworth (ed.), *A Century of British Orientalists 1902–2001* (Oxford, 2001), pp. 123–38, and 'S. R. Driver as an Exegete of the Old Testament', in C. Bultmann, W. Dietrich and C. Levin (eds.), *Vergegenwärtigung des Alten Testaments: Beiträge zur biblischen Hermeneutik. Festschrift für Rudolph Smend zum 70. Geburgstag* (Göttingen, 2002), pp. 285–95.

Free Church leader A. M. Fairbairn (1838–1912), who became Principal of Mansfield College Oxford, the Theological College of the Congregational Church, in 1886, and Edwin Hatch (1835–89) who was appointed Reader in Ecclesiastical History in 1884. Hatch was fully committed to the new historical approach to the development of the early church and its institutions, and in two controversial sets of lectures published as *The Organization of the Early Christian Churches* (1881), which Adolph Harnack translated into German, and *The Influence of Greek Ideas and Usages on the Christian Church* (1890) sought to trace the influence of Greek institutions and speculative thought upon the early church and the development of doctrine. In the second of these two series of lectures, which were the most controversial, Hatch argued that an originally simple primitive Christianity, best illustrated by the teaching of the Sermon on the Mount, had been transformed under the influence of Greek ideas into the post-Nicene elaborate dogmatic system. Such a view would not endure, but it is an indication of the change afoot in Oxford at that time. Hatch's celebrated *Concordance to the Septuagint*, which was unfinished at his early death in 1889, was completed by H. A. Redpath in 1897.

Fairbairn began his theological career as a minister of the Evangelical Union in Scotland, at one stage temporarily lost his faith but regained it through studies in Germany, and in 1877 moved to England to be Principal, first of dissenting Airedale Theological College at Bradford, and then of Mansfield College in 1886.[16] He was among the most zealous converts to historical criticism of his time, and believed that historical research had now made it possible to recover the history of the New Testament through its literature and that in this history the most important achievement was the recovery of the 'historical Christ'.[17] Thus, history rather than inherited doctrine now offered us the way to the knowledge of the historical Christ, that is, we come to doctrine only and properly by way of our historical knowledge of the historical Christ. The use of the word 'Christ' rather than 'Jesus' was fully intended, for though Fairbairn like other 'liberals' was confident that the new historical research would reveal the historical person of Jesus, unlike them 'he believed that that Jesus would be manifestly and unequivocally God.'[18] We may note that the conviction that history could achieve so much was quite the antithesis of the Idealist premise of the limitations that history placed upon a

---

[16] See Hinchliff, *God and History*, ch. 8, 'Knowing God in History'.

[17] His two most important studies were *Studies in the Philosophy of Religion and History* (London, 1876) and his magnum opus *The Place of Christ in Modern Theology* (London, 1883).

[18] Hinchliff, *God and History*, p. 187.

modern understanding of Christianity. What historical research might reveal about Jesus of Nazareth and the origins of 'Christology' was soon to become the subject of a debate that was to run through twentieth century New Testament research.

The same intellectual and cultural developments and changes that emerged in England in the late nineteenth century had their impact upon theological thinking in Scotland. There the 'trial' of William Robertson Smith, which followed his publication of articles in the *Encyclopaedia Britannica* in 1875 adopting the conclusions of recent German historical criticism of the Pentateuch, did more than the instigators of the case against him could have foreseen to bring about the acceptance of critical methods in biblical studies. The charge of heresy was brought against him in 1876 and although in the course of the lengthy procedures the indictment against him was abandoned, in its place there was finally a vote of no confidence in his worthiness to teach men preparing for the ministry of the church, and in June 1881 he was summarily dismissed from his professorship at the Free Church College at Aberdeen. Such was the manner in which, and the conviction with which, he defended himself, however, that he attracted widespread sympathy both in academic circles and in the church, not least among the students and young clergy whom he had taught. Even during the years of his trial he received requests to deliver, in Edinburgh and Glasgow, two popular series of lectures, which were subsequently published as *The Old Testament and the Jewish Church* (1881) and *The Prophets of Israel* (1882). At the cost of his Chair he had in effect won the victory for biblical criticism in Scotland. There were some skirmishes to come, but a new tolerance had been gained and the future was set in favour of the new ideas in biblical study.

Behind that victory, however, stood also Robertson Smith's teacher at New College Edinburgh, A. B. Davidson (1831–1902), who had introduced him to critical methods in biblical exegesis. Davidson has been described as having brought about by his writing but especially by his teaching a 'silent revolution': 'the adoption of a sound critical method in the study of the Old Testament and the presentation of biblical theology in a framework not of traditional dogmatics but of historical development'.[19] Though he did not become directly involved in the long drawn out proceedings against Robertson Smith in 1876–81,[20] Davidson 'by his moral weight was recognised as the real author of the victory which, at the loss of his own Chair,

---

[19] G. W. Anderson, 'Two Scottish Semitists', in *Supplements to Vetus Testamentum* 28 (Leiden, 1975), p. xvi.

[20] For some observations on this see Anderson, 'Two Scottish Semitists', pp. xviii–xix.

Smith won for Scotland'.[21] Davidson was a founding member of the British Academy, though he died just prior to the granting of its Royal Charter in 1902.

Others too contributed to the new intellectual climate in Scotland. Such were, for example, Robert Flint (1838–1910), professor of divinity at Edinburgh University, and John Caird (1820–89) and his younger brother Edward, professor of moral philosophy at Glasgow University from 1866 until 1893, when he became Master of Balliol College in succession to Benjamin Jowett. Flint was thoroughgoing in his philosophical commitment to reason as the test of belief, and wrote of the defence of theology on strictly rational grounds. Both the Cairds, but especially Edward, were the leaders of the newly emerged Idealist movement in Great Britain during the second half of the nineteenth century. The influence of both of them contributed more than any other single factor in creating a new climate of thought in Scotland and in bringing about change in Scottish theological thinking in their time.

The founding of the British Academy

The founding of the British Academy thus came at a propitious time in the development of intellectual change in Great Britain. There had also come about, as in the physical sciences (see below), a 'professionalism' in research and in the methods of research that could only be encouraged and advanced by the creation of an Academy that would bring together researchers in the diverse fields of the humanities. Further, the critical temper of the time, the new-found independence of thought, advances already perceived to have been made, a remarkable overlap in interests between theologians, biblical scholars, philosophers, historians, classicists, students of the study of religions, even the running debates between the protagonists of differing points of view—all this created a new ethos among those engaged in humanistic studies. It is a comment on our own age of increasingly narrow specialisation—even if inescapable because of the colossal expansion of knowledge in the century that has passed—that our forebears at that time were still much more broadly based in their interests within their individual fields of learning and, indeed, much more knowledgeable of other areas of scholarship, learning and research than we are. When it came, therefore, the idea of an

---

[21] The quote is from S. R. Driver's entry on William Robertson Smith in the *Dictionary of National Biography*.

Academy for humanistic learning and scholarship found a well of most willing support.

The idea of a British Academy arose at a meeting at Wiesbaden in October 1899 of representatives of European and American Academies, which resolved to form an International Association of Scientific and Literary Academies throughout the world.[22] In Great Britain the Royal Society, which had been founded in the seventeenth century, had for some time ceased to concern itself with areas of learning that we today refer to as 'the humanities', confining itself instead to the physical and natural sciences. From the 1840s onwards there emerged a distinctly scientific 'community' that increasingly sought and gradually achieved self-definition within Great Britain.[23] In part this had come about as a result of the growing conflict between science and the claims of religion, in part also through an increasing 'professionalisation' of science. Already in 1847 the Royal Society had reformed the rules for membership to favour not only a smaller Society but also one that would henceforth be composed only of practising scientists.

As a result of the meeting in Wiesbaden, the Royal Society in November of 1899 addressed itself to this problem, and in a letter to a number of distinguished scholars (Lord Acton, Richard Jebb and Henry Sidgwick) invited them to make suggestions about the formation of a body that would represent those subjects which are not represented by the membership of the Royal Society. Two suggestions were offered on how this might be achieved: (a) by an enlargement of the scope of the Royal Society so as to include the humanities; or, alternatively, (b) to support the formation of a body external to itself in the attempt to acquire a new Charter.

This proposal was brought to a full meeting of the Fellows of the Royal Society in May 1901, who voted against enlarging the scope of the Society to embrace new areas of study, whilst sympathising with the desire to secure corporate organisation for these subjects. Following this, those whom the Council of the Royal Society had invited to report to it concerning the issue raised at the Wiesbaden meeting resolved with others at a meeting in June to take independent action to form such a new organisation and to this end to petition for a Royal Charter. They constituted themselves as a provisional 'General Committee' with a sub-committee to deliberate and report on how the proposal

---

[22] Sir Frederic Kenyon published an account of the founding of the Academy under the title *The British Academy: The First Fifty Years* (Oxford, 1952).

[23] See Frank M. Turner 'The Victorian Conflict between Science and Religion: A Professional Dimension', in his *Contesting Cultural Authority: Essays in Victorian Intellectual Life* (Cambridge, 1993), pp. 171–200.

for an Academy could best be advanced. In November 1901 the 'General Committee' decided to invite a number of scholars to become the first members of a new body to be called 'The British Academy for the Promotion of Historical, Philosophical, and Philological Studies'.

In December the new body met and drew up a Petition to the King in Council for the Grant of a Royal Charter and was strongly supported by the Royal Society. On 8 August 1902 the Royal Charter was granted.

Accompanying the petition for the Charter was a list of forty-eight members of the proposed new Academy whose names accordingly appear in the Charter of Incorporation. They included S. R. Driver, A. M. Fairbairn, R. Flint, James Frazer, Edward Caird, George Salmon (Provost of Trinity College, Dublin and a New Testament specialist), W. Sanday and H. B. Swete (1835–1917), who succeeded Westcott as Regius Professor of Divinity at Cambridge. A. B. Davidson, who had also been invited, had died before the petition had been submitted, and Bishop Westcott died before the invitation to him arrived. Henry Sidgwick and Lord Acton had also died. Others on the list were Sir Leslie Stephen, who had resigned his orders and became one of the leading agnostics of the time, and wrote on the inadequacy of religious thought in the eighteenth century in the face of the challenge of the Enlightenment (*History of English Thought in the Eighteenth Century*, 1876); James Ward (1843–1925), philosopher and psychologist, who, though he felt unable to continue his ministry in the Congregationalist Church, delivered two sets of Gifford Lectures against scientific naturalism published as *Naturalism and Agnosticism* (1899), and *The Realm of Ends, or Pluralism and Theism* (1911); A. J. Balfour (the statesman, later Earl Balfour, 1848–1930), who, like Ward, also wrote from the perspective of 'personal idealism' against materialist and naturalist philosophies of the time in *The Foundations of Belief* (1895) and in his Gifford Lectures published as *Theism and Humanism* (1914); T. W. Rhys Davids (1843–1922), Honorary Professor of Pali and Buddhist Literature at University College, London, 1882–1912, who was appointed in 1904 to the newly established professorship of comparative religion at Manchester University which he held until 1915; W. M. Ramsay (1851–1939), ancient historian who wrote much on the early church and on St Paul.

At meetings in the course of the year following the granting of the Charter, the members met to increase the membership, having agreed that the number of members should be limited to a maximum of 100. Among those elected in 1903 were F. G. (later Sir Frederick) Kenyon (1863–1952), classicist, who was also to make contributions to the study of the Septuagint text of the Old Testament and to New Testament textual criticism;

M. R. James (1862–1936), remembered among biblical scholars for his publication of *The New Testament Apocrypha* (and for his ghost stories!); J. Armitage Robinson (1858–1933), a New Testament and patristic scholar who also made valuable contributions to the history of the medieval abbey of Westminster and of medieval Somerset. The number of members before the first Ordinary Annual Meeting on 26 June 1903 was seventy. There were four Sections: I. History and Archaeology; II. Philology (Oriental, Biblical, Classical, Medieval, Modern); III. Philosophy (Logic, Psychology, Ethics, Metaphysics, etc.); IV. Jurisprudence and Economics.

The view ahead from 1902: changing agendas

The twentieth century was like all others in one important, if obvious, way: those who, like the founding Fellows of the British Academy, stood on its threshold could not have anticipated the unpredictable twists and turns and the cataclysmic events that time was to bring, and above all the appalling desolation that war was to inflict not far into the new century. The Boer war at the turn of the century brought some sense of disillusion with any breezy optimism in inevitable progress, and it is possible that some already feared that deteriorating relations between Britain and Germany could only end in conflict. But no one could have foreseen the carnage and horrifying loss and the shocking ravages of the First World War that began in 1914. Disillusionment with the optimism of the late nineteenth century was profound, and such was the change that this war effected in western thinking, and such the social, political, and moral upheavals and transformations that came in its grim wake, that it is commonplace in looking back to say that 1914 rather than 1900 marks the beginning proper of the twentieth century.

More immediately, however, at the turn of the century when the Academy was founded, agendas for the diverse subject areas of theological studies had already suggested themselves for both the short and medium term. There was continuing turbulence about the implications of biblical criticism for faith, and especially about critical work on the Gospels. In his contribution to *Lux Mundi* ('The Holy Spirit and Inspiration') Gore had largely confined himself to Old Testament criticism, with no allusion to the far-reaching implications of the application of similarly sharp, historical criticism of the Gospels. The Gospels were still viewed as the citadel itself, not least of all the fourth Gospel, which many scholars, including Sanday, still regarded as the work of the 'beloved disciple'. Thus in 1902 the assessment of scholarly views that seemed to conflict with church tradition on the New Testament books and

Christian origins was soon to be at the heart of the Roman Catholic Modernist controversy and its British ramifications, as William Horbury shows in his contribution to this volume (Chapter 2) and to which we will return below.

In philosophy, the agenda seemed assured for the Idealist movement, which dominated British philosophy in the second half of the nineteenth century, and had exercised such an influence upon theological thought. In the pre-First World War period, the extensive and powerful influence of Idealist philosophy was such that 'many of its practitioners came to believe that it was finally established as the philosophy of the future, allowing of refinements and new applications but no question of its fundamental principles. It had come to stay.'[24]

This was to turn out to be a short-lived conviction. In the twentieth century Idealism rapidly faded in mainstream philosophical circles, finding continuing exponents only at the margins or in the thinking of some theologians.[25] Historians of the subject list a number of reasons for this, but the most important factor in the discrediting of Idealist philosophy and in bringing about the subsequent widespread disregard of it, was the changed and charged intellectual temper that followed the ravages of the First World War. The aftermath was

> a deep sense of disillusionment with the bright, and often superficial, optimism of the late nineteenth century, summarized in a typically sententious way by a leading idealist teacher of the time in the words 'The universe is homeward bound'—all this brought into existence a much tougher temper and an extensive impatience with speculative thinking which could not, like science, be brought to the test of hard fact here and now.[26]

In short, it was no longer thought of as a world in which one could argue that the ideal was recognisable in the empirical.

There was a 'Revolution in Philosophy' that abandoned speculative thinking. The British empiricist tradition, whose founding figure was David Hume, reasserted itself, and analytical philosophy emerged as a significant movement within this tradition, with a preoccupation with language as the way in which philosophical questions were to be handled:

> Philosophers, like other writers, felt it was time they came back to earth, the poetry of Wilfred Owen, Siefgried Sassoon and Herbert Read replaced that of Rupert Brooke as fitting the mood of the time, the cynicism of Lytton Strachey found a ready response, and a realist movement in philosophy . . . found a more explicit and

---

[24] Lewis, 'The British Idealists', p. 271.

[25] Lewis, 'The British Idealists', provides a convenient summary.

[26] Lewis, 'The British Idealists', pp. 272–3.

more boldly acceptable expression in the work of Bertrand Russell and G. E. Moore and in due course of Wittgenstein. . . . With the popularizing of this new mood in the positivist work of the Vienna Circle and its exposition in A. J. Ayer's early masterpiece of exposition, his now celebrated *Language, Truth and Logic*, all metaphysical thinking fell under the general ban as literal nonsense in which no one could indulge and retain the respect of his philosophical colleagues generally.[27]

This 'revolution' in philosophy reset the agenda for much of the philosophy of religion for the remainder of the century. In Great Britain and in the United States of America there was decline of interest in European continental philosophy, and in its place there developed what has come to be known as 'Anglo-American' philosophy. Stewart Sutherland's chapter in this volume narrates the reassertion of the British empiricist tradition and the engagement between the philosophy of religion and this broad movement during the twentieth century.

The agenda for the study of religions, on which Keith Ward writes in this volume, was also to undergo substantial transformation during the twentieth century, not as a result of the war but because of intrinsic weaknesses in the subject as conceived of and studied in the late nineteenth century.[28] At that time it was theory-driven and highly speculative. There was virtually no fieldwork. Thus Frazer, the subject's most celebrated author internationally, carried out his research and wrote his renowned work, *The Golden Bough*, at Cambridge. A theory of the evolution of civilisation, usually a reflection or variation of Auguste Comte's so-called 'law of the three stages'—theology, metaphysics, scientific (or 'positive')—was imposed upon texts narrating ancient myths, religious rites, stories and customs. For Frazer, the stage-by-stage evolution was better formulated and understood as magic, religion and science: magic, the first stage, representing primitive society's endeavour through its magicians to exercise control over the ordered forces of nature; religion, which replaced magic, when societies came to believe in superhuman divine beings as those who had power over nature; and finally the arrival of modern scientific civilisation.

When therefore Frazer published the first two volumes of *The Golden Bough* in 1890—there followed ten further volumes—he hoped that he was helping to found a 'science of religions'. Religions and mythologies would be systematically categorised, traced to their origins in primitive human societies, and explained in such a way that science could now be seen as the

---

[27] Lewis, 'The British Idealists', p. 273.

[28] Edmund Leach, 'Anthropology of Religion', offers a lively discussion of the state of the anthropology of religion in the late nineteenth and early twentieth centuries.

proper intellectual replacement for religion. Just over a century later, as Keith Ward shows in Chapter 10, the study of religions looks very different. Virtually all scholars agree that Frazer's categorisations were naïve and Procrustean, and that he was mistaken in the presumption that the origins of religion can be scientifically discovered, and in thinking that religion can be explained as primitive science. The search for a 'grand narrative' of the rise and fall of religion has been abandoned in favour of detailed localised studies of particular religious practices and beliefs. The search for an 'essence of religion' has been abandoned in favour of attempts to set religious practices in the context of specific cultural forms of life. The conjectural histories of earlier anthropologists have been abandoned in favour of methods of participant observation and an attempt at value-neutrality in describing religious beliefs. In short, the original project of 'comparative religion', whether in its naturalistic, anti-religious form as in Frazer, or in a form that sought the spiritual essence of all religions, as in the work of scholars like Max Müller, came to nothing.

Religious studies is now a complex of cultural studies, history, theology, philosophy and anthropology, which embraces both adherents and opponents of specific religions. It is a focus of inter-disciplinary studies, rather than a distinct science. Its motto might be, 'Do not generalise, but discriminate.' Frazer and his colleagues thought they were founding a new science. They were wrong. But they did generate a discipline which has the capacity for extending awareness of the diverse human forms of life, for establishing more informed and nuanced views of religion, and for deconstructing the often dangerous generalisations about religion which form the rhetoric of much public discourse.

The impact of the First World War upon theological thought was not immediate. At the beginning of the century, as Rowan Williams shows in Chapter 8, English theology was dominated by a set of issues generated by the results of the critical approach to the Bible. There was a growing acknowledgement of the unavoidability of engagement with questions to do with the evolution of religious understanding in different phases of scriptural composition, and not just in the case of the Old Testament, but especially in the New Testament, with the challenges this posed for traditional Christology. In the period up to 1914 Christological controversy played a major part in theological debate.

Much immediate post-war British theology showed remarkably little of the war's effect, and interest in the 'neo-orthodox' theology deriving from Karl Barth was slow to come in the inter-war period. Only very gradually in those years, as Rowan Williams shows, did the new trends from continental Europe begin to make any impression. Perhaps post-war xenophobia was a factor in this. Edwin Hoskyns in Cambridge translated Barth's famous commentary on Romans in 1933, but it made little impact on a somewhat 'baffled English theological public', as Williams puts it. Grounds were being laid, however, notably by Scottish theologians, for a much greater degree of engagement with the theology of Barth, especially in Scotland, in the post-Second World War years when Edinburgh's theological faculty became a centre in the United Kingdom for Barthian theology, under the leadership of T. F. Torrance. In Glasgow University's faculty in the 1960s Bultmann became dominant under the leadership of Ronald Gregor Smith. By contrast there was no similar focus of interest in theologies of modern continental origin in England, where during the middle decades the liberal agenda continued, though the French revival of Thomist theology made some impact not only upon English Roman Catholics but to some extent also in Anglican circles through the work of E. L. Mascall.

The more recent shifts and changes of theology during the second half of the century are sketched by Rowan Williams, including those arising from and stimulated by major and well-remembered landmarks such as *Soundings* (1962) and Bishop John Robinson's controversial *Honest to God* (1963), which signalled an unease about doctrinal orthodoxies, and *The Myth of God Incarnate* (1977), which focused upon a rethinking of classical Christological language. There has followed a variety of 'movements', centring upon liberation theology, feminist theology, approaches centred upon 'post-modernist' ideas, a vigorous critique of liberal methodology from John Milbank and a group of younger theologians who style their theology as 'Radical Orthodoxy', which in turn has evoked a response by those remaining in the liberal tradition.

In Old Testament studies the agenda at the beginning of the century continued to be dominated by source analysis, but other long-term tasks claimed increasing attention, as James Barr's comprehensive chapter shows. Among these was much-needed work on the text of the Hebrew Bible as well as on the other ancient versions of the Old Testament. Archaeological work on sites in the Holy Land, already begun in the latter part of the nineteenth century, called for an accelerated programme of fresh work, which, though interrupted by the First World War, moved into one of its most important and productive stages in the decades that followed. There was much new work also on lexicography and comparative linguistics. Serendipity played its part in yielding such momentous finds as the Ugaritic texts and language, discovered and deciphered in the late twenties onwards, and the Dead Sea Scrolls beginning in 1947, the former shedding so much light upon the religion and mythology of Syria-Palestine in the late Bronze Age, the latter providing invaluable materials for the study of the text of the Hebrew Bible as well as of Second Temple Judaism. Alongside these finds came increasing knowledge of the history, religion and institutions of the Mesopotamian empires as well as of ancient Egypt.

The inter-war years in German scholarship brought a number of new insights, and the work of Albrecht Alt and his most distinguished students Gerhard von Rad and Martin Noth introduced new ways of understanding pre-monarchic Israel and the origin of some central features of Israelite religion and institutions, as well as, for example, offering new approaches to the foundations of the Pentateuch or Hexateuch and the composition of the historical books. There were in all this important conclusions concerning, for example, the origin and nature of the covenant in Israelite religion as well as other cultic and legal institutions. In addition, these years between the wars saw a rebirth of Old Testament theology. W. Eichrodt's celebrated *Theologie des Alten Testaments* (vol. 1, 1933; vol. 2, 1935; vol. 3, 1939) was an auspicious beginning to a new phase in the study of Old Testament theology that was to burgeon in the post-Second World War period.

It was not until after the Second World War, however, that British scholarship took up and assessed these new approaches and results. In the United States also there was acceptance of much of the results of the so-called 'Alt-Noth School', though also controversy, especially on the contribution that archaeology could make in recovering the history of Israelite origins, here the 'Alt-Noth School' arguing a minimalist view as against the 'Albright School' which made larger claims for the light that the findings of archaeology could shed upon that history. Already in the 1960s, however, came the beginnings of a 'revisionist' period that questioned much of the agreed results of the middle decades of the century and has led to new debates on such issues as the dating of the sources of the Pentateuch, and during the last years of the century a vigorous controversy about whether there ever was a pre-exilic Israelite or a Judaean state such as the historical books of the Old Testament narrate.[29] All this, as well as the increasing interest in different literary methods of reading the Old Testament, including approaches from a feminist perspective or from the perspective of liberation theology, has opened up new debates for the years ahead, as Professor Barr shows.

In New Testament studies two long-term trends will have been clear to founding Fellows of the Academy, as William Horbury describes in Chapter 2.

---

[29] For a characteristically incisive and lively review of recent trends such as this see Professor Barr's *History and Ideology in the Old Testament: Biblical Studies at the End of a Millennium* (Oxford, 2000).

One was the already time-honoured effort to interpret the New Testament in its Jewish setting, with special reference to rabbinic literature and to the geography, antiquities and archaeology of Palestine. In was in 1902 that Sanday himself visited Palestine and wrote on the identification of sacred sites of the Gospels, but he had long been active in promoting access to rabbinic and Jewish studies in New Testament scholarship, notably through republication and revision of work by Alfred Edersheim.

Jewish aspects of New Testament interpretation were much considered in British scholarship and developed during the opening decades of the century, especially through the work of such Jewish scholars as C. G. Montefiore, Israel Abrahams, Adolph Büchler and H. Loewe. Non-rabbinic aspects of Judaism were studied by scholars in the Academy such as M. R. James, F. C. Burkitt (1864–1935), and R. H. Charles (1855–1931), who were pioneers in the study of Jewish and Christian apocalypses.

A further trend already manifest at the turn of the century was religio-historical, stimulated in part by the German History of Religions School, in part also by the work of James Frazer outside the biblical field. Interest tended to concentrate on the Greek and Roman world and on the indebtedness of biblical tradition to gentile thought and religion. Sanday had expressed reserve at Hellenistic interpretation of the New Testament, but in the Academy it was developed from varying points of view, notably by another founding Fellow, Sir William Ramsay, with special reference to Paul, and in a later generation by A. D. Nock, C. H. Dodd (1884–1973) and Wilfred Knox. In the 1930s onwards, however, this Hellenistic trend in New Testament scholarship was gradually overtaken by the long-standing but now intensified concern of New Testament interpreters with Jewish sources. As can be seen in the work of Dodd and Knox, those Greek Jewish writings which had been studied with a special eye to the Hellenistic world were now also widely viewed together with rabbinic and apocalyptic texts as witnesses to Judaism. In addition to William Horbury in Chapter 2, Martin Goodman considers this development in Chapter 3.

The future significance of some other trends that were already affecting early twentieth-century New Testament work may have been harder to foresee at the turn of the century. One trend that very soon became clear, however, was the significance of eschatological hope as determinative for the mind of Jesus and Paul. This approach was famously prominent in Albert Schweitzer's celebrated *Quest of the Historical Jesus* (1906) as well as in the work of Johannes Weiss and, in England, of F. C. Burkitt. It conflicted with the liberal emphasis on the timeless value of the teaching of Jesus which was represented at the beginning of the century by Adolph Harnack.

Another trend, which Professor Horbury describes, led away from the source criticism of the Gospels that had reached its high point in British research in the first couple of decades of the century, especially in the work of B. H. Streeter (1874–1937). It could seem at this stage that a main task was now to build upon the results of source analysis for a life of Jesus. At just the same time, however, there was an intensified interest in the form criticism of the Gospels and Epistles. This critical method was often and influentially coupled with doubts on the recoverability of any outline of the life of Jesus, especially in the work of Rudolph Bultmann. Within the Academy in the mid-twentieth century, C. H. Dodd then C. F. D. Moule developed form criticism in a different direction, towards the discernment of continuities between Jesus and the church, but an approach closer to that of Bultmann was represented by R. H. Lightfoot (1883–1953), and there was a vigorous revival of New Testament as well as Old Testament theology.

Discoveries in the middle years of the century, including the paintings of biblical scenes in the Dura-Europos synagogue, and the Dead Sea Scrolls mentioned above, gave added impetus to the intensification of a concern with the New Testament in its Jewish setting which has continued to be central in exegesis. The Nag Hammadi Gnostic papyri, another mid-century find, were correspondingly studied for their Jewish as well as Hellenic and New Testament connections. The later years of the century brought a renewal of the quest of the historical Jesus, a revived interest in Hellenism, and a re-kindled awareness of the importance for the New Testament of studies in literature, society and religion as well as theology.

The centrality of ancient Jewish literature in New Testament interpretation brings us conveniently to Martin Goodman's chapter on 'Early Judaism'. And here too there was great change in the course of the twentieth century. When the century began, interest in early Judaism in British scholarship was motivated largely by the light it could shed upon Jesus and early Christianity. A century later this remains the case among many scholars and, indeed, has been in some measure increased by awareness of the Jewishness of Jesus and many aspects of the early church. There has come also, however, among a growing number of scholars within Jewish studies an interest in early Judaism in the light of the history of Judaism as a whole. Classicists too have become keenly interested in this field of specialisation, because of the insights into themes of change, acculturation and resistance which are prominent issues elsewhere in the Mediterranean world in the late Hellenistic and early Roman imperial period.

The pronounced change in the study of early Judaism over the century has been driven in significant ways by the remarkable new finds, which in turn have prompted new avenues of research, as Martin Goodman shows. These include the texts of the Cairo Geniza, Egyptian texts from *c*.610–390 deriving from a Jewish military garrison in Elephantine, still more Egyptian Jewish papyri from later periods, the Qumran scrolls and additional material discovered in the Judaean desert in the years following the initial finds in the caves by the Dead Sea. Our knowledge of Diaspora Judaism has also been illumined by archaeological finds such as the synagogue at Dura-Europos. These many discoveries have revolutionised our knowledge of early Judaism. For example, the new perspectives that have arisen from the study of these new sources have increased uncertainty about aspects of Judaism that scholars a century ago thought they had mapped out precisely. Thus, much of the Jewish literature composed before 70 CE was ascribed to Essene, Pharisee or Sadducee authors. As Professor Goodman comments, it is difficult to imagine such confidence today.

The abundant new materials for the study of Second Temple Judaism and early Rabbinic Judaism have led to much new research in non-normative Judaism, a subject heralded early in the century by R. H. Charles's monumental edition of the *Apocrypha and Pseudepigrapha of the Old Testament* (2 vols., 1913). The Dead Sea Scrolls themselves provided perhaps the best known insight into a particular brand of non-normative Judaism. Indeed the study of the Scrolls, as Goodman points out, has become a separate subdiscipline of the study of early Judaism during the past half-century or so. Jewish mysticism is a further manifestation of non-normative Judaism that has also received much attention recently.

Other issues of current debate are, for example, the effects of the surrounding culture upon early Judaism, and especially the extent to which Judaism was influenced by Hellenism. A major new trend, however, since the 1970s has been the endeavour to integrate the religion of Jesus and, to a lesser extent, Paul into the general picture of early Judaism itself. Here one thinks immediately of the contributions of G. Vermes on the Jewishness of Jesus and those of E. P. Sanders both on Jesus and on Paul. Finally, as Goodman points out, in recent years has come the suggestion that such integration of Jewish and Christian history should go still further, and that 'the parting of the ways' between Judaism and Christianity should not be seen as having occurred until the time of Constantine.

Modern patristic study began in the nineteenth century when the new critical historical methods of studying the Church Fathers gradually superseded traditional apologetic interpretation. There was a need for accessible texts and these were published through the remarkable industry of the French priest J.-P. Migne, whose *Patrologia Latina* and *Patrologia Graeca* were a significant first landmark.[30] They did not provide, however, the sort of critically established texts that scholars require. Quite apart from this, many new texts were being discovered and, as Maurice Wiles shows in Chapter 4, fresh finds from archaeological excavations in the twentieth century added further and significantly to the materials for study. From the latter part of the nineteenth century new critical editions of texts were undertaken, mostly through the sponsorship of the Vienna and Berlin Academies.

The importance of the Fathers was second nature to Anglican theologians who made their own distinctive contribution. The *Journal of Theological Studies* was founded in 1899 partly for the purpose of being a journal for the publication of patristic studies and texts, whilst just a few years later a project for the compilation of a lexicon of Patristic Greek was launched, though it took many years until its completion and publication under the editorship of Geoffrey Lampe (1912–80).

A creative and productive British contribution to patristic studies, one that arose from interest in the subject but in turn enhanced study and research in the subject internationally, was and remains the Oxford Congress for Patristic Studies launched in 1951 by F. L. Cross. The Congress, which continues to meet every four years, has been a major stimulus of research and publication.

Among the most significant changes during the century, however, was the transformation of patristic studies from being very largely a preserve of theologians and church historians to include students of the later classical ages. Further, from the 1960s onwards classical scholars have taken an interest in later periods, and under the powerful influence of scholars such as Arnoldo Momigliano and Peter Brown there has emerged as a special and thriving field of research the period now commonly referred to as 'Late Antiquity'. In addition, the study of Judaism both during and beyond the patristic period proper, has brought to light varied forms of Judaism as well as the continued interaction between Judaism and Christianity, and these developments have likewise opened up new subjects for research.

At the beginning of the twentieth century there was scarcely a theologian in academic work in Great Britain who could not turn to patristic texts, whether the Latin or the Greek Fathers, with ease, and such was the importance attached to the study of the Church Fathers that, as Professor Wiles writes in Chapter 4, H. B. Swete was concerned to assist the ordinary clergy to study the patristic writings. Whilst writing of the significant British contribution to patristic studies during the twentieth century,

---

[30] For an attractive account of Migne, emphasising not just his shortcomings but his services to scholarship, see Owen Chadwick, *A History of the Popes 1830–1914* (Oxford, 1998), pp. 539–40.

however, Professor Wiles expresses concern that the prospects for maintaining this British tradition of patristic study and research are not encouraging. And he ends on a note of anxiety about how well it will prove possible to sustain the British contribution to this highly important field of research in this new century.

William Stubbs (1825–1901), one of the founders of modern British historiography and among the main providers, especially through the Rolls Series, of the sources for the study of English constitutional history in the medieval period, wrote that 'History knows that it can wait for more evidence and review its older verdicts; it offers an endless series of courts of appeal, and is ever ready to reopen closed cases.' It is of course as true of the history of the church as of constitutional or any other specialised area of historical research. During the first century of the British Academy the study of the history of the church in England was characterised both by the discovery, uncovering and editing of archival sources on an unprecedented scale and by various 'courts of appeal' and the reopening of a number of celebrated 'closed cases'. New sources have stimulated new perspectives with resulting revision of inherited verdicts and a clash of new 'revisionist' conclusions. The three chapters in this volume which focus upon British ecclesiastical history amply illustrate this.

At the beginning of the twentieth century the endeavour to uncover the manifold sources available for the writing of a history of the Church of England in the medieval period lagged far behind the achievement gained by Stubbs for the writing of constitutional history of that period. But the ground has been made up, as David Luscombe shows in Chapter 5, and it is no exaggeration to say that our knowledge of the medieval church has been transformed during the past century.

An abundance of archival materials has been recovered and has been the subject of research, notably in a significant project sponsored by the British Academy (*English Episcopal Acta*) aimed at publishing, diocese by diocese, the documents issued by the bishops in England between the Conquest and the thirteenth century when episcopal registers began to be made. Along with cathedral resources, they have shed light on the reforms introduced by the Normans after the Conquest, relations with the papacy, the development of canon law, medieval libraries, the significance of the study of the Bible in the schools and universities, the development of the universities themselves, and the religious orders and the coming of new orders after the Conquest, and have led to fresh work on leading figures such as Lafranc and St Anselm, councils and synods and their records, editions of the works of medieval historians, as well as fresh studies of medieval art and architecture.

F. W. Maitland in his book on *Roman Canon Law in the Church of England* (1898) overthrew the view of Bishop Stubbs by demonstrating that in the Middle Ages English church law was part of the law of the universal church, whatever anomalies and imprecisions there were in custom or in the workings of the courts. Z. N. Brooke in his *English Church and the Papacy* (1931) explored the relationships between England and Rome in the period between the Norman Conquest and the reign of King John. He presented them in terms that we might see—although the context is of course very differ-ent—as broadly similar to the processes whereby English laws and jurisdic-tions are now being assimilated to those of the European Union, the difference being that then it was papal law and jurisdiction that filtered in, that this authority was exercised on behalf of spiritual, not temporal, power, and that there were at key moments much sharper conflicts between the two. Times of tense conflict include the periods of exile from England of Archbishop Anselm of Canterbury (1097–1100, 1103–7) as well as of Archbishop Thomas Becket (1164–70), and the period of the Interdict of the English church (1208–14) during the reign of King John. The penetration of the barriers raised by the Anglo-Norman and Angevin kings against papal jurisdiction over the English church, and the resurgence in the later Middle Ages of royal resistance to papal control of revenues and patronage in the English church, have proved to be debatable perspectives from which to pres-ent its development from a supposed pre-Conquest insularity to post-Conquest alignment with Europe and eventually to a *de facto* national independence which preceded the Henrician breach with Rome in the 1530s. Such perspectives have created powerful stereotypes, but they continue to receive constant challenges and detailed nuances. A potent example—one among many—is provided by the way in which Z. N. Brooke represented the aftermath of the martyrdom of Becket in Canterbury cathedral on 29 December 1170 as 'the point at which the English Church falls into line with the rest of the Church in respect of obedience to Rome' (p. 215). But C. R. Cheney also showed in *From Becket to Langton* (1956) that in its day-to-day administration the English church continued to rely on royal servants, on sinners as well as on saints, to do its work.[31]

Underlying these and many other debates about the integration of English church governance in the life of the nation and of the church universal has been the accumulation of documentary evidence—including for example the publication already mentioned of episcopal *acta*, episcopal registers and

---

[31] See also Henry Mayr-Harting, 'Henry II and the Papacy, 1170–1189', *Journal of Ecclesiastical History*, 16 (1965), 39–53.

papal decretals—which continue to enrich studies of the medieval English church, as David Luscombe shows.

In his chapter on the Reformation Patrick Collinson describes the English Reformation as having been a subset of political and constitutional history among scholars during the first half or so of the century. It was once, indeed, described as an 'act of state'. Thus, for example, in the early decades of the century A. F. Pollard (1869–1948), the leading historian of Tudor England at that time, played down the religious aspects of the Reformation, and argued that the events of the reign of Henry VIII that so changed England were *sui generis*; he represented the Reformation as social and political change, a natural stage in England's rise to nationhood, not a decisive break with the past. Among historians of the church, the Reformation was also regarded as *sui generis*, though for different reasons. Here the predominant view was the Anglo-Catholic perspective that the Reformation had been an internal English matter that owed nothing to the reformation movements in continental Europe. The tone was set by the monumental work of R. W. Dixon's *History of the Church of England from the Abolition of the Roman Jurisdiction* (6 vols., 1884–1910) whose very title stressed a break with the medieval past that was jurisdictional rather than theological. The most militant phase of religious change under Edward VI was played down or ignored, and attention was focused instead on finding 'Catholic' tendencies in the Elizabethan Settlement. Puritans were treated as outsiders to the established Church, closely allied with post-1662 'Dissent' or Nonconformity, whose study remained largely confined to those with denominational loyalties.

The second half of the century was one of almost continuous 'revisionism'. A new phase in research was famously opened up by Geoffrey Elton whose *The Tudor Revolution in Government* (1952) argued that 'revolution' rather than 'reformation' is the key word for understanding the events of the reign of Henry VIII, which marked the beginning proper of modern methods of government. But the driving force was not Henry but his Chancellor Thomas Cromwell. Elton's work, which dominated the mid-decades of the century, played down the role of religion in the Reformation.

The significance of religious change in the causes of the Reformation was strongly reclaimed, however, in the influential work by A. G. Dickens, *The English Reformation* (1964). It was Dickens who brought a new perspective on the Reformation gained from new archival riches that had lain in the provinces and became available only as local record offices began to open, the first in Bedfordshire in the 1920s, but followed by many more county record offices from the 1950s. These saved many of the country-house collections that were then being dispersed, and gave opportunities for diocesan and cathedral archives to be made available for research. The pioneer in this was Dickens, who from the 1930s began taking a local perspective on the Reformation. While recognising the crucial role of the Tudor monarchy in religious change, Dickens laid emphasis on the popular elements that worked alongside official change.

For Dickens the English Reformation was both a social and a religious event, much more than an 'act of state' or constitutional change, however significant. His case was that the old religion had been in decline and that the English were ready for reformation; that, in fact, the triumph of Protestantism was 'almost predictable'. He thus broke with the Anglo-Catholic consensus on the *Sonderweg* of England in the sixteenth century, and with his knowledge of Germany and the reformation there his perspective was both wider and more concentrated, as much international as local. It was perhaps significant that the other major English historian to take the rest of Europe seriously, Gordon Rupp, was a Methodist and not an Anglican.

As Patrick Collinson shows, Dickens's work met with forceful challenge in J. J. Scarisbrick's monumental work, *Henry VIII* (1968), which argued that the old religion was by no means dead, and that on the whole the English did not want the Reformation and when it came were slow to accept it; that the actions of the state had very much more to do with the Reformation and the decline of the old religion than Dickens's work allowed. Subsequently, and partly stimulated by Scarisbrick's work, and taking their cue also from local research, but with different overall conclusions from Dickens, more recent 'revisionists', such as Christopher Haigh and Eamon Duffy, have also once more emphasised the Reformation as an outcome of state action, with little theological content but also with little popular support. Paradoxically, these revisionists therefore concur with the Anglo-Catholics about the special, insular nature of the English Reformation. Collinson shows how more recent work, notably Diarmaid MacCulloch's magisterial *Thomas Cranmer* (1996), has returned to rediscover the importance of ideas in galvanising support for the Reformation, and to realise that the profile of these ideas was European rather than *sui generis*. This in turn has made the English Reformation look more like its neighbours: even like the Reformation in Scotland. That is, some recent scholars have taken the rest of Europe much more seriously than has been the case in much British study of this period. Collinson in Chapter 6 also draws the larger picture in this respect.

As in the case of the Reformation, so also and for the same reason the Church of England in the eighteenth century had a bad press in 1902. As Jane Shaw shows in Chapter 7, the eighteenth-century church was viewed, from a 'triumphalist' Tractarian perspective, as having been dead on its feet. From this torpor, so Tractarian historians insisted, the church had been rescued by the Oxford Movement. Clerical numbers had now increased and new theological colleges had recently been founded and were thriving.

Such was the new temper of the twentieth century, however, and such the intellectual challenges that faced the church, that the winds of change were not far away. New research into church life in the eighteenth century, and especially new archival research, rediscovered a pastoral efficiency and lively spirituality that had been marginalised under the impact of Tractarian historiography as well as the evangelical view of the eighteenth-century church as spiritually moribund. A landmark in revision was Norman Sykes's *Church and State in England in the XVIIIth Century* (1934). This initiative had only a limited impact during the middle decades of the century, however, as Jane Shaw explains, but during the final two decades of the century there was a veritable 'cottage industry' in histories of the eighteenth-century church, and there is now a wide range of local studies based on extensive archival research, which gives us a rich and multi-layered picture of diocesan and parish life for both clergy and laity.

In a further significant development of the closing decades of the century, other historians began to rethink the relationship between religion and the Enlightenment, questioning the assumption that would have been made in 1902: namely, that the one was antagonistic to the other. Beginning in the 1970s, a new emphasis on the Enlightenment's origins in Britain, and detailed analyses of the relationship between religion and the scientific/philosophical movements of the Enlightenment, led to the conclusion that religion, and the debates about religion, were significant forces in the formation of Enlightenment sensibilities. Yet others came to question the nature of the Enlightenment itself. As the aftermath of two World Wars provoked disillusionment amongst intellectuals about the possibility of progress, so the Enlightenment came to be seen as a less benign force than Victorian agnostic intellectuals had allowed. Building on the influential work of Theodor Adorno and Max Horkheimer, *Dialectic of Enlightenment* (1947), several generations of scholars have explored the 'underside' of the Enlightenment.

The revision of the verdict of earlier generations upon the Church of England in the eighteenth century, dominated as it was by the perspective of the Tractarians, has in turn offered a new basis for a reassessment of the Oxford Movement itself, which, for example, has been freshly examined in a significant study by Peter Nockles in his *The Oxford Movement In Context: Anglican High Churchmanship 1760–1857* (Cambridge, 1994). Here too— though it has not been possible to include a chapter on this period in this volume—a time of revision has begun.

Across the range of subjects included in 'theological and religious studies', this has been a century of work on fresh sources as well as the development of new approaches, and philosophical and doctrinal work has constantly reflected new currents of thought, so that a century after the foundation of the Academy there is much to build on—and much to be done!

CHAPTER ONE

The Old Testament

JAMES BARR

This survey will begin with the Hebrew text of the Old Testament and the ancient versions of it. It will go on to the rise of traditional biblical criticism, and then consider study of the Hebrew language and its cognate Semitic languages. It will then survey various topics in turn, preserving some historical perspective where possible. In general, the centre of the article will seek to describe the dominant position of the mid-twentieth century and the last sections will look at more recent developments.

First, then, the text itself. As it was generally understood in 1902, any printed edition of the Hebrew Bible ought to reproduce, as far as possible, the words and forms of the Bomberg edition (Second Rabbinic Bible) published in Venice in 1524–5, which was believed to be authoritative. The print in common use was the Letteris edition produced for the British and Foreign Bible Society in 1852. Little or no attempt had been made to go behind the Bombergiana and incorporate data from manuscripts that antedated it. New studies of different manuscripts and discoveries of yet others during the eighteenth and nineteenth centuries prepared the way for important changes.

The situation was changed from about 1925 when the third edition of the *Biblia Hebraica* began to appear, in separate fascicles with different editors. It was Paul Kahle more than any other one person who by his studies in the history of the Masorah was able to show that the MS B19a of St Petersburg, datable to 1008 CE, was the best available representative of the work of the Masoretic families at its climax. The *Biblia Hebraica* thus sought to provide a near-diplomatic copy of this one MS. On the other hand its Apparatus Criticus reported different readings, often from ancient translations, primarily from the LXX, and also alternative readings proposed by modern scholars. Another milestone was passed when the Aleppo Codex, dated to 930 CE, was eventually made available to scholarship; it had tragically been damaged, however, and most of its text of the Torah had been lost. And from 1947 on, the discovery at Qumran of a multitude of fragments of biblical text, going back two thousand years or so, along with one or two near-complete books such as Isaiah, revolutionised the scene even more. Most of the editors of books in the later edition, *Biblia Hebraica Stuttgartensia* (1967–77), were German, but editors from the British Isles included D. W. Thomas (Isaiah) and Th. H. Robinson (Ruth, Lamentations). Further editions of the *Biblia Hebraica* have been published or are under preparation.

It is strange that these editions were heavily blamed for allegedly changing, emending or altering the text, for they did no such thing. The text as printed by all of them was exactly the Masoretic Text, subject to limitations of using the medium of a printed book. For most, the MT remained 'the Text'. The apparatus reported readings from other versions, primarily the Greek, later from the Dead Sea Scrolls, and proposals by scholars, but it did not introduce these into the text itself. Especially now since the Scrolls are becoming better known, the MT must become, for academic purposes, only one of the various forms of the Text, even if by far the most complete of them, and all witnesses must be seen on an equal basis. Religion may always require that the MT should be final, but research must take a new path. Only at the end of the twentieth century did this requirement begin to be faced, with an experimental text of Gen. 1–11 edited by R. S. Hendel (*The Text of Genesis 1–11*, Oxford, 1998). Much controversy must be expected before this issue is settled.

Great advances were made in the study of the versions, especially the Greek (LXX) and the Syriac. Cambridge and Göttingen were the homes of major editions of the LXX. The larger Cambridge series, edited by A. E. Brooke and N. McLean, covered the narrative books but was not continued beyond them. H. B. Swete edited a shorter edition of the whole (1895). The Cambridge editions took as their text one particular MS, usually Vaticanus, and alternative wordings (which might include the best) were cited in an apparatus. Göttingen worked in a different way, printing the text that the editor, from his vast knowledge of the characteristics of the version, thought right. Its great names were Lagarde, Rahlfs, Ziegler, Hanhart and Wevers. It was slow at first in making progress, and little had appeared before 1940. In the latter part of the century Ziegler brought out the major prophetic books and Job, and Wevers with great diligence produced the five Pentateuchal books between 1974 and 1991. Though many points of controversy remain, it is now accepted that the Göttingen approach has been the right one. Another major centre has been in Finland, with a stress on grammatical analysis (Soisalon-Soininen, Aejmelaeus, Sollamo). The basic, but incomplete, grammar by H. St. J. Thackeray (Cambridge, 1909) has not been superseded.

As already mentioned, the Dead Sea Scrolls interacted with the LXX, both of them providing ancient evidence for the biblical text. First discovered in 1947, the early finds included a practically complete text of Isaiah, as well as several non-biblical writings of great importance for our knowledge of Hebrew and Aramaic and also, obviously, Jewish life and thought in the Second Temple era. There followed some delay before the countless smaller fragments could be sorted out, classified and published. The person who combined a leadership in LXX studies with one in the Scrolls and who has brought the publication of the latter to a successful conclusion is Emanuel Tov (especially in his *Textual Criticism of the Hebrew Bible*, Assen and Minneapolis,1992). Mention must be made also of the Hebrew University Bible Project and its profoundest thinker, M. H. Goshen-Gottstein.

The all-important working instrument, a bilingual Greek–Hebrew concordance, was published by E. Hatch and H. A. Redpath (Oxford, 1897) and remained essential throughout the century. A more modern dictionary, to the Minor Prophets only, was published by T. Muraoka (Louvain, 1995) and a simple Greek–English one to the entire LXX by J. Lust and associates (2 vols., Stuttgart, 1992, 1996). A computerised bilingual registration of the texts, prepared in Philadelphia, is of the utmost value.

Along with the LXX a high importance attaches to the Syriac text, commonly called Peshitta. Here a complete critical text was badly lacking, and it was not until 1972 that a full edition in many volumes, initiated in many respects by P. A. H. de Boer, began to come from the press of Brill in Leiden. Outstanding in the integration of Syriac studies with LXX and Hebrew biblical text have been S. P. Brock and M. P. Weitzman. Also significant for textual matters is the Bible in classical Ethiopic, and innovative research in this area has been done by M. A. Knibb. Study of the Targums or Jewish Aramaic translations has also greatly advanced: a big advance was the discovery (1956) of the previously unknown Targum Neofiti, published by A. Díez Macho (1968–79). Even more striking has been the discovery of fragments of a Job Targum, and also of one of Leviticus, at Qumran.

We turn next to the place of biblical criticism in the British Isles. In Scotland a position with affinities to that of Julius Wellhausen became well known through W. Robertson Smith back in the later nineteenth century, but the person who more than any other made the new approaches familiar and acceptable was S. R. Driver, with his care, his caution and his avoidance of improbable novelties. His *Introduction to the Literature of the Old Testament* (1892), his commentaries, his *Hebrew Tenses* (Oxford, 1892) and his part in the co-operative production F. Brown, S. R. Driver and C. A. Briggs, *A Hebrew and English Lexicon of the Old Testament* (Oxford, 1907), formed a group of basic statements that well represented the average cross-section of views within Old Testament scholarship until well through the century, in some respects through to its end. The strata within the Pentateuch were J, E, D and P, in that order (Driver and others actually thought of a Hexateuch, the same source analysis applying through Joshua also). Isaiah had three portions, from different periods; Daniel came from the Maccabean period. These formed the typical common ground. Though some parts of the Bible, especially the beginning of Genesis, were mythological, in a broad sense the history of Israel had been as the Bible depicted it: 'historical' criticism was critical more in a literary than in a historical sense. There were other views, both more conservative and more critical, but none showed signs of threatening to replace the critical consensus.

A typical scholarly activity has been the writing of critical commentaries on the various books of the Bible. Such commentaries would apply the critical analysis of texts, their origins, sources, process of composition, philology and textual variations. A major series is the International Critical Commentary (ICC), some volumes of which appeared as early as the 1890s; similar series came from German-language scholarship. Much scholarly work also went into commentary series that were more popular and more aligned with religious needs. Some specialised in particular approaches: that emphasising form criticism is a good example. The ICC was slow to progress and was hardly complete when it was felt to be time to start a new series of the same: W. McKane's *Jeremiah* (2 vols., Edinburgh, 1986, 1996) is a fine example. German scholarship had already led the way with the solid volumes of the Biblischer Kommentar, some of which were translated into English, notably C. Westermann's *Genesis* (German: Neukirchen, 1974; English: London, 1984).

Before pursuing further the movement of criticism in a general sense, we should consider some of the other areas essential to scholarship.

Hebrew language was obviously central and has already been mentioned. In the earlier part of the twentieth century most of the new development in Hebrew language studies came from comparative Semitic studies. Old Testament scholars were expected to achieve some competence in other Semitic languages: at the least, in Aramaic, since part of the Hebrew Bible is in Aramaic, and this would naturally extend into Syriac (the term commonly used for Christian and/or later forms of Aramaic). Arabic was also indigenous to the field, and had had great importance in medieval Jewish tradition. It was not uncommon for biblical scholars to spend time in the Middle East and gain some fluency in Arabic. Analogies from Arab life were quite often used in the explanation of biblical passages. Newer and more promising of change were the languages like Egyptian and Akkadian, discovered in the nineteenth century and now in the twentieth expanding enormously in the exhibition of their riches, with their monuments visible in the museums and their languages coming eventually to be set down and described methodically. These influences grew gradually and unsteadily. A comparative grammar of the Semitic languages by Brockelmann was available quite early (2 vols., Berlin, 1908, 1913). On the other hand there was nothing like a serious dictionary of Akkadian until much later: of the two main dictionaries now recognised, that of W. von Soden was published over 1965–81, and the major *Chicago Assyrian Dictionary* did not commence publication until 1956 and at the time of writing (2002) is still not complete. Since new texts were being discovered all the time and scholarly discussion and interpretation was dispersed over a wide variety of genres and publications, it was not easy for anyone other than a full-time Assyriologist to command the material. To know the language (and its sign system!) was one thing; to understand the texts and see how they helped the understanding of the Old Testament was another. Both were now necessary. In the 1930s the further discovery of Ugaritic was of great importance: its script was a simpler one, it had many words similar to Hebrew, and it had mythological texts clearly relatable to poetic texts of the Bible. For comparative Semitic grammar a simple and clear work was edited by S. Moscati (Wiesbaden, 1964), and its conspectus included all the above, and also classical Ethiopic and Epigraphic South Arabian, these last having marked connections with Arabic and with Hebrew. In the field of Hebrew personal names an essential step forward was taken with M. Noth's *Die israelitischen Personennamen* (Stuttgart, 1928), for it took general Semitic onomastics into account and thus avoided the guesswork on the basis of normal Hebrew meanings which was formerly so common. It has remained the basic work; more recent research has been led by J. J. Stamm. A monumental study of the three commonest Hebrew prepositions was published by E. Jenni (3 vols., Stuttgart, 1992). The slowly increasing corpus of inscriptions in ancient Hebrew and other closely related languages has been closely studied: important publications include those of G. A. Cooke and S. A. Cook early in the twentieth century, later of D. Diringer, and more recently especially of H. Donner and K. Röllig, of J. C. L. Gibson, of A. Lemaire and of G. I. Davies.

G. R. Driver, the son of S. R. Driver, was a personal embodiment of these interests in their application to the Bible. In his earlier days he published in the field of Arabic, and later in that of Akkadian. He brought out a widely used textbook of the Ugaritic texts (*Canaanite Myths and Legends*, Edinburgh, 1956; revised by J. C. L. Gibson, Edinburgh, 1977). But much of his main interest in the Bible lay in the application to it of insights drawn from comparative Semitics. Where Hebrew words were difficult, or where a phrase seemed to make no sense, one could take a Hebrew form and utilise its consonants to identify a relation to a word in the cognate languages, and the meaning of that word could illuminate the identity and meaning of the Hebrew. This method was not peculiar to Driver: all over the world there were scholars who practised it, like W. F. Albright in the United States, but Driver concentrated on it and devoted his energies more entirely to it than any other. He was devoted also to the task of a new translation of the Bible into English and many of his proposals were included in the Old Testament of the *New English Bible* (Oxford and Cambridge, 1970).

His scholarship was very different from his father's, though he revered his paternal heritage very deeply. The literary criticism and the historical ranking of sources which the father had practised did not greatly interest the son. He seemed not to systematise his knowledge. He did not write an Introduction, nor did he write commentaries on biblical books, nor indeed a methodical account of comparative philology. He did not deny the edifice of source criticism, such as J, E, D and P, on which his father had laboured so long; but he did not utilise it much either. He was much more a philologist than a historian or a literary critic. Even textual criticism was often evaded by his approach: a word which had been doubted on textual grounds could often be shown to be entirely right, once one realised that it was a quite different word, identifiable only through Arabic or Ugaritic. Much of his work was published in sets of short notes on biblical passages. His heritage was continued by D. Winton Thomas, J. A. Emerton and others.

Mention of the lexicography of Hebrew may suitably be made at this point. The work of Brown, S. R. Driver and Briggs has already been mentioned above, and it remained the dominant English-language dictionary till near the end of the twentieth century, the main alternative being the German-language dictionary of F. Buhl (1915). Both of these took for their basis the work of the great German lexicographer Gesenius (1786–1842). The first major new approach had its base in Switzerland, where L. Koehler and W. Baumgartner prepared a dictionary (1953), published by Brill in Leiden, which gave both German and English glosses. It was thoroughly revised in later editions; these, however, went back to the use of German only. It was in 1994 that an English translation of the final form of the German began to appear, edited by M. E. J. Richardson. In German a new edition of Gesenius (the 18th) is being prepared under the guidance of H. Donner (vol. 1, Berlin, 1987). In England a dictionary of new format, edited by D. J. A. Clines, began to appear (*The Dictionary of Classical Hebrew*, Sheffield, from 1993). It 'systematically deflects attention from the word to the larger units of meaning', omits all reference to words in cognate languages, and registers material in a way that concerns itself 'not only with meanings, but with syntagmatic and paradigmatic relationships'. It will be a lengthy work, expected to take eight volumes when complete. Another striking phenomenon is the publication by Luis Alonso Schökel of a *Diccionario Bíblico Hebreo-Español* (Madrid, 1994). Full-size dictionaries of Biblical Hebrew had scarcely existed hitherto except in German and English. Interestingly, Clines notes tendencies in this Spanish work that are parallel to the principles of the Sheffield dictionary.

Mention should be made also of grammars of Hebrew for beginners, since Hebrew is a language which many have to learn from zero. A. B. Davidson's *An Introductory Hebrew Grammar* was a classic that went through many editions, the best-known being the 24th (Edinburgh, 1932). In the mid-twentieth century the *A Practical Grammar for Classical Hebrew* of J. Weingreen (2nd edition, Oxford, 1959) was extremely popular. In the United States the *Introduction to Biblical Hebrew* of T. O. Lambdin (New York, 1971) has been widely used. But there were many other elementary grammars, some of them designed for a particular institution and little known outside of it. In the field of syntax the works of A. Niccacci (*The Syntax of the Verb in Classical Hebrew Prose*, Sheffield, 1990) and B. K. Waltke and M. O'Connor (*An Introduction to Biblical Hebrew Syntax*, Winona Lake, Ind., 1990) have had wide acceptance.

Another approach was made possible through archaeology. The discovery of ancient languages and texts has already been mentioned, but the study of ancient cities, fortresses, temples, technologies and land settlement patterns is equally significant. Such explorations were already carried out in the nineteenth century, notably in conspicuous sites such as Jerusalem; but in the twentieth century such investigations became more specialised and professional. Nelson Glueck carried out extensive land surveys. Kathleen M. Kenyon's work in Jericho and Jerusalem made a great impact: in her *Archaeology in the Holy Land* (1960) 'she largely rewrote the history of ancient civilisation in Palestine', wrote Peter J. Parr (*DNB 1971–1980*, p. 463). R. de Vaux was another of the mighty men of archaeology in this period. Later in the century conflicts over archaeology arose, and these will be mentioned shortly.

A dominant figure in the mid-twentieth century was W. F. Albright, who kept in touch with a wide range of archaeological, ethnological, linguistic and textual discovery. Typical of his approach was his *From the Stone Age to Christianity: Monotheism and the Historical Process* (Baltimore, 1940).

Archaeology, the discovery of inscriptions, a wide sweep of ancient history especially in religion, and detailed philological proposals mingled together to show the rather conservative result that Moses was a monotheist. Albright founded a school which kept his heritage alive in the work of pupils, many of whom held teaching posts in strategic institutions of the United States. F. M. Cross has been notable among them (*Canaanite Myth and Hebrew Epic*, Cambridge, Mass., 1973). He and D. Noel Freedman had a position of leadership, and guided such projects as the *Anchor Bible*, a work which, however, included in the same series commentaries of very variable quality, seen at its scholarly best perhaps in P. K. McCarter's *I–II Samuel* (2 vols., New York, 1980, 1984). The *Anchor Bible Dictionary* (6 vols., New York, 1992) has been well appreciated.

A related influence was exerted by the comparative and historical approach to religion. Ideas derived from Sir James G. Frazer were widespread in general intellectual life in the 1920s and 1930s. Robertson Smith drew extensively on traditions of pre-Islamic Arabia and on ideas of totemism derived from Victorian ethnographic studies. The new knowledge of Mesopotamian and Egyptian religion was very important for work on the Bible. Though such influence sometimes moved scholars to see a community of religious insights so that Israel came closer to Mesopotamia or Egypt, or similarly to Greece and Rome, the same comparative study could be used, and later in the century was used, in the opposite direction, with works like H. and H. A. Frankfort and others, *The Intellectual Adventure of Ancient Man* (Chicago, 1946; later reprint *Before Philosophy*, London, 1951). The Frankforts argued that the religious cultures of Egypt and Mesopotamia, though both polytheistic, were extremely distinct in structure, and this left open a gap in which a distinctiveness for Israel's historically based faith might be asserted. G. E. Wright built his *God Who Acts* (London, 1952) on such a basis, and 'the action of God in history' became the watchword of an influential movement.

The approach considered 'historical-critical' and typified by the name of Wellhausen continued to command the acceptance of a majority, at least in general outlines, throughout the twentieth century; but it would be a mistake to ignore the existence of contrary trends. On the one hand there were those whose criticism seemed to be much more 'extreme' than the moderate Wellhausenian positions. One example is T. K. Cheyne. A good illustration is the contrast between two encyclopaedic works, the more extreme *Encyclopædia Biblica* (London, 1899–1903), often guided by Cheyne's approach, and the moderate-critical *Dictionary of the Bible*, edited by J. Hastings (Edinburgh, 1903–5). Again, there were some, like F. F. Bruce (predominantly a New Testament scholar, but his main professorship, at Manchester, covered Old Testament also) or D. J. Wiseman (professionally an Assyriologist), who were able to integrate their scholarship with somewhat conservative views of biblical history and of dates and reliability of the literature. Jewish scholarship also was often dubious about the modern critical views: a strong reaction, especially against Wellhausen, was expressed by Y. Kaufmann, best known from his *The Religion of Israel*, abridged and translated by M. Greenberg (Chicago, 1960).

Quite a different approach came from others, notably in Scandinavia, who in various ways took something of a more transhistorical view, emphasised oral tradition, favoured the Masoretic Text and were uninterested in source criticism. A leading example was the Dane J. Pedersen, whose two-volume work *Israel: Its Life and Culture* (London and Copenhagen, 1926 and 1940) surveyed the 'soul' of ancient Israel, its conceptions, its integration with society, its perception of individual and universe. From similar sources, fertilised by the strong Scandinavian tradition of comparative religion, came an interest in the cultic or ritual aspects and in sacral kingship. Approaches through cult and myth had already been fostered by the influential W. Gunkel in Germany and (from a different point of view) by the Norwegian S. Mowinckel. In Britain, similar lines of thought can be seen in A. R. Johnson, with his *Sacral Kingship in Ancient Israel* (Cardiff, 1955) and *The Cultic Prophet in Ancient Israel* (Cardiff, 1962). He also studied aspects of the Old Testament that came closer to the anthropological, as in his *The One and the Many in the Israelite Conception of God* (Cardiff, 1961). G. W. Anderson is another who did much to interpret the Scandinavian scholarly traditions.

We cannot go further without mentioning H. H. Rowley, who was perhaps the central figure in British Old Testament scholarship in the mid-twentieth century. Rowley was not a particularly original thinker and there are few novel ideas associated with his name, but he typified a central position better perhaps than any other of his time, writing on a wide variety of themes: the Aramaic texts, the historical relations of the Exodus, Old Testament theology, and apocalyptic. He was very active in international relationships and, as Foreign Secretary of the Society for Old Testament Study, did much to rebuild a sense of common international scholarship at the end of the Second World War. He sought to stimulate scholarly publication both in Britain and internationally; with his name might well be linked, in this respect, that of the Leiden scholar P. A. H. de Boer. The periodical *Vetus Testamentum* had its beginning at this time (first publication, 1951), as did also the International Organisation for the Study of the Old Testament (first of its triennial meetings, 1950). The British Isles has its own Society for Old Testament Study, and the United

States has its Society of Biblical Literature. From the 1970s onwards these societies, especially the latter, became enormous clearing-houses for all sorts of research, discovery and discussion.

From perhaps the 1960s a number of problems became more controversial than had been the case earlier on. One of these was the theme of covenant. This theme seemed to some to form a centre for the thought of the Old Testament, and it had indeed been adopted as such a centre in the 1930s by W. Eichrodt, a major exponent of Old Testament theology (to be mentioned again below). Against this it was noted that Wellhausen himself had argued that the covenant motif had emerged only late, around the Deuteronomic period. In the 1950s a new argument emerged (G. E. Mendenhall, *Law and Covenant in Israel and the Ancient Near East*, Pittsburgh, 1955). Increasing knowledge of Near Eastern texts revealed a pattern of treaties between major powers and subsidiaries, a pattern which seemed to have analogies with biblical covenant language. This had support from members of the influential Albrightian tradition in the USA and seemed to many to re-establish the early date and the centrality of covenant. On the other hand a meticulous study of the biblical texts by L. Perlitt (*Bundestheologie im Alten Testament*, Neukirchen, 1969) reinforced the Wellhausenian view that the covenant theme emerged only late. Extensive discussion of this theme continued; a balanced view is offered by E. W. Nicholson in his *God and His People* (Oxford, 1986).

Old Testament theology in general has been a controversial field, some holding that it does not belong within academic biblical studies, others maintaining that without it the Old Testament would be left without importance for religion or for general culture. In the early decades of the twentieth century it was little mentioned, more emphasis being placed upon the history of religion and comparative religion, an approach well typified by W. O. E. Oesterley and Th. H. Robinson, *Hebrew Religion: Its Origin and Development* (London, 1930). S. H. Hooke well represented the 'myth and ritual' approach, connected with anthropology. In the later 1930s Old Testament theology came back into notice, primarily in the German-language area. W. Eichrodt, mentioned above, was the first exponent to be widely influential, and his influence hardly began until after the Second World War. N. W. Porteous was significant as one who had studied in Germany during the seminal period of the subject. As against the historical and analytic approach of critical scholarship, Old Testament theology has been interested in the *entirety* and its unity, in a synchronic perception as against a diachronic, in depth of meaning and conviction as against description, and in relationship with the New Testament. The *distinctiveness* of the Old Testament as against its ancient environment, as against its similarities noted by the history of religion, has thus been emphasised. This fits in to some degree with another tendency, namely the interest in the Hebrew/Greek thought contrast. Hebrew thought was deemed to be highly distinctive when set beside Greek thought. The theological effect of this argument depends on another: namely, the notion that the New Testament, though written in Greek, belongs entirely or almost entirely to Hebrew thought and is thus quite opposed to Greek culture. Arguments along these lines became very influential in the period 1945–60. This approach was attacked by J. Barr, *The Semantics of Biblical Language* (London, 1961). Interest in Old Testament theology has, obviously, had connections with New Testament theology and some have aspired to go further and seek to formulate a theology of the entire (Christian) Bible.

The leading work in Old Testament theology has continued to be continental, and also American. Significant work was done by the Dutchman Th. Vriezen, the Frenchman E. Jacob, the American G. Ernest Wright (who combined this interest with archaeology), and Rowley in his *The Faith of Israel* (London, 1956). But the greatly dominant work was that of G. von Rad in Germany (2 vols., German originals: 1957, 1960; English translations: 1962, 1965).

Von Rad took *history* as the backbone of his theological structure. History was the milieu in which God revealed himself. The core of the Bible was historical narrative. But history was not mere statement of past events. It was confessional reinterpretation of them. Themes from the past were actualised and used for the understanding of the present. This movement of realisation of ancient themes passed through the stages of the Old Testament, continued as the Old Testament was reinterpreted in the New, and continued again as both were interpreted in the later community. Von Rad also wrote a supplementary volume on the Wisdom Literature, a body of material which might have been thought to disagree with this framework.

This approach was theological, but had connections with movements in historical criticism. We have indicated that the Wellhausenian scheme continued to dominate, but alterations certainly took place. Perhaps the fullest classic presentation of traditional criticism in the mid-century was that of O. Eissfeldt (*Das Alte Testament*, Tübingen, 1934, 3rd edition 1964; English translation with additions by P. R. Ackroyd, Oxford, 1965). Wellhausen, and others such as S. R. Driver, had sought to pursue the Pentateuchal strata on into the subsequent historical books, but this came to be discouraged in a later wave, in general terms that of von Rad and M. Noth. According to this scheme, very roughly speaking, the J, E and P identified in Genesis continued only to the end of Numbers. Apart from minor exceptions, they were not present in Deuteronomy or in the following books. E in any case was a minor stratum, not identifiable all through the first four books. From Genesis on, therefore, there were really only two main strands, an earlier (J, plus traces of E) and a later (P). D did not substantially exist in this section. Deuteronomy was now classed as leader of the block of historical books, Joshua to Kings, which came to be known as the Deuteronomistic History. It consisted of a framework which was governed by the principles and theology of Deuteronomy, and within this framework were older stories of people like the various 'judges', kings and prophets.

This critical approach was taken by von Rad into the structure of his theology, and some considered that his theology was in fact the theology of Deuteronomy. One major problem that followed from his work lay in its relation to the critical history of Israel. Theology, as von Rad saw it, had to be anchored to the events as they had been interpreted and 'confessed' by Israel, and could not be transposed into another idiom. But, since it was admitted that historical events had often been other than those depicted in this confession, if theology was to be anchored to history, did it not have to be anchored to the history as it had in fact been, in the perspective of critical history? No easy solution to this dispute was to be found. This has effects on what followed.

From about 1960 a number of changes in the atmosphere of Old Testament study came to take effect. On the one hand the impact of so many environing disciplines was increasingly acknowledged; on the other hand the effect was often that scholars moved into their various specialisms and it became harder for people to hold these different interests and methods together. Archaeology, for example, became a much more distinct professional vocation (cf. the general guidance of R. E. Mortimer Wheeler), and some of the earlier work, vaguely mixing biblical texts with archaeology from the earth, came to be looked on as amateurish. Although the importance of Mesopotamian sources was universally acknowledged, Assyriology had now become an enormously large and complicated field in itself, so that Old Testament scholars could touch only the fringes of it. Among Assyriologists who took an active part in Old Testament studies we must pay tribute especially to H. W. F. Saggs and W. G. Lambert, and to the great lexicographers, W. von Soden and Erica Reiner. Another scholar who has exercised great influence is E. Ullendorff, in three areas: in bringing Ethiopian languages into greater attention, in comparative Semitics, and in introducing modern general linguistics. He often lamented what he called 'the demise of the Hebraist' and the rising interest in theological interpretation. J. Barr also looked for guidance in modern linguistics and semantics, with effect upon both Old and New

Testament and biblical theology; he has worked at different ends of the spectrum, on the one hand in detailed textual and orthographical studies (*The Variable Spellings of the Hebrew Bible*, Oxford, 1989) and in general theory (*History and Ideology in the Old Testament*, Oxford, 2000). J. B. Segal is a general Semitist, who has published much in the area of Syriac language and culture, but also wrote the important book *The Hebrew Passover from the Earliest Times to A.D. 70* (London, 1963).

Old Testament studies have thus been drawing away somewhat from the context of theology in which they had earlier been set. But equally it was becoming difficult for the biblical scholar to keep in touch with the linguistically difficult and scientifically technical subjects that nevertheless remained important for his work. Amateurish dabbling in Egyptology or in archaeology was no longer acceptable. Even in the relations with theology the estrangement could have similar causes: academic theology had its own required history and esoteric technical knowledge. Old Testament studies and New Testament studies seemed to have drawn apart, for similar reasons. Some have been satisfied with this, while others have deplored it.

The apparent gulf between Old Testament and New Testament studies has been modified, however, by an increasing interest in the world of post-biblical interpretation, the reception history of the Hebrew Bible and its function as background for later developments. It became commoner to meet 'biblical' scholars whose interest was much more in the later interpretation of the texts than in their original meaning. The basic edition of the Apocryphal books was done by R. H. Charles (Oxford, 1913) and a new, slightly different, selection by H. F. D. Sparks (1984). Copious new editions have been published in America, notably under the guidance of James Charlesworth.

The Dead Sea Scrolls greatly increased the importance of this, for a number of the books, hitherto known only as 'Apocrypha' of various Christian traditions, were now evidenced in a Jewish setting and in Hebrew or Aramaic. This will be pursued, however, in Chapter 3.

Of more general importance, on the other hand, is the increased interaction of Jewish and non-Jewish scholarship in the later decades of the twentieth century. Y. Kaufmann's work received little attention outside the Jewish context, and this was true of some others such as I. Cassuto. But after the creation of the state of Israel much more of Jewish scholarship came on to the international scene, while non-Jewish scholars took the opportunity to live and study within a Jewish context. Familiarity with Modern Hebrew became much more common among Christian scholars. Among the many important Israeli scholars we may mention Ch. Rabin, I. L. Seeligmann in Septuagint, Moshe Greenberg as a general biblicist, M. Weinfeld for his work on

Deuteronomy, M. Haran for deep learning in the formation of scripture, and many specialists in the history of Hebrew grammar, manuscripts and historical geography. Academic organisations came to recognise more fully their inter-religious character. The Old Testament came to be referred to more often as the Hebrew Bible, or by some other expression ('First Testament' has also been tried). Jewish/Christian cooperation is made visible in powerful composite statements such as those of M. J. Mulder (ed.), *Mikra: Text, Translation, Reading and Interpretation in Ancient Judaism and Early Christianity* (Philadelphia, 1988) and M. Sæbø (ed.), *Hebrew Bible/Old Testament: The History of its Interpretation* (Vol. 1, Göttingen, 1996).

In the later decades of the twentieth century some considerable changes came to affect Old Testament study. We may begin with the field commonly known as 'history of Ancient Israel'. The widely used work of J. Bright (Philadelphia, 1959) kept very close to the biblical text, at times doing little more than to paraphrase it; that of M. Noth (German: Göttingen, 1950; English: London, 1960) was more critical. The two typified the methodological differences between the Albright school and the German school that followed A. Alt. To follow the subsequent changes of opinion we may go first to the related work of archaeology. Much of the older archaeological work had seen itself as 'biblical archaeology': the image of the worker with his spade in one hand and the Bible in the other was sometimes used. The places and artefacts discovered or surveyed were often considered from the start as elements corresponding to things mentioned in the Bible. This, it was now argued, cast a biblical framework over everything. Archaeology should be related not to the biblical names and peoples, but to a geographical area like 'Syria and Palestine' or to a population that might have no biblical identity such as 'Israel'. It was at least possible, therefore, that the people and the past that archaeology revealed might be quite unrelated to the grid imposed upon them by the Bible. This would make it likely that any 'history' basically read off from the Bible would be historically unreal; it would be, rather, the product of ideological drives in the society of the groups who, much later, wrote and edited the texts.

This might seem to be nothing new. Had not biblical critics from the beginning declared that this or that story of the Bible was not historically accurate and expressed rather the theological convictions of later ages? Yes and no. Although biblical critics had declared unhistorical many narratives of the earlier periods, there was a narrative core of which they had remained convinced that it told a real history. There was a real David and Solomon, and Solomon had ruled over a substantial empire; this united kingdom had later split into two states known as Israel and Judah. Israel had been banished and dispersed by the

Assyrians. Later Judah had been exiled by the Babylonians to Mesopotamia, leaving the land more or less vacant. Eventually the exiles had returned and restored a temple and a minor statelet under the Persian Empire. In general outline this had been maintained throughout the critical period, and used as a grid upon which the literary criticism of the books was hung.

Some newer historians questioned all this, leaders being perhaps the Dane N. P. Lemche, the American T. L. Thompson, also working in Denmark, and in Great Britain K. W. Whitelam. Apart from the Bible itself, they argue, there is no evidence for many of these things. The newer archaeology, as mentioned above, cannot verify them. 'Ancient Israel' is a 'construct' required by the needs of Jews striving to construct a community and a tradition in the difficult times of the Persian Empire. Something like this had long been thought, it could be argued, of stories about Abraham or Moses; why should the same not be true of much of the story of the time of the kings? The history of the times and lands surveyed by the Bible had too often been written as 'History of Israel', but this prejudiced it in favour of the Jewish conception. It should be the History of Palestine and Syria (or whatever the area should be called) and of whatever peoples historical investigation finds to have been there.

Naturally, not all scholars assent to these historical opinions, but they have certainly made a difference to the scene of biblical study. A good attempt to bring together the different impacts of history, archaeology, inscriptional evidence, linguistics, literary study, religious structures and sociology, as they bear upon the period of the Israelite/Judahite kingdoms, is Z. Zevit, *The Religions of Ancient Israel* (New York, 2001).

Moreover, there are other elements in the modern scholarly scene that work in a similar direction. Independently of this movement among historians, some critical views of the biblical literature had already been moving towards a later dating of the texts. The Swiss H. H. Schmid argued that the J document was of much later origin than had been supposed. The American J. Van Seters argued that the traditions about Abraham were also of much later date and fitted in very well with a time after the exile. Moreover, the supposition that Deuteronomy was essentially separate from the other four books of the Pentateuch was challenged; and if this was so, then D elements were to be found, after all, in all sorts of places in Genesis and Exodus, and this would potentially bring the dates of many passages down later. Deuteronomy itself, and the Deuteronomistic History, may be seen to have several distinguishable elements and thus not to be a unitary source, and this also might move its date down later (R. Smend, W. Dieterich, T. Veijola). The general idea of three or four clearly distinct sources was now felt to be doubtful, and a new construction of two compositions, KD and KP, was proposed (E. Blum, following

R. Rendtorff). These various approaches are all different from each other and none shows a likelihood of totally replacing the general perspective inherited from Wellhausen but modified in limited ways. Nevertheless a general tendency to date Pentateuchal sources later is now widespread. In addition, some scholars completely denied the whole idea of different sources within the Pentateuch (R. N. Whybray). E. W. Nicholson presents a balanced survey in his *The Pentateuch in the Twentieth Century* (Oxford, 1998).

Biblical law has been a focus of increasing attention (D. Daube, B. S. Jackson, A. Phillips). A distinction between 'casuistic' and 'apodeictic' law, coming from A. Alt, has been widely used. It served to fit a distinction between laws shared with Mesopotamian sources, which were 'casuistic', and others which were distinctively Israelite, which were 'apodeictic'. Recent study, however, seems to have relativised the contrast somewhat. The ritual laws and laws involving expiation have been intensively studied (J. Milgrom, B. Janowski). In general, emphasis on the legal aspects of the Hebrew Bible has tended to increase throughout the twentieth century.

In the latter part of the twentieth century increasing interest began to be paid to the Wisdom Literature. This had never been entirely neglected, of course. O. S. Rankin wrote a general survey in 1936, and the work of B. Gemser was also noted. The commentary of E. Dhorme on Job (1926) was said by some to be the best commentary ever written on any book of the Bible (though only from a limited viewpoint could this be affirmed), and the contacts with Egyptian and Babylonian work in the same genre were taken seriously. But the mid-century emphasis on the 'God Who Acts' had put Wisdom somewhat in the shade. From the 1960s, however, positive appreciation of Israelite Wisdom increased, with major attention coming from W. McKane and R. N. Whybray, later from K. J. Dell, and in the USA from S. Terrien and J. L. Crenshaw. The associated question of schools and education in Israel was approached by A. Lemaire and E. W. Heaton.

In the prophetic books much reconsideration has taken place. The analysis of Isaiah into three great sections continues to be broadly maintained: one still speaks of 'Deutero-Isaiah'. But in detail the division has failed to give satisfaction to many. Much work has sought to show how the sections deemed later were in fact integral with the earlier ones. Even if the three great sections could still be distinguished, portions of each seemed to have affinities with another of the three. In particular the separate identity of the four 'Servant Songs' came under renewed questioning (Barstad, Mettinger), and this particular view, though formerly widespread, must now be considered very doubtful. Quite a different picture is given by B. Sommer, who suggests that Deutero-Isaiah's true connections are not with the earlier Isaiah tradition but with Jeremiah.

In Jeremiah itself the markedly different extent and ordering of the Greek text has come into its own as a major theme, since the Dead Sea evidence makes it clear that this goes back to a Hebrew original. We therefore have two full editions of the book, both from ancient times. In Ezekiel also wide divergence has existed between support of the traditional text (M. Greenberg) and a text-critical approach (W. Zimmerli). Among the Minor Prophets, Habakkuk has been distinguished through the discovery of a *pesher* or interpretation among the Dead Sea documents. In general, interest in the prophets has tended to move towards the way in which later generations looked back on prophets of earlier times, and the books themselves can be seen as influenced and structured by these retroactive forces (J. Barton, *Oracles of God*, London, 1986).

From this it follows naturally that intense interest has been directed towards the literature that seems to belong expressly to the late, post-exilic, period: Ezra, Nehemiah, Chronicles, Esther, Zechariah, Haggai. A basic survey by P. R. Ackroyd (*Exile and Restoration*, London, 1968) marked the more positive approach to the period. Here again, however, there is a division between those who take Ezra and Nehemiah as basically reliable historical sources and those who see them as self-serving ideology-laden works, serving the cause of the group which claimed to be returned exiles against those who had remained in the land throughout. A balanced survey is L. L. Grabbe, *Judaism from Cyrus to Hadrian* (London, 1994). On Chronicles major research has been done by S. Japhet and H. G. M. Williamson. On Daniel and apocalyptic new perspectives have been opened out by P. Hanson, R. Carroll, J. J. Collins and C. C. Rowland: any full discussion requires one to go out into the non-canonical literature, notably Enoch, of which the Aramaic fragments from Qumran were edited by Milik. The theology of Enoch and its relevance for later religion have been studied especially by M. Barker. An interest in LBH or 'Late Biblical Hebrew' has stimulated work by R. Polzin and A. Hurwitz.

Study of the Psalms, and of Hebrew poetry generally, has gone through great changes. W. Gunkel initiated the use of form criticism, in which a limited number of forms were classified and identified as belonging each to a *Sitz im Leben*. These forms were later used by individual poets. S. Mowinckel related the forms to ritual use in the liturgical practice of the temple; this had the effect of dating the poems further back, under the kingdom, for the most part. Study of Hebrew poetic patterns has burgeoned during the twentieth century, stimulated by the Ugaritic literature which appears to offer analogies. M. Dahood sought, in the Psalms and elsewhere, to prove that Hebrew and Ugaritic were more or less the same language. In Hebrew itself two approaches exist, the metricist which seeks to identify a metrical system in Hebrew, and the parallelist which finds the essence of poetry in the very obvious parallelism of half-verses with one another. A. Berlin wrote *The Dynamics of Biblical Parallelism* (Baltimore, 1985). J. Kugel has tried to solve the problem by seeking to show that there was no poetry at all in Hebrew, but only rhetoric (*The Idea of Biblical Poetry: Parallelism and Its History*, New Haven, Conn., 1981). W. G. E. Watson is noted as the central specialist in Hebrew poetry.

An approach that flourished greatly in the last decades of the century was the study of 'inter-biblical exegesis'—the way in which later elements of text were not independent but were composed in order to interpret the meaning of earlier passages. The leading exponent is M. Fishbane (*Biblical Interpretation in Ancient Israel*, Oxford, 1985). Exegesis in this sense, therefore, is not something done after the Bible as a whole is complete: rather, it is done within the biblical books and forms an essential linkage within them. This connects with canonical interpretation, to be mentioned below.

Sociological approaches have greatly increased in influence in the last two decades of the twentieth century. N. K. Gottwald in the USA (*The Tribes of Yahweh*, Maryknoll, NY, 1979) has been something of a leader in this movement and K. W. Whitelam is a good representative in Britain more recently. The movement appears to start from historical questions but holds that these cannot be answered with older methods. The underlying movements of history are sited in social realities, which are indicated by evidences such as demography, kinship, family relations, economic conditions, dwelling types and settlement patterns. All of these were concealed by traditional literature with its interest in great personalities, wars and battles, and religious convictions. The Old Testament is the product of an elite, and an elite of the Second Temple period; it does not tell us how things were, but expresses the ideology of that elite. This is not the only direction in which sociological interpretation can go, but it is the one most noticeable at present in biblical studies.

Feminist interpretation has much kinship with this. On the one hand it points to the sparse information given by the Old Testament about the normal life of women. The patriarchal domination of society has silenced much of the social reality, in which women must have played a much greater role. On the other hand it seems to believe also the opposite, namely that the Old Testament is full of material in which women are the predominant focus of interest. Searches for such material are being actively pursued in numerous doctoral dissertations. Certainly feminist interpretation has enabled new dimensions of texts to be seen. Of particular importance is one aspect in which it is linked with new evidences in the history of religion: namely the inscriptions which, if rightly interpreted, appear to show that Yahweh, the God of Israel, was in some circles worshipped along with a female consort, Asherah (a lively discussion of this exists; see important studies by J. A. Emerton, S. Olyan, Z. Zevit and many others). Much requires to be done to explore the impact of this new evidence upon both theology and social life. Leading feminist scholars specialising in the Old Testament include M. Bal, P. Bird, A. Brenner, J. C. Exum and P. Trible.

Perhaps the most influential and fundamental of the forces bringing change to Old Testament studies towards the end of the twentieth century has been the approach commonly termed 'literary' (the qualification is necessary, because much traditional biblical criticism had also been known as 'literary criticism'). Deep contempt on the part of literary critics for the dullness, meticulous pedantry, lack of imagination and disregard for all reception history and anything other than the 'original writer' on the part of biblical critics is nothing new and can be found two centuries ago. But on the whole it was balanced by the values attached to the original sources and authors. By the mid-twentieth century, however, the importance of the original was being undermined. It does not matter where a poet had got his ideas from, nor does it even matter what he himself thinks to be its meaning: the text is its own meaning, or at least communicates its own meaning. If a text like a biblical book was composed from various strands, that is of no interest; the reader wants to know what it means as it is. The approach should be synchronic rather than diachronic; for applications of this principle to the Bible see D. J. A. Clines, *The Theme of the Pentateuch* (Sheffield, 1978) and D. M. Gunn and D. N. Fewell, *Narrative in the Hebrew Bible* (Oxford, 1993). Reader-response interpretation is another possibility that may have to be considered. These suggestions may provide a useful connection of the newer, literary-based, approach with the older, traditional, religious reading (which had actually had little sympathy with any such literary approach). This literary approach often sees traditional biblical criticism as a sort of archaeology, digging holes in the text in the hope of finding something decisive. Works like R. Alter and F. Kermode (eds.), *The Literary Guide to the Bible* (London, 1987) are representative (though, in this particular case, paradoxically, it seems to have escaped the notice of the editors that a large proportion of the contributors are obviously traditional biblical critics who do not at all belong to the editors' movement and are quite remote from it in their own work). Many of the 'literary' works on the Bible produced thus far have not been purely literary but have incorporated also themes and insights from those other approaches discussed immediately above.

Partially related with these interests is the rise of 'canonical' interpretation, which began in the United States—B. S. Childs is by far the leading
exponent, in a series of works culminating in *Biblical Theology of the Old and
New Testaments* (London, 1992)—and has quickly become widely influential. The emphasis here is on the final form of the text, the text as it lies before
the reader now or at any other time: the word *origin* is a bad word, to be
avoided at all costs. The emphasis is synthetic where the older biblical study
was seen as analytic. A biblical book must be seen as a whole, holistically.
Moreover, the Bible is not a collection of diverse books: it is a canon, an
intended assemblage of books that must be read together. Thus—a typical
case—it should have meaning that Gen. 38, the story of Judah and Tamar,
comes between sections of the Joseph story, though it seems at first sight to
have no connection with it. Textual criticism is also devalued: the authoritative text for interpretation is the Masoretic Text, and attempts to get behind it
only damage the canonical intention. The use of the Bible as historical
evidence, though not erroneous, is of secondary importance for interpretation.

The canonical approach, seen in this way, may well draw support from the
various fairly novel trends in scholarship, especially from the literary
approach. This is not the emphasis of Childs, however. For him its justification is entirely theological. In this respect the relation between Jewish and
Christian interpretation has to be considered. At first sight the canonical
approach might appear to draw a sharp line of separation between
Christianity and Judaism, because the Christian Bible is a two-part canon and
the canonical principle requires the interpretation of Old and New together.
Jewish interpreters therefore could not join in the discussion. This however is
probably not intended. For the Jewish Bible is also a canon, though constructed in a different way from the Christian canon (or, more correctly,
canons, since the various major church traditions have different canons). The
canonical nature of the Jewish Bible means that it is admired and accepted by
the Christian canonical approach, and its canonical character is thought to
provide substantial support to the emphasis on the same in Christianity.

The canonical approach is however not only theological in the general
sense. It is, in the main form expressed so far, rather strictly linked to one particular theological position, and is used very much as a polemical weapon
against other forms of theology. Ideologically, it is linked with a strong hostility towards the Enlightenment. And, apart from theology, its negativity
towards other approaches in Old Testament scholarship is marked.

In any case, whether one approves of canonical biblical theology or not,
the whole discussion has fostered valuable research into the concept of canon,
its history, the mode of its operation, which had been rather neglected in the

past. In this sense it has greatly enriched Old Testament scholarship. The work of J. Barton is outstanding in this regard.

Under theology, the production of 'theological dictionaries' should be noted. Following in some respects the pattern of Kittel's well-known theological dictionary to the New Testament, which was begun before the Second World War, a similar *Theological Dictionary of the Old Testament* was begun under the editorship of G. J. Botterweck and H. Ringgren; later H.-J. Fabry replaced Botterweck after the death of the latter. The German text appeared during 1973–95 in Stuttgart, the English translation in eleven volumes in Grand Rapids, 1974–2001. Meanwhile a more concise work of the same kind had been prepared by E. Jenni and C. Westermann (2 vols., Munich, 1971, 1979), translated into English as *Theological Lexicon of the Old Testament* (3 vols., Peabody, Mass., 1997). In spite of the term 'theological' that occurs in the titles of these works, it should not be ignored that they contain much valuable linguistic and cultural information: see for example the statistical work in Jenni-Westermann. There is also some overlap with the *Anchor Bible Dictionary*, already mentioned above.

Although biblical theology has tended to be opposed to interest in the history of religion, it has not succeeded in overcoming the values perceived in the latter. On the contrary, the approach through the history of religion has enjoyed a substantial revival towards the end of the century. R. Albertz published his extensive *History of Israelite Religion in the Old Testament Period* (2 vols., London, 1994; German original: 2 vols., Göttingen, 1992). He argued that this approach promised to be much more effective than Old Testament theology, even in the tasks which the latter had sought to fulfil. Albertz thus took the arguments which had been thought to favour biblical theology and turned them against it and to the advantage of history of religion. Meanwhile others (J. Day, M. S. Smith, J. C. de Moor, T. N. D. Mettinger) have continued to pursue the setting of Israelite religion within the environment of Near Eastern religion, with an emphasis on the Mesopotamian and the Ugaritic evidence.

In conclusion, it should be recorded that the British Academy's interest in biblical study has been marked, among other things, by the award, normally annually, of a Burkitt Medal in recognition of special services to biblical studies (both Old and New Testaments). The medals were originally struck by Burkitt himself. Since then they have been awarded to numerous leading scholars in Hebrew Bible. Some of these have been Fellows of the Academy themselves, or have already been mentioned in the present article. Among others should be mentioned S. A. Cook, H. Wheeler Robinson, P. Benoit, J. Lindblom, Bonifatius Fischer, Otto Kaiser and A. S. van der Woude.

Mention should also be made of the Schweich Lectures, a series of the British Academy. They are commonly referred to as 'on Biblical Archaeology' but the full specification is that they should be on subjects related to 'the archaeology, art, history, languages and literature of Ancient Civilization with reference to Biblical Study'. They have in fact, as this very open definition invites, been on a very wide variety of subjects related to Bible and religion.

CHAPTER TWO
The New Testament

WILLIAM HORBURY

When the twentieth century began, New Testament study was increasingly regarded as a distinct field. In the meanwhile, workers within it have felt the importance of looking over the hedge.[1] In 1902, however, when the Academy was founded, the movement towards demarcation could be seen at least partly as an assertion of integrity. This field of biblical study was of profound concern to the theological faculties and to the church, and it also attracted students of biblical and rabbinic Hebrew and of Classics; but if it was to flourish it had to attain a certain concentration and detachment.

New Testament work since 1902 is here reviewed with an eye on movements in British scholarship, but with some notice of their continental European and North American background. Scholarly publication and tendencies of thought persisted throughout both the world wars. Hence, although 1918 and to some extent 1945 were perceived soon afterwards as theological turning-points, the epochs in this story can perhaps best be marked by books.[2]

I have taken two books as signs of changing times and new periods: G. Kittel's *Wörterbuch* (1932 onwards) and E. P. Sanders's *Paul and Palestinian Judaism* (1977). German and American respectively, they reflect the importance for Britain of continental and transatlantic developments. An opening sketch of the manifold setting of New Testament study during the century is followed accordingly by comment arising successively from the three periods 1902–32, 1932–77 and 1977–2002. As a thread leading through these times I have kept in view the interaction between the two principal sides of New

---

[1] This need is stressed by M. Hengel, 'Aufgaben der neutestamentlichen Wissenschaft', *NTS* 40 (1994), 321–57. The term *Fakultätszaun*, 'faculty-hedge', was used half jestingly by H. Lietzmann, 'Notizen', *ZNW* 36 (1937), 293.

[2] A. M. Hunter, *Interpreting the New Testament, 1900–1950* (London, 1951), pp. 124–5 (tendencies evident before the First World War first had their full effect from 1918); for 1945 as a threshold of theological revival, J. de Zwaan, 'The Unity of Purpose in New Testament Studies', *JTS* 48 (1947), 129–36 (135–6).

Testament study, the philological—to use the word in its broadest sense—
and the theological.

I

Demarcation

New Testament work is part of biblical study, and also part of the study of the
early church. These two larger areas are in many ways distinct from one
another, but the sequence Old Testament–New Testament–early Christian literature is closely knit, both chronologically and thematically. The Old
Testament with the apocrypha extends into New Testament times, and the
New Testament with the Apostolic Fathers verges on the patristic age. To turn
to major subject-groupings, the New Testament has its place within the fields
of theology and religion, and can also come within the purview of Classics
and Jewish Studies. Towards the end of the nineteenth century all these relationships were manifest in a number of journals and series printing New
Testament work.

In Britain the links of New Testament study with the Old Testament and
the early church, and with Jewish Studies and Classics, could be seen especially in the Oxford series *Studia Biblica et Ecclesiastica* (1885–1903), and
they had also appeared in the Cambridge *Journal of Philology* (1868–1920),
which continued the range of the short-lived *Journal of Classical and Sacred
Philology* (1854–60). Then the Old Testament, the New Testament and the
early church were treated together within the theological field by the new
Journal of Theological Studies (1900–), and in the USA by the *Harvard
Theological Review* (1908–). The biblical field as a whole was served in
Britain by the *Expository Times* (1889–) and the *Expositor* (1873–1925), in
the USA by the *Journal of Biblical Literature* (1886–), and in France by the
Revue Biblique (1892–).

The year 1900 also saw, however, the inception in Germany of a specialised New Testament journal, E. Preuschen's *Zeitschrift für die neutestamentliche Wissenschaft und die Kunde der älteren Kirche*, followed later in
the century by others including *New Testament Studies* (Cambridge, 1954–),
Novum Testamentum (Leiden, 1956–), the *Journal for the Study of the New
Testament* (Sheffield, 1978–) and *Filología Neotestamentaria* (Córdoba,
1988–). The demarcation of New Testament study emerges clearly in these
later titles, which separate the New Testament from the Old Testament on the
one hand, and the early church on the other (Preuschen's reference to the

early church has been dropped). Professional concentration is correspondingly evinced in the sponsorship of *New Testament Studies* by a new international specialist society, Studiorum Novi Testamenti Societas, founded 1937–8.[3]

Throughout the twentieth century this progressively delimited field was cultivated in universities and church institutions, in Britain and overseas, in differing political settings. Its demarcation helped to buffer pressures—ecclesiastical, academic, political or intellectual. For much of this time New Testament study, eagerly followed in the church, was central in a theological curriculum, and closely linked with work on the Old Testament and early church history and doctrine; but by the end of the century it was often one of a more loosely connected series of subjects in theological and religious studies, and scholars in a firmly defined New Testament field had become correspondingly concerned to keep in touch with kindred disciplines.

Early twentieth-century settings overseas

The clearer demarcation of a field had its background in the political as well as the academic developments of the nineteenth and twentieth centuries. Academically, theological study was proliferating, but it did so in political settings which, despite the differences between countries and regions, placed New Testament work mainly in the context of theology and the church.

In continental central and northern Europe New Testament study had its chief home in university theological faculties. These were famous, especially in Germany, for their freedom and fecundity in critical work, but they also by law represented the interests of the ecclesiastical bodies. An influential but debated liberal attempt to bring together New Testament work with service to the church was Adolf Harnack's *Das Wesen des Christentums* (1900), in which this great historian and interpreter of the early church endeavoured to show how synoptic criticism could be united with the Reformation 'liberty of a Christian'; a fresh and simple apprehension of the essence of Christianity could then, he urged, be found in the ethical and spiritual teaching of Jesus.[4] Harnack here shared the 'quest of the historical Jesus' soon to be renewed by

---

[3] G. H. Boobyer, 'Studiorum Novi Testamenti Societas', *NTS* 1 (1954–5), 66–9; formation was discussed on J. de Zwaan's initiative in 1937, and effected in 1938.

[4] Harnack expressed longing to serve 'our churches of the Reformation' in their difficulties ('unsern vielfach kümmerlichen Reformationskirchen') in a letter of 21 October 1899 to M. Rade, discussed by Agnes von Zahn-Harnack, *Adolf von Harnack* (Berlin, 1936), pp. 299–302.

the young Albert Schweitzer.[5] For Harnack the teaching of Jesus was penetrating in its simplicity, for Schweitzer it was challenging in its strangeness, but for both authors the historical Jesus was at the heart of a rethought Christianity, and their links with the church as well as scholarship are clear.

The ecclesiastical setting of the field was paramount, however, in countries such as France and the USA, where the tendency to separate church and state was strong, notably in the French disestablishment of 1905. Here biblical work was equally pursued at high levels, but characteristically within church institutions of various kinds. These included denominational universities in North America, and Instituts Catholiques (originally intended as new church universities) in France; and a directly ecclesiastical setting like that of a seminary could indeed encourage a valuable interaction with all branches of theology. Yet it also became of great moment that biblical criticism, perhaps above all in the New Testament field, was increasingly perceived as a threat to church loyalty.

In the French Roman Catholic community of the early twentieth century these studies aroused interest as intense as the hostility they evoked. Eminent New Testament scholars among the clergy included the judicious M.-J. Lagrange (1855–1938), founder of the École Biblique in Jerusalem, and the outspoken Alfred Loisy (1857–1940), who sceptically questioned Harnack's reliance on a reconstructed body of Jesus's teaching, and urged that the historian inevitably encountered, rather, the church which arose from and presented the teaching. Lagrange, who remained a devoted Dominican, later nostalgically called these years a time of struggle, but also of burning ardour for biblical studies.[6] Prosper Alfaric, a younger priest who eventually became a rationalist lay scholar, remembered how, when teaching dogma in French seminaries at this time, he read with fascination the *Revue Biblique* and the work of Loisy; and how the liberal archbishop of Albi, Mgr Mignot, startled him by an urgent summons to what turned out to be a discussion of Philo in relation with the Fourth Gospel and Hebrews.[7] Similar excitement was felt in Italy, not least in Rome, where in the 1890s a Società romana per gli studi biblici had formed a seed-bed for contributions to the *Revue Biblique*.[8]

---

[5] A. Schweitzer, *Geschichte der Leben-Jesu-Forschung* (2nd edn. of *Von Reimarus zu Wrede* [1906], Tübingen, 1913); Eng. trans. *The Quest of the Historical Jesus, First Complete Edition*, trans. W. Montgomery, J. R. Coates, Susan Cupitt and J. Bowden, ed. John Bowden (London, 2000).

[6] 'Une époque de luttes où les esprits étaient si ardents pour les études bibliques': M.-J. Lagrange, *Évangile selon Saint Marc*, 4th edn. (Paris, 1929), p. iii.

[7] P. Alfaric, *De la foi à la raison* (Paris, 1955), pp. 137–43, 170.

[8] J. (G.) Semeria, 'Chronique d'Italie', *RB* 2 (1893), 431–54 (431–3).

The precarious conditions of New Testament work in this setting became parlous during the conservative church reaction to biblical criticism fostered under the rule of Pius X (1903–14). Loisy formed the main target when propositions termed Modernist were condemned in the decree *Lamentabili* of the Holy Office in 1907, followed up by the encyclical *Pascendi* (1907) and the anti-Modernist oath to be taken by the clergy (1910–67).[9] In 1907, correspondingly, and from 1911 to 1914, the Pontifical Biblical Commission issued responsa upholding widely doubted traditional views on the Fourth Gospel, the synoptic problem, Matthew, Mark, Luke, Acts, the Pastoral Epistles and Hebrews. Defence of biblical criticism was not helped by revival at this time of the 'Christ-myth' theory, suggesting that Jesus had never existed, a suggestion rebutted in England by the radical but independent F. C. Conybeare.[10]

Loisy was excommunicated in 1908. Mignot was eminent among scholarly members of the clergy who kept in touch with him, despite the danger of being stigmatised. Among New Testament scholars in England he won sympathy not only from his faithful friend Baron Friedrich von Hügel, who took a deep interest in biblical subjects from the standpoint of a philosophical theologian and student of mysticism, but also from F. C. Burkitt (1864–1935).[11] The cloud over Roman Catholic biblical study was lifted only after a generation, by Pius XII's 1943 encyclical *Divino afflante Spiritu*. Yet New Testament work went on in France; Lagrange's large-scale commentaries questioned the radicalism of Loisy, vigorous Protestant learning was exemplified by M. Goguel at the Sorbonne, and sceptical non-religious study by P.-L. Couchoud, Alfaric and others implausibly favoured the Christ-myth theory, but led to thorough discussion of Christian origins.[12]

Twentieth-century British settings

There was a somewhat comparable contemporary New Testament struggle in Britain and especially in the Church of England, but the political and

[9] O. Chadwick, *A History of the Popes, 1830–1914* (Oxford, 1998), pp. 346–59.

[10] F. C. Conybeare, *The Historical Christ, or an Investigation of the views of Mr J. M. Robertson, Dr A. Drews, and Prof. W. B. Smith* (London, 1914); these writings were also criticised in 1913 by Schweitzer, *Geschichte der Leben-Jesu-Forschung*, pp. 444–97, Eng. trans. pp. 355–90.

[11] Letters of Burkitt to Loisy written in 1908 and 1934 are quoted by A. R. Vidler, *A Variety of Catholic Modernists* (Cambridge, 1970), pp. 186–7; a sympathetic contemporary account of Loisy was given by F. C. Conybeare, *History of New Testament Criticism* (London, 1910), pp. 72–4 (with plate) and 134–8.

[12] E. Trocmé, 'Exégèse scientifique et idéologie: de l'École de Tubingue aux historiens français des origines chrétiennes', *NTS* 24 (1978), 447–62 (458–60).

academic setting here recalled Germany rather than France. The New Testament had long been studied in universities with an ancient or more recent church connection, including Oxford, Cambridge, the four older Scottish universities, Trinity College, Dublin, and the early nineteenth-century foundations of King's College in London, Durham University, and Queen's College (later University) in Belfast.

Yet by the end of the nineteenth century formal links with the church had become less marked in Britain than in Germany. University religious tests had effectively ceased, and although many chairs retained their ecclesiastical ties academic biblical study was now clearly lay as well as clerical, and also increasingly interdenominational, with a powerful Free Church participation. At the same time important contributions were being made by scholars from the Jewish community. In 1904 a Faculty of Theology was established at Manchester in express independence of any religious test, and this example was followed in a number of university colleges and universities in the early years of the century, and then in a new wave after the Second World War. The New Testament stood out in these developments; among scholars named above and below, F. C. Burkitt and C. H. Turner were early lay divinity professors in Cambridge (1905) and Oxford (1920), respectively, and professors in the Manchester faculty include the Congregationalist C. H. Dodd (1930), who moved in 1935 to a Cambridge chair and was succeeded in Manchester by the Presbyterian T. W. Manson.

Disquiet over New Testament criticism and church loyalty emerged in Britain as well as France, not least in the Church of England, in which the Broad Church or liberal Anglican tradition now became known, in line with the Continent, as Modernism. Tension was bound up with the question whether recital of the creeds required affirmation of physical miracle. The 1905–6 *Declaration on Biblical Criticism by 1725 Clergy of the Anglican Communion* was an effort to show, despite opposition, how substantial was the support for criticism among the clergy. Supporters of Loisy in France valued this document, and New Testament signatories in the Academy included R. H. Charles and B. H. Streeter, but not the more conservative W. Sanday, although his views later changed; among signatories in related fields were J. E. B. Mayor and W. W. Skeat, professors respectively of Latin and Anglo-Saxon in Cambridge.[13] On the other side 'there were many who wished [their]

---

[13] H. Handley (ed.), *A Declaration on Biblical Criticism by 1725 Clergy of the Anglican Communion* (London, 1906) (French newspaper reaction is quoted at p. 26), discussed by A. Houtin, *La Question biblique au XXe siècle* (Paris, 1906), pp. 227–40.

Bishops to give the same relentless reply as the Pope', and they found a leader of formidable spirit and integrity in Charles Gore, bishop successively of Worcester, Birmingham and Oxford.[14]

Feeling of this kind continued: witness for example the charge of teaching contrary to scripture which was formally brought against H. D. A. Major in 1921; for his part he presented his own contested view of resurrection as emerging primarily from 'the application of modern methods of literary and historical criticism to the interpretation of Scripture', exemplified by Charles.[15] Gore's position was relinquished by his successors in the liberal catholic movement in the Church of England, including New Testament scholars mentioned below such as A. E. J. Rawlinson (bishop of Derby), Wilfred Knox and E. G. Selwyn; but the inward tension still felt by critics in this tradition emerges in a comment from E. C. Hoskyns, looking back, on 'the acute pain of our technical work',[16] and later in the ultimately negative retrospect on Loisy as well as Harnack—leading however to a defence of free New Testament criticism as not incompatible with Christian orthodoxy— offered in 1939 by N. P. Williams, who as a young graduate had studied in both the Protestant and the Roman Catholic faculties at Strassburg during the fraught years 1906–7.[17]

Perhaps the last major eruption of controversy on criticism followed the publication in 1947 of *The Rise of Christianity* by E. W. Barnes, FRS, bishop of Birmingham. Barnes's emphasis on the late date and doubtful authorship of New Testament books evoked a form-critically fortified response from Dodd on the early tradition which they preserved.[18] Thirty years later there was a comparable controversy, again as it happened arising from work in Birmingham, over *The Myth of God Incarnate*, edited by John Hick. Now, however, although the debate had a strong New Testament side, public concern was predominantly doctrinal.[19]

---

[14] G. K. A. Bell, *Randall Davidson, Archbishop of Canterbury*, 3rd edn. (London, 1952), p. 671; on Gore's view that biblical criticism would not affect credal affirmation of physical miracle see S. W. Sykes, *The Integrity of Anglicanism* (London and Oxford, 1978), pp. 20–25.

[15] Major in *The Doctrine of the Resurrection of the Body: Documents Relating to the Question of Heresy raised against the Rev. H. D. A. Major, Ripon Hall, Oxford* issued by H. M. Burge, DD, Lord Bishop of Oxford (London, 1922), pp. 48–9.

[16] Letter of Hoskyns (1934) to A. R. Vidler, quoted by Vidler, *A Variety of Catholic Modernists*, p. 188.

[17] N. P. Williams, 'What is Theology?', in K. E. Kirk (ed.), *The Study of Theology* (London, 1939), pp. 3–82 (32–6); E. W. Kemp, *N. P. Williams* (London, 1954), pp. 7–9.

[18] C. H. Dodd, *Christian Beginnings: A Reply to Dr. Barnes's 'The Rise of Christianity'* (London, n.d. [1947]); J. Barnes, *Ahead of his Age: Bishop Barnes of Birmingham* (London, 1979), pp. 395–414.

[19] J. H. Hick (ed.), *The Myth of God Incarnate* (London, 1977); M. D. Goulder (ed.), *Incarnation and Myth: The Debate Continued* (London, 1979).

A new phase of ecumenical church-related scholarship had in fact already begun before the Second World War, and was further strengthened in the aftermath of *Divino afflante Spiritu*. For a considerable period New Testament work was particularly closely integrated into church life. The New English Bible was translated from 1947 onwards at the joint request of major Christian bodies in the British Isles, and New Testament theology was important for the World Council of Churches founded in 1948, and the Second Vatican Council of 1961–5. Dodd was only ten years younger than Barnes, but in his critique he, a Congregationalist academic, represented this new phase of church-related ecumenical scholarship, whereas Barnes, a bishop of the established Church, warmed to the more detached scholarship typical of an earlier phase.

Towards the end of the century the atmosphere in Britain changed again. In the universities the undergraduate syllabus in ancient and modern languages, literature and history was broadening, with greater choice and some fragmentation. Within the theological faculties this trend converged with the increasing importance of religious studies, concentrated on non-Christian religions and sometimes distinguished from theology as a subject. At the same time critical approaches in which subjectivity was taken for granted became more common. Demarcation now perhaps helped to preserve the wholeness of New Testament study as it moved into new settings.

In the USA biblical work was now finding a place not only in denominational universities and colleges but also, under the aegis of the study of religion, in state universities and other places of higher education. Paula Fredriksen writes of a 'new home for New Testament research created, particularly in the United States and Canada, within the religion faculties of liberal arts colleges and universities'.[20] Contrasts in self-awareness arose between scholarship with and without church sponsorship, respectively.

At the same time there was a shift towards the predominance of the English language in scholarship. In 1900 Latin was still in use, then and later French was always important, and in time Spanish, Italian and other languages became prominent; but the main language of New Testament study for most of the century had been German. Now the international impact of the North American scene and the English language was also heightened by the expansion of the USA-based Society of Biblical Literature to include researchers from many other countries.

---

[20] P. Fredriksen, *Jesus of Nazareth, King of the Jews: A Jewish Life and the Emergence of Christianity* (1999, repr. London, 2001), p. 5.

In Britain, affected by these developments together with its own syllabus broadening and concern with world religions, New Testament study could benefit from the wish for choice and diversity and for the representation of religions by their own texts and adherents, but it could also seem less central within theological faculties and departments, and become more isolated from other areas. Reduced opportunities for the learning of Latin and Greek at school increased the difficulty of beginning New Testament study, but were partly countered by widespread interest in archaeology and ancient history. Connections with the church and the Jewish community remained important, but non-religious standpoints regained their early twentieth-century prominence, and the philological side of New Testament work tended to become more separate from the theological side. British scholarship was in a position to feel tension, sometimes perhaps creative, between continental European traditions of study and North American approaches.

By the end of the twentieth century the New Testament was studied in connection with theology and religion in well over twenty of the larger universities in Scotland, Wales, England and Ireland, as well as in the theological and bible colleges and colleges of education which were increasingly connected with the universities. To pick out two centres which were important throughout the period, comparison between histories of twentieth-century Oxford and Cambridge might give the false impression that New Testament scholarship has been more significant in the latter;[21] it had greater nineteenth-century strength in Cambridge, but in the twentieth century it has flourished in both, and in universities old and new throughout the British Isles. A notable aspect of this work was the training of graduates; at the end of the century New Testament candidates for research degrees in Britain included a high proportion from overseas, notably from the USA, the Commonwealth and continental Europe. The former ecclesiastical pressures now mainly took the form of internal tension between scholarship and piety, but political, academic and intellectual movement of course also continued to impinge on the study of theology and religion, within which most New

---

[21] In B. Harrison (ed.), *The History of the University of Oxford*, 8. *The Twentieth Century* (Oxford, 1994), theology is not treated among the areas of study, although New Testament comments in the chapter on 'Religion' (e.g. pp. 298, 309) receive a little supplement in the select list of pre-1939 arts publications (pp. 134–5); but C. N. L. Brooke, *A History of the University of Cambridge*, 4. *1870–1990* (Cambridge, 1993) has a chapter on 'Theology' and separate studies of F. J. A. Hort and C. H. Dodd.

Testament work was carried on. Yet some of the strength of New Testament study has arguably arisen in response to tensions of this kind.[22]

Retrospect

At the beginning of the century, however, New Testament work occupied a sometimes uncomfortably central height in theology and the church. Practical consequences are illustrated by the fate of an early twentieth-century article on 'The Relation of the Discourses in the Fourth Gospel to the Book of Wisdom'. The author was the young J. A. F. Gregg, commentator on Wisdom (1909) and later professor at Trinity College, Dublin (1911) and archbishop successively of Dublin and Armagh. From Greek catena manuscripts he had already edited 'The Commentary of Origen on the Epistle to the Ephesians' in the *Journal of Theological Studies* (3 [1902–3], 233–44, 389–420, 554–76). His piece on the Fourth Gospel was accepted for the *Journal* in December 1904 by the Cambridge editor, J. F. Bethune-Baker, a leading representative of Anglican Modernism. The article reached the stage of a corrected final proof due to be published in 1905, only to be rejected in late March that year on the plea of the other editor, the more traditional F. E. Brightman, who was supported, as Bethune-Baker wrote to Gregg, by 'one of the most influential of the Oxford directors' of the *Journal*.[23] This was probably Sanday, the revered founder of modern New Testament work in Oxford, who united an unrivalled knowledge of German scholarship with deep loyalty to church tradition, above all on the Johannine question. After his death, and despite his adoption later on of more liberal critical opinions, Burkitt suggested that it might now be easier for Sanday's junior Oxford colleagues to express their views freely.[24]

It was in autumn 1904 that Sanday made a heartfelt defence of the Fourth Gospel as apostolic eyewitness testimony, against critics including P. W. Schmiedel and Loisy, in lectures which he issued at Easter 1905 as *The Criticism of the Fourth Gospel*. Gregg's article was rejected just when these lectures were being prepared for publication. Hoskyns later wrote, with special reference to this book of Sanday, that 'it was a widely held opinion in liberal theological circles in Germany before the War that Sanday in Oxford

---

[22] Pressures on academic theology as perceived during the unrest of 1968–9 were discussed by C. K. Barrett, 'Theology in the World of Learning', reprinted from the *Australian Biblical Review* 17 (October, 1969), 9–20 in Barrett, *New Testament Essays* (London, 1972), pp. 144–56.

[23] G. Seaver, *John Allen Fitzgerald Gregg, Archbishop* (London and Dublin, 1963), p. 45, quoting a letter of Bethune-Baker of 28 March 1905.

[24] F. C. Burkitt, reviewing B. H. Streeter, *The Four Gospels* in *JTS* 26 (1925), 278–94 (278).

and [V. H.] Stanton in Cambridge had been appointed by the Archbishop of Canterbury in order to defend orthodoxy; . . . nor is this judgment altogether surprising.'[25] Sanday had given up this view of the Fourth Gospel by 1912.[26] Seven years earlier, however, Gregg's article had touched the same neuralgic point as Mignot's discussion with Alfaric, the relation between ancient Jewish conceptions of divine intermediaries and the Johannine Christology.[27] From April 1905, also, the declaration in defence of biblical criticism was circulating, and Gregg became one of the 1,725 signatories.

II

The early twentieth century

Yet despite pressures the years from 1902 to 1932 formed a golden age of abundance, solidity and variety in New Testament scholarship. Well-known British contributions to it include Sanday's Oxford seminar which brought forth *Studies in the Synoptic Problem by Members of the University of Oxford* (Oxford, 1911). Aspects of the problem, notably the character of Q, were being studied at the same time by Harnack and others, above all J. Wellhausen, outstanding in work on the New Testament as well as the Old. The seminar led ultimately to Streeter's *The Four Gospels* (London, 1924), a book which includes the classic English statement of a four-document hypothesis of the literary interrelationship of the synoptic Gospels.[28]

The immediate background of these studies, which were based on minute first-hand scrutiny, was the uncertainty about the origins of the synoptic material which still remained after wide acceptance of the priority of Mark or a form of Mark. In Britain the lively late-Victorian comments on the synoptic problem by George Salmon, FRS kept in currency, for instance, the thoughts that Q might well stand for Query, and that Mark might be at once early and

---

[25] E. C. Hoskyns, *The Fourth Gospel*, ed. F. N. Davey, 2nd edn. (London, 1947), p. 35.

[26] W. Sanday, *The Criticism of the Fourth Gospel* (Oxford, 1905) and *Divine Overruling* (Edinburgh, 1920), p. 61, discussed by C. H. Turner, *The Study of the New Testament, 1883 and 1920*, 3rd edn. (Oxford, 1926), pp. 33–5. With the reaction to Gregg envisaged here from Sanday, compare Sanday's 1890 warning against misunderstanding of E. Hatch on Greek influence (n. 103, below).

[27] Contrast Gregg's view that John 'drank deeply' of a pre-existent Jewish Wisdom-doctrine (Seaver, *Gregg*, p. 48, quoting a paper delivered by Gregg in 1905) with Sanday's tracing of Johannine Christology (by simultaneous use of and debate with Loisy) above all to the teaching of Christ preserved by the earliest Christians (Sanday, *The Criticism of the Fourth Gospel*, pp. 223–6, 231–3).

[28] On the seminar and Streeter see S. C. Neill, in S. C. Neill and N. T. Wright, *The Interpretation of the New Testament, 1861–1986* (Oxford, 1988), pp. 129–36.

late—preserving apostolic tradition used by Matthew and Luke, but completed in its present form only after them.[29]

Then in Cambridge about 1912 the problems of Christian origins became the work of a similar seminar. Collaboration which was continued later in the USA led to the five-volume work on Acts issued by F. J. Foakes Jackson and Kirsopp Lake under the title *The Beginnings of Christianity* (London, 1920, 1922, 1926, 1933, 1933). As it seemed to the editors, 'the discovery and the general solution of the synoptic problem' had been achieved; we now had 'to translate these results into the language of the historian' and to scrutinise the process whereby 'the preaching . . . begun by Jesus passed into the sacramental cult of the Lord Jesus Christ'. This echo of German religio-historical study (*Religionsgeschichte*), a movement noticed further below, led to a matter-of-fact English conclusion, 'the necessary preliminary to the investigation of these questions is the study of Acts'.[30]

These two large-scale projects both involved textual and source criticism; the study of Acts went on to exegesis and history, and historical interest was also important in the synoptic seminar. This work on the Gospels and Acts then formed as it were a frame for reconsideration of the historical Jesus. Two contrasting presentations of Jesus emerged. On one side stood such scholars as Burkitt and E. C. Hoskyns, following J. Weiss and Schweitzer in presenting Jesus as imbued with eschatological hope; the outline of the ministry, in Burkitt's view, was disclosed by the Marcan sequence of events.[31] Burkitt urged that apocalypses gave the key to Gospel interpretation; the Assumption of Moses, dated soon after the death of Herod the Great, presents the hope reflected in the Gospels that God's 'kingdom shall appear' (Ass. Mos. x. 1), and some sayings of Jesus 'only appear in their true light if regarded as *Midrash* upon words and concepts taken from Enoch'.[32] In its eschatological aspect this approach was not far from that then being followed by Loisy and the young Rudolf Bultmann, but they did not share Burkitt's historical

---

[29] G. Salmon, *An Historical Introduction to the Study of the New Testament: Being an Expansion of Lectures Delivered in the Divinity School of the University of Dublin*, 4th edn. (London, 1889), pp. 155–8; F. C. Burkitt, *Jesus Christ: An Historical Outline* (London and Glasgow, 1932), p. 13, n. 1.

[30] Foakes Jackson and Kirsopp Lake, *Beginnings*, vol. 1, p. vii; cf. vol. 5, pp. vii–viii.

[31] F. C. Burkitt, *The Gospel History and Its Transmission*, 2nd edn. (Edinburgh, 1907), pp. 62–3, 78–81, with other works including id., *Jesus Christ* (n. 29, above), discussed by M. D. Chapman, *The Coming Crisis: The Impact of Eschatology on Theology in Edwardian England* (*JSNT* Supplement Series 208, Sheffield, 2001), pp. 81–101.

[32] F. C. Burkitt, *Jewish and Christian Apocalypses* (Schweich Lectures 1913, London, 1914), pp. 21, 38–40.

confidence.[33] Bultmann in particular had viewed form criticism as precluding any outline of the life of Jesus. This position was to receive much discussion, as noted below; but meanwhile perhaps the most obvious contrast continued to be that between eschatological and other depictions of Jesus.

To turn now to the other side, non-eschatological depictions were offered by Harnack and Wellhausen in Germany—in Wellhausen's case with particular emphasis on the Christian colouring of Mark's narrative—and by B. W. Bacon in the USA.[34] In Germany these would recur to a considerable extent in the work of Gerhard Kittel and Joachim Jeremias, now beginning. In England they would be developed by Dodd, in work also just beginning, which was to form (in the words of a Scottish reader who was not fully convinced) 'a remarkable turning of the tables against the purely futurist eschatology ascribed to Jesus and His disciples by Weiss and Schweitzer'.[35] In the Oxford *Studies* Streeter, following Sanday, had indeed already urged, not without sympathy for the apocalypses, that their significance for the thought of Jesus was strictly limited; Paul and John brought the church back nearer to the mind of the historic Christ.[36] Bacon in Yale would write very similarly that Jesus fully shared 'those apocalyptic ideas native to every Jewish mind', but had 'an inner core of individual faith . . . which made practical the ultimate adjustment to Hellenistic ideas' in Paul and above all in the Fourth Gospel.[37]

These contrasting presentations indicate two broader aspects of the history of study. First, here as often a divergence of opinion traversed national boundaries; realised as well as futurist eschatology found sponsorship in Germany as well as England, and Dodd and Kittel approached the subject similarly at the first of a series of Anglo-German theological conferences with a New Testament orientation (1927 in Canterbury, 1928 at the Wartburg and 1931 in Chichester) which were jointly led by Adolf Deissmann and

---

[33] A. Loisy, *La Naissance du christianisme* (Paris, 1933), pp. 91–7; R. Bultmann, *Jesus* (Berlin, 1926), pp. 29–30.

[34] A. Harnack, *Sprüche und Reden Jesu* (Leipzig, 1907), esp. pp. 170–74, Eng. trans. *The Sayings of Jesus* (London, 1908), esp. pp. 246–52; E. Bammel, 'Der historische Jesus in der Theologie Adolf von Harnacks', *Tutzinger Texte* 1 (1968), 71–97, Eng. trans. 'The Jesus of History in the Theology of Adolf von Harnack', *The Modern Churchman* N.S. 19 (1975–6), 90–112; J. Wellhausen, *Einleitung in die drei ersten Evangelien*, 2nd edn. (Berlin, 1911), pp. 86–104, 147–53 (expressly against both Schweitzer and Harnack); B. W. Bacon, *The Beginnings of Gospel Story* (New Haven, Conn., 1909), reviewed by Burkitt, *JTS* 10 (1909), 604–7.

[35] J. Baillie, *The Belief in Progress* (London, 1950), p. 203.

[36] Streeter, 'Synoptic Criticism and the Eschatological Problem', in Sanday, *Studies in the Synoptic Problem*, pp. 425–36; on Sanday's view see J. K. Riches, *A Century of New Testament Study* (Cambridge, 1993), pp. 27–8.

[37] B. W. Bacon, *Studies in Matthew* (London, 1930), pp. 412–35.

G. K. A. Bell (bishop of Chichester from 1929).[38] Local or national characteristics in scholarship can be too hastily identified. Secondly, in both the contrasting presentations noted above, philological and historical work merged
with religious and theological apprehension; this dimension can also be
detected in other philological trends of New Testament study.

The work just outlined shared in three such trends which have continued
to the present day, but had particular early twentieth-century influence: the
study of ancient versions and apocrypha, the exploration of Jewish and
Palestinian material for exegesis, and the interpretation of Christianity in the
setting of Greece and Rome. These trends were all related to the customary
study of the New Testament in its Old Testament and patristic setting, but they
had independent impetus, and a brief sketch of each will help to characterise
this first phase of twentieth-century study.

Versions and apocrypha

The New Testament versions and apocrypha are among the prime witnesses
to ancient biblical interpretation, but this way of looking at them is more
typical of later study. At the beginning of the century they were mainly
considered with regard to problems of text, history, and language.

The ancient versions, especially the Latin and the Syriac, could often
claim to attest indirectly an earlier Greek text than either the Textus Receptus
as issued by Erasmus on the basis of relatively late minuscule Greek manuscripts, or the text issued by B. F. Westcott and F. J. A. Hort (1881) on the
basis especially of the great fourth-century uncial codices. This claim was to
the fore at the end of the nineteenth century.[39] Sometimes, as scholars such as
F. C. Burkitt and C. H. Turner now emphasised, the Latin translations current
before Jerome (the Old Latin) converged with a probably early Syriac version
(the Old Syriac) to attest not only an earlier but also what seemed a more original text. The 'Western text' of the New Testament, so named in the past on
the basis of its Old Latin support, had been best known from the Greek and
Latin Gospels and Acts in the bilingual Codex Bezae. In Hort's analysis this
form of text had emerged as marked by the tendency, seen in Codex Bezae,
towards what was judged to be paraphrase and interpolation; yet it had also
been recognised as early, and widespread in east as well as west. Fresh Old

[38] C. H. Dodd and G. Kittel, both under the heading 'The this-worldly Kingdom of God in our Lord's
Teaching', *Theology* 14 (1927), 258–60, 260–62.
[39] See for example F. H. Chase, *The Syro-Latin Text of the Gospels* (London, 1895).

Latin and Old Syriac witnesses, however, now converged with one another as 'Western' but less marked by this tendency.[40]

The Latin and Syriac traditions seemed then to promise access to early and unrevised textual material of many-sided interest, often reflecting, as Hort had said of the Western text in general, 'a vigorous and popular ecclesiastical life', but now with a clearer claim also to be of value for textual restoration.[41] Work on these and other versions, notably the Coptic,[42] was aimed first of all at the preparation of reliable editions of versions and particular manuscripts.

Widespread though such textual interests were, they do indeed seem characteristic of Britain. Here the beaten track from Classics to Theology opened eyes to the significance of textual questions, even if it might sometimes allow relative inattention to the Old Testament.[43] Thus C. H. Turner highlighted the significance of textual variation for the synoptic problem, and like the more radical Kirsopp Lake and the classical scholar Friedrich Blass he spoke out for the legitimacy and value of conjectural emendation of the New Testament text.[44] Classicists concerned with the New Testament text include A. C. Clark and editors of the many finds of early papyri, notably F. G. Kenyon and H. I. Bell. A list of eminent names in New Testament textual criticism, in a French handbook of 1935, gives nine from England, as compared with five in the USA, three in Germany, and two each in France, Belgium and Holland.[45]

Pride of place among the ancient versions and in work on them in Britain belongs to the Latin Vulgate. An outstanding achievement, spanning more than half the period considered here, was the large Oxford critical edition of the Vulgate New Testament, issued between 1889 and 1953, and edited by John Wordsworth (1843–1911) and H. J. White (1859–1934)—'each of the two gave all the credit of the work to the other'—and then by H. F. D. Sparks

---

[40] F. C. Burkitt, 'Text and Versions', *Encyclopaedia Biblica* 4 (1907), cols. 4977–5031 (4988–9).

[41] Hort in B. F. Westcott and F. J. A. Hort, *The New Testament in Greek*, 2 vols. (Cambridge, 1881), vol. 2, p. 126; Turner, *The Study of the New Testament*, pp. 58–61 (with five examples from Mark).

[42] G. W. Horner edited at this period both the Bohairic (4 vols., Oxford 1898–1905) and the Sahidic (7 vols., Oxford, 1911–24).

[43] Thus when Charles Raven moved from the Classical to the Theological Tripos as a BA in 1907, despite being taught by J. H. A. Hart he 'never became a Hebraist nor did he ever make an extended study of Old Testament documents', as noted by F. W. Dillistone, *Charles Raven* (London, 1975), pp. 49–51.

[44] Turner, *The Study of the New Testament*, pp. 47, 61–2; K. Lake, review of F. Blass, *Evangelium secundum Matthaeum* (Leipzig, 1901), in *JTS* 3 (1902), 303.

[45] M.-J. Lagrange, with the collaboration of S. Lyonnet, *Introduction à l'étude du Nouveau Testament, deuxième partie: critique textuelle, 2. La Critique rationelle* (Paris, 1935), pp. 16–17.

(1908–96).[46] Its immediate late nineteenth-century background included fundamental work on the history of the Vulgate text by the French Protestant theologian Samuel Berger.

The Oxford New Testament was the first modern attempt to recover the text on the basis of manuscript witness, for the issue of the Clementine Vulgate of 1592 had been accompanied by prohibition of the printing of any other text, or of a text with variants. Work towards a new papally sponsored edition was not authorised until Pius X entrusted it to a commission of Benedictines in 1907; and in view of the Oxford project they courteously began with the immense task of issuing the books of the Old Testament.[47]

Turner and Burkitt, among others, stressed that the Vulgate gospel manuscript tradition represented in Wordsworth and White ascended to the sixth century rather than the fourth. Turner's last work, issued posthumously by A. Souter, Regius Professor of Humanity in Aberdeen, offered evidence from a St Gall manuscript which might help to bridge the gap.[48]

On the other hand, an invaluable feature of the large edition was its registration of Old Latin readings. Jerome's work on the Gospels had been a revision of existing Latin texts, as he says in his prefatory letter to Damasus; and the Vulgate Acts, Epistles and Revelation, although they lack clear attestation from Jerome himself and are unlikely to be his work, are also revisions rather than translations. Other Old Latin work accompanying the edition included editions of manuscripts by E. S. Buchanan and others, and studies of patristic witness by Sanday, Turner, Souter and others.[49] The Oxford series *Old Latin Biblical Texts* founded by Wordsworth (1883 onwards) was matched by the comparable *Collectanea Biblica Latina* (Rome, 1912 onwards), the firstfruits of the Benedictine Vulgate commission, and by German work including

---

[46] *Novum Testamentum Domini Nostri Iesu Christi Latine secundum editionem Sancti Hieronymi* ad codicum manuscriptorum fidem recensuerunt Iohannes Wordsworth et Henricus Iulianus White, in operis societatem adsumto Hedley Friderico Davis Sparks, 3 vols. (Oxford, 1889–1953); see H. J. White, 'The Vulgate New Testament', in E. W. Watson, *Life of Bishop John Wordsworth* (London, 1915), pp. 140–56; A. Souter, 'Henry Julian White and the Vulgate', *JTS* 36 (1935), 11–13 (the quotation in the text is from p. 11); H. F. D. Sparks, 'The Rev. A. Ramsbotham and the Oxford Vulgate', *JTS* 36 (1935), 391; S. P. Brock, 'Hedley Frederick Davis Sparks', *PBA* 101 (1998), 513–36 (520–24, 535).

[47] Pius X paid some expenses personally, and nuns as well as monks shared the work; see F. Stummer, *Einführung in die lateinische Bibel* (Paderborn, 1928), pp. 208–9.

[48] C. H. Turner, *The Oldest Manuscript of the Vulgate Gospels* (Oxford, 1931), reviewed by Burkitt, *JTS* 32 (1931), 67–8; H. N. Bate, 'Cuthbert Hamilton Turner: A Memoir', in C. H. Turner, *Catholic and Apostolic* (London, 1931), pp. 1–65 (28–9, 30).

[49] Thus C. H. Milne, *A Reconstruction of the Old-Latin Text or Texts of the Gospels used by Saint Augustine, with a Study of their Character* (Cambridge, 1926) was undertaken at Souter's suggestion.

H. von Soden's comparison of Old Latin manuscripts with Cyprian.[50] Souter, who inspired others in this field, was himself inspired by teachers including J. E. B. Mayor (mentioned above as one of the 1,725 signatories), a contender for the value of biblical and ecclesiastical Latin in classical study.[51]

The Oxford Vulgate, with White's hand-edition, did much to familiarise those studying the New Testament with the importance of the Latin versions. Further help on this way came from Souter's widely used Oxford Greek Testament (1910); a revised edition appeared in 1947, proof-read by the young F. F. Bruce. Here the text was that followed in the Revised Version, but Souter's apparatus gave greater prominence than had been usual to Latin evidence.[52] The value of the Vulgate itself for textual questions was emphasised by Harnack, who noted that in the Gospels it was a second-century text revised in the light of third- or fourth-century Greek manuscripts; 'we have no other witness of the same value, but this witness we do now know accurately, thanks to the work of Wordsworth and White'—generous words from the second year of the First World War.[53]

The Syriac New Testament had aroused lively western interest ever since the sixteenth century, mainly in the Peshitta translation, that which was most widely current. In the early twentieth century much work, especially by John Gwynn in Dublin, was devoted to the later revisions of the Peshitta; but a great focus of New Testament study in general was what came to be called the Old Syriac version. A fragmentary British Museum text of the Gospels in this version, from the Syrian convent of St Mary in Nitria, had been edited by W. Cureton in 1848, and three leaves identified in a Berlin manuscript were published in 1872. In 1892, however, Mrs Agnes Smith Lewis of Cambridge, with her twin sister Mrs Margaret Dunlop Gibson as photographer, found what was identified as a more complete text of the Old Syriac Gospels in the underwriting of a palimpsest in St Katharine's monastery on Mount Sinai; a first transcript appeared in 1894.[54] Mrs Lewis issued her own edition (London, 1910) after further inspections of the manuscript.

---

[50] H. von Soden, *Das lateinische Neue Testament in Afrika zur Zeit Cyprians* (TU 33A, Leipzig, 1909).

[51] J. E. B. Mayor and A. Souter, *Q. Septimi Florentis Tertulliani Apologeticus* (Cambridge, 1917), p. v (Souter), pp. xii–xiii (Mayor).

[52] *Novum Testamentum Graece,* textui a retractoribus Anglis adhibito brevem adnotationem criticam subiecit Alexander Souter (Oxford, 1910); Lagrange, *La Critique rationelle*, p.15.

[53] A. von Harnack, 'Zur Textkritik und Christologie der Schriften des Johannes', reprinted from *SB Berlin* (1915) in id., *Studien zur Geschichte des Neuen Testaments und der alten Kirche*, 1. *Zur neutestamentlichen Textkritik* (Berlin and Leipzig, 1931), pp. 105–52 (145–6).

[54] Agnes Smith Lewis, *In the Shadow of Sinai: A Story of Travel and Research from 1895 to 1897* (Cambridge, 1898), pp. ii–xv; R. L. Bensly, J. Rendel Harris and F. C. Burkitt, *The Four Gospels in Syriac transcribed from the Sinaitic Palimpsest* (Cambridge, 1894).

Meanwhile Burkitt had presented the Sinaitic evidence in a fresh edition of the Curetonian text (1904), with translation and comment; he judged that the title, which could be rendered 'copy of the separated gospels', distinguished the four Gospels copied as separate works from a gospel harmony, the popular Diatessaron of Tatian (c.170).[55] In the same years the Sinaitic text was translated with full commentary by the Heidelberg Orientalist and theologian Adalbert Merx, who exemplified contemporary fascination with the potential of this new version for historical reconstruction of the life of Jesus.[56]

In the long run the importance of the Old Syriac has seemed rather to lie in the history of the text and early interpretation of the New Testament. Thus, to give examples, in both the Curetonian and the Sinaitic Syriac the bystanders who beat their breasts after the Passion (Luke xxiii. 48) cry out 'Woe to us, what has befallen us! Woe to us for our sins!' This expansion is the first part of a lament found in the Gospel of Peter (vii. 25) and in Codex Sangermanensis I of the Latin Gospels; in these two texts it goes on to foretell the desolation of Jerusalem. The Old Syriac here attests apocryphal influence (direct or indirect) on the reading of the canonical Gospel, as well as the anti-Jewish tendency often seen in early interpretation; Hort's 'vigorous and popular ecclesiastical life' is disclosed.[57] Secondly, however, despite this tendency, the Sinaitic Syriac agrees with the Old Latin Codex Bobbiensis in omitting Matt. ix. 34 'but the Pharisees said, He drives out demons by the prince of demons'—a clause which is not required by the context and is probably a harmonistic addition. Here the Old Syriac, in conjunction with the Old Latin, points towards restoration of the Gospel text.[58] It was especially in view of such indications that C. H. Turner wrote: 'Of all additions, since the publication of Westcott and Hort, to our knowledge of the early texts of the gospels, this Sinai Syriac MS is, take it all in all, the most weighty.'[59]

---

[55] F. C. Burkitt, *Evangelion da-Mepharreshe: the Curetonian Syriac Gospels re-edited, together with the readings of the Sinai palimpsest and the early Syriac patristic evidence; with a translation into English*, 2 vols. (Cambridge, 1904).

[56] A. Merx, *Die vier kanonischen Evangelien nach ihrem ältesten bekannten Texte. Übersetzung und Erläuterung der syrischen im Sinaikloster gefundenen Palimpsesthandschrift*, 3 vols. (Berlin, 1897–1911).

[57] Comment on the Old Syriac by Burkitt, Merx and others was discussed by L. Vaganay, *L'Évangile de Pierre*, 2nd edn. (Paris, 1930), pp. 268–71.

[58] See J. Neville Birdsall, 'A note on the textual evidence for the omission of Matthew 9:34', in J. D. G. Dunn (ed.), *Jews and Christians: The Parting of the Ways, A.D. 70 to 135* (WUNT 66, Tübingen, 1992), pp. 117–22.

[59] Turner, *The Study of the New Testament*, p. 54.

In the related field of apocrypha a central place belongs to a scholar who has retained an aura of glamour and affection, M. R. James (1862–1936).[60] His evergreen repute rests in part on his unequalled ghost stories, and in part on his manuscript catalogues; but it also attests his creative sympathy with a literature which in some sense linked these two sides of his activity, the biblical apocrypha. Gifted contemporary workers in this field included Forbes Robinson on Coptic New Testament apocrypha and J. Rendel Harris and others on the Syriac Odes of Solomon. The Odes, which form an Old Testament pseudepigraph but resemble hymn-like poems in the Acts of Thomas and John, and were treasured for their fresh and vivid mystical piety, are a reminder that New Testament apocrypha cannot well be separated from Old Testament pseudepigrapha, which were opened up in this period above all by R. H. Charles. On their specifically Christian side, the New Testament apocrypha also merge with the Apostolic Fathers; the Didache or Teaching of the Twelve (first edited in 1886), the Epistles of Barnabas and Clement, and the Shepherd of Hermas are all attached to names found in the New Testament. At this period these writings were at the heart of work on the dating of New Testament books, and also of work on early catechesis and liturgy, two subjects which would soon gain still greater prominence.

James like Charles worked in the apocryphal literature of both Testaments, but he is perhaps best known for his repeatedly reprinted *The Apocryphal New Testament* (Oxford, 1924), later supplemented by J. W. B. Barns (1953) and revised and re-edited by J. K. Elliott (1995). James kept in mind inquirers from the fields of medieval literature and art, as well as biblical and patristic study. 'My aim' (he wrote) 'has been to give a fresh translation of everything and hardly any notes. A great deal appears for the first time in English.'[61] As compared with its chief rival, E. Hennecke's bulkier *Neutestamentliche Apokryphen* (1904 and subsequent reissues and revisions), James's one handy volume offers less in the way of introduction and interpretation, but considerably more translated apocrypha.

James's genius was for short publications, in which he commonly produced both new textual evidence from felicitous manuscript discoveries, and new views on the date and contents of sparsely attested writings. He ranged through Old Testament pseudepigrapha—the Greek Psalms of Solomon and Testament of Abraham, and in Latin Enoch, II Esdras, and the Biblical Antiquities of Pseudo-Philo—to apocryphal gospels, acts and revelations,

[60] R. W. Pfaff, *Montague Rhodes James* (London, 1980), with bibliography of James; M. Cox, *M. R. James, an Informal Portrait* (Oxford, 1983).

[61] Letter of September 1923 to R. W. Chapman, quoted by Pfaff, *James*, p. 373.

notably the Apocalypses of Peter and Paul, which witness to conceptions of after-life with a strong Hellenic air.[62] The pseudo-Philonic Biblical Antiquities and the Apocalypse of Peter are among works the importance of which James showed, although they became focuses of study mainly after his death.

German study of New Testament apocrypha included an interest in their value for the life of Jesus which recalled Merx's approach to the Old Syriac. W. Bauer (1877–1960) brought them together with the New Testament text and versions—arguing for instance from the apocrypha against Merx's contention for the historical value of the reduction of Roman responsibility in the Sinaitic Syriac Passion narrative—and he analysed the apocryphal presentation of the life of Jesus.[63] Closer to James's sphere was the treatment of New Testament apocrypha in connection with early and medieval Christian art by E. von Dobschütz (1870–1934).[64]

Jewish and Palestinian material for exegesis

The second great trend of the early years of the century to claim notice is the exploration of Jewish and Palestinian material for exegesis. 'From where did the mass of early Christian conceptual material come if not from Judaism?', asked William Wrede in 1897.[65] This trend has medieval and earlier origins, it readily coalesced with Old Testament study, and in the early twentieth century it appeared in many countries; one of its expressions is in the range of Jewish literature, from the Septuagint to rabbinic texts, which Emil Schürer surveyed in his handbook on New Testament history (revised edition, 1909).[66] In Britain Sanday introduced a revised edition of work by A. Edersheim, a

---

[62] W. Dieterich, *Nekyia* (Leipzig, 1893), and E. Norden, *P. Vergilius Maro, Aeneis Buch VI*, 2nd edn. (Leipzig and Berlin, 1916), p. 6 (the Apocalypse of Peter); E. Maass, *Orpheus: Untersuchungen zur griechischen römischen altchristlichen Jenseitsdichtung und Religion* (Munich, 1895), pp. 254–7 (the Apocalypse of Paul).

[63] W. Bauer, *Das Leben Jesu im Zeitalter der neutestamentlichen Apokryphen* (Tübingen, 1909, repr. Darmstadt, 1967), pp. 204–7, 487–541.

[64] E. von Dobschütz, *Christusbilder: Untersuchungen zur christlichen Legende* (TU 18, 2 vols., Leipzig, 1899); id., *Der Apostel Paulus*, 1. *Seine weltgeschichtliche Bedeutung*; 2. *Seine Stellung in der Kunst*, 2 vols. (Halle, 1926, 1928).

[65] W. Wrede, 'The Task and Methods of "New Testament Theology" ', Eng. trans. in R. Morgan, *The Nature of New Testament Theology: The Contribution of William Wrede and Adolf Schlatter* (London, 1973), p. 114.

[66] M. Hengel, 'Der alte und der neue "Schürer". Mit einem Anhang von Hanswulf Bloedhorn', reprinted from *JSS* 35 (1990), 19–72 in M. Hengel, *Judaica, Hellenistica et Christiana: Kleine Schriften II* (Tübingen, 1999), pp. 157–99 (158–66). Schürer's less than sympathetic view of 'life under the law' (n. 80, below) did not prevent him from indicating the importance of rabbinic texts.

Christian scholar of Jewish birth, with the observation that Schürer's philological judgment was complemented by Edersheim's rabbinic knowledge and imaginative sympathy with Jewish life.[67]

The power of this trend in Britain had particular nineteenth-century antecedents. In the universities, there had been cooperation between gentile biblical scholars and rabbinic scholars from the Jewish community, exemplified in Cambridge by J. B. Lightfoot's debt to S. M. Schiller-Szinessy.[68] Through the church's missionary work there was much interest, strongly represented in Scotland and Ireland as well as in London-based mission, in the Jewish populations of central Europe and the East. In the country more broadly, there was long-standing concern with the Holy Land, focused in the Quarterly issued by the Palestine Exploration Fund from 1869.

The Jewish-Christian cooperation just noted has regularly been important, and in later years it was strongly represented in England on the Jewish side by scholars including H. Loewe, D. Daube and R. Loewe, but it was especially notable in the early years of the twentieth century. It meant that the immersion of New Testament scholars in Jewish texts was stimulatingly matched by Jewish investigation of the New Testament.

Two Anglo-Jewish scholars who involved themselves deeply in New Testament work were C. G. Montefiore (1858–1938), commentator on the synoptic Gospels, and Israel Abrahams (1858–1925), author of *Studies in Pharisaism and the Gospels*.[69] They collaborated (1889–1908) as editors of the *Jewish Quarterly Review*, which welcomed to its pages gentile New Testament scholars including Burkitt, Charles, Conybeare, and J. H. A. Hart—who had himself learned jointly from H. B. Swete, editor of the Septuagint, and the rabbinic scholar Solomon Schechter.[70] It was also a forum for important Jewish New Testament contributions from such scholars as Adolph Büchler, Kaufmann Kohler and Samuel Krauss. The historical discussion of new apocryphal discoveries which was typical of those years is met, for instance, but now with special reference to Judaism, in Büchler's

---

[67] W. Sanday in A. Edersheim, *History of the Jewish Nation after the Destruction of Jerusalem under Titus*, revised by H. A. White (London, 1896), p. vi.

[68] J. B. Lightfoot, *Saint Paul's Epistles to the Colossians and to Philemon* (London, 1875, repr. 1897), p. viii. Adolph Neubauer, whose substantial Oxford cooperation with gentile scholars bore especially on Old Testament work, had earlier in France helped Renan in the New Testament field; see E. Renan, *Vie de Jésus*, 13th edn. (Paris, 1867), pp. xlv–xlvi.

[69] C. G. Montefiore, *The Synoptic Gospels*, 2 vols. (London, 1909; 2nd edn., revised and partly rewritten, London, 1927); I. Abrahams, *Studies in Pharisaism and the Gospels* (*First Series*, Cambridge, 1917; *Second Series*, Cambridge, 1924).

[70] For Swete's work on Septuagintal, New Testament and patristic study, with bibliography, see *Henry Barclay Swete: A Remembrance* (London, 1918).

study of the unknown Greek gospel text presented by a miniature parchment leaf from Oxyrhynchus (P. Oxy. 840). Here a Pharisaic chief priest charges 'the Saviour' with entering the temple court unpurified, and asserts his own purity: 'I have bathed myself in the pool of David and have gone down by the one stair and come up by the other and have put on white and clean clothes.' Büchler urged that this text showed a better knowledge of relevant detail than the synoptic Gospels, and must rest on good sources.[71]

Jewish texts explored for New Testament exegesis included the Septuagint, studied notably in this connection by A. Deissmann, and much else that was familiar in Greek, above all Philo. Debate on resemblances between Wisdom, Philo, and John has already been noticed; a major contribution to perception of the setting of these resemblances had been F. C. Conybeare's 1895 argument that Philo on the Christian-like monastic Therapeutae was a genuinely Philonic description of a Jewish group. Josephus, the most familiar non-biblical Jewish source of all, was considered with reference to the historical Jesus and the New Testament by authors including H. St. J. Thackeray at home, and Adolf Schlatter and Robert Eisler abroad.[72] Greek-speaking Judaism was viewed in its historical setting especially through E. R. Bevan's work on the Hellenistic kingdoms, beginning with *The House of Seleucus* (1902). More recondite were the apocalypses and other pseudepigrapha which now came to the centre of New Testament study, especially in *Leben-Jesu-Forschung*, as noted above, but also, as Sanday emphasised, in interpretation of Paul.[73] The Ethiopic Enoch and many other texts were edited and studied by Charles in a large-scale programme which led to his collective two-volume *Apocrypha and Pseudepigrapha of the Old Testament* (1913), and also prepared for his own monumental exposition of Revelation (2 vols., 1920).

All these Jewish writings, however, from the Septuagint and Philo to the pseudepigrapha, were mainly preserved by church tradition and in Greek and the languages of the Christian East, and they had to be viewed together with the Aramaic Targums and the Hebrew and Aramaic rabbinic texts handed down in the Jewish community—a point underlined in 1910 by Schechter's publication of Cairo Genizah texts of the Damascus Document, widely

---

[71] A. Büchler, 'The New "Fragment of an Uncanonical Gospel" ', *JQR* 20 (1908), 330–46.

[72] H. St. J. Thackeray, *Josephus: The Man and the Historian* (New York, 1929); R. Eisler, ΙΗΣΟΥΣ ΒΑΣΙΛΕΥΣ ΟΥ ΒΑΣΙΛΕΥΣΑΣ, 2 vols. (Heidelberg, 1929–30); A. Schlatter, *Die Theologie des Judentums nach dem Bericht des Josefus* (Gütersloh, 1932).

[73] W. Sanday in G. H. Box, *The Ezra-Apocalypse* (London, 1912), 9*.

recognised as exemplifying, together with Genizah texts of the Hebrew Ecclesiasticus, Hebrew-language literature from the Hellenistic age.[74]

The tradition of collecting material to form a rabbinic commentary on the New Testament goes back to John Lightfoot and Christian Schoettgen in the seventeenth and eighteenth centuries, but it received an unprecedentedly rich development from 1921 onwards in the great commentary written by Paul Billerbeck at the suggestion of H. L. Strack.[75] The keen-eyed and large-hearted Montefiore judged that Billerbeck was over-concerned to show the originality of Jesus (and, one may add, the distinctiveness of Christianity), but that his wealth of rabbinic passages formed a 'magnificent collection', presented with consistent accuracy in translation and reference.[76]

One major question for biblical exegetes then and since has been that of the relative importance for New Testament interpretation of the ancient Jewish literature preserved by the church and the Jewish community, respectively. Under another aspect it is the question of primary sources for a description of ancient Judaism in the early Roman period. At the beginning of the twentieth century Schürer took a characteristically balanced view, in which all are taken into account—a view developed by J. H. A. Hart with echoes and modifications of Schechter's concept of a world-wide 'catholick Judaism'.[77] Wilhelm Bousset (1865–1920), however, a leader in the school of *Religionsgeschichte* and a controversial but brilliant interpreter of ancient Jewish and Christian religion, contended especially for the significance of the Septuagint and Philo, the apocrypha and pseudepigrapha—a view all the more attractive because, as noted already, some of this material was echoed in or contemporary with the New Testament, and was likewise current in Greek.[78] The rabbinic texts, on the other hand, had indeed long been recognised as exegetically indispensable—Israel Abrahams recalled John

[74] S. Schechter, *Documents of Jewish Sectaries, 1. Fragments of a Zadokite Work* (Cambridge, 1910); Charles, *Apocrypha and Pseudepigrapha of the Old Testament*, vol. 2, pp. 785–834; L. Rost, *Die Damaskusschrift* (Berlin, 1933), pp. 4–6 (listing further studies from this period).

[75] H. L. Strack and P. Billerbeck, *Kommentar zum Neuen Testament aus Talmud und Midrasch* (Munich, vol. 1 [1922], 2 [1924], 3 [1926], 4.1 [1928], 4.2 [1928]; index volumes by K. Adolph and J. Jeremias, 5 [1956], 6 [1961]). On Billerbeck see R. Deines, *Die Pharisäer: Ihr Verständnis im Spiegel der christlichen und jüdischen Forschung seit Wellhausen und Graetz* (WUNT 101, Tübingen, 1997), pp. 257–9.

[76] C. G. Montefiore, *Rabbinic Literature and Gospel Teachings* (London, 1930), pp. xv–xx (noting H. Loewe's concurrence on the accuracy of the translations).

[77] J. H. A. Hart, *The Hope of Catholick Judaism: An Essay towards Orientation* (Oxford and London, 1910), pp. 23–30.

[78] W. Bousset, *Die Religion des Judentums im späthellenistischen Zeitalter*, 3rd edn., ed. H. Gressmann (Tübingen, 1926).

Lightfoot's dictum at the Westminster Assembly (1643) that 'there are divers things in the New Testament, which we must be beholden to the Rabbins for the understanding of, or else we know not what to make of them';[79] and yet rabbinic texts were later than the New Testament, and their Christian explorers had often assessed them in ways from which Jews demurred—so Israel Abrahams, again, had differed from 'Professor Schürer on Life under the Jewish Law'.[80]

Doubts were answered succinctly by Abrahams, in an essay addressed especially to exegetes (n. 79, above), and Bousset's view was countered in a defence of the prior claims of rabbinic sources by G. Kittel.[81] A more extended answer was given in the USA by G. F. Moore, who condemned polemic in Christian exegesis, and urged in his book *Judaism* that the Mishnah and contemporary Jewish tradition provided the framework within which both the earlier Jewish writings and the New Testament could best be understood.[82] Within the ecclesiastical and theological context a 'liberal' attitude sometimes turned instinctively towards Philo and the Greek sources, a more 'conservative' one to the rabbis. This debate overlapped with discussion of the influence on Judaism and Christianity of Hellenism in general. In the upshot, although historical reconstruction of Jewish religion and theology continued to vary, the necessity of rabbinic texts for New Testament exegesis was widely admitted. As Stephen Neill wryly put it, 'in this bright post-Strack-Billerbeck epoch, we are all Rabbinic experts, though at second hand'.[83] This development was perhaps aided by the skilful use of rabbinic knowledge in the commentaries (1929 onwards) written late in life by Adolf Schlatter, whose emphasis on the New Testament as revelation won increasing sympathy.[84]

The exploration of Jewish literature for New Testament exegesis was concurrent with concern for Palestinian material, drawn from the languages, literature, topography, customs and antiquities of the land. Study of these subjects for biblical research was among the purposes of various national institutes in Jerusalem, including the École Biblique mentioned already. Here

---

[79] I. Abrahams, 'Rabbinic Aids to Exegesis', in H. B. Swete (ed.), *Essays on some Biblical Questions of the Day by Members of the University of Cambridge* (London, 1909), pp. 159–92 (180).

[80] Abrahams reviewed Schürer under this title in *JQR* 11 (1899), 626–42.

[81] G. Kittel, *Die Probleme des palästinischen Spätjudentums und das Urchristentum* (Stuttgart, 1926), pp. 2–4, 71–87.

[82] G. F. Moore, 'Christian Writers on Judaism', *HTR* 14 (1921), 197–254; id., *Judaism in the First Centuries of the Christian Era: The Age of the Tannaim*, 3 vols. (Cambridge, Mass., 1927–30).

[83] Neill, with footnote by Wright, in Neill and Wright, *The Interpretation of the New Testament*, p. 313.

[84] Schlatter began to prepare his exegetical notes for publication on the advice of Gerhard Kittel; see P. Stuhlmacher, 'Adolf Schlatter's Interpretation of Scripture', *NTS* 24 (1978), 433–46 (437).

archaeology, history and New Testament work were combined especially by L.-H. Vincent and F.-M. Abel, for example in their great study of Emmaus, beginning from the excavation of the ancient Judaean Nicopolis.[85]

At the end of the nineteenth century topographical work was classically embodied in Scotland in Sir George Adam Smith's *Historical Geography of the Holy Land* (1894; 4th edn., London, 1896). This repeatedly reprinted book served the New Testament as well as the Old, and in the campaign which ended Turkish rule in 1917 it interpreted the biblical data for General Allenby.[86] Many themes of Palestinian research were combined in the work of Gustav Dalman of Greifswald (1858–1941) on Aramaic grammar and the language of Jesus, the divine and messianic titles in the sayings of Jesus, and the topography and customs presupposed in the Gospels.[87] Work encouraged by Dalman includes a pioneering corpus of Palestinian Jewish inscriptions, with many from New Testament times, by Samuel Klein, who became Professor of Palestinology at the Hebrew University of Jerusalem.[88] Dalman's own continuator was in many ways Joachim Jeremias, whose *Jerusalem in the Time of Jesus* first appeared between 1923 and 1937.[89]

These Palestinian studies could be linked with work on diaspora Judaism in such areas as epigraphy and synagogue archaeology, bringing together parts of the New Testament setting which were often viewed separately.[90] Meanwhile an approach to the Gospels with emphasis on rabbinic and Palestinian sources (and on the contrast with rabbinic moderation which could be discerned, it was suggested, in the rigorous historical Jesus) had been sponsored in Jerusalem by Joseph Klausner, whose *Jesus of Nazareth*

---

[85] L.-H. Vincent and F.-M. Abel, *Emmaüs: sa basilique et son histoire* (Paris, 1932).

[86] 'Two books he consulted almost daily, the Bible and George Adam Smith's *Historical Geography of the Holy Land*': A. P. Wavell, *The Palestine Campaigns*, 3rd edn. (London, 1931), p. 3. Smith considered the future of the land at the time of Allenby's advance in his pamphlet *Syria and the Holy Land* (London, 1918).

[87] G. Dalman, *Grammatik des jüdisch-palästinischen Aramäisch*, 2nd edn. (Leipzig, 1905); id., *Die Worte Jesu*, 2nd edn. (Leipzig, 1930); id., *Jesus-Jeschua* (Gütersloh, 1922; Eng. trans. by P. P. Levertoff, London, 1929); id., *Orte und Wege Jesu*, 3rd edn. (Gütersloh, 1924); Eng. trans. by P. P. Levertoff of expanded text, *Sacred Sites and Ways* (London, 1935); id., *Jerusalem und seine Umgebung* (Gütersloh, 1929).

[88] S. Klein, *Jüdisch-palästinisches Corpus Inscriptionum (Ossuar-, Grab- und Synagogeninschriften)* (Vienna and Berlin, 1920); Dalman contributed notes and additions.

[89] J. Jeremias, *Jerusalem zur Zeit Jesu*, 3rd edn. (Göttingen, 1962); Eng. trans. of revised text by F. H. and C. H. Cave (London, 1969); id., *Golgotha* (Angelos-Beiheft 1, Leipzig, 1926).

[90] For example, J.-B. Frey, *Corpus Inscriptionum Judaicarum*, 2 vols. (Rome, 1936, 1952), proceeding from Rome and Europe to Palestine and the Middle East; E. L. Sukenik, *Ancient Synagogues in Palestine and Greece* (Schweich Lectures 1930, London, 1934).

(1922) was translated from modern Hebrew into English by Herbert Danby, at that time canon of St George's, Jerusalem.[91]

In Britain topography had been brought into special connection with the Gospels and the life of Jesus by Sanday, and British Academy Schweich Lectures of the 1920s reflect a post-1917 intensification of concern with the Palestinian setting of biblical history.[92] The language and thought of Jesus and the Gospels were further illuminated by the Old Testament scholar C. F. Burney, in two books on the Aramaic substratum of the Gospels, including John (here his work converged with that of Adolf Schlatter); these were followed up by a study of John in the light of mystical rabbinic texts by H. Odeberg, inspired by G. H. Box.[93] In the background of these books was the penetrating consideration of Aramaic in Wellhausen's work on the Gospels. A lasting contribution in the convergence of Palestinian and rabbinic study was made by Danby, the translator of Klausner, in his pioneering English translation of the Mishnah; Danby's judicious discussion of New Testament interpretation in the light of rabbinic texts is a complement to the weighty but decided opinions of G. F. Moore.[94]

Christianity in the setting of Greece and Rome

Finally, a third pervasive trend was to interpret the earliest Christianity with special regard to its Greek and Roman setting. Such interpretation arose read-ily from the classical training already mentioned, and it could range from language through history to religion and theology. All these were within the

[91] J. Klausner, *Jesus of Nazareth: His Life, Times, and Teaching*, translated by H. Danby (London, 1925).

[92] W. Sanday, with the assistance of P. Waterhouse, *Sacred Sites of the Gospels* (Oxford, 1903); I. Abrahams, *Campaigns in Palestine from Alexander the Great* (Schweich Lectures 1922, London, 1927); T. H. Robinson, J. W. Hunkin and F. C. Burkitt, *Palestine in General History* (Schweich Lectures 1926, London, 1929).

[93] A. Schlatter, *Die Sprache und Heimat des vierten Evangelisten* (Gütersloh, 1902); C. F. Burney, *The Aramaic Origin of the Fourth Gospel* (Oxford, 1922) (he did not know Schlatter's work until his own was far advanced); id., *The Poetry of Our Lord* (Oxford, 1925); H. Odeberg, *The Fourth Gospel Interpreted in its Relation to Contemporary Religious Currents in Palestine and the Hellenistic-Oriental World* (Uppsala, 1926).

[94] H. Danby, *The Mishnah* (London, 1933 and reprints); on the problems and history of interpreting the New Testament in the light of rabbinic literature see H. Danby, *Tractate Sanhedrin: Mishnah and Tosefta* (London, 1919), pp. ix–xvi; id., *Gentile Interest in Post-Biblical Hebrew Literature* (Jerusalem, n.d.), also published in N. Bentwich and H. Sacher (eds.), *The Jewish Review* 3 (December 1932 – March 1933), 18–34. Danby's use of rabbinic and later Jewish literature when he was Regius Professor of Hebrew in Oxford is sketched by J. A. Emerton, 'Godfrey Rolles Driver, 1892–1975', *PBA* 63 (1977), 345–62 (361–2).

spectrum of what was commonly called in English 'the Graeco-Roman world' or 'Graeco-Roman culture', but in German with greater precision, as in the title of a famous early twentieth-century aid to New Testament study, 'die hellenistisch-römische Kultur'.[95] The term 'Hellenistic' had been applied to civilisation as well as literature since J. G. Droysen in the early nineteenth century, and it drew attention to special characteristics of the post-classical 'Hellenism' which colonised vast regions under Alexander the Great, and issued in a Greek-speaking Judaism and Christianity and a Hellenised Roman literature and culture.[96]

Interpretation in the context of Hellenism became important in study of the Fourth Gospel and other books, but it had a natural prominence in the case of Acts and Paul. In this period these were the focuses of outstanding New Testament work by classical scholars, and of a struggle in the theological faculties over the relative importance of Judaism and Hellenism in Paul.

The prime need in Acts for the special knowledge of the philologist (in the broad sense) rather the theologian had been stressed in a philological commentary by Friedrich Blass, and Eduard Norden somewhat comparably related how, when discussing the Areopagus speech in the seventeenth chapter, he and other professed students of Classics were determined that here at least, in a scene set in Athens, they would not submit themselves to the judgment of their fellow-Grecians from the theological faculty.[97] Norden himself distinguished the Paul of Romans from the Paul of Acts xvii (here in contrast with Harnack, for whom the affectionate Hellenism of the Areopagus speech was quintessentially Pauline);[98] but he set them both within a Hellenistic literary tradition of Stoic-influenced propaganda which was used by Jews and could attain great heights, as it did in Acts xvii.

---

[95] P. Wendland, *Die hellenistisch-römische Kultur in ihren Beziehungen zu Judentum und Christentum* (Tübingen, 1907); the English phrases are exemplified in W. R. Inge, 'The Theology of the Fourth Gospel', in Swete, *Essays on some Biblical Questions of the Day*, pp. 251–88 (255–7), in connection with 'European civilization'.

[96] How far 'Hellenism' can be judged to culminate in Christianity and a Hellenised Rome is discussed by A. Demandt, 'Hellenismus—die moderne Zeit des Altertums?' and G. Dobesch, 'Die römische Kaiserzeit—eine Fortsetzung des Hellenismus?' in B. Funck (ed.), *Hellenismus: Beiträge zur Erforschung von Akkulturation und politischer Ordnung in den Staaten des hellenistischen Zeitalters* (Tübingen, 1996), pp. 17–27, 561–609.

[97] F. Blass, *Acta apostolorum* (Göttingen, 1895), p. vi; E. Norden, *Agnostos Theos: Studien zur Formengeschichte religiöser Rede* (Leipzig and Berlin, 1913), p. v.

[98] Karl Barth as a student wrote a paper for Harnack's seminar, concluding that 'Acts is and remains a secondary source for Pauline doctrine'; Harnack wrote in the margin 'I would say, a primary source' (E. Busch, *Karl Barth: His Life from Letters and Autobiographical Texts* (Eng. trans. by John Bowden, 1976), p. 39).

To a third classical witness, the ancient historian and archaeologist Sir William Ramsay (1851–1939), it seemed at the time that most scholars were 'sentient only of the Judaic element' in Paul, and, despite their classical training, insufficiently familiar with just that post-classical Hellenism noted above. Leading up to a treatment of 'St. Paul and Hellenism', he complained that 'I rarely find in them any sympathy with, or understanding of, hardly any thought about, the Hellenism that overran the world of Western Asia . . .'; but if we approach Paul from that side, he added, 'we shall feel everywhere in his work the spirit of the Tarsian Hellene'.[99]

Ramsay could note exceptions, such as E. L. Hicks, editor of Ephesian and Coan inscriptions, and later bishop of Lincoln, who stressed the Hellenism of Paul's thought; but in any case the atmosphere was changing.[100] Edwin Hatch, read with enthusiasm by Harnack, had exhibited Christian constitutional arrangements as forms of those usual in Hellenistic guilds (1881), and had brought out *The Influence of Greek Ideas on Christianity* (1889);[101] these perceptions had worked in parallel with Harnack's own thesis of the Hellenisation of Christianity, and with the encouragement given by inscriptions and papyri, and brilliantly expressed by J. H. Moulton, towards classifying New Testament Greek as Hellenistic rather than Semitic or biblical—to touch on two proposals which were to be debated throughout the century.[102] Sanday had warned in his obituary of Hatch against the positing of Hellenistic influence on Christian origins, but Hicks wrote, 'Let us beware of post-dating the influence of Hellenism on Christian thought.'[103] Much indeed tended to suggest that Hellenism would already have been a force in Christian origins, perhaps especially (but here again debate arose) through Hellenised Judaism. Ramsay is remembered for his eminence as an Anatolian explorer and archaeologist, and for his eagerness to show the accuracy of Luke–Acts; but he was

[99] W. M. Ramsay, *The Cities of St. Paul: Their Influence on his Life and Thought* (London, 1907), pp. 6–9.

[100] E. L. Hicks, 'St. Paul and Hellenism', *Studia Biblica et Ecclesiastica*, 4 (Oxford, 1896), 1–14 (stressing influence on thought, but rejecting Hellenistic derivation of sacramental practice).

[101] E. Hatch, *The Organization of the Early Christian Churches* (London, 1881 and later editions), discussed by O. Linton, *Das Problem der Urkirche in der neueren Forschung* (Uppsala, 1932), pp. 20–22, 31–9 and W. G. Kümmel, *The New Testament: The History of the Investigation of its Problems* (Eng. trans. London, 1973), pp. 212–3; E. Hatch, *The Influence of Greek Ideas on Christianity* (London, 1889), discussed by Neill and Wright, *The Interpretation of the New Testament*, pp. 147–50, and J. Z. Smith, *Drudgery Divine* (London, 1990), pp. 59–62.

[102] J. H. Moulton, 'New Testament Greek in the Light of Modern Discovery', in Swete, *Essays on some Biblical Questions of the Day*, pp. 461–505, developing the *Prolegomena* (1906) of his *Grammar of the New Testament Greek*.

[103] W. Sanday, 'In memoriam Dr. Edwin Hatch', *The Expositor*, Fourth Series, 1 (1890), 93–111 (107–9); Hicks, 'St. Paul and Hellenism', p. 12.

also a powerful advocate of a 'Hellenistic-Roman' Paul, an apostle who was mentally a Hellene, and endowed with an almost mystical and thoroughly Hellenistic sense of the significance of Roman world-empire.[104]

In Germany the case for understanding Paul in particular as Hellene was vigorously put by representatives of *Religionsgeschichte*. In biblical work this school of thought concentrated on religion rather than doctrine, and on religion viewed in its historical setting, with special attention to mythology, the undercurrents of religious feeling, and the interaction between Jewish or Christian religion and other cults. Later in the century its influence was evident in the importance of mythology and gnosis for Rudolf Bultmann, despite his opposition to the liberal theology associated with the school, and in Gershom Scholem's rehabilitation of Jewish mysticism.[105] Now together with Bousset, mentioned above, a leader of the *Religionsgeschichtliche Schule* was the great Old and New Testament scholar Hermann Gunkel (1862–1932), best known for work on biblical myth in Genesis and Revelation and on poetic form in the Psalms. Gunkel's first book had related Paulinism to Hellenistic polydaemonism, and he now urged that those Pauline teachings which have no clear Old Testament analogy, such as mystical union with Christ, should be compared not only with the Greek mysteries but also with the dying and rising of oriental gods.[106] The widespread Syrian, Egyptian or eastern mystery cults like those of Adonis, Isis and Osiris, and Mithras were identified as the heart of gentile religiosity in Paul's time, and the Greek Hermetic literature, linked with the cult of Thoth-Hermes, was examined as a great clue to pre-Christian gentile anticipations of Gnosticism.[107]

The Pauline interpretation of religion, above all the Christ-cult with the rites of baptism and 'the Lord's Supper' (a phrase which in this context sounded like an echo of a gentile cult), then appeared as a link in a chain which stretched back into Hellenistic observance and towards oriental religion. It seemed that gentile Christianity had been influenced not simply by Greek tradition, important though this influence was, but by a mingling of Hellenic and oriental religion which could already be identified as Gnosticism. This religio-historical approach coincided with widespread work

---

[104] On Ramsay see W. H. C. Frend, *The Archaeology of Early Christianity: A History* (London, 1996), pp. 93–5.

[105] On Scholem as a 'child of the *Religionsgeschichtliche Schule*' see E. Hamacher, *Gershom Scholem und die Allgemeine Religionsgeschichte* (Religionsgeschichtliche Versuche und Vorarbeiten 45, Berlin and New York, 1999), pp. 73–104.

[106] H. Gunkel, *Zum religionsgeschichtlichen Verständnis des Neuen Testaments* (Göttingen, 1903).

[107] R. Reitzenstein, *Poimandres: Studien zur griechisch-ägyptischen und frühchristlichen Literatur* (Leipzig, 1904).

on Hellenistic and Roman cults, notably in English classical study and anthropology by Jane Harrison (1850–1928) on Orphism and J. G. Frazer (1854–1941) on Adonis, Attis and Osiris, in German Old Testament study by W. W. Baudissin (1847–1926) on Adonis and Esmun, and in ancient history in Belgium by F. Cumont (1868–1947) on Mithraism and other oriental cults in the Greek and Roman world.[108]

Of special note, however, were one big book and one little one. In his great history of early Christology Wilhelm Bousset derived the Pauline cult of *Kyrios Iesous Christos* from pagan cult likewise directed towards a divine *Kyrios* (1913);[109] and Richard Reitzenstein (1861–1931), a classical scholar with theological training, gave a vivid brief sketch of 'the Hellenistic mystery-religions', presenting Paul as a mystic whose experience fully belonged to the pattern of Hellenistic religion (1909).[110]

Otto Pfleiderer (1839–1908), who was among the last of those taught by F. C. Baur, integrated such views into a rounded presentation of Paulinism.[111] For him, Paul at Tarsus learns not only Judaism but also Stoic philosophy and pagan religion, including Mithraism; on the way to Damascus Paul has an ecstatic experience comparable with the 'visions and revelations' of II Cor. xii. 1, and feels himself to be a 'new creature' (II Cor. v. 17); reflection on the questions which now move his soul forms Pauline theology, in which an intuition (Gal. i. 12) bound up with Jewish apocalyptic thought reveals Christ as spirit and heavenly son of God; Paul's understanding of union with Christ, baptism and the Supper is shaped not just by the Mithraism of Tarsus, but also by the cult of Adonis at Antioch; Pauline eschatology remains Jewish, but includes the apocalyptic and Hellenistic hope of a blessed afterlife (n. 62,

---

[108] J. E. Harrison, *Prolegomena to the Study of Greek Religion* (Cambridge, 1903); J. G. Frazer, *Adonis, Attis, Osiris*, 2nd edn. (London, 1907); W. W. Baudissin, *Adonis und Esmun: eine Untersuchung zur Geschichte des Glaubens an Auferstehungsgötter und an Heilsgötter* (Leipzig, 1911); F. Cumont, *Les Religions orientales dans le paganisme romain*, 2nd edn. (Paris, 1909); Dieterich, Norden, and Maass, as cited in n. 62, above.

[109] W. Bousset, *Kyrios Christos: Geschichte des Christusglaubens von den Anfängen des Christentums bis Irenaeus* (FRLANT 21, 1913; 2nd edn. Göttingen, 1921, repr. 1926), pp. 90–104, 117–29.

[110] R. Reitzenstein, *Die hellenistischen Mysterienreligionen nach ihren Grundgedanken und Wirkungen: Vortrag ursprünglich gehalten in dem Wissenschaftlichen Predigerverein für Elsass-Lothringen den 11. November 1909*, 2nd, revised, edn., (Leipzig and Berlin, 1920), pp. 47–66, 185–244, 256–60 (adding over sixty pages on Paul to the twenty relevant pages of the first edition).

[111] O. Pfleiderer, *Die Entstehung des Christentums* (Munich, 1905), Eng. trans. *Christian Origins* (New York, 1906), pp. 155–90; for discussion see E. Hirsch, *Geschichte der neuern evangelischen Theologie*, vol. 5 (Gütersloh, 1954), p. 563; Smith, *Drudgery Divine*, pp. 89–98.

above). Tarsus and its religion, prominent in such reconstructions, were studied by others too with Paul as a 'Tarsian Hellene' in mind.[112]

It was of course realised that resemblances could be over-interpreted. Thus P. Wendland's handbook, already mentioned, notes the Judaism of Paul himself and the limits of his Hellenism—although the final emphasis lies on the importance of the oriental cults for Paul both directly and through their influence on Judaism.[113] Perhaps the most important reaction, however, was formed by another approach which could arguably also do justice to the phenomena, namely an interpretation of Paul and his communities through the Greek literature and epigraphy of Judaism.

Among the classical scholars, this route was followed by E. Norden, who criticised undiscriminating claims for Hellenistic influence (praising Hicks for restraint), mocked over-emphasis on Tarsus, brought out Paul's often strikingly 'un-Hellenic' Greek style, and stressed the importance of Greek Jewish literature for his interpretation.[114] From within New Testament study and *Religionsgeschichte* A. Deissmann took a similar line. He gave prominence to the Septuagint, in the setting of the papyri and the gentile and Jewish inscriptions which brought 'light from the east' upon the language of the New Testament; and he had a strong sense not only for the Hellenised Jews but also for the Judaised Hellenes in the orbit of the Pauline communities. He portrayed the Apostle as a *Septuagintajude*, who indeed preached a cult like the gentile cults of rulers and deities, but did so in a way which suited gentiles already affected by Judaism presented in accord with that cosmopolitan bible, the Septuagint.[115]

Albert Schweitzer in 1911 reacted against all these reconstructions—and implicitly against Hicks and Ramsay—with the motto 'Nothing Greek in Paulinism'; thus he insisted on the awkwardness of the tension between Judaism and Hellenism in Pfleiderer's Paul.[116] He eloquently pressed a widespread contemporary contrast not just between Jew and Greek, but between

---

[112] Ramsay, *The Cities of St Paul*, pp. 84–244; H. Böhlig, *Die Geisteskultur von Tarsos im augusteischen Zeitalter mit Berücksichtigung der paulinischen Schriften* (FRLANT 19, Göttingen, 1913).

[113] Wendland, *Die hellenistisch-römische Kultur*, pp. 138–43, 177–9.

[114] E. Norden, *Die antike Kunstprosa vom VI. Jahrhundert v. Chr. bis in die Zeit der Renaissance*, 2nd edn., 2 vols. (Leipzig and Berlin, 1909; repr. 1923), vol. 2, pp. 465–79, 492–502.

[115] A. Deissmann, *Paulus: eine Kultur- und religionsgeschichtliche Skizze* (Tübingen, 1911; 2nd edn., 1925), Eng. trans. *Paul: A Study in Social and Religious History* (London, 1912), pp. 89, 101–3, 165–70, 210–11.

[116] A. Schweitzer, *Geschichte der paulinischen Forschung* (Tübingen, 1911), pp. 52–8, Eng. trans. *Paul and his Interpreters: A Critical History* (London, 1912; repr. 1956), pp. 66–74; 187, headline 'Nichts Griechisches im Paulinismus', not reproduced over the translation of the relevant passage, Eng. trans. p. 240.

Hellenised and non-Hellenised Jews.[117] At the same time, however, a Hellenistic Paul was finding considerable acceptance in Britain, where the impact of Reitzenstein was strengthened by the influence of Hatch and Ramsay and of the broader interest in Hellenistic cults noted above.[118]

Kirsopp Lake presented a Paulinism influenced by the mystery religions in his searching critical study of the evidence for Paul's earlier life and teaching (1911). Lake judged that in Pauline teaching gentiles 'saw every reason for equating the Lord with the Redeemer-God of the Mystery Religions', and that in baptism and the eucharist they 'found "mysteries" which could immediately be equated with the other "mysteries"', and that 'Gnostic ideas are earlier, not later, than Christianity'.[119] He integrated the 'godfearers' into his work, making these gentile adherents of Judaism who figure prominently in Acts into an example of the penumbra of sympathisers acquired by many oriental cults in the Roman empire. He took these studies further in *The Beginnings of Christianity*, outlined above. Yet for him the attraction of Judaism in the age of Paul was still primarily that of 'a deeply ethical and spiritual austerity', lacking the aesthetic and mystical appeal found in other cults and now incorporated into Pauline Christianity.[120] Here there was room for discussion of the character of Judaism in the early Roman empire.

The sacraments and Hellenism in Paul became a focus of British biblical and theological debate, against the background of this movement in scholarship and also of the rise of the liturgical movement in the church.[121] Overseas the same shift of interest was exemplified by the liturgical theme of Hans Lietzmann, *Messe und Herrenmahl* (1926), rooted in the Pauline discussion

[117] This can perhaps be related to the strong distinction drawn by both Jews and gentiles at this time between traditional Jews from eastern Europe, and assimilated Jews in the West—a Leitmotiv of the periodical *Ost und West: Illustrierte Monatsschrift für Modernes Judentum* (1901–28).

[118] Thus distinctive features of Paul were emphasised in reaction to Reitzenstein and Pfleiderer, before the publication of Bousset's *Kyrios Christos*, in Edwyn Bevan's essay 'The Gnostic Redeemer', reprinted in E. Bevan, *Hellenism and Christianity* (London, 1921), pp. 89–108.

[119] Kirsopp Lake, *The Earlier Epistles of St. Paul, their Motive and Origin* (London, 1911), pp. 44, 46; for the impact of the book see Neill and Wright, *The Interpretation of the New Testament*, pp. 178–9.

[120] Lake, *The Earlier Epistles of St. Paul*, pp. 37–45, 428–36 (quotation from 43).

[121] N. P. Williams, 'The Origins of the Sacraments' (with a section headed 'A Critique of the "Mystery" Hypothesis') and W. Spens, 'The Eucharist', in E. G. Selwyn (ed.), *Essays Catholic and Critical by Members of the Anglican Communion* (1926; 3rd edn., London, 1929), pp. 367–423, 425–48; W. R. Halliday, *The Pagan Background of Early Christianity* (Liverpool and London, 1925); J. W. C. Wand, *The Development of Sacramentalism* (London, 1928); A. D. Nock, 'Early Gentile Christianity and its Hellenistic Background', in A. E. J. Rawlinson (ed.), *Essays on the Trinity and the Incarnation by Members of the Anglican Communion* (London, 1928), pp. 53–156; from the USA, F. Gavin, *The Jewish Antecedents of the Christian Sacraments* (London, 1928).

just noted, and later translated into English and supplemented by R. D. Richardson. By contrast with resistance to the association of New Testament sacraments with pagan mysteries, an influential combination of Hellenistic interpretation with the liturgical movement was developed by O. Casel, of the abbey of Maria Laach.[122] In an amused English comment from the early 1920s on interpretative fashion: 'Bible, creed, ministry, all are derived from the worship of the faithful, and part of that from the earlier worship of the pagan: it is *Kyrios Christos* everywhere.'[123] The measure of sympathy in this comment hints at the theological and liturgical illumination which could be found through Hellenistic renderings of Paul.

Comparison of Pauline sacraments with the mysteries was questioned, however, especially by H. A. A. Kennedy in Edinburgh. The strength of his argument against Lake lay not only in his assertion of Paul's Septuagintal inheritance, but also in his fuller appreciation of the mystical aspect of Jewish religion in the Hellenistic age.[124] A measured reaction to these movements of thought can be seen in C. H. Dodd's first book, *The Meaning of Paul for To-day* (1920), in which a biblical and Hellenic, yet also Roman Paul is presented with what seems a considerable debt to Ramsay. Like Ramsay, Dodd begins from Paul's philosophy of history as expressed in Rom. viii, stresses Paul's combination of a biblical sense of hope with a classical sense of universal degeneration, and presents the Pauline ideal as that of a Christianised society with analogies both to the freedom of the Hellenic city and the universality of the Roman empire.

A more detailed response to the approaches represented by Deissmann and Reitzenstein, respectively, was made by Wilfred Knox (1925); he argued in two close-packed studies for Paul's debt to the Hellenised Jewish teaching best known from Philo, and for a modified acceptance of Reitzenstein's view of the influence of Hellenistic religious conceptions on Paul—and, he adds elsewhere, on gentile Christian perceptions of the eucharist, although he stresses that the Pauline rite itself will not have been an innovation.[125] These views were then later followed in the confrontation of Acts xvii and the

---

[122] O. Casel, *Das christliche Kultmysterium* (Regensburg, 1932), Eng. trans. in Casel, ed. B. Neunheuser, *The Mystery of Christian Worship, and other Writings* (London, 1962), discussed by H. Rahner, *Griechische Mythen in christlicher Deutung* (Zürich, 1945), pp. 29–30, Eng. trans. *Greek Myth and Christian Mystery* (London, 1963), pp. 10–11.

[123] A. Nairne, review of H. StJ. Thackeray, *The Septuagint and Jewish Worship* (Schweich Lectures 1920, London, 1921), *JTS* 23 (1922), 88–91 (91).

[124] H. A. A. Kennedy, *St. Paul and the Mystery Religions* (London, 1913); id., *Philo's Contribution to Religion* (London, 1919).

[125] W. L. Knox, *St Paul and the Church of Jerusalem* (Cambridge, 1925), pp. 126–36 (Hellenistic Judaism), 136–49 (Hellenistic religion), 372–85 (the eucharist).

Epistles with Greek and above all Philonic and other Hellenistic Jewish material in his *St. Paul and the Church of the Gentiles* (Cambridge, 1939).

In Germany G. Kittel pointed out (1926) that Paul's 'I received from the Lord' (I Cor. xi. 23), with its eucharistic reference, could be related not only to mystical concentration on the exalted Christ, but also to Judaean Jewish tradition formulae such as are met later on in the Mishnah.[126] Caution over the identifying of sacraments as mysteries was soon reinforced by A. D. Nock (n. 121, above). Bousset's Hellenic derivation of Christology was opposed, with reference to the Aramaic phrase Maranatha (I Cor. xvi. 22), by scholars including J. Weiss, Burkitt and L. Cerfaux.[127] Similarly, the biblical background of Pauline *mysterion* was brought out by K. Prümm and others.[128]

Finally, Hellenistic interpretation of Paul was totally resisted by Albert Schweitzer in his *Mysticism of Paul the Apostle*, largely complete in 1911 but issued finally in 1930. He urged that although Paul soon received a Hellenistic interpretation, his own wholly Jewish and non-Hellenist 'eschatological mysticism' linked him closely with the apocalypses and the historical Jesus. Paul's Supper-narrative was tradition, as Kittel's point suggested, rather than new revelation, and the heart of his religion was eschatologically oriented union with Christ.[129] Hard though it is to follow Schweitzer's dismissal of the impact of Hellenised Judaism on Paul, his vigorous book has had long-term influence, for example on E. P. Sanders's work (section IV, below).

To this discussion, although it did not appear until 1935, belongs C. H. Dodd's *The Bible and the Greeks*, a reassertion of the prime importance of Hellenistic Judaism for early Christianity. In the first part Dodd examines theological terms in the Septuagint, including *nomos* and *dikaiosyne*, to show how Septuagintal usage is followed by Paul and other Christian writers. In the second he reconsiders the Hermetic treatise *Poimandres* studied by Reitzenstein, urging that it represents not simply the compound of Hellenism and Iranian religion which he emphasised, but a non-Jewish author's interest

[126] Kittel, *Die Probleme des palästinischen Spätjudentums und das Urchristentum*, pp. 63–4.

[127] J. Weiss, *Das Urchristentum*, ed. R. Knopf (Göttingen, 1917), pp. 26–7; F. C. Burkitt, *Christian Beginnings* (London, 1924), pp. 44–52; articles of 1922, 1923 and 1931 reprinted in *Recueil Lucien Cerfaux* (Gembloux, 1954), vol. 1, 3–63, 136–72.

[128] K. Prümm, ' "Mysterion" von Paulus bis Origenes: ein Bericht und ein Beitrag', *Zeitschrift für katholische Theologie* 61 (1937), 391–425; more recent literature is discussed by M. N. A. Bockmuehl, *Revelation and Mystery in Ancient Judaism and Early Christianity* (WUNT 2.36, Tübingen, 1990).

[129] A. Schweitzer, *Die Mystik des Apostels Paulus* (Tübingen, 1930), Eng. trans. *The Mysticism of Paul the Apostle* (London, 1931), discussed by Wright in Neill and Wright, *The Interpretation of the New Testament*, pp. 404–8.

in the Septuagint and Judaism. The mingling of popular philosophy with Jewish tradition in Philo or Paul then appears as not far from the interest shown in Judaism from the standpoint of popular philosophy in *Poimandres*.

Three further examples of the interpretation of early Christianity with special regard to the Greek and Roman world deserve notice in conclusion. First, the ancient historian Eduard Meyer, renowned for Near Eastern as well as classical learning, set Christian origins in the context of Jewish, Greek and Roman history in a three-volume work, much of which was an examination of the Gospels, the Acts and Paul.[130] Meyer's Jesus, like Wellhausen's, is Pharisaic. Meyer's Paul has a superficial Hellenism, but Judaism is more important for his mentality, and in his time Hellenism itself is being overwhelmed by the tendency to mystery cults and turning from philosophy towards religion; in this setting the Pauline Christian rites too are mysteries.[131] Meyer's New Testament criticism, not least his detection of sources and his reassertion against Wellhausen of the historical value of the Marcan narrative, was influential in Britain especially in the work of Wilfred Knox, Vincent Taylor and T. W. Manson; in Jerusalem Klausner both criticised and followed Meyer on Jesus and Paul.

Secondly, from 1907 there appeared the *Dictionnaire d'archéologie chrétienne et de liturgie* (15 vols., Paris, 1907–53), a work initiated under Benedictine auspices and edited jointly by F. Cabrol and H. Leclercq, but very largely written by the latter.[132] This compendium set the earliest Christian writings in the context of the otherwise almost unsearchable riches of the material remains of Christianity in the Roman empire, including Palestine, and the great body of work on liturgy. A famous instance of pursuit of a biblical and liturgical theme through such material was E. Peterson, *Heis Theos* (FRLANT 41; Göttingen, 1926), on the acclamation 'One God' among pagans, Christians and Jews.

Lastly F.-J. Dölger, professor in the Roman Catholic faculty in Breslau and then in Bonn, began in 1929 to issue a series of studies under the heading *Antike und Christentum*. His confrontation of Christian texts with pagan

---

[130] Meyer is called 'perhaps the most learned ancient historian who has ever lived' by H. Lloyd-Jones in his Introduction to U. von Wilamowitz-Moellendorff, *History of Classical Scholarship* (Eng. trans. London, 1982), p. xvi.

[131] E. Meyer, *Ursprung und Anfänge des Christentums* 3 vols. (Berlin, 1921–3), vol. 3, pp. 308–38.

[132] T. Klauser, *Henri Leclercq 1869–1945: von Autodidakten zum Kompilator grossen Stils* (*JAC* Ergänzungsband 5, Münster, 1977), reviewed by W. H. C. Frend, *JTS* N.S. 30 (1979), 320–34.

literature and inscriptions often bore on the New Testament.[133] Dölger initiated this approach in his vast study of Christian fish-symbolism, ΙΧΘΥΣ
(1910 onwards), and his work culminated in the great *Reallexikon für Antike
und Christentum*, still in progress. Its publication was begun by T. Klauser
after his death but on the lines which he had planned (1941 onwards; the first
volume was completed in 1950).

As this instance may suggest, the three trends now outlined did not lose
their importance in the later years of the century; it was never possible to
study the New Testament in any depth without encountering versions and
apocrypha, Judaism and Palestine, and Hellenistic-Roman culture. Yet a certain change in atmosphere was perceived by contemporary scholars during
the 1930s, and some of those whose work had given early twentieth-century
New Testament study its character died in this decade, including Turner,
Burkitt, Charles, Harnack, Reitzenstein and Lagrange.

At least two ideals typical of classical training had been to the fore, on the
one hand to range freely over all ancient literature from Homer to Gregory the
Great—'the ambition was to read everything', M. R. James said of himself as
an undergraduate;[134] and on the other hand to attain *akribeia*, to be accurate,
critical and scholarly. Biblical commentary in this context was marked by 'its
predilection for quotations from the ancient commentators skilfully selected
and worked in, its careful technical treatment of textual criticism, and its
abundant illustration also from ancient sources'.[135] This tradition of *Studia
biblica et ecclesiastica*, to quote a series title stemming from these years,
flowered in work such as that of C. H. Turner, textual critic, patristic as well
as New Testament scholar, ecclesiastical historian, and student of canon law.
It had long come together with the Hebrew and rabbinic study noted above,
which had repeatedly opened a door to the interrelationship between
Christianity and Judaism. Now it was also fruitfully combined with the new
insights and approaches from art and archaeology, Semitic and oriental
research, and the history of religion, in a New Testament study which had
affinities with the conception of *Altertumswissenschaft* in its broadest
sense.[136]

---

[133] See for example F.-J. Dölger, 'Der Feuertod ohne die Liebe: Antike Selbstverbrennung und
christlicher Martyrium-Enthusiasmus. Ein Beitrag zu I Korinther 13, 3', in id., *Antike und
Christentum*, 1 (1929), 254–70.

[134] M. R. James, *Eton and King's* (London, 1926), pp. 140–1.

[135] W. Sanday's remark on H. B. Swete's commentaries, quoted from *JTS* 8 (1907), 483 in *Henry
Barclay Swete: A Remembrance*, p. 106.

[136] This conception as formulated by Wilamowitz, involving union of studies in literature, religion, art and archaeology, is discussed and criticised by Lloyd-Jones in his Introduction to
Wilamowitz-Moellendorff, *History of Classical Scholarship*, pp. xiii–xiv, xvii.

Typical figures, then, despite their intense individuality, were F. C. Conybeare, outstanding in Armenian and patristic study, interpreter of Therapeutic asceticism and New Testament demonology, and a chivalrous supporter of the Rationalist Press Association; and J. H. Moulton, Hellenist and Iranist, reinterpreter of New Testament Greek and historian of Zoroastrianism, a devoted Methodist teacher and Manchester professor who died as a result of submarine action in the Mediterranean. Among the pillars of New Testament study, F. C. Burkitt was comparably also a Hebraist and Semitist, an Old Testament scholar and a student of Gnosticism, the interpreter not only of the Latin and Syriac versions but also of the Syriac-speaking church, the religion of the Manichees, and Franciscan tradition. The impressive cross-disciplinary concentration of scholars working on Christianity in its ancient setting was mirrored among present and future members of the Academy at this time; Sanday, Conybeare, Charles, Burkitt, Turner, Dodd, T. W. Manson and Wilfred Knox were flanked among the classicists and ancient historians by J. E. B. Mayor, F. G. Kenyon, A. C. Clark, Souter, A. D. Nock, Edwyn Bevan and M. P. Charlesworth.

The work reviewed from this first period shows something of the depth and potential of New Testament philological study. At the same time its concurrent theological interest has emerged, for example in the differing Christ-portraits of Burkitt, Streeter and Bacon, in the glimpses of religious impulse and church life in the versions and apocrypha, in the sense of the local and national specificity of the earliest Christianity conveyed by rabbinic and Palestinian study, and in the mystical and liturgical appeal of the Hellenistic Paul. In the following period (1932–77) philological breadth did not disappear, but new prominence was attained by concern for theology and the church.

III

A book which marks this change is the *Theologisches Wörterbuch zum Neuen Testament*, completed under the editorship of G. Friedrich in 1973. Its first volume (1932) was edited by Gerhard Kittel and significantly dedicated to Adolf Schlatter. Its approach to New Testament vocabulary was shared in England by Sir Edwyn Hoskyns. A sketch of Hoskyns, intended to show something of the new outlook, leads below to comment on three features of the forty-five years from 1932: form criticism, the trend from Hellenic towards Jewish interpretation, and the trend towards New Testament theology.

E. C. Hoskyns and the language of the New Testament

'No less than thirty-four competent New Testament scholars', wrote Hoskyns, 'have combined to produce a "Theological Lexicon to the New Testament"— the emphasis lies on the word "Theological".' In this review of the first volume he added that the lexicon built on increased recent knowledge of Hellenistic Greek—here he implies a contrast with J. H. Moulton's understanding of New Testament Greek as ordinary Greek of the day (n. 102, above)[137]—to show how words in the New Testament may be deflected from meanings found elsewhere. 'It is difficult to think', he wrote, 'that the deflection is not a consequence of the specific theme of the New Testament writers—namely, the relation between God and man.'[138]

Just such readiness to link semantic deflection with the theme of divine–human relationship has grated on subsequent users of the *Wörterbuch*, especially since James Barr's critique of its tendency to speak as if seemingly distinctive aspects of biblical and New Testament usage were bound up with theology.[139] In 1933 C. H. Dodd already wrote that 'the theological tone of the work is (as they say in Germany) "sehr positiv" ', and he noted a trace of Barthian cliché.[140] Yet, although linguistic phenomena cannot be derived simply from a theological theme, they may attest the influence of Jewish usage and of the Hebrew scriptures which treat that theme. Thus the Septuagintal and New Testament attestation of *doxa* in the unusual sense of 'glory', associated with biblical Hebrew *kabod*, can be treated as a characteristic arising from bilingualism, in this case in the setting of biblical translation.[141] The lexicon has remained an invaluable indicator of the Hebraic as well as Hellenic setting of New Testament themes and language; as Barr allowed, 'its attention to OT and LXX usage (though uneven in parts) is one of the great things to its credit.'[142] It is probably also often valued for what can be regarded as a fault, the characteristic extension of its purview from vocabulary to subject-matter. The reader needs to look out for continuity in an atmosphere of

---

[137] J. H. Moulton and G. Milligan, *The Vocabulary of the Greek Testament illustrated from the Papyri and other Non-literary Sources* (London, 1914–30) had recently been completed.

[138] E. C. Hoskyns, 'A Theological Lexicon to the New Testament', *Theology* 26 (1933), 82–7 (83).

[139] J. Barr, *The Semantics of Biblical Language* (Oxford, 1961), especially pp. 206–62.

[140] C. H. Dodd, reviewing *TWNT* 1 in *JTS* 34 (1933), 280–5 (281, 283).

[141] This line is followed on New Testament *doxa*, in agreement with Barr that the *Wörterbuch* made too much of etymology, but in disagreement with his reluctance to accept that Septuagintal and New Testament Greek words could have received an additional or technical sense, by C. Mohrmann, *Études sur le latin des chrétiens*, 4 (Storia e letteratura 143, Rome, 1977), 180–2, 198–201.

[142] Barr, *The Semantics of Biblical Language*, p. 241.

contrast, but many articles convey the sense of having been excited by the New Testament.

In 1932 the avowedly theological emphasis of the project was stirring and refreshing to many. In German-speaking scholarship the prominence increasingly given in the 1920s to faith and revelation, grace and sin had a contemporary dimension, such that the writers concerned and outside observers too could link it with German social and political circumstances; N. P. Williams associated the rise of dialectical theology with 'the bitter scarcity and distress' in Germany at the time, and Karl Barth in 1924—writing soon after the French invasion of the Ruhr and German and Swiss devaluation—had indeed presented the tension of faith perceived in Paul as the only counter to 'the tensions of human life, of which to-day we again know more than other times have done'.[143] In these years Barth had issued three remarkable New Testament commentaries, on Romans (1919; 2nd edn., 1922, translated into English by Hoskyns), I Corinthians xv (quoted above), and Philippians (1927). His exegesis formed 'an unequalled assertion of the priority and "otherness" of God'.[144] 'I had to foist all this teaching on Paul', he wrote later. 'But I didn't just foist it on him. It's there in Romans. But I was the one who first drew out those threads.'[145] Barth was *sui generis*, but his biblical work signalled a mood found among a number especially of younger (and not necessarily Barthian) exegetes, involving revitalised reverence for scripture and a rejection of liberal *rapprochements* with western culture.

This mood, however, despite what appeared to be its special links with central European crisis, was to some extent shared in British New Testament study, perhaps above all by Hoskyns and his friends and pupils. Hoskyns's lectures in this period were exciting, A. M. Ramsey wrote, because of 'the clash between the discovery of the New Testament which Hoskyns was making for us and the general ethos of religious culture which his hearers shared'.[146] The serene integration of religion and culture represented by Harnack in Germany or Streeter and Bethune-Baker in England was provocatively called into question.

Common feeling among at least some German and English scholars in this matter had become clear in the 1927–31 series of Anglo-German

---

[143] Williams, 'What is Theology?', p. 57, cf. p. 82; K. Barth, *Die Auferstehung der Toten* (Munich, 1924), p. 125.

[144] R. S. Barbour, 'Karl Barth: The Epistle to the Romans', *ET* 90 (1979), 264–8 (267).

[145] K. Barth, *Der Götze wackelt* (Zollikon, 1961), p. 112, quoted by Busch, *Karl Barth*, p. 120.

[146] A. M. Ramsey, *From Gore to Temple: The Development of Anglican Theology between* Lux Mundi *and the Second World War 1889–1939* (London, 1960), p. 133.

theological conferences noted above.[147] Regular New Testament members included Hoskyns, C. H. Dodd, A. E. J. Rawlinson, A. Deissmann, K. L. Schmidt and Gerhard Kittel (not in 1931). The successive subjects were the kingdom of God, Christology (these papers were published under the title *Mysterium Christi*) and Corpus Christi. The tendency towards New Testament theology is clear, and the papers could display not only international concord (n. 38, above), but also national variations on the same theme, for example in the contrasting fortunes of 'kingdom of God' in Germany and America.[148]

The conferences highlight the international context of Kittel's collaborative enterprise. For the first volume of the *Wörterbuch* he gathered scholars including Bultmann, Jeremias, Peterson, H. Sasse, K. L. Schmidt and H. von Soden—'a massive combination', as Hoskyns said. In the past Kittel had also urged and practised similar cooperation with Jewish scholars, notably in the editing of rabbinic texts.[149] It was a bitter irony that, when Hitler came to power, Kittel argued for the segregation of Jews in his 1933 lecture *Die Judenfrage* (3rd edn., Stuttgart, 1934).[150] This grievous instance of *la trahison des clercs* has overshadowed the impetus given by the *Wörterbuch* towards setting exegesis in a biblical and Jewish as well as Hellenic context.

Hoskyns died aged fifty-two in 1937. He had been Dean of Chapel of Corpus Christi College, Cambridge, since 1919, and his sermons witness to his New Testament work. He is one of a few British New Testament scholars in connection with whom it is possible to envisage something like a school of thought. His inspiration emerges in theologians and exegetes including A. M. Ramsey (quoted above), C. F. Evans, and C. K. Barrett. Different as these are (and although all three went to his lectures, only Evans was a pupil of Hoskyns), they all convey that sense of the New Testament as 'peculiarly related to truth and to human life' which Evans ascribes to Hoskyns.[151]

---

[147] Reports and papers were published in *Theology* 14 (1927), 247–96; 17 (1928), 182–260; 22 (1931), 301–46.

[148] H. Frick, 'The Idea of the Kingdom of God from Luther to the Present Day', *Theology* 14 (1927), 280–86 (283).

[149] Kittel, *Die Probleme des palästinischen Spätjudentums und das Urchristentum* (1926), pp. 19–21, on the 'necessity that the Christian and Jewish scholar should work hand in hand'; the book is dedicated to the memory of I. I. Kahan.

[150] After reading this A. Marmorstein withdrew his collaboration with Kittel in editorship of a series of rabbinic texts, despite two letters from Kittel begging him to reconsider, as related by Marmorstein's son Emile in A. Marmorstein, *Studies in Jewish Theology* (London, 1950), p. xxii. On the argument and reception of the tract see R. J. C. Gutteridge, *Open thy Mouth for the Dumb: The German Evangelical Church and the Jews, 1919–1950* (Oxford, 1976), pp. 111–14.

[151] C. F. Evans, 'Crucifixion-Resurrection: Some Reflections on Sir Edwyn Hoskyns as Theologian', reprinted from *Epworth Review* 10.2 (May, 1983), 15.

Particularly close to Hoskyns was his gifted pupil F. N. Davey (1904–73), jointly with whom he wrote *The Riddle of the New Testament* (London, 1931), often reprinted; in 1959 Faber put it in their new series of 'paper-covered editions', between William Golding's *Lord of the Flies* and Don Marquis's *Archy and Mehitabel*.[152] The 'riddle' was the relationship of Jesus to the primitive church; did the life and death of Jesus control the life of the church, which is known to us from the New Testament documents; or was his life and death, not so certainly known to us, submerged by a piety and faith wholly beyond his horizon? The answer was that Christological interpretation has not been imposed upon an un-Christological history; Jesus was not a humanitarian teacher, but a messiah working on an Old Testament pattern to inaugurate the kingdom of God.[153]

Hoskyns summed up some of the history of study considered here in his own development from a catholic modernism, influenced by Loisy and concentrated on religious experience, to a position which when overstated could provoke the response 'surely the Bible itself cannot be quite so Biblical'.[154] In the collegiate setting which helped to shape his thought his departure from Loisy was expressed in a question which he put to the young C. F. Evans: 'Is there not a dagger pointed at the heart of the Master's position?'—the Master of Corpus, Sir Will Spens (n. 121, above), being then, in Evans's words, 'the most subtle and formidable exponent' of argument from religious experience for a rational faith, on catholic modernist lines. The 'dagger' would have been formed by the lack of criteria for assessing experience which ensues upon a submergence of Jesus in the church.[155]

Throughout this development, however, Hoskyns's insight as well as his vulnerability was bound up with his feeling for words. The study of vocabulary which he saluted in the *Wörterbuch* had long been central in his own teaching. Initially he connected it with the religious experience of the Christians.[156] This study is the subject of the first chapter of *The Riddle*; here the Jewish scriptures and the Semitic-language substratum of the New

---

[152] For assessment from differing viewpoints see C. F. D. Moule, 'Revised Reviews: IV—Sir Edwyn Hoskyns and Noel Davey: The Riddle of the New Testament', *Theology* 64 (1961), 144–6; B. S. Childs, *The New Testament as Canon: An Introduction* (London, 1984), pp. 150–1. On Davey see C. K. Barrett, *The Gospel of John and Judaism* (Eng. trans. London, 1975), pp. viii–ix; Barrett, 'Hoskyns and Davey', in id., *Jesus and the Word* (Edinburgh, 1995), pp. 55–62.
[153] Hoskyns and Davey, *The Riddle of the New Testament*, pp. 14, 206–7.
[154] O. C. Quick, *The Gospel of Divine Action* (London, 1933), p. 109.
[155] Evans, 'Crucifixion-Resurrection', p. 6.
[156] 'We were given a fascinating discussion of New Testament Greek, shewing how the religious experience had affected the character of the language': Ramsey, *From Gore to Temple*, p. 133 (on lectures by Hoskyns c.1925–6).

Testament are identified as contributory causes of its linguistic peculiarity, but awareness of divine action in history is now the creative element, as in the 1933 article quoted above, and this seems already to have been characteristic of Hoskyns's thought for some time.[157] As he came back to the theme of vocabulary in sermons from the time of the issue of the *Wörterbuch*, to some extent he brought together the contrasting emphases on experience and on divine action in his contention that the New Testament spoke 'the language of the church'; through wrestling with such biblical words and themes as tribulation and comfort, crucifixion and resurrection, one could learn what might be called a biblical and ecclesiastical humanism: 'where the Lord was crucified, the whole world—please notice, the *whole world*—comes back to us in all its vigorous energy.'[158]

Hoskyns's fascination with New Testament Greek as a distinctive biblical 'language of the church' could find scholarly support, for example, in the indications of Pauline 'Septuagintalism' gathered by Deissmann and Dodd. It was in any case an instance of a more widely attested contemporary concern with the impression left on language by culture and religion, typically pursued at that time with vocabulary to the fore (a heroic example of this approach is the study of the language of the Third Reich, *Lingua Tertii Imperii*, undertaken at his peril by the Romance philologist Victor Klemperer).[159] Thus in 1929 Erik Peterson, soon to contribute to the *Wörterbuch*, was studying in the manner also followed by Hoskyns the 'history of meaning' (*Bedeutungsgeschichte*) of a watchword of Christian liberty, παρρησία.[160] This concern emerged not only in the *Wörterbuch* and with regard to Christian Greek but also in study of the earliest Christian Latin. Thus in 1932 J. Schrijnen issued a programme for the study of Christian Latin as the language of a community—a line pursued by his disciples, above all Christine Mohrmann, cited above, with allusion to the comparable questions of the background of New Testament Greek.[161] The *Wörterbuch* articles converged not only with their writings but also with the theologically oriented

---

[157] G. S. Wakefield in E. C. Hoskyns and F. N. Davey, *Crucifixion-Resurrection: The Pattern of the Theology and Ethics of the New Testament,* edited with a Biographical Introduction by G. S. Wakefield (London, 1981), p. 57.

[158] The two quotations are from a 1932 sermon on 'The Language of the Church', in E. C. Hoskyns, *Cambridge Sermons* (London, 1938), pp. 90, 93.

[159] V. Klemperer, *LTI: Notizbuch eines Philologen* (dedication dated Christmas, 1946; 3rd edn., Halle, 1957; repr. Leipzig, 1975).

[160] E. Peterson, 'Zur Bedeutungsgeschichte von παρρησία' *Reinhold-Seeberg-Festschrift* 1 (Leipzig, 1929), pp. 283–97.

[161] J. Schrijnen, *Charakteristik des Altchristlichen Latein* (Nijmegen, 1932); C. Mohrmann, *Études sur le latin des chrétiens*, vol. 1 (Rome, 1961), pp. 129–30.

articles of the *Patristic Greek Lexicon* planned by H. B. Swete and completed under the editorship of G. W. H. Lampe (n. 272, below). Much of Hoskyns's view would later reappear, against the background of the *Wörterbuch*, in G. von Rad's declaration that, despite the difference between Hebrew and Greek, 'in a deeper sense the language of the Old Testament and the New are the same'.[162]

Hoskyns did not show the constant overt attention to semantic theory evident in Schrijnen, but he shared with Schrijnen, Mohrmann, Peterson and others an interest in semasiology. This term could then cover the whole range of semantics, but it has sometimes been specialised in the area concerned here, a study of significations which begins from words which express them. Any tendency in Hoskyns to theologise semantics was at least partly countered by his characteristic emphasis on the church; the vocabulary of the New Testament for him always belonged to the language of a community.

Hoskyns has been important in another way as a precursor of the Biblical Theology movement which flourished in the USA, Britain and Scandinavia after his death, and of a broader and more lasting concern with biblical theology.[163] He insists both on the theological nature of New Testament work, and on New Testament study as the central work of theology.[164] He anticipates some features of the Biblical Theology movement in particular, notably an emphasis on the importance of the Old Testament for the New and on the distinctiveness of biblical conceptions, and a style of exegesis which is theological without neglect of the historical; but his sense for the restlessness and particularity of New Testament thought, his ecclesiastical and humanist aspects, and his combination of depth with a fundamental merriment, all help to single him out.[165]

Formgeschichte in Britain

As befits the insular standpoint of this study, I have deferred until now any extended comment on the New Testament form criticism (*Formgeschichte*)

---

[162] G. von Rad, *Old Testament Theology* (Eng. trans., 2 vols., Edinburgh, 1962, 1965), vol. 2, p. 354.

[163] B. S. Childs, *Biblical Theology in Crisis* (Philadelphia, 1976), p. 54; Neill, in Neill and Wright, *The Interpretation of the New Testament*, p. 234.

[164] These emphases correspond to the first two of the prominent aspects of modern biblical theology, in the broader sense, picked out by J. Barr, *The Concept of Biblical Theology: An Old Testament Perspective* (London, 1999), pp. 5–17.

[165] Evans, 'Crucifixion-Resurrection', pp. 7–8, 16 differentiates Hoskyns from the Biblical Theology movement, and picks out 'the delightful divine merriness of the Christians', from Hoskyns on John xv. 10–13, as the phrase which brought the lineaments of Hoskyns again most clearly before him.

which had taken shape in Germany from 1919 onwards in books by K. L. Schmidt, M. Dibelius and R. Bultmann.[166] Among those who thought with the young Karl Barth it was an exciting theological event, securing the Gospels from adoption by Harnackian liberalism.[167] In other circles on the Continent and in Britain it was often viewed primarily as a new critical method, leading to results which could seem debatable as well as beneficial.

In Britain 1932 was still almost within the time 'before the form critics came to power', to use C. N. L. Brooke's phrase.[168] Hoskyns and Davey did not mention *Formgeschichte* in *The Riddle*, although they verged on it with regard to the tradition reshaped in Gospel documents.[169] It had indeed already been used and noted in England, as in the USA and France, but it attained wider British discussion mainly in the 1930s. This process was linked especially with three members of C. H. Turner's seminar on St Mark: A. E. J. Rawlinson (later bishop of Derby), R. H. Lightfoot (later professor in Oxford) and C. H. Dodd (later professor in Manchester and Cambridge).[170] In 1925 Rawlinson in his Marcan commentary urged, following Schmidt, that the chronological order of the narrative was largely valueless, in 1932 Dodd challenged this position, and from 1934 Schmidt and Dibelius were championed by Lightfoot.[171]

M. Dibelius, *Die Formgeschichte des Evangeliums* (1919) was issued in English translation in 1934, and R. Bultmann, *Geschichte der synoptischen Tradition* (1921) in 1963. These English publications roughly mark, respectively, a stage when the achievement of the form critics was first being digested, and a later stage when it was chewed like cud in Bultmann's

---

[166] K. L. Schmidt, *Der Rahmen der Geschichte Jesu* (Berlin, 1919); M. Dibelius, *Die Formgeschichte des Evangeliums* (Tübingen, 1919); R. Bultmann, *Geschichte der synoptischen Tradition* (1921; 2nd edn., 1931; repr. Göttingen, 1964).

[167] K. Barth, 'Rudolf Bultmann—an Attempt to Understand Him' (1952), in H. W. Bartsch (ed.) and R. H. Fuller (trans.), *Kerygma and Myth: A Theological Debate*, vol. 2 (Eng. trans. London, 1962), pp. 83–132 (89), on 'the lead we had been given by the form critics' in 'a new appreciation of the objective character of the New Testament documents'.

[168] Brooke, *A History of the University of Cambridge*, vol. 4. *1870–1990*, p. 147.

[169] Hoskyns and Davey, *Riddle*, pp. 107–10, 162–207; the latter section was developed in an explicitly form-critical study by C. H. Dodd, *History and the Gospel* (London, 1938), pp. 92–110.

[170] Bate, 'Cuthbert Hamilton Turner: A Memoir', p. 53.

[171] A. E. J. Rawlinson, *The Gospel according to St. Mark* (Westminster Commentaries; London, 1925), discussed by C. H. Dodd, 'The Framework of the Gospel Narratives', *ET* 43 (1932), 396–400, reprinted in Dodd, *New Testament Studies* (Manchester, 1953), pp. 1–11. The critique of Dodd's study by D. E. Nineham, 'The Order of Events in St. Mark's Gospel—an Examination of Dr. Dodd's Hypothesis', in Nineham (ed.), *Studies in the Gospels: Essays in Memory of R. H. Lightfoot* (Oxford, 1955), pp. 223–39 is itself criticised by C. F. D. Moule, reviewing *Studies in the Gospels*, *JTS* N.S. 7 (1956), 280–2.

theological heyday. By this time, however, those who fully endorsed form criticism, both inside and outside Germany, had begun to complement it by emphasis on the creativity of editors and evangelists and by a reconsideration of the historical Jesus. In the 1970s, when interpretative method in general was debated, form-critical approaches received renewed criticism.[172] They had then been current in New Testament work for over fifty years. Throughout this time they posed the question of the setting in life (*Sitz im Leben*) of literary and oral forms, and so underlined the importance of a church setting for the origins and development of Gospel traditions.

By the end of the nineteenth century Gunkel's work on Genesis and the Psalms had brought literary forms and their *Sitz im Leben* to the fore in the history of Israelite literature, which in areas like prophecy and psalmody included New Testament material.[173] An English by-product of this interest was R. G. Moulton's *The Literary Study of the Bible* (London, 1896), subtitled 'an account of the leading forms of literature represented in the sacred writings', and a forerunner of many attempts to bring some reflection of differing forms into the printing of the English Bible. Gunkel's Old Testament approach converged among New Testament scholars with broader interest in pre-literary tradition, for example in the concern with a primitive catechetical 'form of teaching' (Rom. vi. 17) which had been intensified by the publication of the Didache.[174] The forms of early Christian literature had been viewed in the setting of Greek literature and tradition by Norden (n. 114, above), with special reference to style, and P. Wendland, for whom, as for some later form critics, Mark was not a writer, but a collector of traditions with sparse knowledge of the outline of events.[175]

Then, however, this work was taken up with special regard to the Christian community before and during the completion of the Gospels, by K. L. Schmidt and M. Dibelius, in books published independently of one another in 1919 (n. 166, above). Dibelius brought out a continuity between Jesus, the traditions from his circle, and further development; but

---

[172] For example M. D. Hooker, 'On Using the Wrong Tool', *Theology* 75 (1972), 571–81; G. N. Stanton, *Jesus of Nazareth in New Testament Preaching* (Cambridge, 1974); G. B. Caird, 'A Re-assessment of Form Criticism', *ET* 87 (1975), 137–41.

[173] For example, H. Gunkel, 'Literaturgeschichte Israels', *RGG* 1 (1909), cols. 1189–94, speaking of 'die Erforschung der Formensprache' and 'die Betrachtung der Formen' without using the term 'Formgeschichte'.

[174] The importance of A. Seeberg, *Der Katechismus der Urchristenheit* (Leipzig, 1903) as a precursor of form criticism is noted by Kümmel, *The New Testament*, p. 450, n. 404; comparison with rabbinic and Greek Jewish instruction was added by G. Klein, *Der älteste christliche Katechismus und die jüdische Propaganda-Literatur* (Berlin, 1909).

[175] P. Wendland, *Geschichte der urchristliche Literaturformen* (Tübingen, 1912), pp. 262–3, 267.

discontinuity between Jesus and the Gospels marked the larger study of the synoptic tradition by R. Bultmann which followed in 1921. As he later put it, the community tradition showed no interest in the human personality of Jesus, or the course of his life, and these cannot now be reconstructed.[176] This critical stance matched Bultmann's theological aversion from the quest of the historical Jesus as an attempt to know Christ after the flesh (II Cor. v. 16)—an aversion recalling Luther on justification by faith. 'I am deliberately renouncing', Bultmann later wrote, 'any form of encounter with a phenomenon of past history, including an encounter with the Christ after the flesh, in order to encounter the Christ proclaimed in the kerygma.'[177]

A contrasting form-critical study by M. Albertz (1921), showing the influence of Gunkel, on the significance of the synoptic dialogues for the historical Jesus, was prefaced by a protest against Bultmann's sceptical application of the method.[178] G. Bertram (1922) treated the Passion narrative form-critically as a document of the Christ-cult, underlining the formative potential of biblical *testimonia* for narrative.[179]

In 1924 E. Fascher examined all these books, criticising Dibelius and Bultmann for their separation from source criticism and neglect of possible settings in the life of Jesus.[180] His comments found response in Germany in Lietzmann's judgment, noted below, in the continuing source-critical work of W. Bussmann, and in a famous presentation of Jesus as a numinous healer by Rudolf Otto, from the *Religionsgeschichtliche Schule* and a senior Marburg colleague of Bultmann.[181] Fascher's criticisms were also influential in Britain. Yet everywhere they were swimming against a strong tide.

Gospel form criticism could be taken, as Bultmann held, to strengthen Wellhausen's scepticism on the historical value of Mark. The Gospel could

---

[176] R. Bultmann, 'Reich Gottes und Menschensohn', *Theologische Rundschau* N.F. 9 (1937), 1–35 (1–2).

[177] R. Bultmann, 'A Reply to the Theses of J. Schniewind' (1944), translated by R. H. Fuller in H. W. Bartsch (ed.), *Kerygma and Myth: A Theological Debate* (Eng. trans. London, 1953), pp. 102–23 (117); God 'makes none rich save the poor', a comment of Luther on Rom. x. 19, is quoted by Bultmann, 'Bultmann Replies to his Critics', ibid., pp. 190–211 (206), without special reference to the historical Jesus but in a general defence of his position.

[178] M. Albertz, *Die synoptischen Streitgespräche: ein Beitrag zur Formengeschichte des Urchristentums* (Berlin, 1921), pp. v–vi.

[179] G. Bertram, *Die Leidensgeschichte Jesu und die Christuskult: eine formgeschichtliche Untersuchung* (Göttingen, 1922).

[180] E. Fascher, *Die formgeschichtliche Methode: eine Darstellung und Kritik. Zugleich ein Beitrag zur Geschichte des synoptischen Problems* (BZNW 2, Giessen, 1924), pp. 54, 212–34.

[181] W. Bussmann, *Synoptische Studien* (3 vols., Halle, 1925, 1929, 1931); R. Otto, *Reich Gottes und Menschensohn* (1934), Eng. trans. *The Kingdom of God and the Son of Man* (London, 1938), reviewed by Bultmann, 'Reich Gottes und Menschensohn'.

now seem to be the piecing together, without chronological discrimination, of a number of communally rounded narratives. This view, echoed in Britain by Rawlinson, was advocated by R. H. Lightfoot, closely following Dibelius. He was opposed especially to F. C. Burkitt's praise for the historical guidance afforded by Mark's framework, but he increasingly affirmed the significance of the Evangelists as teachers, here in line with E. Lohmeyer on the doctrinal aspect of gospel geography and C. H. Dodd on apostolic preaching and realised eschatology.[182] In Scotland William Manson had reasserted the historical value of the messianic gospel depiction of Jesus, with an appeal to Fascher; and the method was critically reviewed by Vincent Taylor and judiciously employed, together with source criticism, in his big commentary on Mark (1952), with a by then unfashionable stress on historical questions.[183] Lightfoot's view was defended, however, by his pupil D. E. Nineham, whose influential Pelican commentary on Mark (1963) sharply differs from Taylor in its stress on the sparseness of the Gospel's historical yield; *Formgeschichte* was more critically viewed in the commentary on Luke (1963) in the same Pelican series by G. B. Caird (1917–84).[184]

In wider church and theological circles a general sympathy with form criticism as echoed by R. H. Lightfoot had been encouraged since the 1940s by the work of Austin Farrer, well-known as a philosophical theologian and an intuitive interpreter of Christian life. He warmly endorsed Lightfoot's apprehension of Mark as a creative theologian, and his own work on Mark and Matthew anticipated study of *Redaktionsgeschichte*, in Germany by H. Conzelmann and others, and in French-speaking scholarship by J. Dupont in Belgium.[185] Farrer's own view of *Formgeschichte*, however, favoured Fascher.[186] He urged that Mark's theological scheme also evinced a historically plausible sequence; here he strikingly differed from both Lightfoot and

---

[182] R. H. Lightfoot, *History and Interpretation in the Gospels* (London, 1934); id., *Locality and Doctrine in the Gospels* (London, 1938), pp. ix–x, 18–23, 108–11; id., *The Gospel Message of St. Mark* (Oxford, 1953).

[183] William Manson, *Jesus the Messiah. The Synoptic Tradition of the Revelation of God in Christ: with special reference to Form-criticism* (London, 1943), pp. 20–32; V. Taylor, *The Gospel according to Saint Mark* (London, 1952), pp. 17–20; review of Taylor by C. F. D. Moule, JTS N.S. 4 (1953), 68–73.

[184] Contrast D. E. Nineham, *Saint Mark* (Harmondsworth, 1963), pp. 27–9 with G. B. Caird, *Saint Luke* (Harmondsworth, 1963), pp. 21–2.

[185] A. M. Farrer, *The Glass of Vision* (Westminster, 1948), pp. 52–4, 136–46; id., *A Study in St Mark* (Westminster, 1951), pp. 6–7; H. Conzelmann, *Die Mitte der Zeit* (2nd edn., 1957), Eng. trans. *The Theology of Saint Luke* (London, 1960), pp. 9–17; J. Dupont, *Les Béatitudes: le problème littéraire, le message doctrinal* (Louvain, 1954).

[186] A. M. Farrer, review of A. E. J. Rawlinson, *Christ in the Gospels* (1944), JTS 47 (1946), 77–8.

Nineham.[187] Through treatment of imagery as well as narrative he also emphasised those links between biblical work and the criticism of literature which were integral to form criticism, and would come to the fore again in the second half of the century; 'I wish to show', he wrote, 'that the sort of criticism of most use for getting to the bottom of the New Testament is often more like the criticism we apply to poetry than we might incline to expect.'[188]

Farrer's brilliance and versatility could seem exasperatingly playful. This aspect of his work injured it among biblical students, but his books were widely found fascinating, and they helped to commend form criticism by showing that it could cohere with imaginative exploration of the Gospels, both for theology and for a historical approach to the ministry of Jesus.

Two modes of more critical response to form criticism in England had been marked by special depth and creativity. One, represented by C. H. Dodd and then by C. F. D. Moule, consisted in further exploration of the potential of the form-critical method itself, so as to show among other things its capacity for shedding light both on the historical Jesus and on early formulations of teaching and apologetic—seen not simply as developed in the church but also as connecting Jesus with the New Testament. In a paragraph on the fruitfulness of form criticism Dodd significantly picked out Schmidt and Dibelius as the founders, without mentioning Bultmann.[189] He developed these form-critical links between the New Testament, the church and Jesus in papers for his Cambridge seminar (1936–49) and in a remarkable series of short books, treating in turn the parables, the apostolic kerygma, the Passion narrative, and the morality of the Epistles, and crowned by a many-sided reinterpretation of testimonia from the Old Testament in the New.[190] In a final work, the second of a pair of big books on John, he studied Johannine narratives form-critically, here in contrast with the source-critical approach to John followed by

---

[187] Farrer, *A Study in St Mark*, pp. 7, 186–202; id., *St Matthew and St Mark* (Westminster, 1954), pp. 159, 228.

[188] Farrer, *The Glass of Vision*, p. 136. His thought on imagery was developed with reference to the Apocalypse in *A Rebirth of Images* (Westminster, 1950) and his commentary *The Revelation of St. John the Divine* (Oxford, 1964).

[189] Dodd, *Christian Beginnings*, p. 14; his silence here on Bultmann was not simply expedient in response to the more sceptical Barnes, but true to the importance of Schmidt and Dibelius as founders and to Dodd's own consistently positive response to their discernment of communal continuity.

[190] C. H. Dodd, *The Parables of the Kingdom* (London, 1935), pp. 43–51, 111–32, 175–202; id., *The Apostolic Preaching and its Development* (London, 1936), pp. 104–18; id., *History and the Gospel* (London, 1938), pp. 90–101, seen as showing that criticism could after all reach towards the historical personality of Jesus by D. M. Baillie, *God Was In Christ* (2nd edn., London, 1955), pp. 57–8; Dodd, *Gospel and Law* (Cambridge, 1951); id., *According to the Scriptures* (London, 1952). G. M. Styler has kindly made the minutes of Dodd's seminar available to me.

Emanuel Hirsch and Rudolf Bultmann in Germany.[191] Paradoxically, Dodd's work is perhaps the single widest-ranging British contribution to *Formgeschichte*.

A second response, represented especially by Wilfred Knox, a leading contributor to Dodd's seminar, consisted partly in questioning—most famously when Knox urged, against R. H. Lightfoot, that precisely from a form-critical perspective an ending at Mark xvi. 8 would be unexpected.[192] Farrer, who had made a lively defence of Lightfoot's view, came to prefer the hypothesis that a sentence had been lost after verse 8; deliberate suppression of an ending was suggested, with reference to Knox, by C. S. C. Williams.[193] Such questions were complemented, however, by further extended study of the literary source criticism of the synoptic tradition. Developing the approach of Eduard Meyer, Knox argued in detail that the Gospels were compiled from a number of shorter tracts, such as would have been in use between the late thirties and the early fifties; these would have been composed for the sake of preaching the gospel, but sometimes primitive and valuable historical material can be discerned in them.[194]

The differing responses of Dodd and Knox had both been envisaged in principle by Fascher.[195] Knox's argument for early written sources was soon paralleled in Sweden by H. Riesenfeld and Birger Gerhardsson, on the likelihood of a relatively fixed pre-gospel oral tradition; Gerhardsson supported this proposal from study of oral tradition in rabbinic Judaism.[196]

The position from which Dodd, Knox and others in Britain began seems broadly comparable with that taken in Germany by Hans Lietzmann, who combined a measured welcome to form-critical insights with reaffirmation of the value of Harnack's source-criticism.[197] Dodd and Moule, however, were also keenly aware of an exegetical and theological dimension of the question;

---

[191] C. H. Dodd, *Historical Tradition in the Fourth Gospel* (Cambridge, 1963).

[192] W. L. Knox, 'The Ending of St. Mark's Gospel', *HTR* 35 (1942), 13–23.

[193] Farrer, *The Glass of Vision*, pp. 136–46; id., *St Matthew and St Mark*, pp. 144–59; C. S. C. Williams, *Alterations to the Text of the Synoptic Gospels and Acts* (Oxford, 1951), pp. 40–5.

[194] W. L. Knox, edited by Henry Chadwick, *The Sources of the Synoptic Gospels* (2 vols., Cambridge, 1953, 1957).

[195] Fascher, *Die formgeschichtliche Methode*, pp. 220–3, 233–4.

[196] H. Riesenfeld, *The Gospel Tradition and its Beginnings: A Study in the Limits of 'Formgeschichte'* (London, 1957), and B. Gerhardsson, *Memory and Manuscript: Oral Tradition and Written Transmission in Rabbinic Judaism and Early Christianity* (Uppsala, 1961), sympathetically criticised by W. D. Davies, *The Setting of the Sermon on the Mount* (Cambridge, 1964), pp. 464–80.

[197] H. Lietzmann, *The Beginnings of the Christian Church* (London, 1961), pp. 45–60, from Eng. trans. by B. L. Woolf of H. Lietzmann, *Geschichte der Alten Kirche*, 1. *Die Anfänge* (2nd edn., Berlin, 1937).

historical criticism must retain its place in gospel study, and the New
Testament should not be presented as an indivisible whole of revelation, but
it was also necessary to avoid a historicism which took no interpretative
account of the biblical intertwining of faith and history.[198] This issue was to
recur in later debate on interpretative method.

In Britain form criticism, with Dodd's study of apostolic kerygma, had
now helped to revive interest in Jewish and Christian catechesis and apologetic (n. 174, above), for example in G. D. Kilpatrick's suggestion that the
special Matthaean material represented expansion current in liturgical use of
the Gospel; the liturgical line of inquiry continued to attract attention.[199]
Notable studies of catechesis, on a pattern of instruction discerned in the
Epistles, were published from 1940 onwards by Philip Carrington, E. G.
Selwyn, and David Daube.[200] Carrington sketched a sympathetic picture of
old Jewish piety as typically marked by realised eschatology, and judged that
much of this piety emerged in the Epistles. Daube, from the Jewish side, was
perhaps the first to follow a form-critical approach in a large-scale study of
the New Testament in the light of rabbinic literature.[201]

The atmosphere of creative Jewish–Christian interaction evident in this
group of writings on form criticism and catechesis can also be felt in the
contemporary series *Judaism and Christianity* edited by W. O. E. Oesterley,
H. Loewe and E. I. J. Rosenthal, with contributors including Wilfred Knox;
and Carrington's view of Jewish piety was perhaps not far from that held by
Dodd when he judged that the Fourth Gospel was akin in thought not only to
Philo (here Dodd was close to Knox) but also to rabbinic literature.[202]

---

[198] Dodd, 'The New Testament', in Kirk, *The Study of Theology*, pp. 219–46 (240–1); id., 'A Problem
of Interpretation', *Studiorum Novi Testamenti Societas Bulletin* 2 (1951), 7–18; Moule, review of
Taylor, *The Gospel according to Saint Mark*, p. 69, and 'Jesus in New Testament Kerygma', reprinted
from O. Böcher and K. Haacker, *Verborum Veritas: Festschrift für G. Stählin* (Wuppertal, 1970) in C.
F. D. Moule, *New Testament Essays* (Cambridge, 1982), pp. 37–49.

[199] G. D. Kilpatrick, *The Origins of the Gospel according to St Matthew* (Oxford, 1946); P. Carrington,
The Primitive Christian Calendar (Cambridge, 1952); Aileen Guilding, *The Fourth Gospel and
Jewish Worship* (Oxford, 1960); M. D. Goulder (n. 222, below).

[200] Philip Carrington, *The Primitive Christian Catechism: A Study in the Epistles* (Cambridge, 1940);
E. G. Selwyn, 'On the Inter-relation of I Peter and other N.T. Epistles' (beginning with pages on
' "Formgeschichte" and its Application to the Epistles' and continuing on 'Baptismal Forms' and
'Catechetical Material'), in id., *The First Epistle of St. Peter* (London, 1947), pp. 363–466; D. Daube,
'Participle and Imperative in I Peter', in Selwyn, *The First Epistle of St. Peter*, pp. 467–88.

[201] See especially the section entitled 'Legislative and Narrative Forms' in D. Daube, *The New
Testament and Rabbinic Judaism* (London, 1956).

[202] *Judaism and Christianity*, 3 vols.: vol. 1, W. O. E. Oesterley (ed.), *The Age of Transition* (London,
1937); vol. 2, H. Loewe (ed.), *The Contact of Pharisaism with other Cultures* (London, 1937); vol. 3,
E. I. J. Rosenthal (ed.), *Law and Religion* (London, 1938), all reprinted in one volume with
Prolegomenon by E. Rivkin (New York, 1969); C. H. Dodd, *The Interpretation of the Fourth Gospel*

Moule at the same time was approaching the birth of the New Testament form-critically, interpreting it as a response to catechetical and apologetic needs, and urging, against the pervasive influence of Bultmann's disciples, that in this context the Evangelists will have wished to provide a reliable narrative of events.[203] In its insistence on this point the book strikingly contrasts not only with Bultmann, but also with a late work of Alfred Loisy which had comparably treated the growth of the New Testament as the development of catechesis.[204] Daube and Moule, each an unmistakably independent scholar, both attended Dodd's seminar and shared his concern with the catechetical aspect of form criticism—Moule coming particularly close to Dodd's sense for links between Jesus, the church and the New Testament.

Especially in Germany it could seem that research into the historical Jesus had been frozen by *Formgeschichte* in combination with Bultmannian theology. The phrase *Leben Jesu*, 'life of Jesus' was now widely dismissed as suggesting an unattainable and undesirable biographical aim. This dismissal was taken for granted in the far-flung school of Bultmann, which was powerful not only in Germany but also, through scholars like D. Georgi, H. Koester and J. M. Robinson, in the USA. A Bultmannian like G. Bornkamm could indeed call the time before the form critics 'the life-of-Jesus era'.[205]

Yet form criticism led in time to renewal of a study of the historical Jesus which had never been entirely given up. So in the 1930s and 1940s Jesus and his eschatology were treated not only by Otto, as noted above, but also by Jeremias and W. G. Kümmel.[206] In 1957 the Bultmannian E. Käsemann noted that E. Stauffer had indeed issued a life of Jesus, and that Jeremias had long engaged with interpretation of New Testament life and thought as a reflection of Jesus's work; moreover—here Käsemann looked towards a development in Bultmannian scholarship which Bultmann did not approve—E. Fuchs and G. Bornkamm as well as Käsemann himself had all been (not writing

---

(Cambridge, 1953), pp. 73–5; W. L. Knox, *Some Hellenistic Elements in Primitive Christianity* (Schweich Lectures 1942, London, 1944), pp. 42–90 (John and Philo).

[203] C. F. D. Moule, *The Birth of the New Testament* (London, 1962; 3rd edn., revised and rewritten, London, 1981); id., 'The Intention of the Evangelists', reprinted from A. J. B. Higgins (ed.), *New Testament Essays: Studies in Memory of T. W. Manson* (Manchester, 1959), pp. 165–79 in C. F. D. Moule, *The Phenomenon of the New Testament* (London, 1967), pp. 100–14; Moule, as cited in n. 183, above.

[204] A. Loisy, *Les Origines du Nouveau Testament* (Paris, 1936, Eng. trans. London, 1950).

[205] G. Bornkamm, '*In Memoriam* Rudolf Bultmann, 1884–1976', NTS 23 (1977), 235–42 ('Leben-Jesu-Aera', 237).

[206] J. Jeremias, *Jesus als Weltvollender* (Gütersloh, 1930); W. G. Kümmel, *Verheissung und Erfüllung: Untersuchungen zur eschatologischen Verkündigung Jesu* (Zürich, 1946; 3rd edn., 1956), Eng. trans. *Promise and Fulfilment* (London, 1957).

biographies of Jesus, but) reviewing the significance of the historical Jesus for faith.[207]

Dodd and his comparably influential friend T. W. Manson were among several British scholars working in this context towards a life of Jesus. A contrast with Germany emerges in Manson's unabashed use of this phrase, and in Dodd's claim, without apology, to give a reading of personality and career.[208] Manson's seminal *The Teaching of Jesus* (1931), later complemented by an outline life, *The Servant-Messiah* (1953), can be set beside Dodd's relatively brief and often dependent *Parables* (1935) and his *Founder* (its first draft was written for public lectures given in 1954). Dodd was above all a form critic, in the distinctive manner just described, but Manson was a source critic, for whom the great post-First World War German work was that of Eduard Meyer.[209] Moreover, Dodd was essentially a Hellenist, but Manson was a Hebraist with an Old Testament training; he took seriously the Aramaic origin and poetic form of the sayings of Jesus, as highlighted by Burney, and he used the Palestinian and rabbinic gospel interpretation of Dalman, Billerbeck, Abrahams and Klausner.

T. W. Manson therefore illuminated important aspects of gospel tradition which are less prominent in Dodd, for example the biblical context of parable. He viewed Jesus's messianic consciousness as shaped by biblical depictions of a faithful minority in Israel, including the servant of God in Second Isaiah, understood collectively (Mark x. 45); correspondingly, the phrase 'Son of man', for Manson (here following Dalman), echoed the canonical Daniel rather than the extraneous Enoch or II Esdras, and by it (here Manson's distinctive view appears) Jesus identified himself with the faithful minority, the suffering but vindicated saints of the Most High (Dan. vii. 13–18, 24–8).[210] This view, accepted by Dodd and in Germany by Jeremias,

---

[207] E. Käsemann, 'Neutestamentliche Fragen von heute' (1957), reprinted in id., *Exegetische Versuche und Besinnungen*, vol. 2 (Göttingen, 1964), pp. 11–31 (21), Eng. trans. in id., *New Testament Questions of Today* (London, 1969), p. 12; G. Bornkamm, *Jesus von Nazareth* (Stuttgart, 1956, Eng. trans. London, 1960); E. Stauffer, *Jesus: Gestalt und Geschichte* (Bern, 1957), Eng. trans. *Jesus and His Story* (London, 1960)—free in speculation, but notable for use of pagan and Jewish sources; E. Fuchs, *Zur Frage nach dem historischen Jesus: Gesammelte Aufsätze*, vol. 2 (Tübingen, 1960).

[208] Dodd, *The Founder of Christianity* (New York and Toronto, 1970; London, 1971), p. 36; T. W. Manson, 'Materials for a Life of Jesus', reprinted in id., ed. M. Black, *Studies in the Gospels and Epistles* (Manchester, 1962), pp. 3–145.

[209] See for example T. W. Manson, *The Servant-Messiah* (Cambridge, 1953), pp. 7, 14–15, 17; id., *Studies in the Gospels and Epistles*, pp. 14, 227.

[210] T. W. Manson, *The Teaching of Jesus* (Cambridge, 1931), pp. 45–86, 211–36, 324–7; his developments of this view and their reception were surveyed by F. H. Borsch, *The Son of Man in Myth and History* (London, 1967), pp. 48–50.

was developed as regards the Son of man by Moule and Morna Hooker, although J. A. Emerton showed that ancient mythological tradition, illuminated by the Syrian legends preserved in Ugaritic, lay behind Daniel and continued to influence the later extra-canonical texts; and Hooker also demonstrated that allusion to the Isaianic servant in the teaching of Jesus was less clear than Manson, Dodd and Jeremias believed.[211]

The ground common to Dodd and Manson included realised eschatology; both set the apocalypses in the broader context of Old Testament and rabbinic teaching on the kingdom, but Manson made the point from detailed study of these sources.[212] Here they were both close to a trend in German study exemplified above by Kittel, but also found in Jeremias and E. Stauffer.[213] Yet for Dodd, by contrast with Manson, messianic hopes at the time of Jesus were varied and imprecise; with a characteristic sense for the Hellenistic-Roman setting Dodd introduces them as an equivalent of ruler-cult, and sees the realised eschatology of the kingdom preaching as genuinely bringing, to individuals and to the community, that sense of 'present deity' which was sought in the cult.[214] Similarly, where Manson's Jesus embodies 'the true Israelite ideal', Dodd, for whom the Old Testament also matters, lays stress on the originality of Jesus and the emergence of a new community.[215]

Towards the end of the form-critical era, therefore, Dodd and Manson exemplify the continuous British study of the historical Jesus, which was continuously countered at home by the form-critical questioning of Lightfoot, Nineham and others, but was now being matched by a certain revival of concern with the historical Jesus in Germany. Manson stands with Knox for continuous British acceptance and development of source criticism of the synoptic Gospels. Dodd, on the other hand, is indeed a form critic, but he does not endorse Bultmann's view of synoptic tradition, and can therefore share Manson's historical reconstruction. Yet there remains a difference between the unified biblical emphasis of Manson and the biblical yet primarily New

---

[211] J. Jeremias, *Neutestamentliche Theologie* I. Teil: *Die Verkündigung Jesu* (Gütersloh, 1971), Eng. trans. *New Testament Theology*, vol. 1 (London, 1971), §§ 23–4; C. F. D. Moule, *The Origin of Christology* (Cambridge, 1977); J. A. Emerton, 'The Origin of the Son of Man Imagery', *JTS* N.S. 9 (1958), 225–42; M. D. Hooker, *Jesus and the Servant* (London, 1959), reviewed by J. Jeremias, *JTS* N.S. 11 (1960), 140–4; ead., *The Son of Man in Mark* (London, 1967).

[212] Manson, *The Teaching of Jesus*, pp. 14–15, 135–41, 244–60; Dodd, 'The New Testament', in Kirk, *The Study of Theology*, p. 234.

[213] Dodd is discussed together with Jeremias and Stauffer by O. Cullmann, *Heil als Geschichte: Heilsgeschichtliche Existenz im Neuen Testament* (1965), Eng. trans. *Salvation in History* (London, 1967), pp. 33–6.

[214] Dodd, *The Founder of Christianity*, pp. 81–5.

[215] T. W. Manson, *The Servant-Messiah*, p. 21 n. 1, pp. 73–4.

Testament outlook of Dodd, with its experiential, ecclesiastical and Hellenic aspects. This difference can be related to two trends of these years exemplified in Manson, towards a Jewish interpretation and towards a biblical theology. Dodd, like Manson, partook in both trends; but he did so with reservation, remaining attached above all to Hellenism and the New Testament.

Towards New Testament interpretation in a Jewish setting

The strength of Septuagintal, Philonic, apocalyptic and rabbinic interpretation of the New Testament in the earlier years of the century has emerged in connection with such names as Deissmann, Knox, Burkitt and Dalman. Awareness of an ever-increasing mass of New Testament interpretation from Jewish sources led, however, to a sense of new movement, as regards the setting envisaged for the New Testament, away from Hellenism towards Judaism. 'In recent years the balance has been redressed', wrote C. H. Dodd in 1950, referring to an earlier predominance of Hellenism in the interpretation of the Fourth Gospel.[216]

Dodd himself could say this partly because he set Philo, closely linked with John by himself and many earlier writers including Knox, within Hellenism as regards the history of religion; but to illustrate the shift in balance he also pointed to much fresh study of the Semitic-language setting of the Gospels, represented by Burney, Schlatter, C. C. Torrey and Matthew Black, and of rabbinic sources, represented by Moore, Billerbeck, Abrahams and H. Loewe. In Pauline study the same trend from Philonic towards rabbinic work stood out in Britain, and within Dodd's seminar, through a comparison between Knox's Philonic *St. Paul and the Church of the Gentiles* (1939) and W. D. Davies, *Paul and Rabbinic Judaism* (1948). The often-reprinted *Rabbinic Anthology*, jointly edited by C. G. Montefiore and H. Loewe, had appeared in 1938, the series *Judaism and Christianity*, mentioned already, was then in progress, and after 1939 came the work on Jewish and New Testament catechesis noted above, by Carrington, Selwyn and Daube. Rabbinic study was part of the atmosphere for a number of Christian students, and it became natural to view the Septuagint and Philo within the

---

[216] Dodd, *The Interpretation of the Fourth Gospel*, p. 74. The Preface is dated January 1950, with a postscript dated June 1952.

Jewish interpretative tradition also represented by the Targums and rabbinic haggadah.[217]

This trend in scholarship in the 1930s and thereafter was strengthened by the centrality of the Jewish community in contemporary European and Middle Eastern history; but New Testament interpretation through the medium of ancient Jewish literature was of very long standing, as noted above, with roots in patristic and medieval exegesis, and a notable early twentieth-century efflorescence. Now it was also encouraged by two major Levantine discoveries.

First, remains of a church and synagogue from early third-century Syria, each with figurative wall decoration, had emerged in excavation carried on until 1937 at Dura-Europos on the Euphrates. Finds included a Greek uncial papyrus fragment from the Passion narrative of a gospel harmony (0212 = P. Dura 10), which with Greek papyrus finds in Egypt cast light on the third-century and earlier period of New Testament textual tradition, hitherto approached indirectly through the Old Latin and the Old Syriac. Even this papyrus, however, and even the church paintings of the Good Shepherd and other subjects, were outshone in New Testament significance by the elaborate synagogue depictions of biblical figures and scenes. Diaspora Judaism in this age, it appeared, could indeed exert the aesthetic appeal which had often been judged, as in Kirsopp Lake on Paul, more characteristic of pagan and Christian cult. E. R. Goodenough combined the Dura synagogue paintings with his interpretation of Philo as witness to a mystical Judaism focused on the living spiritual figures of Moses and the patriarchs, and in a debate which still continues it was asked if the paintings had a messianic theme like that drawn out by treatments of the exodus in the New Testament.[218] Thus from this angle too Philo came to look more clearly Jewish, as did parts of the New Testament with Philonic affinity, notably Paul, John and Hebrews. It was characteristic of twentieth-century concern with Hellenism and Judaism successively that the addressees of Hebrews, traditionally understood as people of Jewish descent, had been reassessed in James Moffatt's commentary (1924) as gentiles, but were now once again taken to be Jewish, in commentaries by C. Spicq (1952) and F. F. Bruce (1965).

---

[217] Thus R. A. Stewart, *Rabbinic Theology: An Introductory Study* (Edinburgh, 1961); he recalls (p. xi) how he began rabbinic reading as a student in 1943.

[218] E. R. Goodenough, *By Light, Light: The Mystic Gospel of Hellenistic Judaism* (New Haven, Conn. 1935), pp. 9, 209–10, 262, and elsewhere; E. Stauffer, *New Testament Theology* (1941; Eng. trans. London, 1955), p. 19.

Secondly, famous finds of Hebrew, Aramaic and Greek texts were made from 1947 onwards in caves near the western shore of the Dead Sea, at the mouth of the Wadi Qumran. In most cases the copying of the texts could be assigned to the period from the Maccabaean age to the time of Christian origins. They showed that in these years in Judaea the books now comprising the Hebrew Bible could be read in Hebrew and in both Aramaic and Greek translation, a point of significance for assessment of the local settings of the New Testament books in Greek, and that they were interpreted through a penumbra of other texts written in the biblical manner, including books known from the Old Testament apocrypha and pseudepigrapha. Another set of texts, scripturally grounded Hebrew rules for communal life accompanied by hymnodic prayers and praises, reflected what was evidently the—Essene or Essene-like—community known since 1910 from the Damascus Document (n. 74, above), and these touched the discussion of New Testament ethics, catechesis and liturgy already noted. Moreover, a series of Hebrew expositions in commentary form, marked by use of the word *pesher*, 'interpretation', explained the scriptures as foretelling the community's special history. This exegesis was related to study of the Old Testament in the New, above all in Sweden by K. Stendahl on the quotations introduced by a fulfilment formula in Matthew.[219]

The theology of the community literature as a whole was viewed together with that of the New Testament in the controversy over identification of the community, notably by G. R. Driver, and in New Testament exegesis, notably, among many others, by two prominent Aramaists, Matthew Black in St Andrews and J. A. Fitzmyer in Chicago; and study of the new texts, by Geza Vermes, formed perhaps the biggest single series of insertions (other comparable series dealt with Jewish epigraphy and Greek Jewish literature) into a new English translation and revision of Schürer's own last revision of his *History*.[220] The extent of this material was perhaps a factor in turning some New Testament interpreters, notably Fitzmyer, away from rabbinic texts

---

[219] K. Stendahl, *The School of St Matthew* (Lund, 1954); E. E. Ellis, *Paul's Use of the Old Testament* (Edinburgh, 1957), pp. 141–7; B. Lindars, *New Testament Apologetic: The Doctrinal Significance of the Old Testament Quotations* (London, 1961), pp. 13–16; Moule, *The Birth of the New Testament* (3rd edn., 1981), pp. 74–106.

[220] M. Black, *The Scrolls and Christian Origins* (London, 1961); H. Ringgren, *The Faith of Qumran* (Philadelphia, 1963); G. R. Driver, *The Judaean Scrolls* (Oxford, 1965); E. Schürer, *Geschichte des jüdischen Volkes im Zeitalter Jesu Christi* (3rd–4th edn., Leipzig, 1901–9); Eng. trans. of 2nd edn. (1886–90), *The History of the Jewish People in the Age of Jesus Christ* (Edinburgh, 1890–1); Eng. trans. of 3rd–4th edn., revised by G. Vermes, F. Millar, M. Black, M. Goodman and P. Vermes (Edinburgh, 1, 1973; 2, 1981; 3.1, 1986; 3.2, 1987), discussed by Hengel (n. 66, above).

towards earlier Jewish sources; but this move is questioned by the importance of rabbinic material for Qumranic as well as New Testament interpretation.

Yet another impulse towards interpretation in the light of Jewish tradition was given by A. Díez Macho's 1956 identification of a complete Pentateuchal Targum of the type current among Jews in Byzantine Palestine, the so-called Jerusalem Targum, in the Roman manuscript Neofiti 1.[221] This discovery complemented texts already known, but it also drew renewed attention to the incorporation of rich new matter of importance for exegesis and communal life into biblical translation, in a fashion already discernible in the Septuagint and Qumran exegesis and in the rendering of the Old Testament in the New. New Testament study of the Targumic tradition became widespread in Britain and Ireland, and intensified existing interest in the relation between the New Testament and midrashic interpretation.[222]

The trend towards interpretation in the light of Judaism could also be seen in study of a major Egyptian discovery in the fields of apocrypha and Gnosticism. Probably fourth-century Coptic copies of apocryphal gospels, apocalypses and other treatises were found in 1945 in the northern Thebaid, not far from modern Nag Hammadi but across the Nile on the right bank, near ancient Chenoboskion, where Pachomius had begun his monastic life in a setting which included Meletians and Marcionites.[223] The Bodmer papyri, including early third-century Greek texts of Luke and John and a third- or fourth-century text of the Protevangelium of James, are also said to have been found in this area.[224] The Nag Hammadi texts bearing names of Old and New Testament authors are largely hitherto unknown, but among them is a Gospel according to Thomas which includes a Coptic version of sayings of Jesus known in Greek from Oxyrhynchus papyri published in 1897 and 1904, and has been to the fore in discussion of the synoptic sayings-tradition and the historical Jesus.[225]

[221] A. Díez Macho, 'The Recently Discovered Palestinian Targum', *SVT* 7 (1959), 222–45; id., *Neophyti 1* (5 vols., Madrid, 1969–78).

[222] For example M. Black, *An Aramaic Approach to the Gospels and Acts* (3rd edn., Oxford, 1967); M. Wilcox, *The Semitisms of Acts* (Oxford, 1965); M. McNamara, *The New Testament and the Palestinian Targum to the Pentateuch* (Rome, 1966); J. Bowker, *The Targums and Rabbinic Literature* (Cambridge, 1969); G. Vermes, *Post-Biblical Jewish Studies* (Leiden, 1975); M. D. Goulder, *Midrash and Lection in Matthew* (London, 1974); id., *The Evangelists' Calendar* (London, 1980).

[223] D. J. Chitty, *The Desert a City* (Oxford, 1966), p. 8.

[224] B. Van Elderen, 'Nag Hammadi', in E. M. Meyers (ed.), *The Oxford Encyclopedia of Archaeology in the Near East*, vol. 4 (New York and Oxford, 1997), pp. 87–9.

[225] Fitzmyer, *Essays on the Semitic Background of the New Testament*, pp. 355–433; C. M. Tuckett, *Nag Hammadi and the Gospel Tradition: Synoptic Tradition in the Nag Hammadi Library*, ed. J. Riches (Edinburgh, 1986).

The Nag Hammadi Coptic apocrypha all show Gnostic traits, and earlier in the twentieth century would therefore perhaps have been viewed primarily in the setting of Hellenism, despite their character as biblical pseudepigraphs. Now their Hellenic aspect was not neglected, but emphasis was laid on the ultimately Old Testament or Jewish influence suggested, for example, by apocalypses under the names of patriarchs, notably a hitherto unknown Apocalypse of Adam.

Philo and Hellenistic Judaism were correspondingly important in discussion of the Nag Hammadi gospels, for example by R. McL. Wilson in St Andrews—which now became a centre for study of the Scrolls, the Targums and the Nag Hammadi texts alike. Philo was likewise to the fore in review of patristic reports on named Gnostics like Valentinus by G. C. Stead and many others, especially in Germany; and there was a widespread tendency, represented by such scholars as E. Peterson and K. Rudolph in Germany and G. W. MacRae in the USA, to find Jewish roots for Gnosticism as a whole.[226] Parallels between Gnostic and Jewish mysticism had long been noted, for example in Marcus Magus as described by Irenaeus.[227] The part played in Gnostic origins by Christian mediation of Jewish tradition was correspondingly debated.[228]

Study of Nag Hammadi apocrypha in the light of Judaism here converged with existing tendencies away from the treatment of gnosticism as Hellenistic mysticism. In work on Paul, for example, W. D. Davies had urged, against Reitzenstein, that 'spirit' was linked with the Old Testament and Judaism rather than a Hellenistic gnosticism, and J. Dupont argued that Pauline conceptions of gnosis arose from the Old Testament, and that even gentile gnosis had its roots in Alexandrian Judaism.[229]

---

[226] For example R. McL. Wilson, *Studies in the Gospel of Thomas* (London, 1960); K. Rudolph, *Die Gnosis* (Leipzig and Göttingen, 1977, Eng. trans. Edinburgh, 1983); G. W. MacRae, 'Why the Church rejected Gnosticism' and B. A. Pearson, 'Jewish Elements in Gnosticism and the Development of Gnostic Self-Definition', in E. P. Sanders (ed.), *Jewish and Christian Self-Definition*, vol. 1 (London, 1980), pp. 126–33, 151–60, respectively; G. C. Stead, 'The Valentinian Myth of Sophia', *JTS* N.S. 20 (1969), 75–104; C. Markschies, *Valentinus Gnosticus?* (WUNT 65, Tübingen, 1992), reviewed by A. H. B. Logan, *JTS* N.S. 45 (1994), 310–13.

[227] G. Scholem, *Major Trends in Jewish Mysticism* (1941; 2nd edn., repr. London, 1955), p. 65; id., *Jewish Gnosticism, Merkabah Mysticism, and Talmudic Tradition* (New York, 1960); cf. H. Graetz, *Gnosticismus und Judenthum* (Krotoschin, 1846; repr. Farnborough, 1971), pp. 104–9. Hellenic links are brought out by N. Förster, *Markus Magus* (WUNT 114, Tübingen, 1999).

[228] The importance of Christian mediation is emphasised by A. H. B. Logan, *Gnostic Truth and Christian Heresy: A Study in the History of Gnosticism* (Edinburgh, 1996).

[229] W. D. Davies, *Paul and Rabbinic Judaism* (1948; 4th edn., 1981, reprinted with Foreword by E. P. Sanders and Biographical Overview by D. C. Allison, Jr, Mifflintown, Pa., 1998), pp. 191–200;

Renewed awareness of Judaism as the prime setting of Christian origins could be seen not only in the discussion of Gnosticism and the New Testament, but also in another trend of this period, towards New Testament theology within revived interest in biblical theology in general.

New Testament theology and biblical theology

J. de Zwaan, speaking expressly against the background of the recently ended Second World War, had appealed at the first General Meeting of Studiorum Novi Testamenti Societas in 1947 for union in study of the New Testament as exemplifying and evoking faith.[230] He caught the mood which was emerging in 1932 and had crossed national and ecclesiastical frontiers; thus in contemporary Uppsala A. Fridrichsen's teaching over the last twenty years was thought to have restored biblical theology to its place of honour,[231] and since *Divino afflante Spiritu* Roman Catholic biblical theology, especially in French, German, Spanish and Italian, had arisen like a giant refreshed. The 'Anglo-Saxon Biblical Theology Movement' was near its zenith, but there was also the broader concern with biblical theology noted above.[232] Throughout the second half of the century awareness of this international field was promoted in Britain by scholar-translators, above all J. S. Bowden, and by scholars who linked Germany, Britain and the USA, such as R. H. Fuller and Norman Perrin.

New Testament theology blossomed throughout Europe and North America. Both regions were represented in a series which evokes the British atmosphere, the Studies in Biblical Theology published by the SCM Press from 1950 onwards, with an Anglo-American group of advisers including two pillars of Biblical Theology in the specialised sense, Floyd V. Filson and G. Ernest Wright. Here work on the theology of particular books and biblical

---

J. Dupont, *La Connaissance religieuse dans les Épîtres de Saint Paul* (Paris, 1949), reviewed by R. Bultmann, 'Gnosis', *JTS* N.S. 3 (1952), 10–26.

[230] de Zwaan, 'The Unity of Purpose in New Testament Studies', (n. 2, above) pp. 134–6.

[231] E. Heen, *Anton Fridrichsen (1888–1953): a Bibliography* (University of Oslo Faculty of Theology Bibliography Series 5, Oslo, 1993), p. 15; see A. Fridrichsen and others, *The Root of the Vine: Essays in Biblical Theology* (Westminster, 1953).

[232] H. Graf Reventlow, *Problems of Biblical Theology in the Twentieth Century* (Eng. trans. London, 1986), pp. 1–9 ('The Anglo-Saxon "Biblical Theology Movement" '); J. Barr, *The Concept of Biblical Theology*, pp. 52–61 (biblical theology more broadly considered); P.-M. Tragan, 'La Théologie biblique: origine, développement, perspectives (avec appendice et complément bibliographique)', in E. Vilanova, *Histoire des théologies chrétiennes* (3 vols., Paris, 1997), vol. 1, pp. 17–133 (enlarged translation of work first issued by Tragan in Vilanova, *História de la Teología cristiana*, vol. 1 (Barcelona, 1984), pp. 21–73).

themes came together with word-studies, some taken from Kittel's *Wörterbuch*; and also in 1950 the same press issued *A Theological Word Book of the Bible*, edited by Alan Richardson, later professor at Nottingham and dean of York, and author of a well-known introduction to New Testament theology.[233] The strength of biblical theology appears yet more clearly in Bavaria at the same time. Here the series Münchener Theologische Studien, also issued from 1950 onwards but covering the whole range of theology, already by 1955 included one 'study in Pauline theology', two books subtitled 'a contribution to biblical theology', another on 'the basic theological question of Hebrews', and another on Psalm cxix 'and its theology'.[234]

Roots of the variously interpreted discipline of biblical theology were now being traced by G. Ebeling in Pietism as well as the Enlightenment, and this perception of origins matched the sense that New Testament theology was not simply a rationalistic exercise.[235] The trend towards theology cohered to a great extent with interpretation of the New Testament in the setting of Judaism, but it was naturally accompanied by revived debate on the Hellenic contribution to ancient Jewish and Christian theology, on early Christian responses to the non-Christian Jewish community and its traditions, and on the relationship between the Old Testament and the New.

The Hellenic question had been lively in the movement away from Greek derivation of Paulinism, primitive Christology and the sacraments noted above from the 1920s. 'The message of the New Testament is in the Hebrew tradition as against the Greek tradition' became a characteristic claim in the Biblical Theology movement.[236] A continuing high valuation of Greek myth and mystery and corresponding elements in Christianity was exemplified, however, in work by H. Rahner and J. Daniélou on patristic interpretation of

---

[233] A. Richardson, *An Introduction to the Theology of the New Testament* (London, 1958), systematically arranged under topics, with emphasis on the church and sacraments, and a tinge of polemic which was both relished and criticised.

[234] R. Schnackenburg, *Das Heilsgeschehen bei der Taufe nach dem Apostel Paulus: eine Studie zur paulinischen Theologie* (Munich, 1950), Eng. trans. *Baptism in the Thought of St Paul* (Oxford, 1964); F. Mussner, *ZΩH, Die Anschauung vom 'Leben' im vierten Evangelium unter Berücksichtigung der Johannesbriefe: ein Beitrag zur biblischen Theologie* (Munich, 1952); E. Pax, *Epiphaneia: ein religionsgeschichtlicher Beitrag zur biblischen Theologie* (Munich, 1955); F. J. Schierse, *Verheissung und Heilsvollendung: zur theologischen Grundfrage des Hebräerbriefes* (Munich, 1955); A. Deissler, *Psalm 119 (118) und seine Theologie* (Munich, 1955).

[235] G. Ebeling, 'The Meaning of "Biblical Theology" ', *JTS* N.S. 6 (1955), 210–25; Enlightenment roots, above all in the work of J. P. Gabler, had been mentioned by T. W. Manson, *The Teaching of Jesus*, p. 4; de Zwaan, 'The Unity of Purpose in New Testament Studies', pp. 130–1. See also L. T. Stuckenbruck, 'J. P. Gabler and the Delineation of Biblical Theology', *SJT* 52 (1999), 139–57.

[236] The quotation is from N. H. Snaith, *The Distinctive Ideas of the Old Testament* (London, 1944), p. 159.

New Testament sacramental and ecclesiological themes, and in the religio-historical aspect of such biblical-theological studies as those of E. Pax or H. Riesenfeld.[237] In Britain there was comparable argument for Greek influence on Jewish eschatology, by T. F. Glasson, and for valuable Hellenic aspects of the New Testament, by C. H. Dodd and F. F. Bruce.[238] Sharp distinctions between Judaism and Hellenism, and between Palestinian and Hellenistic strains within Judaism and within Christianity, remained influential through Bultmann and Jeremias; but they were now questioned again, as they had been by Schürer, notably in Martin Hengel's study of Judaism and Hellenism, showing the extent to which both Judaism and Christianity, even in Judaea, were part and parcel of a Hellenised culture.[239]

Early responses to Judaism, which had formed an important theme for Harnack, were now studied in abidingly important British work from the 1930s by James Parkes and Lukyn Williams, manifesting the concerns also seen in the series *Judaism and Christianity* mentioned above, and then in Switzerland and France by Bernhard Blumenkranz and Marcel Simon.[240] Their reminders of the continuing vigour and prestige of the Jewish community in the Roman empire were taken up in New Testament work, for example by Henry Chadwick on Ephesians as an attempt to claim something of this prestige for the Christians.[241] The integral link between the Jewish and the Christian communities was widely taken to be important, for instance in suggestions that the New Testament reflected the Jewish calendar (nn. 199, 222, above). The negative aspects of New Testament response, however, formed the focus of lively debate from the 1950s onwards, against the background of the Nuremberg and later war crime trials, under such headings as

---

[237] H. Rahner, *Griechische Mythen in christlicher Deutung*, Eng. trans. *Greek Myth and Christian Mystery* (n. 122, above), pp. 6–15; J. Daniélou, *Message évangélique et culture hellénistique aux IIe et IIIe siècles* (Tournai, 1961), Eng. trans. with postscript by J. A. Baker, *Gospel Message and Hellenistic Culture* (London, 1973); Pax, *Epiphaneia*; H. Riesenfeld, *Jésus transfiguré* (Copenhagen and Lund, 1947).

[238] T. F. Glasson, *Greek Influence in Jewish Eschatology* (London, 1961); C. H. Dodd, *According to the Scriptures* (London, 1952), pp. 135–8; F. F. Bruce, 'The New Testament and Classical Studies', *NTS* 22 (1976), 229–42.

[239] M. Hengel, *Judentum und Hellenismus* (Tübingen, 1969; 2nd edn., 1973, Eng. trans. *Judaism and Hellenism*, 2 vols., London, 1974).

[240] J. Parkes, *The Conflict of the Church and the Synagogue* (London, 1934); A. Lukyn Williams, *Adversus Judaeos* (Cambridge, 1935); B. Blumenkranz, *Die Judenpredigt Augustins: ein Beitrag zur Geschichte der jüdisch-christlichen Beziehungen in den ersten Jahrhunderten* (Basel, 1946; repr. Paris, 1973); M. Simon, *Verus Israel* (Paris, 1948; repr. with 'Post-scriptum', 1964; Eng. trans. Oxford, 1986).

[241] H. Chadwick, 'Die Absicht des Epheserbriefes', *ZNW* 51 (1960), 145–53.

'Anti-Semitism in the Gospels' (1965) and *Faith and Fratricide* (1974).[242] These writings, including discussion whether 'anti-Semitism' or 'anti-Judaism' is the more appropriate term for early Christian hostility towards the larger non-Christian Jewish body, were flanked in Britain as elsewhere by intensive work on the trial of Jesus.[243] In these areas of scholarship Jewish members of the Christian community made a special contribution, seen at its most profound in the interpretation of the Passion narrative by Ulrich Simon, *A Theology of Auschwitz* (London, 1967).

Fresh attempts at Christian theologies of Judaism[244] were matched by Jewish study of biblical conceptions of importance in the New Testament.[245] New Testament scholars displayed lively concern with Judaism as a continuing tradition. Within the Academy an outstanding example was W. D. Davies, who pursued rabbinically oriented work towards a New Testament interpretation which held both traditional and contemporary Jewish positions in view. His prolonged study of New Testament understandings of the teaching of Christ as new messianic law touched a great theme of medieval and later Jewish–Christian debate, and he made a New Testament approach to the sources of Zionism.[246] Comparable interest was evident in the concern for the

---

[242] L. Goppelt, *Christentum und Judentum im ersten und zweiten Jahrhundert* (Gütersloh, 1954); W. D. Davies, *The Setting of the Sermon on the Mount*; G. G. O'Collins, 'Anti-Semitism in the Gospels', *Theological Studies* 26 (1965), 663–6; W. P. Eckert et al., *Antijudaismus im Neuen Testament?* (Munich, 1967); D. R. A. Hare, *The Theme of Jewish Persecution of Christians in the Gospel according to St. Matthew* (Cambridge, 1967); R. R. Ruether, *Faith and Fratricide: The Theological Roots of Anti-Semitism* (New York, 1974); R. Kampling, *Das Blut Christi und die Juden: Mt 27,25 bei den lateinsprachigen christlichen Autoren bis zu Leo dem Grossen* (Neutestamentliche Abhandlungen N.F. 16, Münster, 1984).

[243] P. Winter, *On the Trial of Jesus* (Berlin, 1961; 2nd edn., revised and edited by T. A. Burkill and G. Vermes, 1973); E. Bammel (ed.), *The Trial of Jesus* (London, 1970); D. R. Catchpole, *The Trial of Jesus: A Study in the Gospels and Jewish Historiography from 1770 to the Present Day* (Leiden, 1971); further literature from 1966–80 on the trial in W. G. Kümmel, *Dreissig Jahre Jesusforschung* (1950–1980), ed. H. Merklein (Bonn, 1985), pp. 375–419.

[244] J. Jocz, *A Theology of Election: Israel and the Church* (London, 1958), reviewed by R. J. Z. Werblowsky, *JJS* 9 (1958), 225–6; P. Schneider, *Sweeter than Honey: Christian Presence amid Judaism* (London, 1966); C. Thoma, *Christliche Theologie des Judentums* (Aschaffenburg, 1978), Eng. trans. *A Christian Theology of Judaism* (New York, 1980); F. Mussner, *Traktat über die Juden* (Munich, 1979); H. Graf Reventlow, *Problems of Biblical Theology in the Twentieth Century*, pp. 64–132.

[245] For example R. J. Z. Werblowsky, 'Faith, Hope, and Trust: A Study in the Concept of Bittahon', in J. G. Weiss (ed.), *Papers of the Institute of Jewish Studies, London*, vol. 1 (Jerusalem, 1964), pp. 95–139; R. Loewe, ' "Salvation" is not of the Jews', *JTS* N.S. 32 (1981), 341–68.

[246] W. D. Davies, *Paul and Rabbinic Judaism*, pp. 71–2, 142–6; id., *Torah in the Messianic Age and/or the Age to Come* (Philadelphia, Pa.,1952); id., *The Setting of the Sermon on the Mount*, pp. 109–90, 353–66, 446–50; id., *The Gospel and the Land: Early Christianity and Jewish Territorial Doctrine* (Berkeley, Los Angeles and London, 1974); id., *The Territorial Dimension of Judaism* (Berkeley, Los Angeles and London, 1982).

Zealots and their outlook, with varying degrees of readiness to affirm its influence on early Christianity, shown by such scholars as Bo Reicke in Sweden, W. R. Farmer in the USA, M. Hengel in Germany, and G. R. Driver, G. B. Caird and S. G. F. Brandon in England.[247] The related theme of martyrdom was reconsidered, for example by W. H. C. Frend, with fresh attention to continuities between Jewish and Christian martyr-theology.[248]

The question of relating the Old Testament and the New, noted already in the contrast between C. H. Dodd and T. W. Manson, also emerged in connection with biblical interpretation, both in the New Testament and in present-day exegesis. The use of the Old Testament in the New was now being viewed in the context of a broader Jewish interpretative tradition, which had been in development from the Persian period onwards. This outlook, going back to A. Geiger and the nineteenth-century *Wissenschaft des Judentums*, was re-invigorated in Britain perhaps especially through the work of Paul Kahle, Renée Bloch and Geza Vermes; Kahle integrated study of the Old and New Testament text and versions, including Qumran material, as forms of interpretation, and Bloch and Vermes both significantly applied to Judaism a phrase with Christian resonance, 'Scripture and tradition'.[249]

The New Testament now took its place within a continuous interpretative tradition which also contributed to the earliest patristic Old and New Testament interpretation, then being studied intensively in France and England by such scholars as J. Daniélou, H. de Lubac, J. N. Sanders, R. P. C. Hanson and M. F. Wiles.[250] Lively debate against this background on the New Testament role and contemporary viability of typology and allegory involved

---

[247] B. Reicke, *Diakonie, Festfreude und Zelos in Verbindung mit der altchristlichen Agapenfeier* (Uppsala, 1951); W. R. Farmer, *Maccabees, Zealots, and Josephus* (New York, 1956) (when he read a paper at C. H. Dodd's seminar, 27 April 1949, his main thesis—of New Testament links with Maccabaean sentiment—was welcomed, despite criticisms of detail, according to the minutes); M. Hengel, *Die Zeloten* (Leiden, 1961; Eng. trans. Edinburgh, 1989); Driver, *The Judaean Scrolls* (in agreement with C. Roth, *The Historical Background of the Dead Sea Scrolls* (Oxford, 1958); G. B. Caird, *Jesus and the Jewish Nation* (London, 1965); S. G. F. Brandon, *Jesus and the Zealots* (Manchester, 1967).

[248] W. H. C. Frend, *Martyrdom and Persecution in the Early Church: A Study of Conflict from the Maccabees to Donatus* (Oxford, 1965).

[249] A. Geiger, *Urschrift und Uebersetzungen der Bibel in ihrer Abhängigkeit von der innern Entwickelung des Judenthums* (Breslau, 1857; 2nd edn., with introduction by Paul Kahle, Frankfurt am Main, 1938); P. E. Kahle, *The Cairo Geniza* (Schweich Lectures 1941, London, 1947; 2nd edn. Oxford, 1959); R. Bloch, 'Écriture et tradition dans le judaïsme', *Cahiers sioniens* 8.1 (1954), 9–34; G. Vermes, *Scripture and Tradition in Judaism: Haggadic Studies* (Leiden, 1961; 2nd edn. 1973).

[250] Daniélou and de Lubac, as cited in the following footnote; J. N. Sanders, *The Fourth Gospel in the Early Church* (Cambridge, 1943); R. P. C. Hanson, *Allegory and Event* (London, 1959); M. F. Wiles, *The Spiritual Gospel* (Cambridge, 1960); id., *The Divine Apostle* (Cambridge, 1967).

names as varied as Bultmann, Daniélou, de Lubac, G. W. H. Lampe, and F. F. Bruce, among others.[251] In Britain Beryl Smalley had showed that the literal sense too received continuous attention in patristic and medieval exegesis.[252] For the New Testament itself a similar point was made by C. H. Dodd, who discerned attention to the context and general drift of scriptural passages, in many cases on lines continuous with what may be regarded as their original scope, in the kerygmatic interpretation of the Old Testament in the New; this was a creative but also a historical exegesis.[253]

The question of relationship between the Old Testament and the New also posed itself in the background of the theologies of the New Testament which began to appear again in Germany and became central in British study. Bultmann's (1948–51, Eng. trans. 1952–5) was of prime importance. Doubt as well as discipleship could indeed arise from the very order and clarity of his historical progression from the briefly described proclamation of a primitive church in Judaea, through a fuller account of a Hellenistic church theology with integral gnostic motifs, to Paul and then to John. T. W. Manson, having voiced his admiration of the first volume, added: 'The evidence which has come down to us about the ministry of Jesus and the faith and life of the first Christians in Palestine is so drastically treated that there is sadly little left to say about these vitally important topics. As compensation we are given an imaginary picture of the beliefs and practices of a hypothetical Hellenistic community.'[254] Bultmann gripped a succession of readers, however, by his exposition of Paul and John as theologians of human existence, whose word of faith can be apprehended apart from the mythology of their thought-world, through demythologisation (*Entmythologisierung*). Hermeneutical debate

---

[251] L. Goppelt, *Typos: die typologische Deutung des Alten Testaments im Neuen* (Gütersloh, 1939; Eng. trans. Grand Rapids, 1982); R. Bultmann, 'Ursprung und Sinn der Typologie als hermeneutischer Methode', reprinted from *Festschrift G. van der Leeuw* (Nijkerk, 1950), pp. 89–100 in Bultmann, *Exegetica* (Tübingen, 1967), pp. 369–80, and J. Daniélou, *Sacramentum Futuri: études sur les origines de la typologie biblique* (Paris, 1950), both reviewed by C. F. Evans, *JTS* N.S. 2 (1951), 90–5; H. de Lubac, *Histoire et esprit: l'intelligence de l'Écriture d'après Origène* (Paris, 1950), reviewed by H. Chadwick, *JTS* N.S. 2 (1951), 102–4; G. W. H. Lampe and K. J. Woollcombe, *Essays on Typology* (London, 1957); F. F. Bruce, *This is That* (Exeter, 1968); H. Graf Reventlow, *Problems of Biblical Theology in the Twentieth Century*, pp. 14–37.

[252] B. Smalley, *The Study of the Bible in the Middle Ages* (Oxford, 1941; 2nd edn., 1952; 3rd edn., 1983).

[253] Dodd, *According to the Scriptures*, pp. 130–3, endorsed and developed by Caird (Barr, 'George Bradford Caird', pp. 508, 515); Bruce, *This is That*; id., 'The Theology and Interpretation of the Old Testament', in G. W. Anderson (ed.), *Tradition and Interpretation: Essays by Members of the Society for Old Testament Study* (Oxford, 1979), pp. 385–416 (413).

[254] T. W. Manson, in a review of the first volume of R. Bultmann, *Theologie des Neuen Testaments* (Tübingen, 1948–51; Eng. trans. 1952–5), *JTS* 50 (1949), 202–6 (203).

evoked by this programme extended over the next thirty years. Focal points were myth (for example in the collection cited in n. 167, above) and the nature of language and communication, especially in the parables (for example in work by E. Fuchs and his pupils, taken up by Norman Perrin).[255] British work on New Testament interpretation was very widely affected by this debate, partly echoed in popular discussion of *The Myth of God Incarnate* (1977; n. 19, above), and G. B. Caird's studies of language and imagery constitute one vigorous long-term response.[256]

Bultmann's links between the New Testament and the existentialism of Kierkegaard and Martin Heidegger, left implicit in the *Theology*, matched his explicit concluding stress on the connection between thinking and living in the New Testament writers and ourselves. Bultmann considered the Old Testament at earlier points in the work, but not in this conclusion, and in other writings he treated it not without admiration, but as contributing to Christian faith mainly through a version (with a Kierkegaardian air) of the conflict between law and gospel.[257]

This position contrasted with the affirmation of a history of redemption (*Heilsgeschichte*) which shaped the connection of Old Testament and New for E. Stauffer, O. Cullmann and (in Old Testament theology) G. von Rad. This approach again had its roots in Pietism, and it also had patristic analogies in the catechetical narration and the liturgical remembrances which bound Old Testament and New together in a single sequence; within the New Testament it could appeal especially to Luke and Acts, and its emphasis on the church as well as the Old Testament helped it ecumenically.[258]

---

[255] E. Fuchs, *Studies of the Historical Jesus* (1960, Eng. trans. London, 1964); E. Linnemann, *Parables of Jesus* (1961, Eng. trans. London, 1966); E. Jüngel, *Paulus und Jesus* (Tübingen, 1962); N. Perrin, *Rediscovering the Teaching of Jesus* (London, 1967).

[256] G. B. Caird, 'Towards a Lexicon of the Septuagint', *JTS* N.S. 19 (1968), 453–75; 20 (1969), 21–40; id., *The Language and Imagery of the Bible* (London, 1980).

[257] R. Bultmann, 'The Significance of the Old Testament for the Christian Faith' (1933), Eng. trans. in B. W. Anderson (ed.), *The Old Testament and Christian Faith* (London, 1964), pp. 8–35; id. 'Adam, Where art Thou?' (1945), 'Prophecy and Fulfilment' (1949), 'Christianity as a Religion of East and West' (1949), and 'The Significance of Jewish Old Testament Tradition for the Christian West' (lecture delivered in 1949), Eng. trans. in R. Bultmann, *Essays Philosophical and Theological* (London, 1955), pp. 119–32, 182–208, 209–33, 262–72, respectively; cf. M. Oeming, *Gesamtbiblische Theologien der Gegenwart* (Stuttgart, 1985), pp. 17–18 (estimates of Bultmann's view have ranged from neo-Marcionism to affirmation of Old Testament and Jewish tradition); F. Watson, *Text and Truth: Redefining Biblical Theology* (Edinburgh, 1997), pp. 153–69 (neo-Marcionism); Barr, *The Concept of Biblical Theology*, pp. 68, 183–4, 328, 460.

[258] G. von Rad, *Old Testament Theology* (2 vols., Eng. trans. Edinburgh, 1962, 1965, from originals issued 1957, 1960), vol. 2, pp. viii, 382–4; J. Daniélou, 'The New Testament and the Theology of History', reprinted from *Studia Evangelica*, TU 73 (1958) in K. Aland and others, *The Gospels*

E. Stauffer had begun his New Testament theology (1941, Eng. trans. 1955) with the continuity between Old Testament and New as mediated by the Septuagint and pseudepigrapha, and had also vividly realised the nascent church and its summaries of *Heilsgeschichte*, with reference to archaeology and art.[259] Then the Old Testament and the church were comparably important in the interpretation organized by O. Cullmann (1946, 1957, 1965) around the theme of *Heilsgeschichte*, for him a linear history (contrasted with circular views of time associated with Hellenism) in which Christ is central, but to which the Old Testament and the post-apostolic church also in different ways belong.[260] Cullmann's view was adapted in H. U. von Balthasar's rich New Testament theology of *doxa*, for which the Old Testament is fundamental.[261] Jeremias's unfinished work, turning the Dalman tradition into a fascinating theology, was concentrated on the historical Jesus and his originality; but a larger biblical dimension to some extent emerged here too, focused in the affirmation that Jesus 'lived in the Old Testament'—although out of love he dared to radicalise and criticise the written Torah.[262]

By contrast with both Bultmann and Cullmann, and despite indebtedness to both, much contemporary British New Testament theology could seem unselfconsciously historical and theological at the same time, reflecting the view that critical exegesis is a theological enterprise of importance for the church. As C. K. Barrett put it, 'When applied to the New Testament critical and historical study itself becomes a theological operation.'[263] Thus G. B. Caird intertwines historical re-evaluation and C. H. Dodd-like theological restatement, with a debt also to Stauffer and a response to Bultmann, when he

---

Reconsidered (Oxford, 1960), pp. 58–67; Oeming, *Gesamtbiblische Theologien der Gegenwart*, pp. 159–61; cf. Apostolic Constitutions vii. 39; Augustine, *De catechizandis rudibus*, 3 (5)–(6).

[259] Stauffer, *New Testament Theology* (n. 218, above), pp. 18–19, 51–5, 78–9, 239–41 (on *Heilsgeschichte* and its summaries).

[260] O. Cullmann, *Christus und die Zeit* (1946), Eng. trans. *Christ and Time* (London, 1951); id., *Die Christologie des Neuen Testaments* (1957, Eng. trans. London, 1959), reviewed by C. K. Barrett, *JTS* N.S. 10 (1959), 376–9; id., *Heil als Geschichte* (1965), Eng. trans. *Salvation in History* (London, 1967).

[261] H. U. von Balthasar, *Herrlichkeit: eine theologische Ästhetik*, 3.2. *Theologie*, Teil 2, *Neuer Bund* (Einsiedeln, 1969), Eng. trans. *The Glory of the Lord: A Theological Aesthetics*, 7. *Theology: The New Covenant* (Edinburgh, 1989).

[262] J. Jeremias, *New Testament Theology*, vol. 1 (Eng. trans. London, 1971), pp. 205–7.

[263] C. K. Barrett, 'What is New Testament Theology? Some Reflections', reprinted from D. Y. Hadidian (ed.), *Intergerini Parietis Septum (Eph. 2.14)* (Pittsburgh, 1981), pp. 1–22, in Barrett, *Jesus and the Word*, pp. 241–58 (250).

interprets apocalyptic language as metaphor, used in the manner of the prophets with regard to imminent historical crisis.[264]

Many studies were devoted to New Testament themes which bear immediately on Christian life, such as the Pauline imagery of the church, the death of Christ, the spirit and its gifts, and the eucharist; here British scholars like C. F. D. Moule, J. A. T. Robinson, and E. Best were in discussion with American and European colleagues such as John Knox, L. Cerfaux and E. Käsemann.[265] To single out one such theme, in *The Origin of Christology* (1977) Moule gathered up much of his earlier work in viewing 'all the various estimates of Jesus reflected in the New Testament as, in essence, only attempts to describe what was already there from the beginning'.[266] This 'developmental' view to some extent recalls Sanday on the Fourth Gospel, Hoskyns and Davey in *The Riddle*, and Dodd in *According to the Scriptures*; but it stands out for Moule's emphasis on organic growth as the model, in accord with the importance of nature in his thought, and for his demonstration of the Christological weight of Pauline language on the church.[267] This book, soon complemented by Moule's *The Holy Spirit* (1978), was followed by Christological work from his pupil J. D. G. Dunn on *Unity and Diversity in the New Testament* (1977) and *Christology in the Making* (1980). The second book departed from Moule in judging the concept of Christ's pre-existence to be relatively late (here Dunn's argument was part of a discussion of Jewish pneumatology and messianism which still continues), yet in the end supported Moule's main contention; the prime stimulus towards the doctrine of the Incarnation was taken to be specifically Christian wisdom Christology, itself arising from experience of Jesus as a revelation of God.[268]

Large-scale treatment of New Testament interpretation as a central work of theology can be exemplified within the Academy from C. K. Barrett, in the succession of Hoskyns and Davey and with indebtedness to Bultmann, and G. W. H. Lampe, who acknowledged a debt rather to the writings of the

---

[264] G. B. Caird, *Principalities and Powers* (London, 1956); id., *The Revelation of St John the Divine* (London, 1966); id., *New Testament Theology*, completed by L. D. Hurst (Oxford, 1994); cf. n. 256, above; Barr, 'George Bradford Caird, 1917–1984', *PBA* 71 (1985), 493–521 (515).

[265] For example C. F. D. Moule, *Essays in New Testament Interpretation* (Cambridge, 1982); J. A. T. Robinson, *The Body* (London, 1952); E. Best, *One Body in Christ* (London, 1955); J. Knox, *The Death of Christ* (London, 1959); L. Cerfaux, *La Théologie de l'Église suivant Saint Paul* (Paris, 1947); E. Käsemann, *New Testament Questions of Today* (Eng. trans. London, 1969).

[266] C. F. D. Moule, *The Origin of Christology* (Cambridge, 1977), pp. 2–3.

[267] For these aspects of his thought see C. F. D. Moule, *Man and Nature in the New Testament: Some Reflections on Biblical Ecology* (Ethel M. Wood Lecture, London, 1964); id., *The Phenomenon of the New Testament* (London, 1967).

[268] Dunn, *Christology in the Making*, pp. 258–63.

liberal Charles Raven (n. 43, above). Barrett came to envisage New Testament
theology as a releasing of the theological content of the New Testament, with
all its authentic difficulty, into a form which can confront contemporaries; this
theology will be related to the immediate and personal in religion, but will
bear the intrinsic authority of the New Testament as the decisive witness to
Jesus.[269] These aspects stand out in Barrett's study in Pauline theology, *From
First Adam to Last*, with its rejection of *Heilsgeschichte* in favour of a dialectical interpretation of the Pauline role of Old Testament figures, and in his
Pauline commentaries, with the prefatory comment that, 'like most people, I
sometimes wonder if Christianity is true; but I think I never doubt that, if it is
true, it is truest in the form it takes with Paul, and, after him, with such
interpreters of his as Augustine, Calvin, Luther, Barth.'[270]

Lampe (1912–80), who combined patristic and New Testament scholarship (p. 93 and n. 251, above), presented a reshaping of Chalcedonian doctrines of God and Christ mainly in the form of a New Testament theology
focused on spirit; trinity gives way to one loving spirit, incarnation to inspiration.[271] Lampe's historical New Testament work, for example on discipline
and persecution and on the theology of Luke–Acts, had gone side by side with
New Testament treatments of such vexed doctrinal topics as baptism and justification.[272] His *God as Spirit* (Oxford, 1977) begins with an argument that
the best way of expressing traditional belief that the historical Christ remains
a present Lord is through New Testament apprehensions of the abiding presence of the kingdom of God (here Lampe was close to Dodd and T. W.
Manson) and the spirit of God; through ongoing interpretation of biblical and
especially New Testament conceptions of spirit, with attention to the synoptics, Acts, Paul and John, it is concluded that the subtle and manifold New
Testament presentation of spirit in connection with Jesus Christ can express
all that is signified by confession of the descent and ascension of a pre-
existent Christ (here there is Bultmann-like demythologisation). Lampe offers

---

[269] Barrett, 'What is New Testament Theology? Some Reflections', pp. 253–5.

[270] C. K. Barrett, *From First Adam to Last: A Study in Pauline Theology* (London, 1962), pp. 4–6, 111;
id., *The Second Epistle to the Corinthians* (London, 1973), p. vii, discussed by R. Morgan, 'The
Significance of "Paulinism" ', in M. D. Hooker and S. G. Wilson (eds.), *Paul and Paulinism: Essays
in Honour of C. K. Barrett* (London, 1982), pp. 320–38.

[271] A remarkable summary of his proposal is G. W. H. Lampe, 'The Essence of Christianity: A
Personal View', *ET* 87 (1976), 132–7, reprinted in G. W. H. Lampe, *Explorations in Theology*, ed.
G. M. Newlands (London, 1981), pp. 119–29.

[272] C. F. D. Moule, 'Geoffrey William Hugo Lampe, 1912–1980', *PBA* 67 (1981), 399–409 (402–5);
for Lampe's bibliography see G. M. Newlands in Lampe, *Explorations in Theology*, pp. 138–42, supplemented by C. F. D. Moule in Moule (ed.), *G. W. H. Lampe: Christian, Scholar, Churchman. A
Memoir by Friends* (London and Oxford, 1982), pp. 3–4.

not only a doctrinal proposal, but also a fresh integration of New Testament theology. This book indeed recalls the Enlightenment roots of biblical theology, seen in England in such as a book as Samuel Clarke's *The Scripture-Doctrine of the Trinity* (London, 1712), and the efforts to gain through scripture a 'better dogmatics', as de Zwaan put it (n. 230, above); but, like Barrett's work, it also has to an impressive degree the quality of personal religion.[273]

In Britain the attraction of New Testament theology was perhaps more obvious than reflection on its method, but methods were discussed, with regard especially to *Heilsgeschichte* and the contrast between historical and theological interpretation, and this discussion merged with the broader debate on biblical interpretation noticed above.[274] Particularly important in the end was a change in atmosphere, felt in all study of ancient literature, which meant that empathy with the biblical writers now seemed harder to attain. The mythical character of their thinking was indeed widely accepted in the work just surveyed, and Bultmann's response to it, although not widely accepted *in toto*, was by no means without influence; but there was also a strong sense of the immediacy and perspicuity of scripture, such that—not by facile historicism, but through critical exegesis—the New Testament writers could address us directly. Barr wrote that for Caird 'the apostles were not remote beings from another planet; . . . provided that one could listen sympathetically, one could be very close to them', and this also seems true of Moule, Lampe and others (but a stress on distance appears in Barrett).[275] Yet anthropological awareness of the limits of our understanding of other cultures was just one factor in a growing sense of dissociation from ancient writers, voiced in Britain especially by D. E. Nineham.[276]

---

[273] Clarke's work too had depth and piety as well as learning; see M. F. Wiles, *Archetypal Heresy: Arianism through the Centuries* (Oxford, 1996), pp. 110, 125.

[274] Dodd, *History and the Gospel*; A. Richardson, *History Sacred and Profane* (London, 1964), discussed by A. M. Farrer, *Faith and Speculation* (London, 1967), pp. 86–103; R. Morgan, *The Nature of New Testament Theology* (London, 1973); D. E. Nineham, *The Use and Abuse of the Bible: A Study of the Bible in an Age of Rapid Cultural Change* (London, 1976); C. F. Evans, *Explorations in Theology* (London, 1977).

[275] Barr, 'George Bradford Caird', p. 507; contrast Barrett, 'What is New Testament Theology?', p. 252: 'Yet, when all is done, we are not contemporaries of the apostles.'

[276] See discussion of Nineham, *The Use and Abuse of the Bible* by R. P. C. Hanson, 'Are we cut off from the past?' (1981), reprinted in id., *Studies in Christian Antiquity* (Edinburgh, 1985), pp. 3–21; the anthropological observation is applied to New Testament theology, with reference to E. Evans-Pritchard, *Theories of Primitive Religion* (Oxford, 1965), by Heen, *Anton Fridrichsen*, pp. 26–8.

New Testament theology such as that just discussed may itself implicitly question notions of radical dissociation, but opinion in the 1970s was moving in the other direction. The almost seamless robe of an exegesis at once both philological and theological, and interpretation through themes like 'spirit' or *Heilsgeschichte* which could be held to arise from the texts, gave way to intense consideration of interpretative theory, and to exegesis which was more decidedly in a philological or a theological mode.

IV

Paul and Judaism

The eventful publishing year 1977 also saw the appearance of *Paul and Palestinian Judaism: A Comparison of Patterns of Religion*, by E. P. Sanders, a Texan scholar, in his own words 'a liberal, modern, secularized Protestant', who became professor in Oxford and then in Duke University, North Carolina.[277] This book signalled further changes of atmosphere in placing Judaism and Paulinism side by side, and in rejecting some respected earlier interpretation of the New Testament through rabbinic literature. It also represents the importance of North American as well as European scholarship for British study in this last period.

Sanders shares W. D. Davies's deep love and knowledge of rabbinic literature. Davies, however, was concerned with the question of the Judaism or Hellenism of Pauline thought. Paul, he judged, was a Pharisee who had come to hold that Jesus was messiah, and the Pauline gospel was a Christian Pharisaism with a messianic law. Sanders, by contrast, was comparing Paul and Judaism. He agreed that the sources of Paul's thought were Jewish, but he urged that Paul was now possessed by his new conviction of salvation by participation in Christ. Paul attacked his native faith not because of any shortcomings commonly yet debatably found in Judaism by Christian scholars, but simply for one important characteristic: Judaism presented law rather than Christ as necessary to salvation.[278]

Thus for Davies there were strong bonds of unity between Judaism and Paul, and moreover Paul, when interpreted with attention to his historical

---

[277] E. P. Sanders, *Jesus and Judaism* (London, 1985), p. 334.

[278] E. P. Sanders, *Paul and Palestinian Judaism* (London, 1977), amplified in his *Paul, the Law, and the Jewish People* (Philadelphia, 1983) and in Sanders's warmly appreciative 'Foreword to the Fiftieth Anniversary Edition', in Davies, *Paul and Palestinian Judaism* (1998), pp. vii–xvii (xii–xvii).

setting in the Jewish community, emerged with fresh force as a contemporary teacher of Christianity. These aspects of Davies's work seem typical of the period just described. In Sanders, however, despite his admiration for Paul as well as Judaism, Paul is most prominently related to Judaism as a sweeping critic who now attacks it because it is not Christianity, and Pauline Christianity as a way of salvation differs essentially from Judaism. Hence in Sanders Paulinism and Judaism seem largely independent, and continuity between them moves into the background.

This discernment of two independent patterns of religion placed side by side posed a question to biblical-theological claims for continuity between the Old Testament and the New, and also suited the late twentieth-century educational context of the study of various world religions concomitantly.[279] Sanders, echoing G. F. Moore, sharply rejects exegesis by those Christian students of rabbinic literature whom he judges to misrepresent Judaism by presenting it as a religion of works. This critique is bound up with much detailed argument, especially against Billerbeck and Jeremias (whose writings none the less remain rewarding when used with discrimination).[280] Sanders roots his own work, however, in a broader discussion of the scholarly tradition, attaching himself especially to Schweitzer's assertion of the centrality of participation in Christ (rather than justification by faith) in Pauline thought (n. 129, above).

Sanders complemented his Pauline works with equally notable studies of Jesus and ancient Judaism.[281] These books together constituted a fresh historical approach to the New Testament and Judaism, with a challenge particularly to some strands of scholarship within the Lutheran tradition and biblical theology. Especially fascinating was Sanders's rehabilitation of Josephus, read together with rabbinic texts, as a great source for Judaism at the time of Christian origins, a method in which one of his predecessors was Adolf Schlatter (n. 72, above). Discussion of Sanders's monumental oeuvre was central in the debate on all aspects of the relation between the New

---

[279] J. K. Riches illuminatingly suggests that the book 'can be seen as a reaction to the cultural over-confidence of American Protestantism and an attempt to give a reading of the New Testament which reflects more nearly the multicultural environment in which religions are studied in American Liberal Arts colleges and schools' (Riches, *A Century of New Testament Study*, p. 116).

[280] Sanders, *Paul and Palestinian Judaism*, pp. 4–12, 234–5, with reference to the strictures of G. F. Moore; E. P. Sanders, *Judaism: Practice and Belief, 63 BCE–66 CE* (London, 1992) can almost be called an extended dialogue with Jeremias, *Jerusalem in the Time of Jesus* (n. 89, above).

[281] E. P. Sanders, *Jesus and Judaism* (London, 1985); id., *Jewish Law from Jesus to the Mishnah* (London, 1990) and *Judaism: Practice and Belief*, reviewed jointly by M. Hengel, 'E. P. Sanders' "Common Judaism", Jesus, and the Pharisees', *JTS* N.S. 46 (1995), 1–70; E. P. Sanders, *The Historical Figure of Jesus* (London, 1993).

Testament and Judaism which marked the closing years of the century.[282] This included topics which are less prominent in Sanders, for instance the mysticism and eschatological hope attested in the apocalypses, picked out as the mother of all Christian theology by Käsemann.[283] Whereas Käsemann reopened German discussion, the reconsideration of apocalypses by scholars such as C. Rowland, Margaret Barker, J. J. Collins and R. Bauckham continued an English-language tradition of apocalyptic study which had been unbroken since the time of Charles and Burkitt.[284]

The specifically Pauline discussion renewed by Sanders centred on the place of the law in Paul, traditionally understood more negatively by Lutherans but affirmed in Reformed interpretation, and a topic to which British contributions were being made, for example by C. E. B. Cranfield, N. T. Wright and J. D. G. Dunn.[285] Pauline ethics more generally were reconsidered, with debate on their Greek or Jewish character which showed that the controversies of the early twentieth century were still alive.[286] Sanders's work also helped to reactivate broader debate, to which Jews as well as non-Jews contributed, on Paul's understanding of his work, its social and economic setting, and seemingly gentile aspects of his outlook; in Britain subjects which had interested Ramsay and Deissmann were now taken up by scholars such as A. J. M. Wedderburn, Hyam Maccoby and J. J. Meggitt.[287]

---

[282] For example C. Rowland, *Christian Origins: An Account of the Setting and Character of the Most Important Messianic Sect of Judaism* (London, 1985; 2nd edn., 2002); M. Casey, *From Jewish Prophet to Gentile God* (Cambridge, 1991); J. D. G. Dunn (ed.), *Jews and Christians: The Parting of the Ways A.D. 70 to 135* (WUNT 66, Tübingen, 1992); J. P. M. Sweet and J. M. G. Barclay (eds.), *Early Christian Thought in its Jewish Setting* (Cambridge, 1996); J. M. G. Barclay, *Jews in the Mediterranean Diaspora: From Alexander to Trajan (323 BCE–117 CE)* (Edinburgh, 1996).

[283] Käsemann, 'The Beginnings of Christian Theology', translated from a text first published in *ZTK* 57 (1960), 162–85 in id., *New Testament Questions of Today*, pp. 82–107 (102).

[284] For example C. Rowland, *The Open Heaven* (London, 1982); M. Barker, *The Older Testament* (London, 1987); J. J. Collins, *The Apocalyptic Imagination* (London, 1989); R. J. Bauckham, *The Climax of Prophecy* (Edinburgh, 1998); earlier British links in the chain of apocalyptic study include T. W. Manson, H. H. Rowley, S. B. Frost, T. F. Glasson and D. S. Russell.

[285] C. E. B. Cranfield, *Romans* (International Critical Commentary, 2 vols., Edinburgh, 1975, 1979), discussed together with Sanders by Wright in Neill and Wright, *The Interpretation of the New Testament*, pp. 421–30; Wright, *The Climax of the Covenant: Christ and the Law in Pauline Theology* (Edinburgh, 1991); J. D. G. Dunn, *The Theology of Paul the Apostle* (Grand Rapids, Mich. and Edinburgh, 1998).

[286] On biblical and Jewish elements see for example B. S. Rosner, *Paul Scripture and Ethics: A Study of I Corinthians 5–7* (Leiden, 1994); M. Bockmuehl, *Jewish Law in Gentile Churches: Halakhah and the Beginning of Christian Public Ethics* (Edinburgh, 2000); on continuity with earlier debate see T. Engberg-Pedersen (ed.), *Paul in his Hellenistic Context* (Edinburgh, 1994), pp. xvii–xviii.

[287] G. Theissen, *The Social Setting of Pauline Christianity* (Eng. trans. Edinburgh, 1982) and W. Meeks, *The First Urban Christians* (New Haven, Conn., 1983), both critically discussed by J. J. Meggitt, *Paul, Poverty and Survival* (Edinburgh, 1998); A. J. M. Wedderburn, *Baptism and*

Lastly, this broader dimension of Pauline study converged with fresh perceptions of the New Testament in the context of what was now more widely seen as a continuing interrelationship, within the Hellenic and Roman environment, between the ante-Nicene church and the Jewish community. In Britain a series of studies by Henry Chadwick (n. 241, above) have helped to evoke much further work in this area.[288]

Jesus and the New Testament

A second great question of this period was that of continuity and discontinuity between Jesus and the New Testament, once again given fresh impetus by Sanders but already being reconsidered in the 1960s and 1970s. It was then sharply posed in Britain by S. G. F. Brandon (n. 247, above), for whom Jesus was at the heart of anti-Roman resistance, and Geza Vermes, for whom Jesus was a spiritual teacher and healer after the likeness of those called 'the ancient pious men' in the Mishnah (Berakhoth v. 1, and elsewhere), but in contrast with the Christ of the New Testament and the later church.[289] Meanwhile in the Hebrew University of Jerusalem the same question was implied, with a feeling also for continuities, in David Flusser, *Jesus* (Reinbek bei Hamburg, 1968, Eng. trans. New York, 1969). Brandon's theme was important not only for the understanding of Judaism but for the now stronger lines of biblical interpretation linked with Marxian history and liberation theology, influentially presented in France by F. Belo on Mark—who in his debt to the structuralism of R. Barthes also exemplifies the literary approaches noted further below.[290]

Resurrection: Studies in Pauline Theology against Its Graeco-Roman Background (WUNT 44, Tübingen, 1987); H. Maccoby, *Paul and Hellenism* (London, 1991), dedicated to E. P. Sanders; M. D. Goodman, *Mission and Conversion: Proselytizing in the Religious History of the Roman Empire* (Oxford, 1994), discussed by J. Carleton Paget, 'Jewish Proselytism at the Time of Christian Origins: Chimera or Reality?', *JSNT* 62 (1996), 65–103.

[288] For example H. Chadwick, *The Circle and the Ellipse: Rival Concepts of Authority in the Early Church* (Oxford, 1961)—on Jerusalem and Rome—reprinted with other studies in id., *History and Thought of the Early Church* (Aldershot, 1982); id., *The Church in Ancient Society: From Galilee to Gregory the Great* (Oxford, 2001); among other authors R. Murray, *Symbols of Church and Kingdom: A Study in Early Syriac Tradition* (Cambridge, 1974); Goodman (n. 287, above); J. Lieu, *Image and Reality: The Jews in the World of the Christians in the Second Century* (Edinburgh, 1996); J. Carleton Paget, 'Josephus and Christianity', *JTS* N.S. 52 (2001), 539–624.

[289] G. Vermes, *Jesus the Jew* (London, 1973); cf. A. Büchler, *Types of Jewish-Palestinan Piety from 70 B.C.E. to 70 C.E.: The Ancient Pious Men* (London, 1922), presenting the piety with which Vermes links Jesus.

[290] F. Belo, *Lecture matérialiste de l'évangile de Marc: récit, pratique, idéologie* (Paris, 1974), discussed by Trocmé, 'Exégèse scientifique et idéologie: de l'École de Tubingue aux historiens français

These books heralded what has become a celebrated outburst of writing on the historical Jesus in the last quarter of the century. The succession of North American and British contributors has included Morton Smith in New York (1978) on Jesus as magician, recalling Stauffer in the use of hostile accounts of Jesus, but in outlook at the opposite pole; B. F. Meyer in Ontario (1979), on the aims of Jesus as at least partly fulfilled by the church; and in Britain John Riches (1980), uniting theology with anthropology to present Jesus as, through his teaching and way of life, an effective symbol of transformation in Judaism. Then A. E. Harvey (1982) sketched a prophetic teacher and healer, and E. P. Sanders (1985) set Jesus more firmly than Riches within Jewish opinion, as (not messiah, but) viceroy of the heavenly king in national restoration, a view sometimes recalling B. W. Bacon (n. 37, above).

B. L. Mack (1988) found, by contrast, a sapiential Jesus, a Cynic-like Galilean, and J. D. Crossan (1991, 1998) 'a peasant Jewish Cynic'; here Jesus is a sage, detached from apocalyptic prophecy, but Judaism and especially its wisdom literature remains important as his setting. With renewed concentration on the synoptics and Jewish eschatology J. P. Meier (1991 onwards) displayed a teacher and miracle-worker; G. Vermes (1993, 2000)— complementing Jesus the Jew and at times recalling Otto (n. 181, above)—a numinous Jewish teacher of individual *imitatio Patris*; J. C. O'Neill (1995) presented a Jesus who thought of himself as messiah designate and so as eternal son of God; N. T. Wright (1996)—in a large-scale integration of this enquiry with New Testament theology—one inwardly moved to be messianic king; and P. Fredriksen (1999) a prophet of the coming kingdom.[291]

Among all these, Mack and Crossan, with R. W. Funk and others, are linked with the Jesus Seminar, in which Q and the Gospel of Thomas have

---

des origines chrétiennes', pp. 461–2 (n. 12, above), and Riches, *A Century of New Testament Study*, pp. 171–4.

[291] M. Smith, *Jesus the Magician* (New York, 1978); B. F. Meyer, *The Aims of Jesus* (London, 1979); J. Riches, *Jesus and the Transformation of Judaism* (London, 1980); A. E. Harvey, *Jesus and the Constraints of History* (London, 1982), reviewed by C. F. D. Moule, *JTS* N.S. 34 (1983), 241–7; Sanders (n. 281, above); B. L. Mack, *A Myth of Innocence: Mark and Christian Origins* (Philadelphia, 1988); id., 'The Christ and Jewish Wisdom', in J. H. Charlesworth (ed.), *The Messiah* (Minneapolis, 1992), pp. 192–221; J. D. Crossan, *The Historical Jesus* (1991, repr. Edinburgh, 1993) and *The Birth of Christianity* (1998, repr. Edinburgh, 1999); J. P. Meier, *A Marginal Jew* (New York, 1991–); G. Vermes, *The Religion of Jesus the Jew* (London, 1993), reviewed by J. K. Riches, *JTS* N.S. 47 (1996), 201–8; G. Vermes, *The Changing Faces of Jesus* (London, 2000); J. C. O'Neill, *Who Did Jesus Think He Was?* (Leiden, 1995); N. T. Wright, *Jesus and the Victory of God* (London, 1996); Fredriksen (n. 20, above).

been taken to offer two early presentations of Jesus as sage.[292] Crossan and Funk were well-known representatives of the literary approaches to exegesis noted below. Despite emphasis in this group on a new start, their approach is in broad continuity with Harnack and with important elements in Dodd's reconstruction, notably his Hellenic awareness and realised eschatology. As J. Carleton Paget puts it, 'Harnack and his ilk stalk the land in the garb of late twentieth-century American liberals.'[293] These scholars have been described by N. T. Wright as renewing the Bultmann-influenced 'new quest' inaugurated by Käsemann (n. 207, above), whereas Vermes, Sanders, Wright and others for whom Judaism and Jewish hope are primary form a 'third quest' in the line of Albert Schweitzer; the same groups are contrasted by Sanders simply as those who oppose and accept, respectively, an understanding of Jesus in the light of Jewish eschatology, and this formulation implicitly recalls the importance of—non-eschatological—Judaism for interpreters such as Mack.[294]

From this side of the Atlantic F. G. Downing on Cynicism comes near to Mack and Crossan, but others question their use of sources and their view of conditions in Galilee.[295] Again, when Mack interprets Mark as Christian myth, in a manner recalling D. F. Strauss and Bruno Bauer, his English counterparts include Brandon on the synoptics and J. Enoch Powell on Matthew, although they (especially Powell) give fuller and more precise historical and philological discussion; and there is also some convergence with views of the Gospels as free compositions put forward by Goulder and Drury.[296] On the other hand Riches, Harvey and Vermes all view Jesus within Judaism and the synoptic tradition, but like Crossan they stress his work as teacher and his realised eschatology. For O'Neill and Wright, still from a 'third quest' perspective, the crucifixion is central, and Jesus voluntarily dies as messianic

---

[292] Thomas was translated with the four canonical gospels in *The Five Gospels: The Search for the Authentic Words of Jesus*, New Translation and Commentary by R. W. Funk, R. W. Hoover, and the Jesus Seminar (New York, 1993); on Q and Thomas see for example Crossan, *The Birth of Christianity*, pp. 239–56.

[293] J. Carleton Paget, 'Quests for the Historical Jesus', in M. Bockmuehl (ed.), *The Cambridge Companion to Jesus* (Cambridge, 2001), pp. 138–55 (148, with n. 30).

[294] Wright, *Jesus and the Victory of God*, pp. 83–4; W. D. Davies and E. P. Sanders, 'Jesus: from the Jewish Point of View', in William Horbury, W. D. Davies and John Sturdy (eds.), *The Cambridge History of Judaism*, vol. 3 (Cambridge, 1999), pp. 618–77 (624, n. 13).

[295] F. G. Downing, *Cynics and Christian Origins* (Edinburgh, 1992); C. M. Tuckett, *Q and the History of Early Christianity* (Edinburgh, 1996); S. Freyne, *Galilee and the Gospel: Collected Essays* (WUNT 125, Tübingen, 2000).

[296] Brandon, *Jesus and the Zealots*, 221–321; Mack, *A Myth of Innocence*; J. Enoch Powell, *The Evolution of the Gospel* (New Haven, Conn. and London, 1994).

king. O'Neill judges that he held himself to be messiah designate and there-
fore the eternal son of God; the implied Trinitarian reconstruction of ancient
Judaism, even if over-pressed, draws on some widely recognised aspects of
Jewish theology and angelology, studied in Britain by Rowland, Hurtado and
others.[297] For Wright Jesus represents Israel as prophet and messiah (compare
T. W. Manson), and stress is laid again, with Caird and Dodd and against
Schweitzer, on his realised eschatology and the symbolic character of
apocalyptic prophecy.

A third contrast thus begins to emerge, this time among those who can be
linked with Wright's 'third quest'. Sanders and Fredriksen see Jesus's expectation of suffering and death as a church creation, but for B. F. Meyer, O'Neill
and Wright it is genuine and historically central, and it is also significant for
Brandon, Vermes and Riches, widely as they differ from one another. The relatively matter-of-fact figure presented by Sanders thus differs not only from
reconstructions closer to the theme of *Christus victor*, but also from the
numinous spiritual teacher envisaged by Vermes.

British contribution to this work on the historical Jesus has therefore been
far from uniform, but has included emphasis on the primacy of Jewish tradition and the synoptics, on Jesus as teacher against this background, and on the
significance for Jesus and Judaism of the mentality of martyrdom, on the
importance of the many as well as the one in Old Testament and Jewish conceptions of deity, and on theological dimensions of the historical enterprise.[298] To put it broadly, in British scholarship the quest of the historical
Jesus has been clearly linked not only with Roman Galilee and Judaea, but
also with the study of the Old and New Testaments as a whole.

Exegesis and its principles

The late twentieth century abounded both in exegesis and in exegetical theory. Associated study of the text and versions, notably once more the Latin
and the Syriac, continued to flourish, encouraged in the Academy especially
by M. Black (n. 222, above), H. F. D. Sparks (n. 46, above), and S. P.

---

[297] Rowland, *The Open Heaven*; L. W. Hurtado, *One God, One Lord* (2nd edn., Edinburgh, 1998);
William Horbury, *Jewish Messianism and the Cult of Christ* (London, 1998); R. J. Bauckham, *God
Crucified* (London, 1998).
[298] This last point is brought out by R. Morgan, 'From Reimarus to Sanders: the Kingdom of God,
Jesus, and the Judaisms of His Day', in R. S. Barbour (ed.), *The Kingdom of God and Human Society*
(Edinburgh, 1993), pp. 80–139 (134–5).

Brock.[299] The stream of early New Testament papyri permitted important attempts to reconstruct the book-culture of the earliest Christians, represented in the Academy especially by E. G. Turner, T. C. Skeat and C. H. Roberts.[300] Above all, however, these were years of exposition, including in Britain contributions to the International Critical Commentary and large-scale exegetical studies.[301] Commentators not picked out as such so far include W. D. Davies and D. Allison on Matthew (1988–97), J. Marcus on Mark (1999–), C. F. Evans on Luke (1990), T. L. Brodie on John (1993), A. C. Thiselton on I Corinthians (2001), Margaret Thrall on II Corinthians (1994–2000), A. Lincoln (1990) and E. Best (1998) on Ephesians, M. Bockmuehl on Philippians (1998), I. H. Marshall, with P. H. Towner, on the Pastoral Epistles (1999), P. Ellingworth on Hebrews (1993), and J. P. M. Sweet on the Revelation (1979). Much of this work was summed up in the one-volume Oxford Bible Commentary edited by John Barton and John Muddiman (2001). Its mainstream was formed by critical interpretation of the kind familiar throughout the twentieth century, often merging with theological comment; but the importance of other approaches is also obvious, for example in the literary approach of Brodie on John, and in the appreciation of both canonical and literary emphases offered by Davies and Allison in a commendation of their own historical criticism of Matthew.[302]

Yet these remarks give but a pale reflection of the fierce hermeneutical debate. It had a continuity with the recent past which was sometimes neglected, perhaps because of a strong sense of reorientation. Recent debate, however, had likewise involved a questioning of the sufficiency of historical exegesis. This was an element, as noted above, in discussion of Bultmann's biblical interpretation and of typology and allegory; and it had been matched by fresh emphasis not only on the New Testament roots of the latter, but also

---

[299] See among others J. Neville Birdsall, 'The New Testament Text', in G. W. H. Lampe (ed.), *The Cambridge History of the Bible*, vol. 1 (1970), pp. 308–77; J. K. Elliott (ed.), *Studies in New Testament Language and Text* (Leiden, 1976) (in honour of G. D. Kilpatrick); S. P. Brock, *Syriac Perspectives on Late Antiquity* (London, 1984); D. C. Parker, *Codex Bezae* (Cambridge, 1992); D. G. K. Taylor (ed.), *Studies in the Early Text of the Gospels and Acts* (Birmingham, 1999); P. Burton, *The Old Latin Gospels* (Oxford, 2001).

[300] For example, E. G. Turner, *The Typology of the Early Codex* (Philadelphia, Pa., 1977); C. H. Roberts, *Manuscript, Society and Belief in Early Christian Egypt* (Schweich Lectures, London, 1979); C. H. Roberts and T. C. Skeat, *The Birth of the Codex* (London, 1983).

[301] Studies include G. N. Stanton, *A Gospel for a New People* (Edinburgh, 1992); D. R. Catchpole, *The Quest for Q* (Edinburgh, 1993); J. Ashton, *Understanding the Fourth Gospel* (Oxford, 1991); M. G. W. Stibbe, *John as Storyteller* (Cambridge, 1992); B. W. Winter and others (eds.), *The Book of Acts in its Historical Setting* (6 vols., Grand Rapids, Mich., 1992–7); J. M. G. Barclay, *Obeying the Truth* (Edinburgh, 1988); J. Lieu, *The Second and Third Epistles of John* (Edinburgh, 1986).

[302] W. D. Davies and D. C. Allison, *Matthew* (ICC, 3 vols., Edinburgh, 1988, 1991, 1997), vol. 1, 1–5.

on the continuity of present-day historical exegesis with strands of interpretation in medieval and patristic exegesis and in the New Testament itself. In the 1970s continued questioning in Britain was exemplified in the work of C. F. Evans and D. E. Nineham, and Bruce (1979), having discussed New Testament interpretation of the Old, judged that 'the adoption of the historical method does not exclude the validity of a *sensus plenior*'—although this must be rooted 'in the primary meaning of the text, established by the historical method'.[303] In 1977 R. C. Morgan seeks freedom for theological exegesis, but still takes historical exegesis to be prevalent; Hughes in 1979 takes note of long-standing and now renewed protest against its primacy; and at the same time in the systematic field in Germany a theological exegesis in the form of 'Trinitarian hermeneutics', in some tension with Bruce's criterion, is freely applied to the New Testament by J. Moltmann.[304]

In non-biblical literary study a movement away from historical interpretation had underlined the importance of the text as received, and was now converging with postmodern perceptions of the fluidity of signification in texts. Within biblical study doubt concerning the ideal of objectivity and the prime importance of authorial intention had been similarly matched for some time by appreciation of the part played by the subjectivity of those who receive, transmit and interpret texts, and of the importance of the text itself.

Attempts to integrate such appreciation into New Testament study are illustrated in Canadian work in the 1970s when the interpreter's subjectivity is treated very positively, but in the course of a quest for objectivity which is still not thought to be futile, in the theological method of Bernard Lonergan followed by B. F. Meyer (n. 291, above). Correspondingly, in liberation theology and feminist theology, biblical interpretation by various methods could now be practised advisedly from the point of view of the interpreter and of the disadvantaged, and with keen awareness, as in Belo's structuralism, of the political dimensions of exegesis. The value of historical exegesis was particularly questioned, however, in argument for literary and canonical approaches to the Old and New Testaments. In combination they could help, as F. Watson

---

[303] Bruce, 'The Theology and Interpretation of the Old Testament', p. 414; cf. R. E. Brown, *The 'Sensus Plenior' of Sacred Scripture* (Baltimore, 1955), reviewed by J. M. T. Barton, *JTS* N.S. 7 (1956), 294–5.

[304] R. C. Morgan, 'A Straussian Question to "New Testament Theology"', *NTS* 23 (1977), 243–65; G. Hughes, *Hebrews and Hermeneutics* (Cambridge, 1979), pp. 114, 184–5 (nn. 29–30); J. Moltmann, *The Trinity and the Kingdom of God* (1980, Eng. trans. London, 1981), pp. 61–96.

put it with some relish, 'to wrest the text from the grip of historical-critical hypothesizing'.[305]

Literary approaches gained New Testament prominence especially in connection with the parables, already at the centre of the hermeneutic of E. Fuchs, and they continued the literary element in form and redaction criticism which has already been noted; F. Kermode on Mark saluted Austin Farrer.[306] Typically, however, these approaches were viewed by their earlier sponsors in the USA (to quote J. D. Crossan, who allowed the legitimacy of historical criticism) as an American challenge to 'the monolithic ascendancy of historical criticism in biblical studies'; he noted ironically that in the literary approach historical criticism could be Oedipally viewed either as the father to be slain, or the mother to be embraced in an abhorrent marriage.[307]

Later forms of this 'theoretical challenge' were presented with particular zest by S. D. Moore, linking Dublin, Sheffield and the USA.[308] Their 'synchronic' reading of the text as transmitted was commonly joined with eschewal of 'diachronic' attention to its history and historical setting.[309] They have ranged from structuralist concern with encoded meaning and with exegesis as an exercise of power to postmodern perception of fluidity. In gospel study they bore especially on the interpretation of narrative, and contributed to reassignment of the Gospels to the genre of Greek and Roman biography; in work on the Epistles they rekindled interest in rhetorical and epistolary convention, and in the patristic exegesis written when such convention still prevailed.[310]

The importance of the canon as a dimension of interpretation had been underlined in the context of New Testament theology by E. Käsemann and

---

[305] F. Watson, *Text, Church, and World: Biblical Interpretation in Theological Perspective* (Edinburgh, 1994), p. 77.

[306] F. Kermode, *The Genesis of Secrecy: On the Interpretation of Narrative* (Cambridge, Mass., and London, 1979), pp. 60–4, 70–2; the point was stressed by J. Barton, *Reading the Old Testament* (London, 1984), p. 219, n. 17.

[307] J. D. Crossan, *Raid on the Articulate: Comic Eschatology in Jesus and Borges* (New York and London, 1976), pp. xiii–xiv; he associates the Oedipal alternatives with Germany and America, respectively.

[308] S. D. Moore, *Literary Criticism and the Gospels: The Theoretical Challenge* (New Haven, Conn., and London, 1989).

[309] Landmarks in German and American literary approaches to the Gospels were surveyed by R. C. Morgan, 'From Reimarus to Sanders: the Kingdom of God, Jesus, and the Judaisms of His Day', in R. S. Barbour (ed.), *The Kingdom of God and Human Society* (Edinburgh, 1993), pp. 80–139 (125–9).

[310] R. A. Burridge, *What are the Gospels? A Comparison with Graeco-Roman Biography* (Cambridge, 1992), reviewed by F. G. Downing, *JTS* N.S. 44 (1993), 238–40; M. Bockmuehl, *A Commentary on the Epistle to the Philippians* (London, 1997), pp. 38–9.

others, but in the closing years of the twentieth century canonical approaches received their major specifically New Testament impulse from Brevard Childs.[311] His *The New Testament as Canon: An Introduction* (London, 1984) shows how an approach to the New Testament in general and to each separate book and its exegesis can be reshaped by canonical considerations; emphasis now falls on the biblical text as received and on its continuous reception and understanding in the church. Childs presents this approach as a challenge to any claim that historical exegesis always has priority, but also as a complement to the indispensable insights of such exegesis; it is not intended as an alternative method.[312]

An important aspect of canonical concern reflected in Britain was renewed historical study of the biblical canon.[313] In exegesis its influence, with that of other theologically oriented methods, can be seen in F. Watson and M. Bockmuehl.[314] Watson exemplifies not simply a rejection of historical-critical in favour of literary and canonical approaches, but the involvement of both Old Testament and systematic theology in a Trinitarian New Testament exegesis which starts from the final form of the text. The development of theological exegesis into a major dimension of recent British interpretation was also to some extent a counterpart of German movement from those New Testament theologies described above which could seem detached from the Old Testament, towards a 'biblical theology of the New Testament' (a title used by both H. Hübner and P. Stuhlmacher), in which the interconnection of Old and New has become integral, following G. von Rad and H. Gese; in

---

[311] Barr, *The Concept of Biblical Theology*, 378–95; with Barr's vigorous critique of Childs compare the warm appreciation by R. W. L. Moberly, 'The Church's Use of the Bible: the Work of Brevard Childs', *ET* 99 (1988), 104–9.

[312] See especially Childs, *The New Testament as Canon*, pp. 34–47.

[313] J. Barr, *Holy Scripture: Canon, Authority, Criticism* (Oxford, 1983); R. Beckwith, *The Old Testament Canon of the New Testament Church* (London, 1985); J. Barton, *Oracles of God* (London, 1986); id., *The Spirit and the Letter: Studies in the Biblical Canon* (London, 1997); G. M. Hahneman, *The Muratorian Fragment and the Development of the Canon* (Oxford, 1992). Beckwith's view that the books now found in the Hebrew Bible were authoritative for New Testament writers contrasts with arguments for fluidity by Barton and Hahneman, but can appeal to the number of twenty-two or twenty-four books given in Josephus and II Esdras; a supernumerary group of approved books such as Ecclesiasticus should also probably be envisaged.

[314] Bockmuehl, *Philippians*, pp. 42–5; id., ' "To Be Or Not To Be": the Possible Futures of New Testament Scholarship', *SJT* 51 (1998), 271–306 (289–91, 295, 299); Watson, *Text, Church, and World*, pp. 16–17, 30–45; id., *Text and Truth*, pp. 209–19; id., *Agape, Eros, Gender: Towards a Pauline Sexual Ethic* (Cambridge, 2000).

English and from the Old Testament side Brevard Childs moved at the same time towards a *Biblical Theology of the Old and New Testaments*.[315]

The end of the twentieth century was marked by a need for lists of the pro-liferating current exegetical methods.[316] Some methods, for instance the social–scientific approaches exemplified in Theissen, Meeks or Freyne (nn. 287, 295, above) and continuing earlier socio-economic New Testament work, can be called lines of enquiry as much as modes of exegesis. In any case, it has been argued that the main methods are not so varied as may appear. Thus John Barton has repeatedly recalled that the newer literary approaches and the older source criticism and *Formgeschichte* are, all alike, manifestations of the study of literature.[317] Various combinations of historical, literary and theological interpretation have been mooted and practised.[318] Historical exegesis has consistently received an important but subordinate role in proposals developed over many years by R. C. Morgan; it is needed to correct interpretative flights of fancy, but literary readings are singled out as those with which theology can primarily engage.[319] Somewhat comparably, but with a sense for historical interpretation as more than simply corrective, M. Bockmuehl endorsed the need for history, and in practice regarded a his-torical exegesis as important; he suggested, however, that historical interpre-tation without hermeneutical reflection cannot form a focus of New

[315] H. Hübner, *Biblische Theologie des Neuen Testaments* (2 vols., Göttingen, 1990, 1993); P. Stuhlmacher, *Biblische Theologie des Neuen Testaments*, vol. 1 (Göttingen, 1992), discussed by Oeming, *Gesamtbiblische Theologien der Gegenwart*, pp. 119–34; B. S. Childs, *Biblical Theology of the Old and New Testaments* (London, 1992); H. Graf Reventlow, *Problems of Biblical Theology in the Twentieth Century*, pp. 145–78.

[316] A list of six was needed by U. Schnelle *et al.*, 'Bibelkritik II. Methoden der Bibelkritik im Neuen Testament', *RGG*⁴1 (1998), cols. 1480–6; more are often distinguished.

[317] Barton, *Reading the Old Testament*, pp. 3, 141; id., 'Historical Criticism and Literary Interpretation: Is There any Common Ground?', in S. E. Porter, P. Joyce and D. E. Orton (eds.), *Crossing the Boundaries: Essays in Biblical Interpretation in Honour of Michael D. Goulder* (Leiden, 1994), pp. 3–15; Barton, 'Historical-critical Approaches', in id. (ed.), *The Cambridge Companion to Biblical Interpretation* (Cambridge, 1998), pp. 9–20; cf. Riches, *A Century of New Testament Study*, p. 226, on historical interpretation as illuminating the present literary context of exegesis.

[318] Watson, *Text and Truth*, pp. 95–126, notes an indifferentism, manifest in loss of the primacy of the literal sense and authorial intention, which can accompany 'interpretative pluralism'; proposals noted below, like that of F. F. Bruce (n. 303, above), seek to avoid this pitfall.

[319] R. C. Morgan, ' "Nothing more negative . . . ": a Concluding Unscientific Postscript to Historical Research on the Trial of Jesus', in Bammel, *The Trial of Jesus* (n. 243, above), pp. 135–46 (141); id., 'A Straussian Question to "New Testament Theology" ' (theological and historical interpretation should be separate, but the latter should retain a corrective function); id., with J. Barton, *Biblical Interpretation* (Oxford, 1988), pp. 177–200, 286–8 (literary rather than historical work should form the frame), discussed by Riches, *A Century of New Testament Study*, pp. 222–6; R. C. Morgan, 'The Bible and Christian Theology', in Barton (ed.), *The Cambridge Companion to Biblical Interpretation*, pp. 114–27 (126).

Testament study, and for this looked rather to theological interpretation linked with literary approaches and investigation of the history of the impact of the text (*Wirkungsgeschichte*).[320]

At the end of the century a broad significance for historical interpretation was widely recognised, as the exegetical work noted above suggests. James Barr urged that the adjective 'historical' was too limiting a description of what was also and pre-eminently a literary and linguistic enterprise—a philological interpretation, in the vocabulary employed above.[321] Such criticism, as others emphasised, is sometimes narrowly envisaged and inappropriately identified simply with the Enlightenment, whereas it has continuities with older exegesis;[322] and in an earlier phase of debate, as noted above, these were found to extend to interpretation presented in the New Testament itself. Barton urged with force that a broadly conceived critical exegesis is the way to an independent interpretation, which can meet pressures like those noted at the beginning of this chapter.[323]

V

The struggle of a classical sense of degeneration with a biblical sense of hope which Ramsay and Dodd saw in Paul, and the conflict between linear and circular views of time which was presented by Cullmann, can both readily occur to anyone who looks back over this century of New Testament work. Thus it is tempting to say that the most recent period, in its lively diversity and in the prominence of religion, society and nihilism as well as theology, closes the circle with the similarly diverse beginning of the twentieth century. On the other hand, the designation of the early twentieth century as a golden age, for its varied achievement fostered by the classical culture of scholarship, inevitably suggests the thought of later degeneration—which the more unified theological achievement of the following period then at once calls into question. Again, in recent years the ecumenical theological interest which was a force for unity in study remained effective in continental Europe, but in North America and Britain came rather to suggest a contrast with secularised

---

[320] Bockmuehl, *Philippians*, pp. 42–5; id., ' "To Be Or Not To Be" ', pp. 295–302.

[321] Barr, *Holy Scripture*, pp. 105–7.

[322] Barton, 'Historical-critical Approaches', pp. 12–15; from within Jewish scholarship, F. E. Greenspahn, 'How Modern are Modern Biblical Studies?', in M. Brettler and M. Fishbane (eds.), *Minhah le-Nahum: Biblical and Other Studies Presented to Nahum M. Sarna in Honour of his 70th Birthday* (JSOT Supplement Series 154, Sheffield, 1993), 164–82.

[323] Barton, 'Historical-critical Approaches', pp. 18–19; cf. Barr, *Holy Scripture*, pp. 107–14.

exegesis; yet in all these regions New Testament work has continued in its full breadth, theological as well as philological.

Some room is then left for hope, but can it be associated with particular characteristics of British work? Contrasts between Britain and elsewhere are often debatable, even in respect of *Formgeschichte*, and overseas developments have regularly been formative for Britain. One or two clearer differences in the short term have emerged. Thus in Britain in the first half of the century a particular strength in study of the text and versions was perceptible (n. 45, above), and in the second half the influence of Bultmann and his school was less marked than in Germany and the USA, although it was by no means absent. Again, from about 1920 to 1960 the apocalypses were more central in British than in German study.

This example points to a characteristic of greater long-term significance. In Britain the New Testament has usually been studied not just in a Jewish and Greek setting, but in relation with the Old Testament before it and the Church Fathers and early Christian writers after it. Throughout there have been scholars who combined New Testament with patristic and early Christian study, exemplified in the Academy by Salmon, C. H. Turner, Burkitt, Lampe and Wilson. Others have worked in both the Old and the New Testaments or have brought to the New Testament an Old Testament and Semitic training, including Burkitt once more, T. W. Manson, Black, Bruce and Caird. These interconnections of study in areas that are indeed integrally related have countered the inward-looking tendency sometimes associated with demarcation of the subject, as noted above, and they can perhaps be claimed as a characteristic strength of British work.

This feature can in turn play a part in hope, but hope for fruitful development is based essentially on the subject-matter of New Testament study, a body of texts and associated archaeological and epigraphic remains. To express such hope primarily in philological terms, these texts, like any other influential body of texts from antiquity, require and evoke continuous re-appropriation. The intrinsic fascination of this task in the case of the New Testament books lies especially in their interconnection with the whole context to which British scholarship has characteristically been sensitive—with the Old Testament in its full Septuagintal extent, with Philo, Josephus and the rabbinic tradition, with the Greek and Latin culture of the Hellenistic age and the Roman empire, and with early Christian authors from the Apostolic Fathers, Valentinus and Basilides down to Tertullian, Origen, Eusebius and Ephrem Syrus. The source-material for study is itself constantly shifting and expanding, not merely through great discoveries like those on the western shore of the Dead Sea but also through the continual accretion of new excavations, papyri and inscriptions. Continuous reassessment is needed, within the whole context just outlined, from the Old Testament to rabbinic Judaism and early Christian literature and doctrine. This in turn will continue to demand the feeling for the sources exemplified by W. D. Davies and Wilfred Knox in rabbinic and Philonic interpretation, respectively.

To identify some New Testament work of this kind as 'only' philological is unduly to reduce the dimensions of philology, as these have appeared from Eduard Norden and F. C. Burkitt to Martin Hengel or Henry Chadwick. The significance of theology for these studies, bound up as it is with the content of the texts, has continued to find recognition. Hope can perhaps look also for renewed engagement in the philological enterprise, envisaged in its fullness.

Note. I am most grateful for help received in discussion with M. N. A. Bockmuehl, J. N. B. Carleton Paget, J. A. Emerton, N. Förster, M. D. Hooker and G. M. Styler.

CHAPTER THREE
Early Judaism

MARTIN GOODMAN

In a chapter dedicated to the discussion of changing scholarly perspectives during a century of endeavour, it is appropriate to begin with the observation that any decision as to what to include under the rubric of 'Early Judaism' must itself be the product of a distinctive perspective. I shall discuss in this chapter the work that has been done on Judaism in the late Second Temple period and in late antiquity down to the closure of the Talmud—that is, roughly from 200 BCE to c.500 CE. Descriptions of this Judaism as 'early', though common in British scholarship, is not universal. In the eyes of orthodox Jews who trace the origins of Judaism to the giving of the Torah to Moses on Mt Sinai, the late Second Temple period lies a long way down the continuous stream of halakha. In contrast, scholars who view Second Temple Judaism as a prelude to Christianity and rabbinic Judaism after 70 CE as theologically insignificant may describe the last days of the Temple as 'Spätjudentum'. A well-meaning effort to mediate between these attitudes by describing this period as 'Middle Judaism' has not proven popular.[1]

It may justify my retention of the term 'Early Judaism' for this chapter to note that I am thereby reflecting the mainstream perspective of British scholars in Second Temple Judaism over the past century, since most still come from a background in biblical studies, in which a sharp break between the Israelite religion of the First Temple and Judaism of the Second Temple is taken for granted.[2] That late Second Temple Judaism is seen as 'early' is testimony to the appreciation among such scholars that there were to be authentic later forms of Judaism from the early rabbis down to the modern day.

---

[1] G. Boccaccini, *Middle Judaism: Jewish Thought, 300 B.C.E.–200 C.E.* (Minneapolis, Minn., 1991).

[2] Note, for instance, the implications of the decision to begin the *Cambridge History of Judaism* with the Persian period (vol. 1, ed. L. Finkelstein and W. D. Davies, Cambridge, 1984). Vol. 2 (1989) of the *Cambridge History* covers the Hellenistic period; vol. 3 (1999), jointly edited by W. D. Davies, W. Horbury and John Sturdy, covers the early Roman period.

In contrast to Britain, in the world of scholarship outside the United Kingdom the main institutional changes influencing approaches to early Judaism have been the creation of two new academic contexts for such study, namely Jewish studies and religious studies. Neither context was known at the beginning of the twentieth century but there are now numerous departments, courses, periodicals and academic posts dedicated to Jewish studies, particularly in the great centres in the United States and Israel. Departments of religious studies have similarly been established in many universities in the United States, with Judaism of all periods studied in the context of other faiths and religion in general.

Academic study of Jewish culture began in nineteenth-century Germany as a form of affirmation of the place of Jews within European culture. These pioneers of the *Wissenschaft des Judentums* were all themselves Jews and wrote for a Jewish readership. Almost all were either independent scholars or based in Jewish theological institutions. In the United Kingdom, University College London appointed a Jew as Goldsmid Professor of Hebrew in the mid-nineteenth century, and Cambridge had a lecturer in rabbinics soon after, but it was only in the twentieth century that Oxford established the Cowley Lecturership in Post-biblical Hebrew and then, in 1939, the Readership in Jewish Studies. In this respect British universities differed little from other Western institutions, with the notable exception of the Hebrew University of Jerusalem, which had been established in the 1920s as a university 'for the Jewish people'.

There was to be drastic change with the general expansion of university teaching in Western Europe and the United States in the 1960s. This general expansion coincided, especially in the United States, with a demand for greater attention to be paid to study of previously ignored social groups, in particular women and ethnic minorities. The incorporation of Jewish studies into the curricula of many American universities over the past forty years has owed much to the search by American Jews for a Jewish identity, both in the case of the students who take these courses and the donors through whose munificence academic posts have been established. Hence their academic concentration has generally been in the history of the Jews in comparatively modern times. Nonetheless, study of early Judaism, particularly the story of the last days of the Second Temple and its aftermath, has much contemporary resonance and exerts a strong hold on many students and teachers in these departments.

The United Kingdom has not witnessed a similar explosion in Jewish studies in universities. Anglo-Jewry is among the larger populations of diaspora Jews but the size of the community is dwarfed by the number of Jews in the United States, even allowing for the considerable difficulties inherent in establishing precise figures when the definition of Jewish identity is itself disputed. English Jews have been less inclined than Jews in North America to stress their Jewishness as part of their identity, preferring instead a low profile within English society. There is only one university department in the United Kingdom devoted to Hebrew and Jewish Studies, in University College London. In recent years some universities have established centres or programmes as a way to coordinate the teaching of staff already in post with an interest in Jewish subjects but, with the exception of the privately funded Oxford Centre for Hebrew and Jewish Studies, the initiatives have been fuelled less by the interests of donors or potential students than by the desire of university authorities to make a gesture towards incorporation of a new academic field made fashionable by its popularity in the United States.

The pattern for university teaching of religious studies is also set in the United States, where to some extent it is the product of the institutionalised separation of church and state. Since state-funded universities are forbidden to teach Christian theology, study of religions has to be carried out in a more neutral fashion than is standard in the divinity schools or in European universities, and this separation has led quite naturally to study of religions other than Christianity, including Judaism. A similar pattern has begun to spread in the United Kingdom in recent years, but only slowly. For a long time the Religions Department in the University of Lancaster provided a rare British example of the teaching of religions on the model of departments in the United States. Much more common has been the accretion of religious studies to existing departments of Christian theology, with the self-evident risk that non-Christian religions, studied dispassionately from the outside, would emerge as pale and formulaic in comparison with the Christian doctrines discussed with committed passion by adherents from within the Christian tradition.

These institutional changes have affected in different ways the study of Second Temple Judaism and the study of Judaism in the early rabbinic period. In 1900 most scholarship on Second Temple Jews was written by New Testament scholars whose primary interest lay in the background to Jesus. In 2000 this motivation remained strong among many in the field and has, if anything, been increased over the past quarter-century by awareness of the Jewishness of Jesus and many aspects of the early church (see below). But there are also more and more scholars from within Jewish studies who view this period of Judaism in the light of the history of Judaism as a whole, and some (though few in the United Kingdom) who take the quite abundant evidence for the religion of Jews in this period as a starting point for wider explanations of the nature of religion as a whole. The century has also seen incursions into this field by classicists aware that the Jewish material, apart from its intrinsic interest, provides particularly abundant insights into themes of change, acculturation and resistance which are prominent issues elsewhere in the Mediterranean world in the late Hellenistic and early Roman imperial period.

The later period of 'early Judaism', from *c.*70–500 CE, has concerned classicists less, for the simple reason that too much of the evidence is in Hebrew or Aramaic. In 1900 most New Testament scholars lost interest in the history of Judaism after the end of the first century CE: in terms of Christian theology, the history of Judaism ceased to be a concern once the history of Israel was safely in the hands of the church. The third/fourth edition of Emil Schürer's *Geschichte*, published in 1901–11, took the story of Judaism to the defeat of Bar Kokhba in 135 CE, after which, he implied, nothing of any importance occurred.[3] The efforts of the pioneers of the *Wissenschaft des Judentums* to study early rabbinic Judaism as a theological system comparable to the great monuments of systematic Christian theology of the patristic period were continued for the most part only in Jewish theological seminaries and were largely ignored in the universities. In this respect the position has much changed. First, the Jewish theological colleges of 1900 were almost entirely based in Europe and were destroyed in the Holocaust along with much of the rest of European Jewry; those that survived, including Jews' College in London (later renamed the London School of Jewish Studies), did not exert in later years the same influence in this field that they did in the first thirty years of the twentieth century. Secondly, there has been a concerted effort, mostly (but not only) in departments of religious studies in the United States, to build on the pioneering efforts made by early twentieth-century scholars to subject rabbinic materials to the same sort of critical scrutiny as other religious texts, by the publication of translations of the texts into European languages and the application to the texts of techniques originally used to analyse other literatures.[4] The essentially pietistic approach to these writings, which was almost universal in the Jewish seminaries in 1900, is still

---

[3] E. Schürer, *Geschichte des Jüdischen Volkes im Zeitalter Jesu Christi*, 3rd/4th edn. (Leipzig, 1901–11).

[4] Earlier in the twentieth century, much of this work was carried out in Germany by H. Albeck and others, but note, in particular, the voluminous studies in more recent years by Jacob Neusner, in some of which, e.g. *Torah from our Sages, Pirke Avot: A New American Translation and Explanation* (Dallas, Tex., 1984), the location of this approach in the United States is specifically stressed.

to be found in some current scholarship,[5] but many rabbinic scholars in universities now come to the subject without the benefit (and drawbacks) of previous immersion in a traditional *yeshiva* training in study of the Talmud, which is almost indispensable for real familiarity with these very complex texts but brings with it a tendency to ahistorical conflation. This lack of traditional training is itself a symptom of the deepening division between religious and secular Jewish society, particularly in Israel, where those devoted to Talmud study often see no value at all in an academic approach to the texts. The upheavals of the twentieth century produced a series of great scholars who, after a traditional training, left orthodoxy behind on their entry into the university world.[6] Such transitions are of course still possible, but they are increasingly rare. It is worth noting how many of the leading Jewish scholars in this field in the United Kingdom have been émigrés from elsewhere in Europe.

Change over the twentieth century has largely been a product of a change of perspective: different sorts of scholars are tackling the field, for different reasons. But this change has been fuelled by a series of remarkable new finds over the course of the century, which have themselves led research in new directions.

In the first half of the twentieth century, the bulk of the new documents to have had such an impact were all found in Egypt, preserved by the dry climate. Near the beginning of the twentieth century the most important finds were of material composed after antiquity, which nonetheless had an importance for study of this period also. These were the documents from the Cairo Geniza, of which the bulk were brought from Egypt to Cambridge in the 1890s. These texts had all been deposited in the Cairo synagogue between the ninth and twelfth centuries CE, and revolutionised study of the medieval Mediterranean world, but it seemed clear quite early in their study that some of the texts were based on much older materials, some of them from late antiquity. Already in 1910, Schechter published as *Fragments of a Zadokite Work* what turned out to be a late copy of the Damascus Rule eventually to be found in Qumran.[7]

The same period of discovery around 1900 unearthed a great number of papyrus documents from Egypt, which, although not religious texts

---

[5] For a current critique, see S. Schwartz and C. Hezser in M. Goodman (ed.), *The Oxford Handbook of Jewish Studies* (Oxford, 2002) pp. 79–140.

[6] For an illuminating and reflective description of this process in his own case, see the autobiography of David Halivni, *The Book and the Sword: A Life of Learning in the Shadow of Destruction* (Boulder, Col., 1998). Halivni, a Holocaust survivor, teaches at Columbia University in New York.

[7] S. Schechter, *Documents of Jewish Sectaries*, 2 vols. (Cambridge, 1910).

themselves, shed much new light on the religious lives of Egyptian Jews. In the 1920s, Sir Arthur Cowley published the Aramaic texts from Elephantine which revealed the distinctive religious customs of a Jewish military garrison in Egypt from c.610 to c.390 BCE, shedding much light on the varied nature of Judaism at the very end of the biblical period,[8] and over the course of the century plentiful Egyptian Jewish papyri from later periods down to the upheavals in the Egyptian Jewish community in the early second century CE, most of them unearthed in the course of excavations at the beginning of the century, were published as they were deciphered, culminating in the magisterial corpus published by Tcherikover, Fuks and Stern,[9] with an appendix on the Egyptian Jewish inscriptions on stone by David Lewis.

Many of the Egyptian documents were concerned with the social, legal and political status of Jews rather than Judaism, but the same was not true of the great cache of religious documents found in the caves above Qumran by the Dead Sea in the late 1940s.[10] Here was a mass of biblical texts, hymns, rules, prayers and psalms, hidden for safekeeping in antiquity and never recovered until accidentally discovered by bedouin in 1947. Initial disputes over the dates when the documents were written were resolved in the 1990s by carbon-14 dating of the leather and papyrus, so that no scholar doubts any longer that they were written by Jews in the late Hellenistic or early Roman period.

Publication of the scrolls languished during the 1960s, 1970s and 1980s, both because of the difficulty inherent in their decipherment and because of the political volatility of the region where they were found, which made it hard to put pressure on recalcitrant editors. Conspiracy theories about the reason for delay abounded in the popular press but have proven groundless now that the final fragments have been made fully available both on CD-Rom and in the official series of the *Discoveries in the Judaean Desert* published by Oxford University Press.

The Qumran texts have generally been taken as evidence for the history of late Second Temple Judaism up to 70 CE. In contrast, the private legal documents found further south in the Judaean Desert and in Jericho have had an important role in reassessments of Judaism in the years following the destruction of the Temple. These papyri, discovered partly by accident in the 1950s

---

[8] A. E. Cowley, *Aramaic Papyri from the Fifth Century B.C.* (Oxford, 1923).

[9] V. Tcherikover, A. Fuks and M. Stern (eds.), *Corpus Papyrorum Judaicarum*, 3 vols. (Harvard, Mass., 1957–64).

[10] See the influential translation by G. Vermes, *The Complete Dead Sea Scrolls in English* (London, 1997).

and partly through controlled archaeological searches in the early 1960s (and, to a lesser extent, also since then),[11] contain marriage contracts, divorce deeds, records of debt and property transfers and other documents clearly of great importance to the individuals who, apparently during the Bar Kokhba war of 132–5, secreted them away in the caves where they were found. Their significance for the history of Judaea lies in the eclectic systems of law apparently adopted by these Jews in central areas of their personal lives, and the discrepancies between the law they used and that advocated in the rabbinic corpus.[12]

The enterprising and energetic approach exhibited in the search for documents in the Judaean Desert caves by Yigael Yadin in the early 1960s has characterised Israeli archaeology more generally over the past fifty years. The main impulse to archaeological research (as in many other countries) has often been a desire to bolster nationalistic claims in the new state, and Israelis continue to have a fascination for the archaeology of the land, which outstrips their general interest in the ancient past. But, whatever the motives, the increase in knowledge brought by the explosion of excavations over half a century has been great. For the Second Temple period, most significant have been finds of, for instance, great numbers of stoneware bowls in the excavations of Jerusalem.[13] For knowledge of Palestine in the late-Roman period, the first excavations of the Beth Shearim necropolis in the 1930s, and the discovery in the 1920s of a late-Roman synagogue floor at Beth Alpha depicting the signs of the zodiac, have had a huge impact (see below, pp. 144–5).

Finally, the study of Judaism in the diaspora has been revolutionised by new discoveries in the twentieth century. Before 1900 diaspora Judaism was known primarily through the voluminous treaties of Philo and the ambiguous evidence from the Jewish catacombs in Rome. Excavations in the early 1930s in Dura-Europos on the Euphrates by a team from Yale University unearthed a synagogue building precisely dated to the mid-third century, when the building was covered with earth as part of the defensive measures taken by the city when it was under siege.[14] The earth covering protected an

---

[11] Most of the documents are now available in *Discoveries in the Judaean Desert*, vols. 2, 27 and 38; see *DJD* 39, published in 2002, for the definitive guide to publication details of all these texts. For an account of the archaeological explorations of the early 1960s, see Y. Yadin, *The Finds from the Bar Kokhba Period in the Cave of Letters* (Jerusalem, 1963).

[12] See H. M. Cotton, 'The Rabbis and the Documents', in M. Goodman (ed.), *Jews in a Graeco-Roman World* (Oxford, 1998), pp. 167–79.

[13] N. Avigad, *Discovering Jerusalem* (Oxford, 1984).

[14] C. H. Kraeling, *Excavations of Dura-Europos, Final Report* VIII.I: *The Synagogue* (1956, augmented 2nd edn., New York, 1979).

extraordinary series of frescoes depicting biblical scenes, opening up the possibility that such Jewish art was long established outside this one building which happened to survive. No other diaspora finds have had quite the impact of the Dura-Europos synagogue, but identification as a synagogue of a huge late-Roman basilica in Sardis in the 1960s has encouraged much speculation about the possible relationship of Jews to the surrounding culture, particularly because the Sardis synagogue occupied so prominent a position in the fourth-century city.[15] Less spectacular new evidence has accumulated gradually over the century as inscriptions on stone have been unearthed and published. First collected by J. B. Frey in the 1930s, the texts of these inscriptions have been re-edited and augmented in more recent editions,[16] and have formed the basis of some major claims about the nature and distribution of religious authority among Jews, particularly in the context of synagogues.[17]

The combination of different sorts of scholars approaching the subject and the availability of this mass of new evidence has produced quite new perspectives on much of early Judaism. These new perspectives may be said to have some things in common. All of them reflect increased uncertainty about aspects of Judaism that scholars one hundred years ago thought they knew precisely. Much progress has consisted in the dismantling of such 'knowledge'. So, for example, in 1900 much of the Jewish literature composed before 70 CE was unhesitatingly ascribed to an Essene, Pharisee or Sadducee author, on the flimsiest of grounds. It is difficult to imagine such certainty now.

An interest in these non-normative early Jewish texts was signalled early in the twentieth century by R. H. Charles, through the publication of a magisterial edition of the Apocrypha and Pseudepigrapha of the Old Testament, and the research on the Samaritans by Moses Gaster.[18] Charles's edition, which brought together the efforts of a number of scholars who had spent the previous decades unearthing and editing a series of medieval manuscripts of these early texts, itself encouraged further similar research in the same area,

---

[15] A. B. Seager and A. T. Kraabel, 'The Synagogue and the Jewish Community', in G. M. A. Hanfmann, *Sardis from Prehistoric to Roman Times* (Cambridge, Mass., 1983), ch. 9.

[16] See especially W. Horbury and D. Noy, *Jewish Inscriptions of Greek and Roman Egypt* (Cambridge, 1992); D. Noy, *Jewish Inscriptions of Western Europe*, 2 vols. (Cambridge, 1993–5).

[17] See, for example, B. Brooten, *Women Leaders in the Ancient Synagogue* (Atlanta, Ga., 1982).

[18] R. H. Charles (ed.), *Apocrypha and Pseudepigrapha of the Old Testament*, 2 vols. (Oxford, 1912–13). Compare the more cautious comments of the editors of the volume published in the 1980s, partly to replace Charles (H. F. D. Sparks (ed.), *The Apocryphal Old Testament* (Oxford, 1984)), and the more eclectic collection in J. H. Charlesworth (ed.), *Old Testament Pseudepigrapha*, 2 vols. (London, 1983–5). For Gaster's work, see M. Gaster, *The Samaritans: Their History, Doctrines and Literature* (Schweich Lectures, London, 1925).

mostly by biblical scholars. Arguments for the significance of this material were reinforced when some of the pseudepigrapha, notably Jubilees and parts of I Enoch, were found in their original Hebrew and Aramaic forms among the Dead Sea Scrolls, thus confirming their early date and Jewish authorship and providing an invaluable insight into the extent and nature of any changes made to such texts in the process of transmission by Christian scribes and translation into Greek (and, often, from Greek into other languages).[19]

The Dead Sea Scrolls themselves of course have provided an excellent insight into a particular brand of non-normative Judaism, and a huge literature has been devoted to study of the organisation, theology and history of the community responsible for the sectarian documents. British scholars were among the earliest to attempt such interpretation in the 1950s, with important work by Chaim Rabin, Cecil Roth, Sir Godfrey Driver, J. L. Teicher, John Allegro, H. H. Rowley, and (most influentially) Geza Vermes.[20] Study of the Scrolls has become almost a separate sub-discipline of study on early Judaism, with two specialist journals devoted to them and widespread public interest in every revelation of their contents. Much of this interest (from scholars as much as the general public) has been in the significance of the Scrolls for the history of early Christianity, and a recent analysis of the law to be found in the sectarian writings even claimed to be 'rescuing' the Scrolls for the study of Judaism.[21] Some of the theories promulgated about the origins of the sect have pushed to the edges of plausibility in a search to establish for them a greater significance than perhaps they have. In fact, the size and influence of the sect, and its relation to the other varieties of Judaism in the late Second Temple period, remain still disputed despite all this effort.[22] It is to be hoped that in due course, as their novelty wears off, the texts will take their rightful place along with the rest of the evidence for Judaism in this era.

The main impulse to much of the study of non-normative Judaism in the diaspora has also been archaeological discovery, but in fact its greatest exponent in the first half of the twentieth century, Erwin Goodenough, had already

---

[19] Among such contributions, see M. Black, *The Book of Enoch* (Brill, 1985); M. A. Knibb, *Translating the Bible: The Ethiopian Version of the Old Testament* (Oxford, 1999).

[20] The bibliography on Dead Sea Scrolls research is huge. See among recent general introductions, G. Vermes, *An Introduction to the Complete Dead Sea Scrolls* (London, 1999). For the site at Qumran, the best introduction is still the 1959 series of Schweich Lectures: R. de Vaux, *Archaeology and the Dead Sea Scrolls* (London, 1973). See also J. Magness, *The Archaeology of Qumran and the Dead Sea Scrolls* (Grand Rapids, Mich., and Cambridge, 2002).

[21] L. H. Schiffman, *Reclaiming the Dead Sea Scrolls* (Philadelphia, Pa., 1994).

[22] See, for example, N. Golb, *Who wrote the Dead Sea Scrolls? The Search for the Secret of Qumran* (London, 1995); M. Goodman, 'A Note on the Qumran Sectarians, the Essenes and Josephus', *JJS* 46 (1995), 161–6.

written an investigation into diaspora Judaism as expressed in Justin Martyr's *Dialogue with Trypho* (one of the earliest D.Phil. theses to be examined in Oxford, in 1921) when his view that Greek diaspora Judaism in late antiquity continued to be radically different from the Judaism of the rabbis was apparently dramatically confirmed by the excavation of the Dura-Europos synagogue in the early 1930s. Goodenough's own reconstruction of a mystical Jewish theology to be ascertained by interpretation of the images used in Jewish art has not convinced many,[23] but the general principle that archaeology might provide insights into types of late-Roman Judaism not known from the rabbinic texts continues to have a powerful attraction. In particular, excavation in the 1960s of a large basilica in the centre of Sardis decorated with mosaics which exhibited Jewish iconography (see above, n. 15) has encouraged speculation that in Asia Minor Jews practised a distinctive, self-confident synagogue-based Judaism quite different from that of the rabbis,[24] but whether so much can really be validly deduced from mute archaeological remains is unclear. The history of synagogue excavations within the land of Israel induces salutary caution. When in the 1920s a charming, if somewhat rustic, mosaic carpet from a synagogue floor was unearthed in sixth-century Beth Alpha in the Jezreel valley, the central motif of the mosaic, a depiction of the signs of the zodiac with the sun-god at the centre of the circle, was explained as an alien intrusion into synagogue art: perhaps the Roman emperor had insisted on its incorporation.[25] Finds of further zodiac mosaics in conjunction with unambiguously Jewish symbols (menorah, lulav, incense shovels, shofar) at other Galilean synagogue sites over the course of the twentieth century have made it abundantly clear that the zodiac was a distinctively Jewish symbol.[26] Any argument that zodiacs provide evidence of non-rabbinic Judaism is weakened by the names of the donor of one of the finest mosaics, that in the fourth-century synagogue at Hammat Tiberias. This donor, a certain Severus, described himself in Greek as a member of the household of the illustrious patriarchs.[27] There is no room for doubt that the patriarchs to whom he refers were the descendants of Rabbi Judah haNasi, the

[23] E. R. Goodenough, *Jewish Symbols in the Graeco-Roman Period*, 13 vols. (New York and Princeton, NJ, 1953–68).

[24] See among recent studies, P. Trebilco, *Jewish Communities in Asia Minor* (Cambridge, 1991); J. Barclay, *Jews in the Mediterranean Diaspora: From Alexander to Trajan* (Edinburgh, 1996).

[25] For an early discussion, see the volume published by the Academy: E. L. Sukenik, *Ancient Synagogues in Palestine and Greece* (London, 1934).

[26] See now the comprehensive catalogue of the current state of scholarship on ancient synagogues in L. I. Levine, *The Ancient Synagogues: The First Thousand Years* (New Haven, Conn., and London, 2000).

[27] M. Dothan, *Hammat Tiberias: The Ancient Synagogue* (Jerusalem, 1984).

compiler of the Mishnah, the central text of rabbinic Judaism. It is just possible that by the fourth century the patriarchs had drifted away from rabbinic Judaism,[28] but it is not very likely, since the Palestinian Talmud, in the form of an elucidation of, and commentary on, Judah haNasi's Mishnah, was probably the product of Galilean rabbis in precisely this region at precisely this period. To many scholars it now seems preferable to admit to the possibility that rabbinic Jews were more tolerant of acculturation into the wider Roman world than might be apparent from the texts they produced for the consumption of insiders.

The final type of non-normative Judaism to be examined here because it evoked attention for the first time in the twentieth century has been the study of mysticism. Credit for the emergence of the study of Jewish mysticism as a distinct field belongs almost entirely to the Jerusalem scholar Gershom Scholem, whose insistence on taking seriously texts which had been sidelined by the *Wissenschaft des Judentums* as insufficiently rational to deserve study revealed a long-lasting strand of Judaism that stretched from late antiquity through the medieval kabbalah up to modern times.[29] Among the aspects of Scholem's pioneering work most questioned in more recent years has been precisely the extent of such continuity, in particular, the justification for asserting that the roots of the mystical texts preserved in medieval hekhalot manuscripts lie in late antiquity.[30] A fruitful field of enquiry has been the relationship between such mystical traditions preserved by the rabbis and the accounts of heavenly visions found in the Jewish apocalyptic traditions preserved by Christians. In the study of all such texts, there is still much disagreement as to whether they reflect mystical practices or only literary genres, and to what extent they represent deviant Judaism or a mystical aspect of the mainstream.[31]

The same logic that has prompted some to extreme scepticism about the possibility of getting back from the evidence of medieval manuscripts to learn something about late-antique mysticism has also been applied to more mainstream texts, in particular the bibles (Hebrew and Greek) used by Jews in late antiquity and the transmission of rabbinic literature.

---

[28] See most recently, S. Schwartz, *Imperialism and Jewish Society, 200 B.C.E. to 640 C.E.* (Princeton, NJ, 2001).

[29] Most influential of Scholem's many works in this area has been *Major Trends in Jewish Mysticism* (Jerusalem, 1941).

[30] See P. Schäfer, *Synopse zur Hekhalot-Literatur* (Tübingen, 1981).

[31] See, for example, F. C. Burkitt, *Jewish and Christian Apocalypses* (London, 1914); C. C. Rowland, *The Open Heaven: A Study of Apocalyptic Judaism and Early Christianity* (London, 1982).

Discussions of the nature of the Hebrew biblical text in late antiquity have been transformed by the discovery of large numbers of biblical manuscripts at Qumran. In many cases these texts are close in wording to the text copied by the medieval masoretes, but some variations are considerable, sometimes demonstrating the nature of the Hebrew text underlying the LXX translation, sometimes providing readings previously wholly unknown. Arguments about the extent to which the biblical text was still fluid in the late Second Temple period are bedevilled by the difficulty of showing when a text is a biblical fragment or part of a biblical commentary or paraphrase. Many British bible scholars, such as Paul Kahle and James Barr, have been much engaged in these discussions about the biblical texts.[32]

Fragments of Greek biblical texts found at Qumran (in particular the Psalms Scroll) have also had an impact on Septuagint studies. The Septuagint was an area of much interest to British scholars already in 1900; the great Septuagint expert H. B. Swete was a founding fellow of the Academy, and the tradition was carried on throughout the century by others, such as Sir Frederick Kenyon. The Qumran texts provide evidence that some Jews were engaged in an exercise to bring their Greek bible closer to the Hebrew already by the first century CE and that the attitude expressed by Philo (*Vita Mosis* 2.44), that the LXX had itself been divinely inspired, was presumably not shared by all other Jews.[33]

Both the Dead Sea Scrolls and the Cairo Geniza documents stimulated in the second half of the twentieth century an upsurge in interest by textual scholars such as Paul Kahle in the targumim, the Aramaic translations of the Hebrew bible. Since the targumim often paraphrase the original text and add new material, their elucidation can illuminate post-biblical Judaism.[34]

The revolution in the treatment of rabbinic texts has also in part been based on the history of the manuscripts. Scholars in the nineteenth and early twentieth century succeeded in bringing to public attention a number of rabbinic texts previously unknown, but publication tended to be only of the readings of a single manuscript,[35] and neither in these cases, nor in the printing of

---

[32] For example, J. Barr, *The Variable Spellings of the Hebrew Bible* (Schweich Lectures, Oxford, 1989).

[33] See H. B. Swete, *An Introduction to the Old Testament in Greek* (Cambridge, 1900); H. St. J. Thackeray, *The Septuagint and Jewish Worship* (Schweich Lectures, London, 1921; 2nd edn., London, 1923); F. G. Kenyon, *Recent Developments in the Textual Criticism of the Greek Bible* (Schweich Lectures, London, 1933); S. P. Brock, C. T. Frisch and S. Jellicoe, *A Classified Bibliography of the Septuagint* (Leiden, 1973), and N. Fernández Marcos, *The Septuagint in Context: Introduction to the Greek Version of the Bible* (Leiden, 2000).

[34] P. Kahle, *The Cairo Geniza* (Schweich Lectures, London, 1947).

[35] For example, W. H. Lowe (ed.), *The Mishnah of the Palestinian Talmud* (Cambridge, 1883).

the traditional rabbinic texts, was there any attempt to produce scholarly editions such as are standard for the Greek and Latin literary texts of classical antiquity, nor have many such editions appeared over the past century. There is still no critical edition of the text of the Babylonian Talmud. Instead, scholars can now consult on CD-Rom readings from a huge number of talmud manuscripts and are left to decide on their own the significance of the many variants.[36] This lack of editions is not simply a reflection of the magnitude of the task, given the size of many of the texts. Attempts in the 1980s to produce a scholarly edition of the Palestinian Talmud revealed such wide discrepancies between manuscripts that the team responsible resolved instead to publish the variant readings in synoptic form.[37] The extent of variation has encouraged some scholars to doubt whether the whole notion of an original text of such documents is valid. Whole sections of texts found in the manuscripts of the Palestinian Talmud are also found in the manuscripts of Genesis Rabba, and some have suggested that rabbinic material circulated in late antiquity in units smaller than the composite medieval texts. Others have protested that such radical scepticism is not justified in the case of all late-antique rabbinic texts, and a few scholarly editions have begun to appear.[38]

In the first half of the twentieth century a number of scholars, most influentially the Harvard theologian George Foot Moore, tried to extract an overall theology from the rabbinic corpus.[39] The few scholars in the United Kingdom to contribute in this area were mostly expatriate Jews based in Jews College, such as Adolf Büchler and Arthur Marmorstein.[40] The middle of the twentieth century saw the publication of a monumental study of the whole of rabbinic thought based on a mass of diverse rabbinic sources,[41] but this monument was not left unchallenged for long. Its publication was rapidly followed by a strong reaction against such conflation as 'ahistorical', and most work on rabbinic theology in the second half of the twentieth century was less ambitious.[42]

---

[36] *Lieberman Institute: The Sol and Evelyn Henkind Talmud Text Databank with Search Capability* (1998).

[37] P. Schäfer *et al.* (eds.), *Synopse zum Talmud Yerushalmi* (Tübingen, 1991–).

[38] For the debate on the principles involved, see P. Schäfer and Ch. Milikovsky in *JJS* 37 (1986), 139–52; 39 (1988), 201–11; 40 (1989), 89–94.

[39] G. F. Moore, *Judaism in the first Centuries of the Christian era: The Age of the Tannaim* (Cambridge, Mass., 1927–30).

[40] A. Büchler, *Studies in Sin and Atonement in the Rabbinic Literature of the First Century* (London, 1928); A. Marmorstein, *The Old Rabbinic Doctrine of God*, 2 vols. (London, 1927–37).

[41] E. E. Urbach, *The Sages: Their Concepts and Belief* (Jerusalem, 1975).

[42] See the strong criticism of Urbach in J. Neusner, *The Rabbinic Traditions about the Pharisees before 70*, 3 vols. (Leiden, 1971).

A few scholars have applied form criticism in an attempt to find the basic units of rabbinic reasoning[43] and determine the history of development of rabbinic law.[44] This latter approach has proved compatible with redaction criticism. In its extreme form, this involves the claim that it is impossible to generalise about rabbinic thought in any way beyond the Judaism of a particular text.[45] This extreme approach has not been adopted by many, but interest in the final layer of each text, including its process of redaction, is increasing. Among the most acute analysts has been Louis Jacobs, the leading light in Anglo-Jewish scholarship on halakhic rabbinic texts now for some three decades, and a prolific author of works on contemporary as well as early Jewish thought. More general has been increasing awareness that study of rabbinic texts should allow for the possibility (indeed probability) of change between the tannaim (of the first two centuries CE) and the amoraim (of the third to fifth centuries), and of different influences on the rabbis of Palestine and those of Babylonia, not least in the development of traditions of midrashic exegesis of the biblical texts.[46]

The effects of the surrounding culture on early Judaism was in general a continuing scholarly preoccupation in the twentieth century. The prime issue has been the extent to which Judaism was influenced by Hellenism. In 1937 Elias Bickerman suggested in his book *Der Gott der Makkabäer* that some Jews welcomed and internalised a Greek interpretation of their ancestral religion, and that the revolt of the Maccabees in the 160s BCE should be seen as a reaction to such Hellenising.[47] In 1974 Martin Hengel compiled evidence of many different kinds (including much archaeological and epigraphic material) to demonstrate that Judaism during the third and early second century BCE was as much a part of wider Hellenistic culture as other regions which had been conquered by Alexander the Great.[48] The evidence is incontrovertible and has effectively ended the distinction, common in the nineteenth century, between Hellenised diaspora Judaism and the semitic Judaism of the homeland, but its significance, as assembled by Hengel, has been much debated, with challenges both to the notion that this spread of Greek culture

---

[43] See recently, A. Samely, *Rabbinic Interpretation of Scripture in the Mishnah* (Oxford, 2002).

[44] Most voluminously, J. Neusner, *A History of the Mishnaic Law of Purities*, 22 parts (Leiden, 1974–7), and his equally detailed studies of the other branches of Mishnaic law.

[45] J. Neusner, *Judaism: The Evidence of the Mishnah*, 2nd edn. (Atlanta, Ga., 1988).

[46] L. Jacobs, *Structure and Form in the Babylonian Talmud* (Cambridge, 1991); on midrash, see, for example, G. Vermes, *Scripture and Tradition in Judaism: Haggadic Studies* (Leiden, 1961; 2nd edn., Leiden, 1973).

[47] E. J. Bickerman, *Der Gott der Makkabäer* (Berlin, 1937).

[48] M. Hengel, *Judaism and Hellenism*, Eng. trans. (London, 1974).

provides a religious explanation of the Maccabean revolt,[49] and to the general assumption that the use of Greek artefacts and language will necessarily have had an effect on the religious outlook of Palestinian Jews.[50] Research into the impact of Greek culture on the rabbis has been less intensive, and most scholars have been less inclined to suggest that the adoption of Greek terms and ideas are likely to have had any deep effect on rabbinic Judaism,[51] although the synagogue art of late-Roman Palestine has itself sometimes been seen as evidence of Hellenisation.[52]

In other respects too, study of early Judaism has been illumined by research into the realia of Jewish life. In the last years of the nineteenth century, Sir George Adam Smith published his historical geography of the Holy Land[53] and Emil Schürer in a series of editions his monumental history of the Jews in the time of Jesus Christ.[54] Schürer's study, and that of Joachim Jeremias published in 1969, were somewhat schematic, in the tradition of nineteenth-century German classical scholarship, but they laid the foundation for future research, and the revised English Schürer, published between 1973 and 1987, remains a standard resource for scholarship.[55] The first really imaginative reconstruction of the nature of their religious life for late Second Temple Jews was the synthetic study by E. P. Sanders, published as *Judaism: Practice and Belief.*[56] Here, for the first time, is an attempt to empathise with the Jews who saw the Temple in its last days as the centre of their religious lives. It is symptomatic of the accretion of detailed and often recondite scholarly disputes about some of the more important issues about the Pharisees and the nature of the purity laws that Sanders felt it necessary to hive off such issues into a whole second volume, published in fact before the synthetic account.[57]

For Schürer and Jeremias interest in the nature of first-century Judaism was explicitly as the background for the life of Jesus, and Hengel and Sanders

---

[49] Fergus Millar, 'The Background to the Maccabean Revolution', *JJS* 29 (1978), 1–21.

[50] M. Goodman, 'Epilogue', in J. J. Collins and G. E. Sterling (eds.), *Hellenism in the Land of Israel* (2001), pp. 302–5.

[51] S. Lieberman, *Hellenism in Jewish Palestine*, 2nd edn. (New York, 1962).

[52] See Sukenik, *Ancient Synagogues*.

[53] George Adam Smith, *The Historical Geography of the Holy Land* (London, 1894).

[54] Originally published as E. Schürer, *Lehrbuch der neutestamentlichen Zeitgeschichte* (Leipzig, 1874).

[55] J. Jeremias, *Jerusalem in the Time of Jesus*, Eng. trans. (London, 1969); E. Schürer, rev. G. Vermes, F. Millar, M. Black and M. Goodman, *The History of the Jewish People in the Age of Jesus Christ*, 3 vols. (Edinburgh, 1973–87).

[56] E. P. Sanders, *Judaism: Practice and Belief, 63BCE–66CE* (London, 1992).

[57] E. P. Sanders, *Jewish Law from Jesus to the Mishnah* (London, 1990).

also entered the field originally as New Testament scholars, and retain a strong interest in the history of early Christianity. Realisation during the second half of the twentieth century that early Christians are best understood with a full appreciation of the Jewish background has been a catalyst for much further research, especially into the relation of specific New Testament texts to the Jewish writings of the period. Such links were already being made before the twentieth century, but new since the 1970s has been the attempt to integrate the religion of Jesus and less frequently Paul into the general picture of Judaism itself. That Jesus was a Jew to be understood fully within his Jewish environment was the claim of the highly influential study by Geza Vermes, *Jesus the Jew*.[58] Despite widespread acknowledgement of the rationale behind the approach this implies, integration has in fact been sporadic, hindered in part by the great edifice of New Testament scholarship, which discourages straightforward use of the New Testament evidence. In very recent years some scholars have suggested that integration of Jewish and Christian history should go still further, and that the 'parting of the ways' between Judaism and Christianity should not be seen as having occurred until the time of Constantine.[59] This reassessment of the history of the two traditions is based on a radical refusal to view Jewish and Christian material primarily through the lens of later Judaism and Church history, but it flies in the face of much evidence that rabbinic Jews and mainstream Christians in fact defined themselves, at least in part, by what they were not, this being, by definition, a prime concern of patristic heresiologists and (of less obvious importance, given the rare use of the word) of the rabbis who invented the term *minut* to describe the wrong opinions of all those Jews whose religious ideas did not agree with theirs.[60]

Where does this leave current study of early Judaism? It is fair to say that more regular attention is being paid to its elucidation than in any previous period, and with more awareness of the possible extent of variety. Where British scholarship may be thought to have a special role to play may be in the continuing strength of classical studies within the United Kingdom and the increasing readiness of classicists, encouraged by the example of polymaths such as Arnoldo Momigliano, to accept Jewish studies as pertinent to

---

[58] G. Vermes, *Jesus the Jew: A Historian's Reading of the Gospels* (London, 1973).

[59] D. Boyarin, *Dying for God: Martyrdom and the Making of Christianity and Judaism* (Stanford, Calif., 1999).

[60] M. Goodman, 'The Function of Minim in early Rabbinic Judaism', in H. Cankik, H. Lichtenberger and P. Schäfer (eds.), *Geschichte-Tradition-Reflexion: Festschrift für Martin Hengel zum 70. Geburtstag* (Tübingen, 1996), vol. 1, pp. 501–10.

the wider classical world.[61] Classical scholars have played a major role in putting the Jewish evidence properly into the context of the Greek and Roman world. Too much remains disputed for syntheses of current knowledge to retain authority for long. It is not unreasonable to hope that when new syntheses are produced at the end of the twenty-first century, both British scholars and the British Academy will be seen to have played a significant part.

[61] See A. Momigliano, *Alien Wisdom: The limits of Hellenization* (Cambridge, 1975); J. Reynolds and R. Tannenbaum, *Jews and God-Fearers at Aphrodisias* (Cambridge, 1987); F. Millar, *The Roman Near East*, 31BC–AD337 (Cambridge, Mass., 1993); T. Rajak, *The Jewish Dialogue with Greece and Rome: Studies in Cultural and Social Interaction* (Leiden, 2000).

CHAPTER FOUR

British patristic scholarship in the twentieth century

MAURICE WILES

In the centuries following the Reformation, patristic study was an important aspect of British theological scholarship. It was a period during which the Church of England played a dominant role in the life of the universities; and patristics had an important role to play in that church's self-definition. Where other Protestant bodies justified their particular positions by appeal to some form of *sola scriptura*, the Church of England appealed not only to scripture but also to early church tradition as providing the true interpretation of those scriptures. The Roman Catholic Church, on the other hand, ascribed great importance, on the basis of later church tradition, to certain beliefs and practices which Anglicans firmly repudiated. In this respect too, therefore, detailed knowledge and careful interpretation of early church tradition was a matter of great importance. Wherever a period of past history is of crucial significance for some issue of intense contemporary debate, that fact is sure to prove a stimulus to serious and concentrated study of the period. But the contemporary importance of the outcome of such study is also almost equally certain to skew the way in which the historical evidence is read and interpreted.

This tension between the apologetic and the scholarly approaches to the patristic period can be readily illustrated from Newman's famous study of *The Arians of the Fourth Century*, published in 1833. Newman undertook the study by way of preparation for a work that he had been asked to write on the Thirty-nine Articles, a subject of vigorous controversy at the time. That contemporary issue was never far from his mind as he studied the history of the fourth century. In the figures of the ancient Arians he continually saw the faces of the liberal churchmen of his day with whom he was locked in sharp debate. Later, after his conversion to Rome, he put the point even more precisely, saying that he had come to see that while 'the pure Arians were the Protestants, the semi-Arians were the Anglicans'.[1] But while apologetic is clearly the dominant force in the writing of the book, Newman was too good a scholar simply to ride roughshod over the historical evidence. So far indeed was he from doing so that Rowan Williams can even describe him as the real starting-point of 'the modern historical study of the subject [Arianism]'.[2] The tension between the two approaches stands out on almost every page.

With the growth of critical historical scholarship in the course of the nineteenth century, the balance in the tension between apologetics and critical scholarship in patristic study was slowly but steadily tilting in favour of critical historical scholarship. This is most clearly evident in the work of German patristic scholars in the second half of the nineteenth century. But the nature of the shift in Britain can be well illustrated by the founding of the *Journal of Theological Studies*, whose first number appeared in October, 1899. Although not restricted to patristics, it was the main British journal for the publication of patristic scholarship throughout the twentieth century. Its founding father H. B. Swete, and his chief collaborator, William Sanday, were both fellows of the British Academy from its inception, and both J. F. Bethune-Baker and F. E. Brightman, joint editors of the *Journal* for most of its first thirty-five years, were also subsequently elected fellows. Their expressed aim in starting the *Journal* was to provide in Britain a vehicle for the scientific historical study of theology, especially of the Bible and the early church, of the kind that they saw and admired in Germany. At the same time they remained confident that conscientious and unprejudiced study of that sort, carried out with more caution and moderation than was in their eyes characteristic of much German scholarship, would in fact turn out to reinforce the truth of the moderate catholic Anglican faith that most of them professed. Critical historical study, properly pursued, would not, they believed, turn out to be in conflict with apologetic concerns.[3]

The fundamental requirement for any form of historical study is the availability of texts; the fundamental requirement for critical historical study is the availability of good texts, based on a careful study of the available manuscript evidence. The middle years of the nineteenth century had seen a

---

[1] J. H. Newman, *Apologia*, ed. M. J. Svaglic (Oxford, 1967), p. 130.

[2] Rowan Williams, *Arius* (London, 1987), pp. 2–3. See also Maurice Wiles, *Archetypal Heresy* (Oxford, 1996), pp. 166–72.

[3] See Maurice Wiles, 'The Journal of Theological Studies: Centenary Reflections', *JTS* 50 (1999), 491–514.

marked advance in the accessibility of patristic texts. This was the fruit of a remarkable feat of publishing by a French Roman Catholic priest, J.-P. Migne. Being in conflict with his bishop, Migne moved to Paris where he embarked on a career as a publisher with the primary aim of making the works of the Fathers more readily accessible to the clergy. For this new self-appointed task he proved to have an unusual entrepreneurial flair. Between the years of 1844 and 1864 he published *Patrologia Latina* consisting of 221 volumes of the works of the Latin Fathers; this was followed by 162 volumes of the Greek Fathers (with Latin translations) in *Patrologia Graeca*, which appeared between 1857 and 1866. How far this achieved its intended goal of encouraging the clergy to become conversant with the writings of the Fathers is hard to say. What is beyond question is that it made the works of the Fathers far more abundantly and far more readily available for scholarly use. But from a scholarly point of view this great gain had been achieved at a price. The versions of the texts used were in general not ones critically established in the way desired by the scholar, and there were numerous printer's errors. In addition there was a considerable number of newly discovered texts becoming available, not to be found in Migne. So at the start of the twentieth century there was a great need for critical editions of new texts and for better editions of many familiar texts which existed only in unsatisfactory versions.

A start on both these formidable tasks had already been made in the later years of the nineteenth century. Swete himself, for example, had produced a fine critical edition of the newly identified Latin version of Theodore of Mopsuestia's commentaries on the minor epistles of St Paul in the early 1880s. By the beginning of the twentieth century there were many scholars of outstanding ability involved in a great burst of critical editorial work—men such as Brightman (liturgical texts), C. H. Turner (especially canon law), W. E. Crum (Coptic texts) and F. C. Conybeare (Armenian). Edited versions of many shorter patristic texts appeared in the early numbers of the *Journal of Theological Studies*, not only in Greek and Latin but in Syriac, Coptic and other languages also. A particularly rich supply of Syriac texts had been acquired in the nineteenth century, which were still awaiting editing and publication. Robert Curzon and Henry Tattam had brought back a vast number of such manuscripts in the ten years following Curzon's visit in 1837 to the Syrian monastery in the Wadi Natrun in Egypt. A few important texts, Syriac translations of Greek texts which had survived only imperfectly or not at all in their original Greek form, appeared with remarkable speed—such as Eusebius's *Theophaneia* (published in 1842 by Samuel Lee) and Athanasius's *Festal Letters* (published in 1848 by William Cureton). But the great majority were still awaiting an editorial hand as the new century began.[4]

The most basic need, however, was not just for individual editions of this kind, but for a more systematic series of critical editions of the principal writings of the patristic age. For the undertaking of this massive task the world of patristic scholarship is deeply indebted to continental scholars. This aspect of the vital work of publishing good critical texts also had its beginnings in the nineteenth century with the Vienna Academy's inauguration of the *Corpus Scriptorum Ecclesiasticorum Latinorum* in 1866. That was followed in due course by the Berlin Academy's collection of the works of the ante-Nicene Greek Fathers in *Die griechischen christlichen Schriftsteller der ersten drei Jahrhunderte*, which began to appear in 1897. By the beginning of the century 45 volumes of the two series had appeared, and the twentieth century has seen the publication of some 130 more, despite the severe disruption of the Second World War. But it was only in the second half of the century, at the initiative of the monks of Steenbrugge, Belgium, that a set of critical editions with the same kind of comprehensive goal that had inspired Migne was launched. The first two series of *Corpus Christianorum* were, as with Migne, a *Series Latina* (from 1954) and a *Series Graeca* (1977). Both are well established and continue to put out a steady flow of volumes. The first decade of the century had seen the start of two other new series, both published in Paris—the *Corpus Scriptorum Christianorum Orientalium* (1903) and the *Patrologia Orientalis* (1907). These were both devoted to patristic texts in oriental languages, thus covering ground that Migne had not attempted to deal with and providing a vehicle for the publication of many of the great collection of manuscripts brought to light in the nineteenth century. The *CSCO* has Syriac, Coptic, Arabian and Ethiopian series, with the Syriac alone producing more than 200 volumes in the course of the century; the *PO* includes Armenian and Georgian as well. Important British contributors to the early stages of these two series were E. W. Brooks (Syriac) and W. E. Crum (Coptic). Both ventures have proved substantial and successful undertakings, even though in some instances the editorial principles followed have not always satisfied those accustomed to the style of critical editorial work commonly used with classical Greek and Latin texts today. One other series, again

---

[4] For these and subsequent references to Syriac scholarship I am indebted to the advice and writings of Sebastian Brock. See especially his 'The Development of Syriac Studies', in K. J. Cathcart (ed.), *The Edward Hincks Bicentenary Lectures* (Dublin, 1994), pp. 94–112, and his 'Syriac Studies in the Last Three Decades', in R. Lavenant, S.J. (ed.), *VI Symposium Syriacum* (Orientalia Christiana Analecta 247, Rome, 1994), pp. 13–29.

emanating from Paris, has made such a great contribution to the accessibility of good patristic texts that it too calls for mention, even though it does not set out to provide a new critical text in every case. The first volume of *Sources Chrétiennes* appeared in 1942, a time of exceptional difficulty for a venture of that kind in France. The credit for getting the series started and seeing it through its difficult early years belongs to three outstanding Jesuit scholars, de Lubac, Daniélou and Mondésert. Each volume contains a good (but not necessarily new) critical text, a French translation on the facing page, and valuable but succinct introduction and notes. By the end of the century it was just approaching its 450th volume.

Important new editions have not been restricted to these major series. There have been other smaller and more selective series, such as the *Oxford Early Christian Texts*, which include an introduction, facing translation and brief but informative notes as well as a critical text. This series was initiated and edited by Henry Chadwick, and the first volume to appear was Robert Thomson's *Athanasius'* Contra Gentes *and* De Incarnatione (1971). An outstanding recent example of a newly edited text, appearing in the *Vetus Latina* series, is Caroline Hammond Bammel's masterly execution of the highly complex task of producing a critical text of Rufinus's translation of Origen's commentary on the Epistle to the Romans in three volumes, the last two published posthumously (Herder, 1990–8). But in the later years of the century, after the heady days of the rapid appearance of so many new texts in its first decades, it has been through the steady growth of the major series that the bulk of editorial work has been channelled. All in all they constitute a remarkable achievement, the foundation on which all other aspects of twentieth-century patristic scholarship rest.

But if critical texts are the foundation on which all other scholarship rests, there is also need for good tools with which to do the building. One significant British contribution in that respect provides another example of an initiative originally begun for clerical and pastoral reasons which, like Migne's *Patrologia*, has ended up as a standard tool of patristic scholarship. Once again Swete was the founding father. In a little book, written in 1902, he outlines a prospective course of patristic study for clergy. He does acknowledge, with a touch of regret, that they may have difficulty in either finding or affording a complete set of Migne for their own studies, and will therefore almost certainly need to resort to libraries. But in spite of such difficulties his book is powerful in its advocacy and practical in its advice.[5] Four years later a clerical society, entitled the Central Society for Sacred Study, which Swete had

---

[5] See H. B. Swete, *Patristic Study* (London, 1902), esp. p. 181.

founded in 1899 and of which he was still Warden, launched a project for a
Lexicon of Patristic Greek by arranging for some eighty clergymen and some
other interested people to read through the volumes of Migne's *Patrologia
Graeca* and certain other texts with a view to assembling material for the
Lexicon. With no editor appointed at the outset, it sounds, and was, a dubious
start to the production of a major work of reference. But in 1915, by which
time most of the initial reading had been done and recorded on slips, an
Oxford Committee was set up to oversee the project and Darwell Stone was
appointed editor. His original appointment was as 'theological' editor, with a
view to the appointment of a co-editor to deal with the 'non-theological'
aspects of the Lexicon. But no further appointment was made and Darwell
Stone continued to work on the Lexicon until his death in 1941. By this time,
with Liddell and Scott's abandonment of all Christian writings (apart from the
New Testament) in its ninth (LSJ) edition, which appeared between 1925 and
1940, the need for the Lexicon had become greater than ever. Whatever
Swete's initial hopes of its value to a learned clergy, it was clear by this stage
that its only possible destination would be the academic market, and towards
the end of his long labours with it Darwell Stone had begun to have doubts
whether even that market would still be there by the time it was finished. In a
letter to a friend dated 4 December 1937, he is to be found musing whether
'perhaps it ought to have been in Latin, as the chief interest in it is from
abroad, though most foreign scholars read English after a fashion, Latin is
easier to them', and expressing the fear that 'by the time the Lexicon is finished there would be no one in England who knew Greek and no one who
cared what the fathers taught'.[6] After his death Leslie Cross had editorial
responsibility for a short time, but when Geoffrey Lampe took over the editorship in 1948, it still required Herculean efforts on his part and that of his
small band of assistants (sometimes known as 'slaves of the lamp') to bring
it to any sort of completion, let alone one appropriate for the scholarly world
which was now clearly its only possible market. The resultant *Patristic Greek
Lexicon* (published by OUP in 1961–8) has many weaknesses and uneven-
nesses of treatment, arising out of its strange and lengthy period of gestation.
It is fundamentally based on Migne's text; but the steady stream of new critical editions appearing in the final years of the Lexicon's preparation and in
the years following its publication means that for many writings Migne's text
has now long been superseded. Moreover, like a mirror image of LSJ, it iso-
lates Christian vocabulary and usage from that of the wider world of which

[6] F. L. Cross, *Darwell Stone* (London, 1943), pp. 119–21, 338.

Christians were a part. Its corresponding strength is the degree to which it serves not merely as a philological, but also as a theological dictionary of Christian literary usage in the period. But whatever its shortcomings, it has proved itself, and continues to prove itself, an invaluable aid to every reader of Greek patristic texts.[7]

The discovery and publication of newly discovered texts and the production of more reliable versions of well-known texts were not the only sources of material with new light to offer on the early history of the church. The early years of the twentieth century saw the discovery and excavation of many new archaeological sites with buildings and inscriptions significant to the patristic age, especially in North Africa and Asia Minor. William Ramsay's extensive work in the latter of those two regions was a notable British contribution. Methods of excavation and the recording of the finds often left much to be desired, but the century has seen steady improvements in those respects. The cumulative evidence from these various finds have added an important new dimension to our understanding of early Christianity, particularly in its social relations with its Jewish and pagan environment. It has also greatly enhanced our understanding of dissident movements, such as Donatism in North Africa and Montanism in Asia Minor, where the available literary evidence is both limited and one-sided. Some individual finds have been of outstanding interest, either because of the extent of what has been preserved in particular cases or because of the intrinsic importance of the site. The excavation in the years between the two world wars of Dura-Europos, for example, a Roman garrison town on the banks of the Euphrates which was abandoned about 256 CE, revealed extensive remains of many pagan temples, a Mithraeum, a Jewish synagogue and a Christian church. The church, complete with baptistery, not only bore the marks of its interior transformation from domestic to church use, but also contained striking examples of Christian art. And the shrine of St Peter, under the great altar in St Peter's in Rome, was the subject of systematic excavation between 1939 and 1951. Archaeological evidence, for all its apparent solidity, is, of course, always as open to divergent interpretation as the evidence of literary texts. In a case of such special religious sensitivity as St Peter's shrine, the interpretation of the evidence was bound to involve complex critical discussion—a process to which Jocelyn Toynbee and John Ward Perkins made a judicious contribution. Now, by the end of the century, archaeology is firmly recognised as a significant contributing aspect of

---

[7] See H. Chadwick, 'The Greek Patristic Lexicon' in C. F. D. Moule (ed.), *G. W. H. Lampe: A Memoir* (London, 1982), pp. 66–72.

patristic study, even if not as fully integrated into it as its leading advocates, such as William Frend, would like to see.

One further source of new first-hand evidence about the patristic age, which provided rich material around the middle of the century, could equally well be classified as literary or archaeological finds. Important new texts were found, not overlooked or unidentified in one of their natural habitats such as a monastic library, nor in the course of any formal process of excavation, but hidden away in caves and discovered by sheer chance. The Dead Sea Scrolls, which are much the best known of such finds, relate primarily to biblical rather than patristic studies, though they have contributed valuable new insights into the contemporary Jewish culture, whose importance for understanding patristic thought has been increasingly recognised in the course of the century. But two other comparable finds, both in Egypt, impinge much more directly on patristic scholarship. Codices containing works of Origen and of Didymus the Blind were discovered in 1941 at Toura, just south of Cairo, in a cave that was being prepared as an ammunition store for the eighth army. The texts have served to provide interesting new insights into the thought of both writers. Origen's *Dialogue with Heraclides*, for example, is a particularly fascinating text; it provides a first-hand account of Origen at an episcopal synod in discussion with Heraclides, a bishop whose orthodoxy had been called into question, and does so in a way that brings Origen and the theological debates of his day very much to life. Even more important was a peasant's chance find in 1945 of a large number of Coptic texts of Gnostic provenance at Nag Hammadi, stowed away in a large storage pot at the site of a cemetery near the monastery founded by Pachomius. Complications in the acquisition of the documents for the scholarly world and failures in co-operation between the different people and institutions who did acquire them led to a delay of over thirty years before their eventual publication and availability to the scholarly world at large. But their significance for the understanding of Gnosticism can hardly be overstated. It has not led to any firm consensus in how to understand the confusing range of beliefs and practices that are grouped together under that umbrella title, but at least the debate can now draw on first-hand sources rather than having to rely exclusively on the polemical descriptions of their orthodox opponents.

The main theme of this account so far has been the steady accumulation of new sources of knowledge and improved editions of familiar texts bearing on the history of the patristic age. It was work that required linguistic and textual skills of the highest order; and it was work of that kind that was particularly characteristic of British patristic scholarship in the first half of the twentieth century. But it did not stop there. Most of those involved in these studies were Christian theologians, whose underlying motivation that had led them to pursue such studies was the conviction that they would enhance our understanding and evaluation of the Christian doctrines and practices developed during that formative period. Grand theories which might call into question the value of the resultant pattern of church doctrines and practices—such as Harnack's Hellenisation thesis which saw the emerging doctrines as an adulteration of the original gospel by an alien philosophy—were generally regarded as misguidedly speculative. Confidence that historical scholarship would illuminate rather than undermine the religious validity of the course of development that Christian doctrine had taken in the early centuries remained strong. But the sharp distinction between the truth of orthodoxy and the erroneous character of the writings of the heretics began to be called into question by some of the monographs appearing from the pens of British scholars. Bethune-Baker's *Nestorius and his Teaching* (1908), making use of Nestorius's *Bazaar of Heraclides* recently discovered in a Syriac translation in 1895, claimed that there was no fundamental difference between his Christology and that of his orthodox opponent, Cyril of Alexandria. And Charles Raven's *Apollinarianism* (1923) argued that Apollinarius's condemnation for heresy was not based on his actual teaching, but on a grave distortion of it perpetrated by his orthodox opponents. Revisionist works of this kind were not enough in themselves to shake the underlying attitude to the subject which had been so clear at the start of the century, but they were early intimations of changes to come. The prevailing attitude finds attractive expression in Leonard Prestige's beautifully written Bampton Lectures, *Fathers and Heretics* (1940). The two heretics to whom direct attention is given are the same two—Apollinarius and Nestorius. Both receive thoroughly positive and appreciative treatment, but the truth of the main Catholic tradition is firmly maintained.

By 1950, the half-way point of the century, with the major disruption of the Second World War over, there was the opportunity for the resumption of wider international contacts and greater concentration on the work of scholarship. One feature of the second half of the century, which is both a result of and a contributory factor to the great expansion of patristic studies during that period, is the series of International Patristic Conferences that have been held in Oxford every four years since 1951—and still continue. They were set in motion by Leslie Cross, though at the outset he had neither the intention nor the expectation of starting something of the magnitude or durability that have been their hallmark. Appointed Lady Margaret Professor of Divinity at Oxford towards the end of the war, Cross was concerned to promote an ecumenical and international approach to scholarship. In particular, as one who had studied in Germany before the war, he was keen to see German scholars brought back into the forum of scholarly interchange. Moreover, his own subject of patristic research, dealing with a period before the great divisions of the church arose, seemed well suited to the ecumenical aspect of his concerns. So he planned to hold a small international gathering of around twenty-five scholars at Christ Church, Oxford, in September, 1951. The response, especially from overseas, was so enthusiastic that the numbers grew to around 250. An extremely shy and reclusive man, Cross was somewhat alarmed at the size to which his venture had grown; but, having recruited a recent Oxford graduate, Elizabeth Livingstone, to assist him with the administration, all went well. One hitch on the ecumenical side was a last-minute ban on the attendance of Jesuits, issued by the head of the Order. This was a serious blow as the Jesuits included among their number many outstanding patristic scholars: eighteen had signed up to attend, a majority of them due to give a paper. But other Roman Catholic and Orthodox scholars were there in good numbers—and there were even two Jesuits present (Grillmeier and Mondésert, one having already arrived before the ban was issued and the other having studiously avoided collecting any post when he heard a rumour of it while on his way across the Channel). At the last minute Cross, who had originally conceived of the conference as a one-off event, added the word 'First' to the title of International Patristic Conference as an encouragement to some other scholar, or national group of scholars, to carry on at some future date and in some other location the momentum of what he had started. But when the issue was formally discussed at the conference his own suggestions and desires were overruled, and the popular will had its way: the next conference was to be again in Oxford in 1955. And so it has continued at four-yearly intervals ever since. Cross, with Livingstone's invaluable and devoted assistance, remained sole organiser and director of this sequence of conferences until his death in 1969. After that Livingstone continued to do all the ever increasing volume of organising that the conferences entailed, under the overall direction of a shifting series of one or more scholars from the Oxford University Theology Faculty, until 1995—since when the Theology Faculty has taken full responsibility for them.

Numbers have grown over the years, so that they now attract an attendance of some 700 scholars. The selections of papers published after each conference now make up thirty-eight volumes of the *Studia Patristica* series. The conferences have fulfilled for patristics one of the essential functions more commonly supplied in other disciplines by a formally constituted society. They have provided the main opportunity for meetings between scholars from a variety of countries, and have been the starting-point of many valuable collaborations and lasting friendships. Other groupings, such as the Origen and Gregory of Nyssa conferences with their resultant published symposia, have grown out of the Oxford conferences and furthered their objectives in more specific ways than the larger, more wide-ranging conferences are able to do. Other more local societies have also sprung up with their own pattern of regular meetings, like the North American Patristic Society, which after a struggle to establish itself through its early years in the 1970s, is now a lively and flourishing organisation. The format of the Oxford conferences has remained very much the same over the years, but there have also been gradual but significant changes and developments. In running the conferences Cross, like Migne and Swete before him when starting their scholarly patristic undertakings, had also in mind a desire to strengthen a knowledge of the Fathers among the parochial clergy, and the early conferences were attended by a small number of parish priests as well as by specialist scholars. But in the course of time the increasing cost of the conferences and the increasingly technical nature of most of the papers given at them led to the virtual disappearance of that strand of participants. The academic character of the enterprise was underlined from the start by the presence of the Vice-Chancellor of the University at the opening session—a tradition still continued by either the Vice-Chancellor in person or one of the Pro-Vice-Chancellors. But in the beginning the conferences had a distinctly ecclesiastical character as well. Some of the earlier conferences, for example, included a liturgical occasion, such as the singing of vespers, as an integral part of the programme, but that tradition has not continued. Nevertheless Cross's ecumenical intentions have borne fruit. The kind of scholarly cooperation between Protestants and Catholics that he set out to promote is now simply taken for granted in the world of patristic scholarship, as it is in other aspects of theological scholarship.

The transformation of patristic study as a whole from being simply a subdivision of theology into a discipline which engages the attention not just of theologians but also of a substantial number of students of the later periods of the classical age is a primary feature of the way the subject has developed in the second half of the century, with major implications for the nature of the discipline. Before that time the concentration of patristic theologians was predominantly directed at the clarification of the central Christian doctrines in the period of the third to fifth centuries. Classical scholars, on the other hand, when they did venture outside the earlier 'classical' period to which pride of place was almost universally given, were primarily concerned with the fall of the empire, and showed little interest in the doings of the Christian church. We have already seen a reflection of that form of academic apartheid in the division of spheres of interest between Liddell and Scott on the one hand and the *Greek Patristic Lexicon* on the other. But the 1960s and 70s were to see a breakdown of that dividing wall of partition. An increasing number of classical scholars began to take an interest in the later periods of the ancient world. Moreover the post-war world had nurtured a growing interest in anthropology and cultural history, which helped to give rise to a greater interest in religion. So the concept of 'Late Antiquity' was born, and the study of it began to flourish. Peter Brown, following in the footsteps of his teacher, Arnold Momigliano, was the key figure in breaking down the barriers between the two disciplines. He has been described as having 'virtually destroyed the frontier [the barrier between secular and ecclesiastical in the study of the Late Empire], passing this way and that until all the marks were gone'.[8] At the same time theologians were learning that the history of doctrine, like any other aspect of the history of ideas, needed to be studied in close conjunction with the wider cultural history of the time.

This basic change of attitudes on both sides of the 'secular' and 'ecclesiastical' divide in the study of the ancient world has been reflected in the wider range of academic disciplines represented among the participants in more recent Oxford International Patristic Conferences and other similar gatherings, many now coming from departments of late antiquity as well as from departments of theology. Two illustrations from the very end of the century show clearly the nature and extent of the change. The editors of an excellent series of essays entitled *Apologetics in the Roman Empire* argue that the Apologists are even more remote today from their modern equivalents than at any time in the past, and end their introduction by affirming that 'The only modern scholars, therefore, to whom the apologists mean anything are those who take a sympathetic interest in the culture and the interplay of religious traditions in the Roman Empire, and only in the late twentieth century has this interest become at all widespread.'[9] The turn of the century has also seen Brepols, the publisher of the various *Corpus Christianorum* series, producing a revised form of Newsletter, whose first issue appeared in October 2001, and choosing to give it the title of 'Late Antiquity and Patristic Studies Newsletter'.

Peter Brown's influential work has shown from the start the value of his approach for topics at the heart of traditional patristic study. His first book,

---

[8] Alexander Murray, 'Peter Brown and the Shadow of Constantine', *Journal of Roman Studies* 73 (1983), 191.

[9] Mark Edwards, Martin Goodman and Simon Price (eds.), *Apologetics in the Roman Empire* (Oxford, 1999), p. 13.

Augustine of Hippo (1967), added a new and refreshing dimension to the interpretation of one of the most studied of historical figures. A collection of papers that underlay that biography were published shortly afterwards as *Religion and Society in the Age of St Augustine* (1972), and reveal in more detail the kind of material and questions that could profitably be explored in this style of cultural study. His subsequent work, particularly on the ascetic tradition as in *The Body and Society* (1981), has continued to provide valuable insights into important areas of long-standing concern among patristic scholars. But it would be wrong to describe these significant changes as the achievement of a single individual. Other scholars have followed in his wake and, each with their own independent stance, have written with a similar breadth of approach. Important examples are Robert Markus's *The End of Ancient Christianity* (1990) and Averil Cameron's *Christianity and the Rhetoric of Empire: The Development of Christian Discourse* (1991).

It is not only the contemporary religions and culture of Greece and Rome whose significance for the understanding of early Christian thought and life has been brought home to patristic scholars with new force by this increased interest in ancient cultural history. The same is true of contemporary Judaism. The Old Testament and first-century Judaism have, of course, always been regarded as crucial for the understanding of the New Testament—even if not always very well understood or applied. But the varied nature of Judaism in the later empire and of its continuing interrelation with the growing Christian church have more recently come to be seen as much more significant for patristic studies than was recognised in the past. Major contributions to this development within the subject have come from the historical writings of Martin Goodman and from William Horbury's *Jews and Christians in Contact and Controversy* (1998).

This emphasis on the way in which cultural historians of the ancient world have contributed to bringing about a major shift in much patristic scholarship in the later years of this century should not be allowed to suggest that before that time patristic scholarship had paid no attention to such matters. In the more historical aspects of the discipline, for example, the importance of the church's setting within the wider life of the empire was self-evident. But recent years have seen a more perceptive and more penetrating attention to that setting. John Kelly's *Jerome* (1975) is a fine example of a biography enriched by its sensitivity to the culture of the time. Henry Chadwick, whose outstanding erudition and encouragement of the discipline through his many editorial and advisory roles have made him the leading figure on the British patristic scene for many years, has shown himself a historian of the early church well able to integrate the cultural approach of recent years with the more traditional strengths of patristic scholarship. That feature of his work finds appropriate expression in the title of his latest book, a large and highly readable survey of the early history of the church, *The Church in Ancient Society: From Galilee to Gregory the Great* (2001). A similar shift of emphasis is to be seen in recent writing on patristic exegesis of the Bible, a subject which has always been an important theme within patristic studies—and rightly so, since the Fathers themselves consistently claim that scripture is the basis of all their teaching, and the church over the centuries has regularly appealed to the Fathers as guides to the true meaning of scripture. There is an interesting contrast to be seen here between the two outstanding contributions to the topic from British scholars in the second half of the century. Richard Hanson's discussion of Origen's exegesis in *Allegory and Event*, published in 1959, is immensely thorough and a fine, scholarly exposition of what is to be found in Origen's voluminous texts. But Frances Young's *Biblical Exegesis and the Formation of Christian Culture*, published in 1997, draws more deeply on the exegetical practices of the Graeco-Roman schools, in a way which adds an illuminating new dimension to the subject.

The heart of patristic study in the past has generally been seen to reside in the development of doctrine, especially the doctrines of the Trinity and Christology. Even before the century began, the growth of critical history had, as we have already seen, made the traditional understanding of a smooth path from the beginnings of Christianity to the affirmation of Trinitarian and Christological orthodoxy at the ecumenical councils of Nicaea and Chalcedon increasingly difficult to maintain. The more recent extension of that historical approach to take in a broader, cultural history has raised a further set of questions for those older ways of viewing the story of the emerging pattern of Christian belief. But the fact that the history of ideas is always culturally conditioned does not mean that there is no genuine development of ideas at all. So the widening scope of historical study now devoted to the period has not undermined the validity of studying the intellectual aspects, philosophical and historical, of that story. Significant studies of the early history of doctrine have continued to appear. John Kelly's first book, *Early Christian Creeds* (1950), is a meticulous historical study of how the early creeds came to receive their precise formulations. It draws extensively on the findings of German scholarship, where the main work on the subject had been done earlier in the century, at the same time making some new and decisive contributions of its own. Christopher Stead's *Divine Substance* (1977) makes a contribution of similar style and calibre to another central and much-studied topic—the historical roots and philosophical intention of 'substance' or 'ousia' language, with particular reference to its use in the ecumenical creeds.

These two books have helped to ensure that critical reflection on the central doctrinal tradition will be in a position to fulfil that task with ready access to the best available historical and philosophical resources. Two important books, both published in the 1980s, did undertake radically revisionary approaches to the all-important debates around the figure of Arius that gave rise to the Nicene and Constantinopolitan Creeds. Rowan Williams's *Arius: Heresy and Tradition* (1987) continues the tradition of offering a positive and Christian interpretation of the great heresiarchs that we have already seen to be a characteristic of British scholarship in the first half of the century, and takes it a stage further by applying it to the arch-heretic of all time, Arius. Richard Hanson's *The Search for the Christian Doctrine of God* (1988) offers a similarly positive and Christian (though significantly different) account of Arius, setting it in the much wider context indicated by the title of Hanson's magisterial work. This rehabilitation of Arius's religious credentials constitutes a big change from attitudes earlier in the century. Prestige, for example, in his sympathetic treatment of Apollinarius had explicitly distinguished him from Arius, who is described as 'weaving every pre-existent strand of heresy into one vast system of theological depravity'.[10] So these new evaluations of Arius and Arianism constitute the sharpest of challenges to the way in which the work of the Fathers has traditionally been seen as providing a true unfolding of Christian doctrine over against the evil falsehoods of the heretics. Both Williams and Hanson, for all their respect for and sympathy with the religious intentions of Arius, make clear that they have no doubt that the decision of the church in favour of the orthodoxy determined at the Councils and embodied in the Creeds was both justified and vitally important. But the extent of the challenge, implicit in their work, to traditional ways of reading the story of the development of Christian doctrine cannot be denied.

But matters of doctrine have never been the only area of concern about the early, formative years of Christian history. Other issues, such as church order, liturgy, and relations with the state have always been matters of great moment for the church. In recent years the range of issues to which concentrated attention has been given within the international community of patristic scholarship has grown a lot wider still, taking in such topics as homiletics, pastoral care, and the social mix and demography of the early church.

The primary reason that patristic study has been regarded for so long as of great importance for the work of Christian theologians generally is the contribution it has been understood to offer to our present understanding of

---

[10] G. L. Prestige, *Fathers and Heretics* (London, 1940), p. 94.

Christian belief and practice. One of the problems raised by the critical, historical approach to the subject, which has dominated this past century, has been that it tends to make the relevance of the patristic age to our own religious understanding appear increasingly distant and indirect. The more we come to understand early Christian belief and practice in terms of the thought-forms and culture of their own time, the less directly do they seem to bear on the religion and theology of our own day. This is more clearly evident in some aspects of the discipline than in others. One reason for the growing interest in the spirituality of the patristic age, which is a marked feature of the present time, is that that is felt to be an area of study in which this sense of the increasingly remote significance of patristic scholarship for the contemporary church does not apply with the same force. Without any abandonment of the valid principles of historical research, it is widely held, the study of spirituality can provide a much closer link between the fundamental religious concerns of the ancient world and those of our own time than other spheres of patristic study. Thus, while many scholars are inclined simply to dismiss traditional allegorical understandings of scripture as thoroughly misguided, the significance of scripture lections as they are still used in the liturgy often depends on just such an allegorical interpretation. In that context, therefore, it is possible to claim that we are made aware of a real affinity between our world and that of the patristic era; the relevance of the thought and faith of the Fathers appears more immediate than at other moments in our historical investigations. This whole approach is one that comes particularly naturally to members of the Eastern Orthodox churches, whose contemporary spirituality is so much closer to that of the patristic age than is that of the Western churches. An emphasis of this kind, alongside the highest standards of historical scholarship, is to be found in a number of British scholars, such as Kallistos Ware, Andrew Louth and John McGuckin—all members of the Eastern Orthodox church. But how successfully these two ways of approaching patristic study can in fact be held together in a coherent unity remains open to question.

One further area of contemporary patristic scholarship calls for separate comment. We have already noted that the early years of the century saw the new availability and publication of a considerable number of Syriac manuscripts. Many of them were Syriac translations of Greek originals, and it was these that tended to be brought first to the attention of the wider patristic world, as by R. H. Connolly in his scholarly presentation and translation of the *Didascalia Apostolorum* (1929). The original Syriac literature itself and its distinctive tradition roused less interest. F. C. Burkitt, for example, an outstanding Syriac scholar whose primary interest was in Syriac versions of the

New Testament, described Ephrem as 'extraordinarily prolix' and his popularity as showing 'a lamentable standard of taste'.[11] Moreover, modern Syriac users in the Syriac churches were generally regarded as outside the world of contemporary scholarship. It is only within the second half of the century that these attitudes have changed, and a strong scholarly interest in the Syriac tradition has grown up. A critical edition of Ephrem's writings appeared in *CSCO* between 1955 and 1975. Ecumenical relations with the Syriac churches improved and scholarly contact with the Middle Eastern churches began to be established. An international Syriac Symposium was held in Rome in 1972, and further symposia have been held every four years since. In Britain a lively interest in the Syriac tradition, and especially in Ephrem's hymns and theological stance, was set in motion by the publication of Robert Murray's book, *Symbols of Church and Kingdom* (1975). But the predominant influence in initiating and sustaining this highly creative branch of patristic study has been the work of Sebastian Brock, through his teaching, the wide range of his scholarly writings and his personal encouragement of other scholars.[12]

The account that I have given has been restricted almost entirely to British patristic scholarship. But it has been impossible to do so without some reference to the work of other scholars, particularly in relation to the large-scale publication of critical texts which has figured so prominently among the achievements of patristic scholarship in the course of the century. And the obvious fact that, in discussing the inspiration of new ideas and new directions of study in the later part of the century, the important contributions of many scholars from many different countries has had to be passed over in silence in so brief a survey also needs to be made explicit. British patristic scholarship today has to be seen as one contributory stream within a single international community of patristic scholars. The most recent of the Oxford conferences, held in 1999, drew its members from thirty-six different countries, and the bulletin of the *Association Internationale d'Études Patristiques* for that same year lists members from forty.

The British contribution, though an increasingly small part of the whole, has continued to be a significant one, including work of the highest quality. But the prospect of being able to maintain that tradition is not so encouraging. There have been some very able doctoral students working on patristic topics in British universities in recent years, but most of them have come from and returned to countries overseas. And at the undergraduate level the subject

---

[11] F. C. Burkitt, *Early Eastern Christianity* (London, 1904), pp. 96 and 99.
[12] See n. 4 above.

plays a much smaller role in theological degrees than it used to do. At the beginning of the century patristics, along with the Bible, constituted the bulk of the syllabus, and most of those starting on the course already had a sound knowledge of Latin and Greek. Today the character of theology and religious studies courses has radically changed. Even in courses still devoted exclusively or primarily to the study of Christianity, the emphasis tends to be on contemporary issues, with a range of different academic approaches to belief and practice, leaving little room for anything beyond the Bible in the study of Christian origins. The result is little room for patristics and little call for specialist patristic teachers. So despite the vitality of the subject at the level of scholarly writing and research internationally at the present time, there is ground for anxiety how well it will prove possible to sustain the British contribution through the century that is just beginning.

Note. I am grateful to Sebastian Brock, Henry Chadwick, Brian Daley, Elizabeth Livingstone and Rowan Williams for reading an earlier draft of this paper and for their helpful suggestions.

CHAPTER FIVE

The medieval church

DAVID LUSCOMBE

The main thrust of this chapter concerns the contributions made by former Fellows of the Academy to the study of the medieval church. Perhaps above all it was devotion to the Church of England and to its past, or birth into a family which included a vicar among its members, that inspired numerous twentieth-century scholars to unearth the records of the *ecclesia anglicana*, to read its medieval historians and to study its architecture and art. Not every antiquarian scholar or ecclesiastical historian was a religious devotee (though many were); nor have scholarly, communicant members of the Christian churches all been admirers of what they confronted in the past. G. G. Coulton (1858–1947), himself ordained but not active as an Anglican priest, displayed massive prejudices that were as irritating and as uncompromising as they could be magnificent and inspiring. He wrote about medieval life on an encyclopaedic scale. His books ranged widely from *Chaucer and his England* (London, 1908; 4th edn., 1927) to *The Medieval Village* (Cambridge, 1925), from *Art and the Reformation* (Oxford, 1928; 2nd edn., 1953) to *Medieval Panorama* (Cambridge, 1938). He was fascinated by medieval art and architecture and wrote, for example, an introduction to the English translation of the book by M. Aubert on *Stained Glass of the XIIth and XIIIth Centuries from French Cathedrals* (London, 1937). He was also fascinated by medieval biographies and autobiographies and provided an introduction to the translation by H. von E. Scott and C. C. Swinton Bland of *The Dialogue on Miracles by Caesar of Heisterbach* (2 vols., London, 1919). But his magnum opus was *Five Centuries of Religion*,[1] the first volume of which T. F. Tout described as an 'anti-clerical pamphlet on a massive scale'.[2] In his autobiography Coulton recounted how in 1932, when he 'was privileged to give the Raleigh

[1] Vols. 1–4 (Cambridge, 1923–50); 2nd edn. of vol. 1 (Cambridge, 1929). Vol. 4 was published posthumously.
[2] Cited by H. S. Bennett in *PBA* 33 (1947), 278.

Historical Lecture before the British Academy', he concluded the lecture with the remark 'that what History needs is not less but more controversy'. 'The acting chairman on that occasion', Coulton continued, 'as soon as I had ended, rose to say, "I cannot feel that controversy can ever be respectable," and left the chair.'[3] The chairman's exasperation may be best measured by reading not the lecture itself but Coulton's voluminous polemics against Roman Catholic writers such as Hilaire Belloc, Cardinal Gasquet[4] and Herbert Thurstan. Yet he was not always unfriendly to churchmen, medieval or other, and his portraits of such figures as St Benedict and St Bernard are unforgettable. He described Hastings Rashdall's (1858–1924) *Universities of Europe* (Oxford, 1895) as 'one of the books to which I have owed most' because—he wrote with universities in his mind—'I feel that our modern problems can often be studied best in the Middle Ages, not as a golden reign of Saturn but as a period during which men like ourselves were struggling for objects of which many have nowadays been attained.'[5]

More typically, study of the medieval church has proceeded by way of unpolemical but still critical investigation of the sources resulting in continuous debates or revisions of received interpretations. For the periods immediately before and after the Norman Conquest Frank Barlow has provided the most widely read recent guides in *The English Church, 1000–1066* (London, 1963) and *The English Church, 1066–1154* (London, 1979). Study of the relations between England and the papacy in the century and more following the Norman Conquest was an especial concern of Z. N. Brooke (1883–1946)

---

[3] G. G. Coulton, *Fourscore Years* (Cambridge, 1943), p. 326. In the Lecture Coulton asked: 'Might not the Academy do something . . . to render controversy respectable?', 'Some Problems in Medieval Historiography', printed in *PBA* 18 (1932), 155–90 (177).

[4] On Gasquet see David Knowles, 'Cardinal Gasquet as an Historian', in Dom David Knowles, *The Historian and Character and Other Essays* (Cambridge, 1963), pp. 240–63, e.g. 'from c.1900 Gasquet's pages crawl with with errors and slips . . . Towards the end of his life, indeed, Gasquet's capacity for carelessness amounted almost to genius' (p. 254); 'The academic victory lay certainly with Coulton . . . when he died in 1947 . . . Gasquet's writings had been blown upon and all but driven into oblivion' (p. 258). Knowles accepted Coulton's 'most serious charge of intellectual dishonesty' against Gasquet's failure to enter a caveat following the demonstration of his flawed efforts to procure—successfully—the recognition by Rome of the cult of the last abbot of Colchester, Abbot Marshall, as a martyr to the faith for opposing the Royal Supremacy: 'Vengeance came limping after in the person of George Gordon Coulton' (p. 258). But 'On the wider view he (Coulton) was unfair to Gasquet. He ignored altogether—as controversialists often do—the real merits of some of his books and, still more, the numerous discoveries which he had made; he also ignored the judgements of values and institutions with which he did not agree, but which were none the less defensible' (p. 259).

[5] Coulton, *Fourscore Years*, pp. 183, 224. Coulton also founded *Cambridge Studies in Medieval Life and Thought*, a series in which eighteen volumes appeared between 1920 and 1950 under his editorship.

whose most abiding and also now very much built-upon achievement is his book on *The English Church and the Papacy from the Conquest to the Reign of John* (Cambridge, 1931). This absorbing work arose from detailed and original researches into manuscripts containing correspondence and canon law texts found in England and on the Continent. No study of the canon law in medieval England can dispense with the work of F. W. Maitland, whose *Roman Canon Law in the Church of England* (London, 1898) remains fundamental. But neither can studies of Archbishop Lanfranc[6] or of Archbishop Thomas Becket[7] avoid building upon Brooke's exciting assessments both of Lanfranc's reforms following the Norman Conquest of England and of the changing and growing relationships between England and the papacy— relationships which have, however, come to be seen in a less confrontational light since Brooke wrote.[8] Brooke collaborated closely with C. W. Previté Orton (1877–1947) in the editorship of *The Cambridge Medieval History* in eight volumes during the 1920s and 1930s and succeeded Previté Orton as professor of medieval history in Cambridge in 1944. Previté Orton's abridgement, *The Shorter Cambridge Medieval History* (1952), is even more ubiquitously encountered in libraries, but the *History* is now almost completely replaced by *The New Cambridge Medieval History* (1995–), which is also to be in eight volumes. Brooke's own contributions to the old *History* included chapters (in volume 5) on Pope Gregory VII and on Germany under Henry III and IV. His Raleigh Lecture to the British Academy, given in 1939, remains a fundamental statement of the relationship between the so-called Investiture Contest and the wider, papal reform movement that began earlier in the eleventh century.[9]

Zachary Brooke's work has been notably and vastly extended by his son Christopher. Zachary began study of the letters and charters of Gilbert Foliot—abbot of Gloucester from 1139, bishop of Hereford from 1148, and bishop of London from 1163 to 1187—as a part of his enquiry into the Becket crisis of 1164–70; the edition was completed, magnificently, by Christopher and by Dom Adrian Morey.[10] Christopher Brooke also

[6] For example, M. Gibson, *Lanfranc of Bec* (Oxford, 1978).

[7] There recently appeared the magnificent edition and translation by Anne Duggan of *The Correspondence of Thomas Becket, Archbishop of Canterbury 1162–1170*, 2 vols. (Oxford, 2000).

[8] C. N. L. Brooke in his Foreword to the reissue of Z. N. Brooke's book in 1989 has commented in detail on the revisions that have taken place.

[9] 'Lay Investiture and its Relation to the Conflict of Empire and Papacy', *PBA* 25 (1939), pp. 217–47; repr. in L. S. Sutherland (ed.), *Studies in History: British Academy Lectures* (London, 1966), pp. 50–77.

[10] *The Letters and Charters of Gilbert Foliot* (Cambridge, 1967). In *Gilbert Foliot and his Letters* (Cambridge, 1965) Brooke and Morey study Foliot's life and works.

masterminded an exceptionally fine edition and translation of *The Letters of John of Salisbury*, John being secretary to Archbishop Theobald before becoming secretary to Archbishop Thomas Becket as well as Becket's tireless and skilful champion.[11] The dating of Gilbert's letters and those of John, and the identification of their correspondents and other persons and events found in their substantial letter collections, have wide ramifications for further studies.

The late Sir Richard Southern was also a towering influence in this field of study. His two books on Anselm—*Saint Anselm and his Biographer* (Cambridge, 1963) and *Saint Anselm: A Portrait in a Landscape* (Cambridge, 1990)—are especially notable for their treatment of spirituality as well as of administration, of Anselm's religious philosophy as well as of his struggles with kings and popes. Southern also presented editions of texts, notably *The Life of St. Anselm by Eadmer* (London, 1963), and (with F. S. Schmitt) *The Memorials of St Anselm* (Oxford, 1969), which include Anselm's *dicta* or 'table talk'. His genius for capturing all sides of a great person is also evident in his book on *Robert Grosseteste: The Growth of an English Mind in Medieval Europe* (Oxford, 1986). Southern presents Grosseteste as one of the greatest English scholars of the thirteenth century, situated within an English scientific tradition but moving through it to theology and through this to action. As bishop of Lincoln between 1235 and 1253 Grosseteste applied his thought about (for example) the place of Jews in the history of salvation, about ecclesiastical hierarchy, and about prophecy in the course of his vigorous episcopate.

Christopher Cheney (1906–87) focused upon this same period of the history of the medieval English church and also studied relationships with the papacy from the Conquest to the thirteenth century. A research student under F. M. Powicke (1879–1963), then Bishop Fraser Lecturer in Ecclesiastical History at Manchester from 1933 to 1937, reader in diplomatic at Oxford from 1937 to 1945, and (like Powicke until 1928 and also like Tout from 1890 to 1925) professor of medieval history at Manchester from 1945 to 1955, finally professor of medieval history at Cambridge from 1955 to 1972, Cheney was *par eminence* a student of diplomatic. His first book, published at Manchester in 1931 and again with revisions in 1983, was on *Episcopal Visitation of Monasteries in the Thirteenth Century*, a subject which hardly sets hearts racing now any more than do the titles of his other books, *English*

---

[11] *The Letters of John of Salisbury*, 1. *The Early Letters (1153–1161)*, ed. W. J. Millor, H. E. Butler and C. N. L. Brooke (Walton on Thames, Nelson, 1955; rev. edn., Oxford, 1986); vol. 2, *The Later Letters (1163–1180)*, ed. W. J. Millor and C. N. L. Brooke (Oxford, 1979).

Synodalia of the Thirteenth Century (London, 1941; reprinted with a new introduction in 1968), *English Bishops' Chanceries, 1100–1250* (Manchester, 1950) and *Notaries Public in England in the Thirteenth and Fourteenth Centuries* (Oxford, 1972). But all these, as well as being exemplary documentary studies of routines of administration in medieval England, were expertly built platforms from which wider horizons—the spread of canon law, the interaction of royal and ecclesiastical jurisdiction, the role of magistri or graduates in bishops' households—could be espied. Cheney's book *From Becket to Langton: English Church Government 1170–1213* (Manchester, 1956) studies the growth of papal power over the Church of England from the later twelfth century, but its focus was not politics or law but the 'unexampled activity in building the machinery of church government' (p. 175). *Episcopal Visitation of Monasteries in the Thirteenth Century* (1931) was published in the year in which Powicke recommended, in his Raleigh Lecture to the British Academy on 'Sir Henry Spelman and the "Concilia" ', a project to prepare a new edition of Wilkins's *Concilia*.[12] Powicke's enthusiasm for this followed upon his pioneering book on *Stephen Langton* (Oxford, 1928). Cheney was a member of the *Concilia* project group from the beginning. His *English Synodalia* was presented (p. v) as 'prolegomena to the edition of the English Church Councils which is now in preparation'. Cheney thanked (on p. vii) R. W. Hunt, W. A. Pantin, F. M. Powicke, R. W. Southern and his wife Mary for their collaboration. This book as well as *Episcopal Visitation of Monasteries* and *English Bishops' Chanceries 1100–1250* were harbingers of Cheney's growing involvement in the project which was achieved over thirty years later with the publication in two parts of *Councils and Synods with other Documents relating to the English Church, 2. A.D. 1205–1313* (Oxford, 1964).[13] Moreover, *English Bishops' Chanceries* prepared the way for the magnificent project that was adopted in 1973 by the British Academy, *English Episcopal Acta*. Adumbrated by F. M. Stenton in a paper published in the *Cambridge Historical Journal* in 1929, the project aims to publish, diocese by diocese, the documents issued by bishops in England between the Norman

---

[12] The Lecture was read on 18 March 1931, and published in *PBA* 16 (1930), 345–79; see p. 371 and D. Wilkins (ed.), *Concilia Magnae Britanniae et Hiberniae AD 446–1717*, 4 vols. (London, 1737).

[13] Vol. 1 of *Councils and Synods with other Documents relating to the English Church 871–1204* (Oxford, 1981) was brought to port under the editorship of D. Whitelock (1901–82), M. Brett and C. N. L. Brooke. Powicke's work on *Stephen Langton* (1965) led to several projects to study ecclesiastical administration and particularly the reorganisation of the church following the fourth Lateran Council held in 1215. Notable fruits are *Acta Stephani Langton*, ed. K. Major, Canterbury and York Society 50 (1950), and M. Gibbs and J. Lang, *Bishops and Reform 1215–72 with special reference to the Lateran Council* (Oxford, 1934).

Conquest and the thirteenth century when episcopal registers began to be made. Cheney was chairman of the project committee from 1973 to 1986 and himself published two volumes of Canterbury Acta from Thomas Becket to Hubert Walter.[14] His Ford lectures *From Becket to Langton*, published in 1956, his life of *Hubert Walter* (London, 1967), and *Pope Innocent III and England* (Stuttgart, 1976) reflect his attachment to the documentary records of ecclesiastical administration, to penetrating study of what was actually done and of how things really worked, whatever the clouds of rhetoric or of polemic may tempt one to believe, and all this was based on thorough, critical enquiries into how documents were constructed and copied. To the study of the medieval papacy Cheney brought to bear an immense knowledge of the documents containing canon law, papal letters and papal decretals. His wife Mary and he also published together an edition of *The Letters of Pope Innocent III (1198–1216) concerning England and Wales* (Oxford, 1967) and, in 1979, *Studies in the Collections of Twelfth-Century Decretals* (Vatican City).

A. Hamilton Thompson (1873–1952), who was professor of medieval history in the University of Leeds from 1924 to 1939, specialised in the history of the English church in the fifteenth century, in particular the clergy and their bishops,[15] and in publishing their records as well as writing studies of church architecture.[16] H. S. Offler (1913–91), who spent much of his life as professor of medieval history in the University of Durham and who devoted himself principally to the study of the relations between the Roman curia and the Empire in the late Middle Ages, also did much to promote the study of the church in the North of England. He was secretary of the Surtees Society from 1950 to 1966 and president from 1980 to 1987, and he published *Durham Episcopal Charters 1071–1152* in 1968.[17] Interest in the history of the church

---

[14] *English Episcopal Acta: Canterbury 1162–1190* (with B. E. A. Jones); *Canterbury 1193–1205* (with E. John). Under the currently dynamic teamwork of Christopher Brooke, Barrie Dobson, David Smith and others the project has surged forward.

[15] See his Ford Lectures, *The English Clergy and their Organisation in the Later Middle Ages* (Oxford, 1947).

[16] *Visitations of Religious Houses in the Diocese of Lincoln*, Lincoln Record Society (1911 onwards); *Registers of the Archdeaconry of Richmond* (1919, 1930, 1935); *Liber Vitae Ecclesiae Dunelmensis*, Surtees Society 136 (1923); *Rotuli Ricardi Gravesend, episcopi Lincolniensis, AD mcclviii–mcclxxix* (with F. N. Davis and C. W. Foster), Canterbury and York Society 31, and Lincoln Record Society 20 (1925); *Register of Archbishop Thomas Corbridge, Part II*, Surtees Society 141 (1928); *The Register of William Greenfield, Lord Archbishop of York 1305–1315* (with W. Brown), Surtees Society 145, 149, 151–153 (1931–40).

[17] Surtees Society 179. His papers on medieval northern history were collected and published by two of his colleagues, A. J. Piper and A. I. Doyle under the title *North of the Tees: Studies in Medieval*

in the North of England has also been promoted to a remarkable degree by Barrie Dobson who has specialised, in particular, in the history of Durham Cathedral and of York Minster.[18] Likewise, E. F. Jacob (1894–1971) devoted himself, and increasingly so throughout his career, to the history of the church in England and also in Europe in the late Middle Ages. Jacob had been taught history at New College, Oxford, by Ernest Barker (1874–1960) just after the First World War and, as his interests developed, he showed, like Barker, an abiding interest in medieval political theory, along with interests in the *devotio moderna* and the writings of the late medieval mystics, in humanism before and in the fifteenth century, in the great councils of the late Middle Ages and the movements for reform, as well as in the careers of great churchmen and in their administration and their relations with Rome and the curia.[19]

The Canterbury and York Society is the leading producer of editions of the registers of the medieval English bishops. Especially noteworthy outside this series are the already mentioned editions made by A. Hamilton Thompson and the edition by C. W. Foster and K. Major, in ten volumes with two volumes of facsimiles, of *The Registrum Antiquissimum of the Cathedral Church of Lincoln* (Lincoln Record Society, 1931–73). Along with the publication of English bishops' registers, the listing of holders of ecclesiastical office has held an important place in the study of medieval church history. Yorkshire has been particularly favoured through the work of Hamilton Thompson, Charles Clay (1885–1978) and Nora Gurney. They listed the parochial clergy,[20] and Clay in particular, amid all his work as the editor of *Early Yorkshire Charters* (10 vols., Yorkshire Archaeological Society, 1935–65), listed the dignitaries and archdeacons of York[21] and the office holders of York Minster.[22] In the

---

British History (Aldershot, 1996). This volume also contains the memoir written by P. Harvey which first appeared in *PBA* 80 (1991).

[18] See Dobson, *Durham Priory: 1400–1450* (Cambridge, 1973); Dobson (ed.), *Church and Society in the Medieval North of England* (London, 1996), a collection of thirteen essays written by himself. Also *The Church in Medieval York: Records Edited in Honour of Professor Barrie Dobson*, general ed. David M. Smith, University of York: Borthwick Institute of Historical Research, Borthwick Texts and Calendars 24 (York, 1999).

[19] Among Jacob's most prominent publications are his *Oxford History of England* volume on *The Fifteenth Century, 1399–1485* (Oxford, 1961), his *Essays in the Conciliar Epoch* (Manchester, 1943; 2nd edn., 1953) and his edition in four volumes of the *Register of Archbishop Henry Chichele* for the Canterbury and York Society (1937–47).

[20] *Fasti parochiales*, vols. 1 and 2, ed. A. Hamilton and C. T. Clay, Yorkshire Archaeological Society, Record Series 85, 107 (1933–43); vol. 4, ed. Nora K. M. Gurney and C. T. Clay, ibid., 133 (1971); vol. 5, ed. N. A. H. Lawrance, ibid., 143 (1985).

[21] *Yorkshire Archaeological Journal*, 34 (1939), 361–78; 35 (1940–3), 7–34, 116–38; 36 (1944–7), 269–87, 409–34.

[22] *York Minster Fasti*, Yorkshire Archaeological Society, Record Series 123–4, (1958–9 for 1957–8).

1950s the Institute of Historical Research in London decided to commence the revision of the lists of ecclesiastical office holders in the cathedral churches of England and Wales found in J. Le Neve's *Fasti Ecclesiae Anglicanae* (London, 1716; revised in three volumes by T. Duffus Hardy, Oxford, 1854). The title has been preserved while the evidence has been investigated in far greater depth and scope in three new series, *1066–1300, 1300–1541* and *1541–1857*. The first of these series has largely been driven forward by Diana Greenway, the second and third by J. M. Horn. No less ambitious and magnificent as works of reference and fundamental tools of research are the two volumes listing the heads of religious houses in England and Wales from the tenth-century reform to the death of Edward III and giving their chronology as precisely as possible and their careers in brief outline: *The Heads of Religious Houses: England and Wales, 940–1216*, edited by David Knowles, C. N. L. Brooke and Vera C. M. London (Cambridge, 1972; 2nd edition with substantial additions by Christopher Brooke, 2001) and *The Heads of Religious Houses: England and Wales, 1216–1377*, edited by David M. Smith and Vera C. M. London (Cambridge, 2001).

The study of medieval English monasticism and the religious orders in England is dominated by the great achievement of David Knowles (1896–1974) in his graceful volumes on *The Monastic Order in England, 940–1216* (Cambridge, 1940; 2nd edn., 1963) and on *The Religious Orders in England* (3 vols., Cambridge, 1948–59). It would be inadequate to call these volumes works of synthesis. They are also works of vision and of great literary quality reflecting deep sympathy with organised religious life as well as mastery of the historical evidence made available down the centuries by others such as William of Malmesbury, Matthew Paris, John Bale, William Dugdale and J. Armitage Robinson. Knowles's work crowns their labours.[23]

Armitage Robinson (1858–1933), who was Norris Professor of Divinity at Cambridge from 1893, dean of Westminster Abbey from 1902 to 1911 and dean of Wells from 1911 to 1933, was a patristic scholar who also made valuable contributions to the history of the medieval abbey of Westminster and of medieval Somerset. He edited *The History of Westminster Abbey* written in the fifteenth century by John Flete (Cambridge, 1909), wrote a life of Gilbert Crispin (d.1117), *Gilbert, Abbot of Westminster* (Cambridge, 1911), and a history of *The Abbot's House at Westminster* (Cambridge, 1911). At Wells he published *The Saxon Bishops of Wells* (London, 1918) and *The Times of St Dunstan* (Oxford, 1923). He was as familiar with the history of the

---

[23] See *David Knowles Remembered* by Christopher Brooke, Roger Lovatt, David Luscombe and Aelred Sillem (Cambridge, 1991).

pre-Conquest English church as with the church after the Norman Conquest. His studies in *Somerset Historical Essays* (Oxford, 1922) of William of Malmesbury's own studies of the antiquities of Glastonbury (*De antiquitate Glastoniensis ecclesiae*) were acclaimed by F. M. Stenton as 'brilliant examples of the results to be obtained by the comparison of Anglo-Norman historiography with the scattered materials which have survived from the Old English time'.[24]

The history of religious foundations includes the history of schools and universities. H. E. Salter (1863–1951) was particularly active in publishing the records of religious houses in England[25] as well as the records of medieval Oxford—both the city and the university.[26] A. G. Little (1863–1945) made the ecclesiastical as well as the academic history of the Franciscan or Grey Friars (the Friars Minor) in England the centre of numerous studies. Among his earliest works is *The Grey Friars in Oxford. Part 1: A History of the Convent, Part II: Biographical Notices of the Friars* (Oxford Historical Society 20, Oxford, 1892). Here he did not consider the contributions of the friars to scholastic philosophy 'for that clearly forms a subject by itself' (p. v). But elsewhere Little often wrote about these contributions along with the history of the lives and writings of the friars and the histories of their houses, especially at Oxford. The third and fourth chapters of *The Grey Friars in Oxford* underpin his studies of Oxford theology with their accounts of the Franciscan schools at Oxford and of their books and libraries. For Little the history of the Franciscan movement, and of the Mendicant orders in general, was both part of the larger history, on the Continent as well as in England, of medieval thought and religion, and also a matter of local history. Little published an edition of Eccleston's account of the coming of the friars, *Tractatus de adventu fratrum minorum in Angliam* (Paris, 1909).[27] He wrote for the *Victoria County History* accounts of the houses of Franciscan and other houses of friars in several counties, for the *Dictionary of National Biography* lives of sixteen friars and many articles in the *English Historical Review*. His

---

[24] *PBA* 20 (1934), 307.

[25] *Eynsham Cartulary*, 2 vols. (Oxford, 1907); *Cartulary of the Hospital of St John the Baptist*, 3 vols. (Oxford, 1914–17); *Cartulary of Oseney Abbey* (Oxford, 1929, 1931, 1934–6); *Chapters of the Augustinian Canons*, Canterbury and York Society (1922); *Register of St Augustine's Abbey, Canterbury, commonly called the Black Book* (with G. J. Turner, London, 1915, 1924). Salter also wrote on religious houses in the *Victoria County History: Oxfordshire*, vol. 2 (Oxford, 1907).

[26] *Oxford Deeds of Balliol College* (Oxford, 1913); *Medieval Archives of the University of Oxford* (Oxford, 1920–1); *Munimenta Civitatis Oxonie* (Oxford, 1920); *Medieval Oxford*, Ford Lectures (Oxford, 1936). Salter's *Survey of Oxford* was edited and published by W. A. Pantin in two volumes (Oxford, 1960). In total Salter produced thirty-four volumes for the Oxford Historical Society.

[27] A revised edition was published posthumously in 1951.

Ford lectures at Oxford, published under the title *Studies in English Franciscan History* (Oxford, 1917), remain essential reading on their subject. He prepared for the press the second edition of the *Speculum perfectionis* written by Friar Leo and containing a biography, written in 1227, of St Francis that had been left unpublished by Paul Sabatier on his death in 1928 (2 vols., Manchester, 1928, 1931).

W. A. Pantin's (1902–73) gem of a book on *The English Church in the Fourteenth Century* (Cambridge, 1955) rested on extensive work with ecclesiastical and particularly monastic records. Between 1931 and 1937 Pantin published in the Camden Series of the Royal Historical Society (London) three volumes of *Documents illustrating the Activities of the General and Provincial Chapters of the English Black Monks 1215–1540*. In the first volume, where he acknowledges his debts to H. E. Salter and to F. M. Powicke, Pantin described (pp. vii–viii) the documents as 'revealing in progressive stages the mentality and the general policy of the English monks, their attitude towards the big and permanent problems, like the relations between monastery and monastery, or between abbot and convent, the relative claims of Prayer and Study, and many other points of observance'. Pantin had an especial interest in the Black monks who studied in Oxford in the later Middle Ages. *Canterbury College, Oxford* (4 vols., Oxford, 1947–85) brings together monastic and academic history in presenting the inventories of the college which housed monks of Canterbury. So did his edition (with Dom Hugh Aveling) in 1967 of 170 letters written in Latin in the last years before the Dissolution by Robert Joseph, a monk who was a member of another monastic college, Gloucester College, and who was enraptured both by Oxford and by the study of humane letters.[28] To the study of the records of the medieval university Pantin, who became keeper of the university archives in 1946, also contributed substantially through editions of records, including *Formularies which bear on the History of Oxford c.1204–1420* (with H. E. Salter and H. G. Richardson, 2 vols., Oxford, 1942) and *The Register of Congregation 1448–1436* (with W. T. Mitchell, Oxford, 1972). The latter virtually completed the publication, pioneered by Salter, of the surviving archives of the university before 1500. In addition, Pantin and W. T. Mitchell published the *Survey of Oxford* (2 vols., Oxford, 1960–9), which Salter had compiled over the course of fifty years but left unpublished at his death in 1951, and which is a topographical survey of the wards, streets and tenements

---

[28] *The Letter Book of Robert Joseph, Monk-Scholar of Evesham and Gloucester College, Oxford, 1530–3* (Oxford, 1967). See also Knowles, *The Religious Orders in England, 3. The Tudor Age*, ch. 7: 'Humanism at Evesham.'

of Oxford from the twelfth century. Pantin brought together some of his knowledge of Oxford's medieval records, and of what they reveal of teaching and administration and of life in general, in *Oxford Life in Oxford Archives* (Oxford, 1972).

For the history of medieval schools and universities the landmark study is that written by Hastings Rashdall: *The Universities of Europe in the Middle Ages* (2 vols., Oxford, 1895). A new edition was made by F. M. Powicke and A. B. Emden (1888–1979) in three volumes in 1936 (Oxford), Powicke being principally responsible for the continental universities and Emden for the chapters on Oxford and Cambridge. They made many revisions and attracted to their enterprise many advisors. Emden in particular was able to utilise, as Rashdall was not, the publications of Salter. But Rashdall's account of the intellectual life of medieval universities was now outdated. The first two volumes of the new *History of the University of Oxford* devote more attention to the content of teaching and learning in the medieval university than did Rashdall.[29] The monumental achievement of Emden were his *Registers* which meticulously but succinctly brought together from a wide range of sources the known facts concerning the careers of 27,600 men who belonged to the two medieval English universities, including magistri who could not be confidently assigned to either. The *Biographical Register of the University of Oxford to A.D. 1500* (3 vols., Oxford, 1957–9), the *Biographical Register of the University of Oxford A.D. 1501–1540* (Oxford, 1974) and the *Biographical Register of the University of Cambridge to 1500* (Cambridge, 1963) filled the vacuum left by the *Alumni Oxonienses* of Joseph Foster (Oxford, 1887–92), and went far beyond the information given in the *Alumni Cantabrigienses* of J. and J. A. Venn (Cambridge, 1922–7, 1940–54). Emden's work has been supplemented for Scotland by D. Watt in his *Biographical Dictionary of Scottish Graduates to A.D. 1410* (Oxford, 1977)—1410 being the year in which a papal bull permitted the foundation of the first Scottish university at St Andrews.

Owen's College in Manchester, later the University of Manchester, was for many historians of the medieval English church the place where a distinguished academic career was launched, examples being Pantin and Little, Powicke and Beryl Smalley. Powicke studied there under Tout and held a research fellowship there from 1902 to 1905 and an assistant lectureship from 1906 to 1908, becoming professor of medieval history at Manchester from

---

[29] *The History of the University of Oxford*, general ed. T. H. Aston. Vol. 1, *The Early Oxford Schools*, ed. J. I. Catto with the assistance of R. Evans (Oxford, 1984); vol. 2, *Late Medieval Oxford*, ed. J. I. Catto and R. Evans (Oxford, 1992).

1919 to 1928, and then Regius Professor of Modern History at Oxford from 1928 to 1947. He would not be best described as a historian of the church but, as seen already, he did much to promote interest in it. He edited and translated Walter Daniel's biography of St Ailred (1109–67), the Cistercian abbot of Rievaulx.[30] And more importantly he opened doors to the wider study of aspects of ecclesiastical history as well as writing large-scale studies of thirteenth-century political history. And among the many historians whom he encouraged was Beryl Smalley (1905–84).

That the Bible held a central position in the work of schools and universities is far more clearly evident now than it was before Beryl Smalley published *The Study of the Bible in the Middle Ages* (Oxford, 1941). Her book had been preceded by a number of studies of commentaries on the Bible written around and after 1100. These studies are difficult to follow, for Miss Smalley was trying to navigate in a fog: the manuscripts of the period gave few clear indications of their origins or their interdependence. Nonetheless, she succeeded in showing that the *Glossa ordinaria*, which had previously been thought to have appeared in the Carolingian period, struggled into life at this time and was especially linked with the teaching and practical vision of Master Anselm of Laon. Somewhat later and around the middle years of the twelfth century, the fog having started to lift, she saw how Peter Lombard brought to completion a continuous, unified gloss on most parts of the Bible. Thereafter for centuries, as has always been known but as has also often been overlooked, the *Glossa ordinaria* was used in universities to anchor the study of the Bible at the centre of instruction in theology. Smalley's findings still dominate the field, and her book, revised in 1952 and reissued with supplementary notes in 1982, remains unsurpassed. After it first appeared Beryl Smalley continued to hunt after and to bring to light manuscript copies of other unstudied commentaries and to write about their characteristics, with her eagle eye latching on to the topical and personal information that they also contained. In this connection she brought to life Andrew of St Victor (d.1175) whose contacts with living Jewish exegetes enabled him to state what the Old Testament meant to Jews. She was convinced that the twelfth century saw the triumph of a literal approach to understanding the Bible and a turning away from allegory, a view that has many ramifications for the general understanding of the place of the Bible in the medieval world as well as of the practical outlooks of schoolmen. In the second edition of her

---

[30] *The Life of Ailred of Rievaulx by Walter Daniel*, Nelson's Medieval Classics (London, 1950); reissued with an introduction by Marsha Dutton, Cistercian Fathers series 57, Cistercian Publications (Kalamazoo, Mich., 1994).

work (Oxford, 1952) there were two principal additions. The first was Herbert of Bosham, one of Becket's companions, who, she revealed, was an influential exegete and a Hebraist like Andrew. When in later years Smalley gave the Ford lectures on *The Becket Conflict and the Schools* (published at Oxford in 1973) she showed how crucial biblical interpretation was proving to be for scholars engaged in administration and government, for Becket's opposition to double punishment of criminous clerks by church and crown was underpinned by Herbert's (and his own) experience of biblical study in the schools. The second major extension concerns the friars of the thirteenth century and their commentaries. The friars emphasised the literal sense and based their pastoral aims on the experience of teaching and of being taught the Bible in the classroom. From her wide-ranging study of the friars' commentaries emerged a book on *English Friars and Antiquity in the Early Fourteenth Century* (Oxford, 1960) which presented some of the friars, including Thomas Waleys and Robert Holcot, who had developed antiquarian interests. Beryl Smalley's voyages of discovery perhaps culminated in her finding of an almost complete record of the lost lectures on the whole of the Bible by John Wycliffe.

Medieval libraries, their books and their catalogues have become far better known since the beginning of the last century. At that time M. R. James (1862–1936), working at high speed, was adding prodigiously to his series of descriptive catalogues of manuscripts. He published catalogues of the manuscripts in the Cambridge College libraries and in the Fitzwilliam Museum, Cambridge, but his catalogue of the manuscripts in the Cambridge University Library is unpublished. Outside Cambridge James also published catalogues of the manuscripts at Eton, Lambeth, Westminster, Aberdeen and the John Rylands Library at Manchester. A few years after James's death N. R. Ker (1908–82) produced *Medieval Libraries of Great Britain* (London, 1941; 2nd edn., 1964; *Supplement* ed. A. G. Watson, London, 1987) in which the book collections of medieval libraries were listed with indications of the current locations of surviving manuscripts. Ker's *English Manuscripts in the Century after the Norman Conquest* (Oxford) followed in 1960, his *Catalogue of Manuscripts containing Anglo-Saxon* (Oxford) in 1967, and then, from 1969 to 2002, his five volumes describing uncatalogued or barely catalogued collections of the present day, *Medieval Manuscripts in British Libraries* (Oxford).[31] Some of the collections of medieval manuscripts still held in the libraries of English cathedrals and colleges were catalogued by Sir Roger

---

[31] The third and fourth volumes were published posthumously.

(R. A. B.) Mynors (1903–89).[32] All this work is now extensively complemented by Richard Sharpe's *Handlist of the Latin Writers of Great Britain
and Ireland before 1540* (Brepols, 1997); in this volume Sharpe inventorises
the writings of medieval British Latin writers and lists medieval manuscript
copies as well as modern printed editions. Both he and Michael Lapidge had
earlier produced their *Bibliography of Celtic-Latin Literature 400–1200*
(Dublin, 1985), which similarly is fundamental to the study of the literature
of the early medieval church in the British Isles.

The fine editions of the works of some medieval church historians have been
made and remade in the past half-century in the Oxford (formerly Nelson's)
Medieval Texts series where *en face* translations into English accompany the
Latin text. R. A. B. Mynors edited (with B. Colgrave) the *Ecclesiastical
History* of Bede (1969) in this series.[33] Marjorie Chibnall's edition and translation of the *The Ecclesiastical History of Orderic Vitalis* (6 vols., Oxford,
1969–80) is one of the main foundations of Anglo-Norman studies. Dr
Chibnall also provided a revised edition with translation of the *Historia pon-
tificalis* written by John of Salisbury in the mid-twelfth century (London,
1956), the edition she revised being that published by R. L. Poole (Oxford,
1927). The English title which she provided was brilliantly chosen: *John of
Salisbury's Memoirs of the Papal Court*. Diana Greenway's edition and translation of *Henry, Archdeacon of Huntingdon, «Historia Anglorum»* (Oxford,
1996), and the edition and translation by R. A. B. Mynors, R. M. Thomson
and M. Winterbottom of the *Gesta Regum Anglorum* of William of
Malmesbury, with an introduction and commentary by Thomson (2 vols.,
Oxford, 1998, 1999), are considerable contributions to making accessible the
best historical writing by medieval churchmen in England.

The history of the churches outside England during the Middle Ages has
not received the same concentrated attention as the church in England. The
disparity is great and even uncomfortable. For Byzantium in its earliest phase,
rooted in the Greek tradition and in a Roman administrative framework but
transformed by Christian belief, the work of Norman Baynes (1877–1961),
one of the editors of volume 12 of *The Cambridge Ancient History* (1939) and
the author of *Constantine the Great and the Christian Church* (1972),[34] stands

---

[32] *Durham Cathedral Manuscripts to the End of the Twelfth Century* (Oxford, 1939); *Catalogue of the
Manuscripts of Balliol College* (Oxford, 1963); *Catalogue of the Manuscripts of Hereford Cathedral
Library* (with R. M. Thomson, Cambridge, 1993). Mynors's catalogue of the manuscripts of
Peterhouse, Cambridge, is unpublished.

[33] J. M. Wallace Hadrill also wrote a *Historical Commentary* on the work which was published after
his death (Oxford, 1988).

[34] Raleigh Lecture in History, *PBA* 15 (1929); repr. London, 1972.

out. The historic reality of Christian culture and its creativity during the early Middle Ages were brilliantly depicted by Christopher Dawson (1889–1970) in *The Making of Europe* (London, 1932). *The Frankish Church* (Oxford, 1983), written by J. M. Wallace-Hadrill (1916–85), is a *magnum opus* which focused on spiritual centres, religious life, ideas and learning, and the great missionaries of the seventh and eighth centuries. A still fundamental introduction to the workings of the papal curia are the *Lectures on the History of the Papal Chancery down to the time of Innocent III* (Cambridge, 1915) by R. L. Poole (1857–1939). John Cowdrey, too, has provided substantial studies of the 'Gregorian' reform papacy, including a great work on *Pope Gregory VII, 1073–1085* (Oxford, 1998).[35] Peter Linehan has successfully found ways into Spanish ecclesiastical archives to produce *The Spanish Church and the Papacy in the Thirteenth Century* (Cambridge, 1971); and he has written about his experiences of Spanish history and historians in *History and the Historians of Medieval Spain* (Oxford, 1993). The history of the Crusades has been dominated in the twentieth century by the *History of the Crusades* (3 vols., Cambridge, 1951–4) by the late Sir Steven Runciman whose interests have been sustained and extended by many scholars such as D. M. Nicol[36] and Jonathan Riley-Smith.[37]

The history of the medieval church is clearly inseparable from the general history of the Middle Ages; the church shaped society and society shaped the church.[38] No hard and fast distinction can always be made between works by ecclesiastical historians in the twentieth century and contributions made to general history by other historians from, say, Arnaldo Momigliano (1908–87) for late antiquity to Sir Geoffrey Elton for the end of the Middle Ages in England. I have failed to touch on many aspects ranging widely from early

---

[35] See also Cowdrey, *The Cluniacs and the Gregorian Reform* (Oxford, 1970) and *The Age of Abbot Desiderius: Montecassino, the Papacy and the Normans in the Late Eleventh Century* (Oxford, 1983).

[36] His many titles include *Byzantium and Venice: A Study in Diplomatic and Cultural Relations* (Cambridge, 1988); *Collected Studies*, 1. *Byzantium: its Ecclesiastical History and Relations with the Western World* (London, 1972); 2. *Studies in Late Byzantine History and Prosopography* (London, 1986).

[37] For example, *The First Crusade and the Idea of Crusading* (London, 1986; rev. edn., 1993); *The First Crusaders 1095–1131* (Cambridge, 1997); *Hospitallers: The History of the Order of St John* (London, 1999).

[38] For an example of a study of the medieval church considered from the standpoint of society see R. W. Southern, *Western Society and the Church in the Middle Ages*, The Penguin History of the Church, vol. 2 (London, 1970).

Britain[39] to studies of religious practice. However, of the study of learning, thought and doctrine in the Middle Ages I have written separately in an accompanying British Academy Centenary volume entitled *Medieval Studies in Twentieth-Century Britain* and edited by Professor Alan Deyermond.

Note.   I am grateful to Professor Michael Bentley for comments he made on an early draft of this chapter.

---

[39] A collection of memoirs of twenty-eight interpreters of early medieval Britain, all late Fellows of the British Academy, has been edited by Michael Lapidge in *Interpreters of Early Medieval Britain* (Oxford, 2002).

CHAPTER SIX
The Reformation

PATRICK COLLINSON

The decades before the foundation of the British Academy were marked by scholarly endeavours on the grand scale, not least in the attention paid to the age of the Reformation, when modern historical studies of a character and quality set in Germany came of age. The founding father of this heroic epoch was Leopold von Ranke (1795–1886), who held the chair of history at the University of Berlin for sixty years, according to Lord Acton's opinion expressed in his inaugural lecture at Cambridge, 'the most astonishing career in literature'.[1] In 1879, at the age of eighty-three, Ranke embarked on a Universal History and managed seventeen volumes of it. Ranke's method was to narrate the story of the past as it 'evidently' was, 'wie es eigentlich gewesen', an injunction often misunderstood, as if he was even more of a historical positivist than he really was, claiming the infallibility of a total command of the facts.[2] But the dictum certainly conveyed the conviction that the task of the historian was one of 'explanation by narration', a narration as 'true' as he could make it. Experts differ over Ranke's indebtedness to earlier generations of historians, compared with his own Herculean feats in the archives of Germany's many princely and civic states. (Compare II Maccabees ii. 30: 'For to collect all that is to be known, to put the discourse in order and curiously to discuss every particular point, is the duty of the author of a history.')

It was these principles which governed the six volumes of Ranke's *Deutsche Geschichte im Zeitalter der Reformation* (Berlin, 1839–47), a work misrepresented in the very title of its (incomplete) English translation by Sarah Austin, *The History of the Reformation in Germany*, (3 vols., London, 1845–7). For Ranke's Reformation was a story of the interaction of politics

[1] Lord Acton, *Essays in the Liberal Interpretation of History*, ed. W. H. McNeill (Chicago, 1967), p. 136.
[2] Michael Bentley, 'Approaches to Modernity', in M. Bentley (ed.), *Companion to Historiography* (London and New York, 1997), pp. 419–23.

(and not only high politics, as some critics have thought) and religion, the proper concern of historians of the Reformation ever since.[3] To compare Ranke's Reformation with that of Sir Geoffrey Elton (*Reformation Europe, 1517–1559*, London, 1963; 2nd edn., Oxford, 1999) would be, of course, to find some advance in substantive knowledge of the subject. The reputation of history as a subject in which research-grounded progress is possible would be even lower than it is if that were not so. But there is little difference between Ranke and Elton as Reformation historians so far as the fundamental epistemology of the subject is concerned, their respective views on the nature and purpose of historical knowledge. And so far as understanding the interactive processes which made up the German Reformation, there was essentially no progress in the more than hundred years which separate Ranke and Elton, least of all in this country. Oh, and by the way, it was Ranke who introduced to mainstream historiography the concept of a Counter-Reformation, although he pluralised the word, 'Gegenreformationen', which implies a sensitivity to the localism of resurgent Catholicism in many parts of late sixteenth-century and seventeenth-century Germany.

But Ranke was most deficient, by more recent standards, in his account of the theology of the Reformation, which a great many twentieth-century studies would make absolutely central, consciously or unconsciously agreeing with Cardinal Manning's dictum that all great questions are ultimately theological. That is as much as to say that Ranke wrote about the German Reformation before the Luther renaissance associated with such names as Albrecht Ritschl and, in the next generation, Karl Holl (1866–1926), author of a landmark essay, 'Was verstand Luther unter Religion?' (1917).[4] That essay, and much of Holl's other scholarly work, rescued a more authentic Luther from the liberalising Ritschlians and re-established the truly theological character, in the truest sense, of his religious outlook. It was no accident that this was the time when Karl Barth (1886–1968) was inviting Ritschl's pupil Adolf von Harnack to retire to the mountain-top with his reductively liberal version of the essence of Christianity (*Das Wesen des Christentums*, Leipzig, 1900), and of Protestantism. Meanwhile, from 1883, three years before Ranke's death, that great definitive edition of Martin Luther's *Werke* was under way, the *Kritische Gesamtausgabe*, always known as the *Weimarer Ausgabe*, or simply 'WA', its close on a hundred volumes the basis of a huge Luther industry in the twentieth century.

---

[3] A. G. Dickens and John Tonkin, *The Reformation in Historical Thought* (Oxford, 1985), pp. 167–75.
[4] In his *Gesammelte Aufsätze zur Kirchengeschichte*, 1. *Luther* (Tübingen, 1921), pp. 1–110.

Max Weber wrote, in 1904, with the British Academy still in its cradle, that 'the modern man is in general, even with the best will, unable to give religious ideas a significance for culture and national character which they deserve.'[5] We might say 'Amen', although at the cusp of the third millennium Islamic fundamentalism and other religiously inspired nationalisms are sounding a wake-up call. But this was a somewhat surprising judgment at the time, since Weber lived and did his intellectual work in a Germany whose politics were dominated by the cultural, and political, differences between Protestantism and Catholicism. His famous (or infamous) essay *The Protestant Ethic and the Spirit of Capitalism* was very far from inventing the thesis that there is a connection between Protestantism and Progress, which was a commonplace in the eigheenth century and a notion which Weber's friend Ernst Troeltsch went out on a limb in denying.[6] (But it may be that Weber's 'the modern man' was indeed quite specific, and referred to his colleague Werner Sombart, whose account of the origins of modern capitalism allowed too little room, in Weber's judgment, for the religious factor.[7])

But to leave that aside, if 'religious ideas' (which he was careful never to define, or at least to presume to explain) were increasingly marginal to Weber's 1904, what were their prospects to be in the remainder of the twentieth century, as church attendance declined to a shadow of its former self in all western countries (with the exception of the United States), an age of progressive de-Christianisation (in marked contrast to the situation in the continent of Africa, where the Christian future seems to lie)? Surprisingly, the answer to that question is that accounts of religion and of its history, whether in books or in television and radio programmes, have never been more popular with the general public. Religion, it appears, has become a spectator sport. So the prospects are now better than they have ever been for getting the religious factor in history right, and not least in the history of that huge process, or, in Rankean terms, series of events, the Reformation.

But it would be naïve in the extreme to suppose that to get the Reformation 'right', theologically, could ever be a simple matter of objective scholarly application. In the early twentieth century the rights and wrongs of the matters at stake were almost as hotly contested across what we might call the confessional 'line of control' as they had been in the sixteenth century

---

[5] Max Weber, *The Protestant Ethic and the Spirit of Capitalism*, trans. Talcott Parsons (London, with many impressions since 1930), p. 183.

[6] Ernst Troeltsch, *Protestantism and Progress*, trans. W. Montgomery (London, 1912).

[7] H. Lehman and G. Roth (eds.), *Weber's Protestant Ethic: Origins, Evidence, Contexts* (New York, 1993).

itself. That great nineteenth-century German Catholic Ignaz von Döllinger (1799–1890) was as fascinated by Luther as any Catholic could be, but his account was a pathology of its subject (*Die Reformation*, Regensburg, 1846–8; *Luther: Eine Skizze*, Freiburg im Breisgau, 1851). And then the Dominican Heinrich Denifle (1844–1905), archivist at the Vatican, launched an altogether more savage and passionate attack in his *Luther und Luthertum* (Mainz, 1904), a study in the sin of pride. The Jesuit Hartmann Grisar's three volumes on *Luther* (Freiburg and St Louis, 1911–12, translated in six volumes by E. M. Lamond as *Luther*, 1913–17) professed to employ more empathy, but the result was no less denigratory. It has been said that Grisar showered the great reformer 'with the sympathy appropriate to a diseased soul', where Denifle 'could manage only scorn and contempt for a degenerate wallowing in his bestiality'.[8] Yet these too were children of Ranke, at home in the archives, and they were far from making it all up; while their *odium theologicum* was a stimulus to Protestant scholarship which, as we have seen, was no less provoked by deep disagreements among Protestants themselves over what, essentially, their religion consisted of.

With the horrors of the Third Reich demonstrating what unimaginable depths de-Christianisation might reach, and with a communist regime soon to be installed in East Germany, it was time for Christians of all persuasions, Catholics and Protestants, to kiss and make up. Joseph Lortz's *Die Reformation in Deutschland* (Freiburg, 1939–40, translated by Ronald Walls as *The Reformation in Germany*, 2 vols., New York and London, 1968), was written in that spirit. Luther was now portrayed as morally and even theologically not guilty, an earnest Christian soul who was honestly misled by the errors and confusions of late medieval theology, the distortions of Nominalism, above all by the treacherous semi-Catholicism of Erasmian humanism. The Dutch-American historical theologian Heiko Oberman (a Corresponding Fellow of the Academy and a sad loss to scholarship when he died in 2001) made it his business to defend the Nominalist tradition against this rather subtle form of scapegoating, particularly in his *The Harvest of Late Medieval Theology: Gabriel Biel and Late Medieval Nominalism* (Cambridge, Mass., 1963); and in the published work of several of his pupils in the series published by Brill of Leiden, *Studies in Medieval and Reformation Thought*. In 1962, Erwin Iserloh published *Luthers Thesenanschlag: Tatsache oder Legende?* (translated as *The Theses Were Not Posted*, London, 1968). The Ninety-five Theses were not 'posted' on the

---

[8] Dickens and Tonkin, *The Reformation in Historical Thought*, pp. 200–2.

church door in Wittenberg in a mood of defiance, but respectfully 'posted' in the more ordinary and modern sense of being put in the post to Luther's archbishop, Albert of Mainz, material for consideration and discussion. But Luther was not heard. So the fault was more with the church than with him. (Iserloh may well have been right as to the facts of what happened, or did not happen, on 31 October 1517, but his ecumenically motivated argument seriously distorted the provocative rhetoric of the Theses.) In 1969, an American Catholic scholar, Harry McSorley, published *Luther: Right or Wrong?* (New York and Minneapolis, Minn.). McSorley concluded that Luther was right, and a good Catholic, at least so far as concerned his dispute with Erasmus about the freedom or bondage of the human will. This was some of the historical-theological infrastructure to the substantial agreement which theologians from both sides would reach on the crucial issue of justification, towards the end of the twentieth century.

At this point the reader may well want to ask what this discussion has had to do with British historical-theological scholarship, and with the British Academy; and whether 'Reformation' is no more than a synonym for Martin Luther. So far as the second question is concerned, as Robert Graves might have said, I am just coming to that. But the answer to the first is, until quite late in the piece, not much. To stay with Luther: the considerable dependence of English Protestantism on the Reformed ('Calvinist') Protestant tradition rather than on the Evangelical, Lutheran confessions, followed by the anti-Protestant reaction we know as Tractarianism, meant that for centuries after the Reformation Luther was almost inaccessible to English Christians, except for readers, like Samuel Taylor Coleridge, Julius Hare and F. D. Maurice, who were able to read and appreciate him in German. Until the nineteenth century only a tiny proportion of Luther's writings had been translated into English: notably the 'comfortable' theology of his Commentary on Galatians, first published in 1575, and important for John Bunyan and the Wesleys; and the version of the Table Talk launched by the worthy if somewhat eccentric Captain Henry Bell in 1646, which introduced Luther to Coleridge and Thomas Carlyle, who, of course, gave us his English version of 'Ein feste Burg'. But in 1883, to mark the fourth centenary of Luther's birth, the principal of King's College London, Henry Wace, and the professor of German, C. A. Bucheim, published the collection known as *Luther's Primary Works*, consisting substantially of the Ninety-five Theses and the three great treatises of 1520.

This was most of what would be known of Luther until well into the twentieth century, a valuable but restricted view. Between 1925 and 1930 James Mackinnon published four volumes on *Luther and the Reformation*, which opened a window for English readers on the beginnings of the Luther renaissance, but was otherwise an example of the kind of stodgy and unilluminating liberalism which will always let Luther slip through its fingers. There is no doubt that the countries where Lutheranism was the established, or a well-represented, religion were to have more interesting things to say about the subject. In Scandinavia there was Anders Nygren (*Agape and Eros*, so translated by P. S. Watson, London, 1938) and Gustav Aulen (*Christus Victor*, London, 1931), to which a fine study by the Swedish-reading English theologian P. S. Watson (*Let God Be God*, London, 1947) was indebted.[9] From the United States, and those fortresses of Lutheranism St Louis Missouri and Philadelphia, has come, since 1955, the American edition of Luther's *Works*, 55 volumes; but only two really outstanding studies of their author, Roland Bainton's *Here I Stand* (London, 1950) and Heiko Oberman's *Luther: Mensch zwischen Gott und Teufel* (Berlin, 1982), translated by Eileen Walliser-Schwarzbart as *Luther: Man between God and the Devil* (New Haven, Conn., 1989). Oberman dedicated his book to Bainton, 'who combined the gifts of profound penetration and powerful presentation to make Martin Luther come alive for generations of students of the Reformation, on both sides of the Atlantic'.

It no doubt says something about the English tendency in religion, undogmatic, moralistic, and, when educated, trained in the classical tongues, that the most substantial contribution to the study of the Reformation in the broader sense has been P. S. Allen's superb edition in twelve volumes of the letters of Erasmus, *Opus Epistolarum Desiderii Erasmi Roterodami* (Oxford, 1906–47). It was J. A. Froude, in the nineteenth century, who in his lectures on Erasmus said that if you wanted to see the sixteenth century, you should look at it through the eyes of Erasmus. Allen made it possible to look back through those hooded eyes to the elusive mind behind, at least for the competently Latinate. But soon the great series of *Collected Works of Erasmus* in English translation would begin to appear (Toronto, 1974–), making Erasmus accessible to a wider audience, which was also served by Craig R. Thompson in his edition in translation of the *Colloquies* (Chicago, 1965), and by Margaret Mann Phillips and Sir Roger Mynors in their edition of the *Adages* (Toronto, 1982–).

No sooner have we begun to escape from the clutches of Martin Luther than he claws us back, in the work of one of the two most distinguished academicians to have engaged with the subject, Gordon Rupp (1910–86). Rupp

---

[9] Gordon Rupp, *The Righteousness of God: Luther Studies* (London, 1953), pp. 33–6.

was a Methodist (he served as President of Conference and would have been a bishop if the Methodist–Anglican negotiations of the 1960s had come to fruition) who studied in Germany in the 1930s and, having begun to establish himself as a historian of the early English Reformation while fire-watching in the Second World War (*Studies in the Making of the English Protestant Tradition*, London, 1947), reaped the harvest of those studies in his Birkbeck Lectures in Cambridge (also 1947), published in 1953 as *The Righteousness of God: Luther Studies*. In the Preface, Rupp remarked disarmingly that 'in this country we have some leeway to make up in our study of the Continental Reformation, and particularly in awareness of the intricate field known as "Luther Research".' He also quoted a distinguished Norwegian Lutheran, Einar Molland, as warning him that on no account should he, as an Englishman, attempt to write a book on Luther.[10]

In *The Righteousness of God* the leeway was more than made up, although Rupp told one of his students that his book merely introduced Karl Holl to those who could not read German.[11] It is true that the theological guts of the book consists of 177 pages entitled 'Coram Deo', the vehicle for most of us of our knowledge of what Luther research was about. In 1951 came *Luther's Progress to the Diet of Worms*, still the best book to put into the hands of a student who wants to know, in not too many pages, how it all happened.

Rupp wrote in the midst of an ongoing Luther renaissance. The years of his greatest productivity were a time when the annually published *Luther-Jahrbuch* (1919–) could contain as many as a thousand titles; the period when an international conference on the tricky problem of Luther's 'Turmerlebnis' (his conversion to his mature and protestant theological position) ended inconclusively. Landmark studies included Ernst Bizer, *Fides ex auditu: Eine Untersuchung über die Entdeckung der Gerechtigkeit Gottes durch Martin Luther* (Neukirchen, 1961), Gerhard Ebeling, *Luther: Einführung in sein Denken* (Tübingen, 1964), translated by R. A. Wilson, *Luther: An Introduction to his Thought* (London, 1970), and Heinrich Bornkamm, *Martin Luther in der Mitte seines Leben* (Göttingen, 1979), translated by E. T. Bachmann, *Luther in Mid-Career* (London, 1983). Erik Erikson's *Young Man Luther: A Study in Psychoanalysis and History* (London, 1959) caused a minor sensation and was the source for John Osborne's play *Luther* (1965). But although it raised legitimate questions, the answers were a mere distraction, and Erikson contributed less to our historical understanding than a

[10] Ibid., pp. ix, xi.
[11] Memoir by P. N. Brooks, 'Gordon Rupp', *PBA* 80 (1991), 495.

scarcely noticed book by Ian Siggins, *Luther and His Mother* (Philadelphia, Penn., 1981).

Of greater significance for Reformation studies in general than the Luther renaissance has been the growing recognition that 'the Reformation' is no more than a back-projected historical construct, and that insofar as 'it' happened, it was a multi-headed hydra, a vast and complex congeries of movements led and orchestrated by a great many leaders and voices, who were neither simply derivative from Luther, nor to be judged, as orthodox Lutheran scholarship has tended to do, by the standard set by Luther. For example, it is not helpful to categorise the radical reformer Thomas Müntzer who perished in the Peasants' War of 1525, which his preaching helped to provoke, as a deviant Lutheran, since Müntzer's chiliastic ideology was derived from many sources, including the late medieval German mystical tradition to which Luther was himself indebted, and even from the Koran. Luther was not really entitled to tell the insurgent peasants that they had misunderstood his gospel, and that there was nothing Christian about their revolt. Yet it remains possible that if there had been no Luther we should never have heard of Müntzer, and that the Peasants' War would not have been such a cataclysmic event. Counterfactual history is a delightful but risky game.

At the same time, we have been told by those whose approach to the sixteenth century is more social, and cultural, than theological, that the notion of 'leadership', and especially of the leading role of theological propositions, is itself dubious. 'The Reformation' was characterised by convulsive popular movements which were often inspired by preachers and pamphleteers but which had their own momentum and rationale, manifested particularly in the phenomenon of iconoclasm.

When literature on the non-Lutheran Reformation was still scarce, Gordon Rupp contributed a valuable collection called *Patterns of Reformation* (London, 1969), studies of Luther's awkward colleague, Andreas Bodenstein von Karlstadt, Thomas Müntzer, Oecolampadius of Basle and Vadianus of St Gall. But English readers still had to wait until 1976 for an adequate account of the great Zürich reformer Huldreich Zwingli, the culmination of the lifelong interest in the subject of Professor George Potter of Sheffield, *Ulrich Zwingli 1484–1531* (London, 1976); while only in 2002 was a fully rounded English history of *The Swiss Reformation* published by Bruce Gordon (Manchester, 2002). Strassburg and its leading reformer Martin Bucer had been rather better served.[12] The annals of the Anabaptists

---

[12] Hastings Eells, *Martin Bucer* (New Haven, Conn., 1931); M. U. Chrisman, *Strasbourg and the Reformation* (New Haven, Conn., 1967); Tom Brady, *Ruling Class, Regime and Reform at Strasbourg*

have been attended to almost to excess, thanks to the proprietorial interest of the Mennonite denomination in the United States and the world-wide community of Baptists. There is a *Mennonite Quarterly Review* and a *Mennonite Encyclopedia* (Hillsboro, Kan., 1955–). Here the landmark study was G. H. Williams, *The Radical Reformation* (London, 1962), its title more all-embracing than the pejorative and denominationally restricted 'Anabaptists', even if 'radical' has distracting, even anachronistic resonances.[13]

John Calvin and Calvinism take us around the corner into another world. Here, as we should expect, the running has been made by Francophone scholarship, the place of the great Luther studies occupied by the seven volumes of Emile Doumergue's *Jean Calvin, les hommes et les choses de son temps* (Lausanne, 1899–1927). Accounts in English of Calvin and of this or that aspect of his thought and practical achievement abound, including biographies by T. H. L. Parker (Berkhamstead, 1977), William Bouwsma (New York, 1987) and Alister McGrath (Oxford, 1990), and a variety of aspectual studies.[14] But few books on Calvin and Calvinism in English attain the stature of memorable greatness, or have the capacity to expunge forever the mistakenly negative assessment of Calvin typically entertained by the liberal intelligentsia. If John T. McNeill's *The History and Character of Calvinism* (New York, 1954) is now somewhat dated, Francois Wendel's *Calvin: The Origins and Development of his Religious Thought* (trans. Philip Mairet, London, 1963) has stood the test of time.

In recent years the study of 'international Calvinism', the cross-borders transcendency of a kind of religious Comintern, has become a minor industry in its own right. If the collection edited by Menna Prestwich, *International Calvinism 1541–1715* (Oxford, 1985) (which included an invaluable essay on 'Calvinism in East Central Europe' by Robert Evans) was more of a collection of individual national studies than of 'internationalism', the emphasis has become increasingly and more genuinely international, as in the essays in Andrew Pettegree *et al.* (eds.), *Calvinism in Europe 1540–1620* (Cambridge, 1994).

Other continental European regions have never found themselves in the premier league of Reformation studies. Robert Evans's *The Making of the*

(Leiden, 1978); L. J. Abray, *The People's Reformation: Magistrates, Clergy and Commons in Strasbourg 1500–1598* (Oxford, 1985).

[13] See also C. P. Clasen, *Anabaptism: A Social History 1525–1618* (Ithaca, NY, and London, 1972).

[14] R. M. Kingdon, *Geneva and the Coming of the Wars of Religion in France, 1555–1563* (Geneva, 1956); William Monter, *Calvin's Geneva* (New York, 1967); Harro Hopfl, *The Christian Polity of John Calvin* (Cambridge, 1982); W. G. Naphy, *Calvin and the Consolidation of the Genevan Reformation* (Manchester, 1994).

Habsburg Monarchy, 1550–1700 (Oxford, 1979) is the necessary starting point for any onslaught on Eastern Europe. But now there is a collection edited by Karin Maag, *The Reformation in Eastern and Central Europe* (Aldershot, 1997). A helpful symposium on the Nordic Reformation is edited by Ole Grell, *The Scandinavian Reformation* (Cambridge, 1995). For the Netherlands, the easiest approach is through Alistair Duke's essays, *Reformation and Revolt in the Low Countries* (London and Roncoverte, W. Va., 1990).

While the biographies and monographs have continued to flow from the press (but precious few of them, we notice, authored by Fellows or Corresponding Fellows of the British Academy) the basic infrastructure of edited texts and documents has steadily grown, like concrete or tarmac laid across the landscape of the past. In addition to the great Weimarer Ausgabe of Luther's *Werke*, Calvin's *Opera* fill fifty-nine volumes of the *Corpus Reformatorum* and took thirty-seven years (1863–1900) to compile. Huldreich Zwingli needed but fourteen volumes of *CR*. For Martin Bucer, there are as yet incomplete series of *Opera Latina* and *Deutsche Schriften*. The correspondence of Calvin's successor in Geneva, Theodore Beza, runs to nine volumes (Geneva, 1960–78). Much attention is now concentrated on the project to publish all of the European-wide correspondence of Zwingli's successor at Zürich, Heinrich Bullinger, the most eloquent testimony of all to the pan-European scope of the Reformation.[15]

We need someone to rescue us from what is threatening to become a mere and tedious catalogue. Let that someone be A. G. ('Geoff') Dickens, some-time Foreign Secretary of the Academy, who turned his Birkbeck Lectures of 1969–70 into *The German Nation and Martin Luther* (London, 1974). Dickens had made his name as the leading historian of the English Reformation (and especially of the sixteenth-century religious history of his native Yorkshire) and he will figure very largely in our discussion of British Reformation Studies. But Dickens knew Germany, its language and its culture, well, and in 1947 had written a remarkable memoir of his career in the aftermath of the fall of the Third Reich, *Lübeck Diary*. In the 1974 book he brought to the subject of the German Reformation the same interest in the religion of the common man, as well as in the propagation of the Reformation, printers, pamphleteers and polemicists, which he had pioneered in his English studies. And there was a special emphasis on the Reformation in the imperial cities and other German towns. He wrote that he saw the creative and irrevocable events of the Reformation as a social event 'largely in

---

[15] 1972 was the starting point for the ongoing Zürich project to publish all of Bullinger's *Werke*.

terms of the urban Reformation, a movement effectually springing from the new dynamic added by the preachers, pamphleteers, and printers to the old turmoil of city politics'.[16] This owed a good deal to a paradigmatic study by Berndt Moeller, *Reichstadt und Reformation* (Gutersloh, 1962, translated by H. C. Erik Midelfort and Mark U. Edwards as *Imperial Cities and the Reformation*, Philadelphia, Penn., 1972), which represented the adoption of the Reform by a majority of the larger German cities as an expression of communal solidarity, in which the ruling magistrates followed rather than led: a 'Gemeindereformation'.

Dickens was happy to acknowledge that he owed no less a debt to his own pupil, the Australian Bob Scribner, 'whose recent researches at Erfurt and elsewhere have enabled me to sample vicariously the excitement of new discovery among German manuscript-sources'. If this was frank, Dickens's adaptation of the old saying about Luther and Nicholas Lyra was most elegant: 'Si Scribnerus non scripsisset, Dicens non dixisset.'[17] The half-dozen pages which Dickens was able to devote to Erfurt, Luther's university town, were in effect written by Scribner, emphasising the extreme complexity of the process of reformation in just one city, and they would be followed a year later by Scribner's own essay on the subject, 'Civic Unity and the Reformation in Erfurt'.[18] This rendered altogether more problematic and complicated the relatively simple model of urban reformation offered by Moeller, as did subsequent essays on 'Why was there no Reformation in Cologne?', 'Preachers and People in the German Towns', and 'Social Control and the Possibility of an Urban Reformation'.[19] Much of this work was subsequently brought together in a reflective and critical article 'Paradigms of Urban Reformation: Gemeindereformation or Erastian Reformation'.[20]

What should a social history of the Reformation consist of? I am not sure that this was a question which greatly troubled Geoff Dickens. But his answer might have been that it was what happened to ideas, partly propagated, partly generated in society, as they impacted on people's aspirations and needs. Although the name of Max Weber was anathema to him (he called the Protestant Ethic thesis 'a specious theory' and thought that 'nowadays no one

---

[16] A. G. Dickens, *The German Nation and Martin Luther* (London, 1974), p. v.

[17] Ibid., p. vi.

[18] *Past and Present*, 66 (1975), 29–60; reprinted, R. W. Scribner, *Popular Culture and Popular Movements in Reformation Germany* (London and Roncoverte, W. Va., 1987), pp. 185–216.

[19] All reprinted in ibid., pp. 217–41, 123–43, 175–84.

[20] In Leif Grane and Kai Horby (eds.), *The Danish Reformation Against its International Background* (Göttingen, 1990).

has a kind word for it'),[21] I think that he would have been quite comfortable with the Weberian formula that 'material without ideal interests are empty, but ideals without material interests are impotent'.[22] Bob Scribner, who was more consciously indebted to Weber's formula of 'elective affinity', can be said to have immersed himself in the social turmoil of the Reformation, in its language of speech, gesture and direct action, which Dickens only observed from the outside. He once told me that Dickens was like Moses, who was never permitted to enter the Promised Land but viewed it from the summit of Mount Pisgah.

The Promised Land was the Reformation seen from the other side of the tracks, and it was first extensively explored by Scribner in his monograph *For the Sake of Simple Folk: Popular Propaganda for the German Reformation* (Cambridge, 1981). Dickens's Reformation was something which happened in the spoken word of the sermon and in print, which for him certainly included the 'popular' print of the pamphlet, or 'Flugschrift', which the Reformation invented. It was almost, but not quite, Reformation by Print Alone. Scribner's Reformation was explored in the world of images, satirical cartoons, ritual and play, the world inhabited by the vast majority of six-teenth-century Germans who were illiterate, but not without their own agency. These studies were closely connected to the major historical enter-prise of explaining the most convulsive movement in early modern Europe, the Peasants' War of 1525,[23] and to understanding what it might mean to call the Reformation a movement, at times a mass movement.[24] When Bob Scribner, newly appointed to a chair in the Harvard Divinity School, died in 1998, the loss to Reformation studies in this enhanced sense was immeasur-able, since it had no longer been a case of England catching up with Germany. Scribner's research was as good as, and perhaps better than, anything hap-pening in either of the two Germanies of pre-1989, where he had been at home in the archives for many years. He was one of the most accomplished of the Fellows of the British Academy whom we never had.

---

[21] A. G. Dickens, *Reformation and Society in Sixteenth-Century Europe* (London, 1966), p. 178.

[22] H. H. Gerth and C. Wright Mills (eds.), *From Max Weber* (New York, 1948), pp. 63, 280.

[23] P. Blickle, *Die Revolution von 1525* (revised edn., Munich, 1981), Eng. trans. T. A. Brady Jr and H. C. Erik Midelfort, *The Revolution of 1525* (Baltimore, 1981); G. Franz, *Der deutsche Bauernkrieg* (11th edn., Darmstadt, 1977); T. Scott and B. Scribner (eds.), *The German Peasants' War: A History in Documents* (Atlantic Highlands, NJ, 1991); J. M. Stayer, *The German Peasants' War and Anabaptist Community of Goods* (Montreal, 1991).

[24] R. W. Scribner, 'The Reformation as a Social Movement', in his *Popular Culture and Popular Movements*, pp. 145–74.

But there are plenty of younger scholars to carry the torch of the 'new' social and cultural history of the Reformation. Gender plays a role to which Dickens's generation paid little attention. If Steven Ozment thought that the Reformation was on the whole a good time to be a woman, Lyndal Roper, another brilliant Australian historian of the sixteenth century, is quite sure that it was not.[25] Even more recent studies go somewhat beyond these parameters into the far frontiers of what might be called Reformation studies: witness Ulinka Rublack of the Faculty of History in Cambridge on 'Pregnancy, Childbirth and the Female Body in Early Modern Germany' (*Past and Present*, 150 [1996], 84–110), and Alison Rowlands on 'Witchcraft and Old Women in Early Modern Germany' (*Past and Present*, 173 [2001], 50–89).

Witchcraft! In the view of some sceptics the fixation on this undoubtedly fascinating topic has been somewhat disproportionate to its real extent and significance in early modern Europe. But that is not, could not be, to disparage the major intellectual achievement of several Fellows of the British Academy who have made a major impact on the subject: first Hugh Trevor-Roper's ground-breaking 'The European Witch-craze of the Sixteenth and Seventeenth Centuries',[26] and Sir Keith Thomas's *Religion and the Decline of Magic* (London, 1971), which was much more than a study of witchcraft and magic, indeed a whole map, or atlas, of early modern beliefs; then there was Thomas's pupil Alan Macfarlane with *Witchcraft in Tudor and Stuart England* (London, 1970), and something of a climax in a nearly definitive exploration of the mentality of the subject, Stuart Clark's *Thinking with Demons: The Idea of Witchcraft in Early Modern Europe* (Oxford, 1997).[27]

Another as it were collateral subject to have risen to a new prominence towards the end of the twentieth century has been martyrdom and martyrology, first treated as a pan-European, pan-confessional 'big picture' in Brad S. Gregory, *Salvation at Stake: Christian Martyrdom in Early Modern Europe* (Cambridge, Mass., 1999). And here the British Academy can declare an interest, for since 1992 it has sponsored a major project to publish,

[25] Steven Ozment, *When Fathers Ruled: Family Life in Reformation Europe* (Cambridge, Mass., 1983); Lyndal Roper, *The Holy Household: Women and Morals in Reformation Augsburg* (Oxford, 1989).

[26] Published in more than one form in more than one place, including the magazine *Encounter*. Best consulted in H. R. Trevor-Roper, *The Crisis of the Seventeenth Century: Religion, the Reformation and Social Change* (London, 1967), pp. 90–192.

[27] This is not to forget the important contributions from this country of those not (yet) Academicians: Robin Briggs, *Communities of Belief: Cultural and Social Tensions in Early Modern France* (Oxford, 1989), and *Witches and their Neighbours: The Social and Cultural Context of European Witchcraft* (London, 1996); and James Sharpe, *Instruments of Darkness: Witchcraft in England 1550–1750* (London, 1996).

electronically, a critical and scholarly edition of the four versions of the English martyrologist John Foxe's *Acts and Monuments* (popularly *The Book of Martyrs*) published in his lifetime, in 1563, 1570, 1576 and 1583. The effect will be to shed a wholly new light on Foxe's intentions, which developed and changed from edition to edition, his sources and his methods, and to render totally obsolete the nineteenth-century editions of Foxe, to which it is already acknowledged to be academically incorrect to refer. The first tranche of this edition can be expected to appear in 2004, and in the meantime the OUP has released a facsimile of *John Foxe's Book of Martyrs: 1583 Actes and Monuments* (Oxford University Press for the British Academy, 2001), a CD-Rom derived from a copy of the 1583 edition in the possession of Patrick Collinson. The Foxe Project has so far held four international colloquia on Foxe and related matters, and three volumes of the proceedings have been published.[28]

If A. G. Dickens would have been keenly interested in such dramatic progress in the understanding of a text which was of fundamental importance for his own understanding of the Reformation in England, he would have been no less pleased with an ever greater concentration on the history of print and of reading practices in the age of the Reformation. This has followed the seminal lead of the classic studies by Lucien Febvre and H.-J. Martin, *L'Apparition du livre* (Paris, 1958), English translation by D. Gerard, *The Coming of the Book: The Impact of Printing, 1450–1800* (London, 1976), and Roger Chartier, *The Cultural Uses of Print in Early Modern France* (Princeton, NJ, 1987); not to speak of the pioneering book by Elisabeth Eisenstein, *The Printing Press as an Agent of Change*, (2 vols., Cambridge, 1979). A particularly important collection of essays was published in 1990: *La Réforme et le livre: L'Europe de l'imprimé (1517–v.1570)*, edited by Jean-Francois Gilmont (Paris, 1990), translated by Karin Maag, *The Reformation and the Book* (Aldershot, 1998).

In 1946, Hubert Jedin, the historian of the Council of Trent,[29] asked the question in a book title, *Katholische Reformation oder Gegenreformation?* (Lucerne, 1946): was the renewal of Catholicism in the sixteenth and seventeenth centuries to be understood as Catholic Reformation or

---

[28] David Loades (ed.), *John Foxe and the English Reformation* (Aldershot, 1997); id. (ed.), *John Foxe: An Historical Perspective* (Aldershot, 1999); Christopher Highley and John N. King (eds.), *John Foxe and his World* (Aldershot and Burlington, Vt., 2002).

[29] Hubert Jedin, *Geschichte des Konzils von Trient*, 4 vols. (Freiburg im Bresgau, 1949–75), 2 vols. trans. E. Graf, *A History of the Council of Trent* (London, 1957, 1961); Hubert Jedin, *Krisis und Abschluss des Trienter Konzils 1562/3* (Freiburg im Bresgau, 1964), translated as *Crisis and Closure of the Council of Trent* (London, 1967).

Counter-Reformation; was it merely reactive to the Protestant Reformation or a kind of Reformation in its own right, springing from the same sources of renewal which nourished both great movements? The question was neatly side-stepped by A. G. Dickens in the second sentence of his textbook, *The Counter Reformation* (London, 1968): 'Was it not quite obviously both?' 'Counter-Reformation' was another of those historical constructs of the nineteenth century which, as H. O. Evennett observed in his Birkbeck Lectures of 1951, tend to imprison those who employ them within their own categories. As we have seen, Ranke continued to pluralise the concept and ended his *Deutsche Geschichte im Zeitalter der Reformation*: 'Auf das Zeitalter der Reformation folgte das der Gegenreformationen.'[30]

More recent historians have escaped from these trammels, as they have attempted to understand what was happening to Western Christian civilisation on the cusp of the modern world without being tied by the strings of 'Reformation' and 'Counter-Reformation'. Thus Jacques Delumeau in *Le Catholicisme entre Luther et Voltaire* (Paris, 1971), English translation, *Catholicism Between Luther and Voltaire* (London, 1978), stressed the essential similarity of the two movements, which were both about an almost primary Christianisation of the rural population of medieval Europe which had comprehended very little of the innerness of the Christian faith and its obligations. On the other hand, John Bossy, while he scouted that very dubious proposition, has argued in many of his writings that this was an age when, in all the divided confessions, consciences were activated and the essential duties defined in the Ten Commandments were internalised as never before; while regretting the necessity of using the Reformation/Counter-Reformation terminology. In *Christianity in the West 1400–1700* (Oxford, 1985), Bossy wished to jettison 'Reformation' (while knowing very well that he could not), not only because it tended to suggest that a bad form of Christianity was being replaced by a good one, but because it was 'too high-flown to cope with actual social behaviour, and not high-flown enough to deal sensitively with thought, feeling, or culture'.[31] In his own Birkbeck Lectures of 1995 he set 'Counter-Reformation' on one side, and vowed to use even 'reform' sparingly, if at all. 'On the Catholic side at least, and from where I shall be standing, we can readily get along without them.'[32]

---

[30] H. Outram Evennett, *The Spirit of the Counter-Reformation*, ed. John Bossy (Cambridge, 1968), pp. 2, 5.

[31] John Bossy, *Christianity in the West 1400–1700* (Oxford, 1985), p. 93.

[32] John Bossy, *Peace in the Post-Reformation* (Cambridge, 1998), p. 2. See an important article by Bossy, 'The Counter-Reformation and the People of Catholic Europe', *Past and Present*, 47 (1970).

Until Evennett's Birkbecks of 1951 such speculative and hermeneutical philosophisings never arose. We knew what the Counter-Reformation was, and we dealt with it in the stodgy, positivist English way. In B. J. Kidd's *The Counter-Reformation* (Oxford, 1933), the subject was neatly dissected into its distinct and substantial parts: Spanish and Italian proto-reform, the new religious orders, above all the Society of Jesus, the Inquisition and the Index, the Council of Trent, the Counter-Reformation papacy and its achievements, Catholic mission, all those saints. Dickens's *The Counter Reformation* was more deft, but did not depart from these time-honoured parameters.

Just as Virginia Woolf said that *Middlemarch* was the first English novel written for grown-ups, so we might say that the Counter-Reformation first became an interesting subject, for English readers, with the publication of H. Outram Evennett's Birkbecks, *The Spirit of the Counter-Reformation*, which John Bossy brought to the press (Cambridge) posthumously in 1968, with a Postscript of his own. Evennett was another fine Fellow of the British Academy who, for some reason, never was. Although he spent some of his time writing rather nasty little pamphlets about the Reformation for the Catholic Truth Society, as well as playing the piano to a professional standard, he was also the author of a historical classic, *The Cardinal of Lorraine and the Council of Trent* (Cambridge, 1930).

But in *The Spirit of the Counter-Reformation* Evennett hardly mentioned Trent, for he believed that 'spiritual rebirth and enlightenment . . . are not achieved at ecumenical councils'. The 'spirit' of the thing in his view was 'the evolutionary adaptation of the Catholic religion and of the Catholic Church to new forces both in the spiritual and material order', ensuring 'the survival into the post-medieval world of a still-persuasive, still-expanding, world form of Christianity under a single centralised control'. That applied even to the Counter-Reformation popes, who were doing for a new sort of Church what the 'new monarchies' were doing for the state. But the essence was spirituality, and that had most to do with the Jesuits, who were also more about embracing than fighting the general tendencies of the age.[33]

In his Postscript, Bossy suggested that these adaptations only postponed the historic declension of Catholicism, and that Evennett ought to have paid more attention to elements of morbidity which he believed the Counter-Reformation to have contained. This may have been in large part a consequence of a crisis in Mediterranean civilisation, a shift of the centre of gravity to an Atlantic world destined to be predominantly Protestant. The

---

[33] Evennett, *The Spirit of the Counter-Reformation*, p. 3 and *passim*.

Counter-Reformation was a Latin invention, not readily transportable north of the Alps, except in the lands where the Habsburgs and Wittelsbachs ruled. (As for France, it had its own rather special kind of Counter-Reformation, Gallican rather than ultramontane.) But why was that? In his own Birkbecks, published as *Peace in the Post-Reformation* (Cambridge, 1998), Bossy focused on what has been a lifelong interest of his: the role of religion in maintaining the social peace, what in *Christianity in the West* he had called 'the social miracle' (for brotherhood always implied otherhood). Religion as social reconciliation he now called 'the moral tradition', which in different places and at different times adapted forms as various as blood-feuds in Corsica and an inordinate love of organ-playing in Vienna. St Charles Borromeo of Milan was not very interested in this type of Catholicism (we might say that if Harnack defined Christianity as 'the Soul and its God', the paradigmatic Borromeo understood Catholicism as 'the Catholic and the Church'). The conclusion was pessimistic, for Bossy came close to saying that the decline of the moral tradition may account for the decline of Christianity in the West. However, it has to be said that by no means all other scholars working in the field have accepted Bossy's thesis about a radical move from community-centred towards interiorised religion. See, for example, *Penitence in the Age of Reformations*, edited by Katharine Jackson Lualdi and Anne T. Thayer (Aldershot, 2000). And as for the declension of modern Catholicism, the name of Mark Twain is bound to come to mind.

We come, almost finally, to the British Isles, a somewhat special case in both the history and the historiography of the Reformation. In 1591, an Italian Dominican wrote a history of the religious changes in England which he called *Storia Ecclesiastica della Rivoluzione d'Inghilterra*.[34] Only very recently have we begun to refer again to the English Reformation as a revolution, perhaps assisted by the modern Chinese concept of a 'cultural revolution', which undoubtedly it was.[35] For roughly the first half of the existence of the British Academy it was not acknowledged that anything so drastic had happened in sixteenth-century England. A benign continuity was held to be the distinguishing mark of the English constitution, and of its religious culture. Anglicanism held that the religious legislation of Henry VIII had merely corrected some of the more flagrant abuses of the medieval ecclesiastical

---

[34] Quoted in Nicholas Tyacke, *Aspects of English Protestantism c.1530–1700* (Manchester, 2001), p. ix.

[35] See Patrick Collinson, 'Protestant Culture and the Cultural Revolution', in *The Birthpangs of Protestant England: Religious and Cultural Change in the Sixteenth and Seventeenth Centuries* (Basingstoke, 1988), pp. 94–126.

system. Henry himself had established 'Catholicism without the Pope', and if Edward VI and Elizabeth had gone somewhat beyond that, the doctrines enshrined in the Thirty-nine Articles were not to be confused with something called 'continental Protestantism', a formulation tinged with some of the negativity of continental lavatories and continental railway systems, at a time when such things were best avoided. England was both 'Catholic and Reformed'. A map of sixteenth-century religious confessions required a different shading for England, which was 'sui generis', 'Anglican'. Such were the perceptions and perspectives of a religious world in which the modernised form of Tractarianism articulated in *Lux Mundi* (1889) was in the ascendant, and looked down its nose at evangelical and nonconformist tendencies. That learned but robustly Protestant medievalist G. G. Coulton, who used to take his daughters off to the Alps, appropriately shod, was almost a figure of fun, disparaged by Hilaire Belloc as the 'remote and ineffectual don/That dared attack my Chesterton'.

Such appreciations of the English Reformation are not quite a thing of the past. In a major study published from Oxford in 1993, *English Reformations: Religion, Politics, and Society under the Tudors*, Christopher Haigh, a student of Christ Church, insisted, all over again, that the English Reformations (and the pluralisation was significant, for in Haigh's perception the subject consisted of a somewhat disconnected series of political and religious reformations) 'were not the Reformation, exported across the Channel and installed in England by Luther, Calvin, and Co. Ltd. Whatever such English Reformations had in common with Reformation on the Continent, they were not the same thing: not the Reformation.'[36] For those who know Haigh and his work, and where he is coming from, here was no more than an accidental convergence with the Anglo-Catholic scholarship of, for example, Clifford Dugmore, who in his *The Mass and the English Reformers* (London, 1958), a book which secured him the chair of Ecclesiastical History at King's College London, had argued that Cranmer and Ridley had derived their eucharistic doctrines directly from St Augustine and the continuing anti-Ambrosian tradition in the medieval Church, with minimum indebtedness to the continental reformers; a position rendered untenable by the subsequent scholarship of Peter Newman Brooks and of Diarmaid MacCulloch.[37]

---

[36] Christopher Haigh, *English Reformations: Religion, Politics, and Society under the Tudors* (Oxford, 1993), p. 13.

[37] P. N. Brooks, *Thomas Cranmer's Doctrine of the Eucharist: An Essay in Historical Development* (2nd edn., Basingstoke, 1992); Diarmaid MacCulloch, *Thomas Cranmer: A Life* (New Haven, Conn., and London, 1996); Diarmaid MacCulloch, *Tudor Church Militant: Edward VI and the Protestant Reformation* (London, 1999).

Where was Haigh coming from? He was in full reaction against a version of the English Reformation which had been hailed as nearly definitive when first published in 1964: *The English Reformation* by A. G. Dickens. This was an anti-Dickensian 'revisionism', and, like most historiographical revisionisms, productive of a debate which has continued for twenty years, taking us by now into the secondary (or tertiary?) phase of 'post-revisionism': a strenuous and serious attempt, only occasionally and accidentally polemical, to interpret an exceptionally complicated series of events and changes more or less correctly, not a matter of scoring points.

It would be an exaggeration to say that the publication of Dickens's *English Reformation* invented the subject, although it would be correct to say that it had lain dormant for many years. Dickens himself had prepared the way for his magisterial study by twenty years of scholarship in the archives preserved in York Minster, one of the richest sources anywhere in Europe for understanding the detail of sixteenth-century religious change, work productive of many articles and the essays collected in *Lollards and Protestants in the Diocese of York* (Oxford, 1959). But Hull, where Dickens was working, was a far-away university of which we knew little (Philip Larkin was not yet a household name), and when I myself began work on a doctoral thesis on Elizabethan Puritanism in London in 1952, I was aware of very few other young historians who would have defined their field as either 'Reformation studies' or 'Puritan studies'. It is true that much attention had been paid to the dissolution of the English monasteries, but mostly to what happened to the monastic property and to the religious as 'personnel'.[38] Only economic history had yet made any significant penetration of the fortress of English historiography which flew the flag 'Political and Constitutional'. Only the third volume of Dom David Knowles's magisterial *The Religious Orders in England* (Cambridge, 1961) dealt with almost all conceivable aspects of the subject.

The English Reformation was still a subset of political and constitutional history. F. M. Powicke, taking time out from his day job as a medievalist to write *The Reformation in England* (London, 1941), had declared it to be 'an act of state', 'a parliamentary transaction'. What those acts and transactions consisted of constituted a large part of the life-work of the dominant Tudor historian of his day, Sir Geoffrey Elton. The constitutional architecture, laid

---

[38] See G. Baskerville, *English Monks and the Suppression of the Monasteries* (London, 1937); and, on property, H. J. Habakkuk, 'The market for monastic property, 1539–1603', *Economic History Review*, 10 (1958), 362–80, and much secondary discussion in the context of the 'Rise of the Gentry' controversy of the 1950s.

out in *The Tudor Constitution* (Cambridge 1960; 2nd edn., 1982), Elton attributed to his hero, Thomas Cromwell. The legislative conception and achievement were dealt with in *The Tudor Revolution in Government* (Cambridge, 1953), implementation in *Policy and Police: The Enforcement of the Reformation in the Age of Thomas Cromwell* (Cambridge, 1972). Generations of A-level students learned their English Reformation from Elton's heavily political *England Under the Tudors* (London, 1955; 2nd edn., 1974). 'What matters most in the story is the condition, reconstruction, and gradual moulding of a state—the history of a nation and its leaders in political action ... Other matters—economic, social, literary, military [and religious?]—are dealt with but more succinctly: this could not be helped.'[39]

When the Catholic historian Philip Hughes published his three-volume *The Reformation in England* (London, 1950–4), this could not be called 'revisionism', since there was little enough to revise. It was Dickens who established a new mould on which later revisionists have inflicted damage. His book of 1964, discovered, or rediscovered, since as he himself was happy to admit, it was all in Foxe, the character of the English Reformation as both a social and a religious event, much more than 'an act of state'. His revisionist critics should have paid more attention to the balance which he was at great pains to preserve. It was his prime concern to give space to 'ordinary men and women', whom earlier historians had allowed 'to fall and disappear through the gaps between the kings, the prelates, the monasteries and the prayer books'. But he also wrote that it was necessary 'not to lose grip of the conventional themes, for governments and leaders remain important; the story will not cohere in their absence'. So Dickens resented any suggestion that he had had a naïve ambition to write the story entirely 'from below'.[40]

But Dickens had an Achilles heel, and it was not a trivial injury, or handicap. His researches, and perhaps also his Protestant-Anglican leanings which had perhaps moved some way in a Protestant direction from Keble College origins (for, as Catholic historians are liable to complain, why should we call them 'Catholic historians' and regard all others as historians *sans épithète?*), disposed him to believe that Protestantism was an idea whose time had come, that 'the old religion' was losing its grip on the hearts and minds of most people, and was not even defended with much conviction by the clergy themselves. The native Wycliffite heresy, so-called Lollardy, had prepared the

---

[39] G. R. Elton, *England Under the Tudors*, 2nd edn. (London, 1974), p. vi.
[40] A. G. Dickens, *The English Reformation*, 2nd edn. (London, 1989), p. 11. For some of the views reported here, see also Dickens's *Reformation Studies* (London, 1982) and essays in *Late Monasticism and the Reformation* (London and Rio Grande, OH, 1994).

ground for an invasive new religion, rather like the Resistance in occupied Europe in the 1940s. And 'Anticlericalism' was a potent ideology, almost sufficient in itself to explain the success of the Reformation.

Both these 'factors' have received attention. Lollardy is another minor academic industry, but towering over many other studies is the work of Anne Hudson, the major authority on the manuscript literature of Wycliffism, which she has uncovered in Czech as well as English repositories (evidence in itself of the interrelation of the Wycliffite and Hussite movements). Hudson is the editor of the Lollard sermon cycle,[41] and author of a major study, *The Premature Reformation: Wycliffite Texts and Lollard History* (Oxford, 1988). Whereas many historians have emphasised the eclectic incoherence of Lollard beliefs, Hudson, on the contrary, has discovered a remarkable consistency of what Lollards knew and taught with the basic elements of John Wycliffe's teaching. Equally important work on later Lollardy and its connection with the beginnings of English Protestantism has been done by the historian of heretical and Protestant iconoclasm, Margaret Aston.[42] But the Lollard–Protestant link can never be an explanation of why and how the English Reformation happened. It was a necessary argument employed by Foxe and other early Protestant propagandists, countering the charge that their religion was a 'new broached' thing, to point to the Lollards as a 'secret multitude of true professors' long before the Reformation. If the Lollards had not existed it would have been necessary to have invented them. And Aston suggests that to a considerable extent that is what happened.[43] Hudson's significantly titled *The Premature Reformation* concludes with an analysis of the failure of Lollardy to become a Reformation on a national scale (which its correlate in Bohemia, Hussitism, did), the reasons including intrinsic weaknesses in its religious culture as well as in the lack of the kind of political encouragement and support which Protestantism secured from Henry VIII and his successors. The revisionists, Scarisbrick and Duffy (see below), found it possible almost entirely to omit the Lollards from their accounts of the religion of England on the cusp of the Reformation.

---

[41] *English Wycliffite Sermons*, vol. 1, ed. Anne Hudson (Oxford, 1983); and see also her *Selections from English Wycliffite Writings* (Cambridge, 1978).

[42] See some of the essays in Aston's *Lollards and Reformers: Images and Literacy in Late Medieval Religion* (London, 1984), and *Faith and Fire: Popular and Unpopular Religion, 1350–1600* (London and Rio Grande, OH, 1993); and for her work on English iconoclasm and the Reformation, *England's Iconoclasts: Laws Against Images* (Oxford, 1988), and *The King's Bedpost: Reformation and Iconography in a Tudor Group Portrait* (Cambridge, 1993).

[43] Margaret Aston, 'Lollardy and the Reformation: Survival or Revival?', in *Lollards and Reformers*, pp. 219–42.

Anticlericalism is a problematical category, the very term imported, perhaps anachronistically, from the politics of late nineteenth-century France, where it was virtually a synonym for anti-Catholicism. Whatever we may call it, hatred of the clergy, and especially of the higher, princely clergy, was undoubtedly a major factor in the continental Reformation, and especially in Germany.[44] But while English ecclesiastical archives contain as many cases of friction between clergy and laity as the historian may care to sample, especially concerning the payment of tithe, there is insufficient evidence of a generalised anticlericalism to allow this to be an adequate explanation for what happened to the English Church and its clergy in the Reformation.[45]

A. G. Dickens's account of the state of English Catholicism in the early sixteenth century and of the almost predictable triumph of Protestantism, 'a formidable and seemingly ineradicable phenomenon',[46] was first challenged by J. J. Scarisbrick, the biographer of Henry VIII (and, yes, Scarisbrick is a Roman Catholic) in his Ford Lectures of 1982, published as *The Reformation and the English People* (Oxford, 1984). Scarisbrick opens with a manifesto statement which has become famous: 'On the whole, English men and women did not want the Reformation, and most of them were slow to accept it when it came.' But the validity of that judgment remained to be justified by an exploration of 'traditional religion' and its demise on the grand scale, in a book which in its entirety has become no less famous, *The Stripping of the Altars: Traditional Religion in England c.1400–c.1580* (New Haven, Conn., and London, 1992), by Eamon Duffy, who is another Catholic historian. It now appears that what was to become, by the early seventeenth century, the most virulently anti-Catholic country in Europe began the sixteenth century as one of the most Catholic, a society which invested, heavily and literally, in the fabric and the institutions of its piety.[47] *Pace* Dickens, the old religion did not die of natural causes, and forensic revisionists, led by Duffy and Haigh, are regarding the death as suspicious. According to Haigh, 'it was the break

---

[44] I. A. Dykema and H. Oberman (eds.), *Anticlericalism in Late Medieval and Early Modern Europe* (Leiden, 1993).

[45] Or so according to Haigh in 'Anticlericalism and the English Reformation', in id. (ed.), *The English Reformation Revised* (Cambridge, 1987), pp. 56–74. Dickens responded in 'The shape of anticlericalism and the English Reformation', in E. I. Kouri and T. Scott (eds.), *Politics and Society in Reformation Europe* (Basingstoke, 1987), reprinted in *Late Monasticism and the Reformation*, and restated in the second edition of *The English Reformation*, 'Anticlericalism, Catholic and Protestant', pp. 316–25.

[46] See especially Dickens's essay 'Early Protestantism and the Church in Northamptonshire', in *Late Monasticism and the Reformation*.

[47] And see, more recently, Eamon Duffy's micro-historical study, *The Voices of Morebath: Reformation and Rebellion in an English Village* (New Haven, Conn., and London, 2001).

with Rome which was to cause the decline of Catholicism, not the decline of Catholicism which led to the break with Rome.'[48]

But decline and die it did, a strange death, and what has been called 'the riddle of compliance' remains to be solved—and perhaps never will be. If Scarisbrick's 'English men and women' really believed that their dead parents and children were in Purgatory, but could be helped out of that condition by the prayers and propitiatory masses in which they invested so heavily, the rich by the endowment of chantries, the rest through membership of gilds and fraternities, how did they submit so rapidly and without major protest to the confiscation by the state of the assets which sustained those religious practices? A fair analogy from the modern world might be the suppression of hospices for the terminally ill, or the rendering of private pension schemes worthless. The critical historian may be tempted to suspect that there was a difference between belief in Purgatory and belief in the money which paid for masses, to the extent that hard-headed 'English men and women', who, Scarisbrick conceded, and with regret, were prepared to benefit from the dissolution of the monasteries, were reluctant to send good money after bad. He is also almost bound to attempt the following syllogism: If the Protestant Reformation was as totally unacceptable and violent a change as it has been represented, it could not have happened. But it did happen. Ergo, it was not a totally unacceptable and violent change. Enter the post-revisionists, to whom we shall pay attention presently.

But in the meantime, revisionism was threatening to divert attention unduly from the beginnings and development of English Protestantism, something which certainly was taking place in the second quarter of the sixteenth century. Dickens's mistake, an error of his methodology as well as of surmise, was to suppose that to document this process would be to explain how it was that the nation as a whole became predominantly Protestant. Wherever local researches, of the kind which he himself had pioneered, established the presence of pockets of evangelical religion, pins were stuck in the map, and soon the map was fairly bristling with pins.[49] But the same local researches have by now established that almost everywhere, and not only in the conservative county most studied by Christopher Haigh, Lancashire, but in East Anglia and

---

[48] Haigh, *English Reformations*, p. 28.

[49] Dickens was particularly dependent on a *Biographical Register of Early English Protestants c.1525–1558*, compiled by John Fines, published from A to C by the Sutton Courtenay Press (Appleford, 1981), and the remainder made available by the West Sussex Institute of Higher Education: a deceptive source, since the criterion for inclusion was a criminal (heretical) record, and it can neither be assumed that all those included were 'Protestants', nor that all early Protestants are included.

even London itself, these were no more than minority pockets, up to the early years of Elizabeth I.[50] But the formation of these evangelical cells, which became what in Scotland were called 'privy kirks' in the reign of Mary and which were somewhat uneasily absorbed into an established Protestant Church under Elizabeth, is an important subject in its own right, now attended to in a collection of essays, *The Beginnings of English Protestantism*, edited by Peter Marshall and Alec Ryrie (Cambridge, 2002). The formation of what Gordon Rupp called 'the English Protestant Tradition' is a story which begins with William Tyndale and his New Testament (1526), a neglected subject until Tyndale's quincentenary in 1994, an event marked by many publications, including David Daniell, *William Tyndale: A Biography* (New Haven, Conn., and London, 1994). But as early evangelicalism gelled into the Protestantism of the Prayer Book and Articles, the definitive works are Diarmaid MacCulloch's *Thomas Cranmer: A Life* (New Haven, Conn., and London, 1996) and his Birkbeck Lectures of 1998, *Tudor Church Militant: Edward VI and the Protestant Reformation* (London, 1999). The theology of the English Reformation, often misconstrued, especially in its beginnings, has been greatly clarified by Carl R. Trueman in *Luther's Legacy: Salvation and English Reformers 1525–1556* (Oxford, 1994).

MacCulloch is also the author of a book on *The Later Reformation in England, 1547–1603* (2nd revised edn., 2001) and, in the opinion of the present writer, this 'later reformation' was the real Reformation, as the ministry of the church became, by degrees, a Protestant preaching ministry, which was not until the 1570s in the more developed and progressive regions of the country, the early 1600s elsewhere. This was the thrust of many of Patrick Collinson's publications, including his *The Elizabethan Puritan Movement* (London and Berkeley, Calif., 1967; Oxford, 1990), *The Religion of Protestants: The Church and English Society 1559–1625* (Oxford, 1982), and *The Birthpangs of Protestant England: Religious and Cultural Change in the Sixteenth and Seventeenth Centuries* (Basingstoke, 1988). The absorption and interpretation of Protestant religion in rural communities, in the secondary

---

[50] Christopher Haigh, *Reformation and Resistance in Tudor Lancashire* (Cambridge, 1975); Caroline Litzenberger, *The English Reformation and the Laity: Gloucestershire, 1540–1580* (Cambridge, 1997); John Craig, *Reformation, Politics and Polemics: The Growth of Protestantism in East Anglian Market Towns, 1500–1610* (Aldershot and Burlington, Vt., 2001); Susan Brigden, *London and the Reformation* (Oxford, 1990).

and tertiary stages of the reformation process, is a subject presided over by Margaret Spufford and her pupils.[51]

Post-Reformation English Catholicism became, in the second half of the twentieth century, a thickly sown historiographical minefield. In 1976 John Bossy partially broke with the time-honoured tradition of martyrological and hagiographical recusant history in his *The English Catholic Community 1570–1850*, which came at the subject from its devotional and sociological inside. But it was still the 'community', an essentially recusant community, which was the object of study, and the origins and nature of that community, whether in continuity with the Catholic past or, as Bossy argued, substantial discontinuity, was a bone of contention.[52] Other historians have demonstrated that the world of resistant English Catholicism was considerably larger and more complicated than any neatly defined recusant community: especially Alexandra Walsham in *Church Papists: Catholicism, Conformity and Confessional Polemic in Early Modern England* (2nd edn., Woodbridge, Va., 1999) and Michael Questier in *Conversion, Politics and Religion in England, 1580–1625* (Cambridge, 1996). The relation of the Church of England to Catholicism on the polemical and apologetical front is the subject of a major study by Anthony Milton, *Catholic and Reformed: The Roman and Protestant Churches in English Protestant Thought 1600–1640* (Cambridge, 1995).

What do we mean by 'post-revisionism' in English Reformation Studies? It is a recognition that Christopher Haigh's dictum that towards 1600 England was becoming a Protestant nation but not a nation of Protestants,[53] and much of what Collinson has written, employ too exalted a notion of what it might have meant to be a Protestant, almost equating Protestantism with Puritanism; and making arduous entry qualifications of literacy, an intelligence capable of coping with difficult theological propositions, and a preparedness to adopt the 'singular', often antisocial, lifestyle of the Puritans. A more realistic portrayal of the culture, the mentalities and the moral universe of what might be called non-virtuoso Protestantism will be found in Alexandra Walsham's *Providence in Early Modern England* (Oxford, 1999), and Tessa Watt's *Cheap Print and Popular Piety 1550–1640* (Cambridge, 1991); while the complexity of the relations between Puritanism and the world it inhabited is penetrated in Peter

---

[51] Margaret Spufford, *Contrasting Communities: English Villagers in the Sixteenth and Seventeenth Centuries* (Cambridge, 1974); Margaret Spufford (ed.), *The World of Rural Dissenters, 1520–1725* (Cambridge, 1995).

[52] Christopher Haigh, 'The Continuity of Catholicism in the English Reformation', in *The English Reformation Revised*, pp. 176–208.

[53] Haigh, *English Reformations*, pp. 279–80. But see, more recently, Haigh's article, 'Success and Failure in the English Reformation', *Past and Present*, 173 (2001), 28–49.

Lake's *The Boxmaker's Revenge: 'Orthodoxy', 'Heterodoxy' and the Politics of the Parish in Early Stuart London* (Manchester, 2001) and *The Antichrist's Lewd Hat: Protestants, Papists and Players in Post-Reformation England* (New Haven, Conn., and London, 2002).

Towards the end of the twentieth century, it became the fashion to subsume the history of the constituent parts of the British Isles in a newly conceived 'British History', a necessary procedure if one is to make any sense of the Civil War of the mid-seventeenth century, more properly called 'the War of the Three Kingdoms'. Sensitivity to religious interaction between England, Wales, Scotland and Ireland characterises Diarmaid MacCulloch's chapter on 'The Change of Religion' in *The Short Oxford History of the British Isles: The Sixteenth Century*, edited by Patrick Collinson (Oxford, 2002).

It is not clear that historiographical 'Britishness' will survive either the devolutionary disintegration of the United Kingdom or ever greater integration in continental Europe, and it is neither desirable nor likely that the religious histories of England, Wales, Scotland and Ireland will be subsumed and lost to sight in some British ecclesiastical pudding. However, we can be sure that future historians of England will no longer feel free to neglect the histories of those other parts of these Atlantic Isles which have had so much impact on the whole, and on the wider world, not least in this period of the Reformation. Wales has found a superb historian of its sixteenth century in Glanmor Williams, the author of the more or less definitive *Wales and the Reformation* (Cardiff, 1997). Scotland has I. B. Cowan's *The Scottish Reformation: Church and Society in Sixteenth Century Scotland* (London, 1982); and another version by the sometime Historiographer Royal of Scotland, Gordon Donaldson. Donaldson was a somewhat quirky Episcopalian whose account of the Scottish Reformation downgraded the Presbyterian element and stressed the considerable conformity with England which characterised the Kirk in the era of John Knox.[54] The generation of Cowan and Donaldson has some notable successors, who have expanded the scope of the subject. One thinks especially of Margo Todd's *The Culture of Protestantism in Early Modern Scotland* (New Haven, Conn., and London, 2002), and the outstandingly important *Holy Fairs: Scottish Communions and American Revivals in the Early Modern Period* (Princeton, NJ, 1989) by the sociologist Leigh Eric Schmidt, which demonstrates that the religion of revivalism which spread to Ireland and North America in the eighteenth century had its origins, in part, in Scottish Presbyterianism, and specifically in

---

[54] Gordon Donaldson, *The Scottish Reformation* (Cambridge, 1960).

the great and solemn open-air communions typical of that tradition, which had their not-so-solemn periphery, famously characterised by Robert Burns as 'holy fairs'. Schmidt may want to remind us, if we want to be reminded, that this chapter on Reformation studies ought to have a section devoted to the secondary and tertiary Reformation histories of the North American continent. But of the making of books on that subject there has been no end and it is, regretfully, omitted.

What of what we are no longer allowed to call the Celtic Fringe? It is not often that a scholarly article tells us something that we absolutely did not know. But in 1994 Jane Dawson in an essay called 'Calvinism and the Gaidhealtachd in Scotland' (in Pettegree, Duke and Lewis's *Calvinism in Europe 1540–1620*, Cambridge 1994) told us about the remarkable success of Calvinist Protestantism in establishing itself in the Western Isles. Soon godly ministers wearing long hair and little more than the plaids which failed to cover all aspects of the subject were scandalising their southern, Scots-speaking brethren when they met together in synod. There was as yet no Gaelic Bible, but the evangelism of the Kirk appropriated the oral, bardic culture of the region, and so successfully that Franciscan friars who arrived in the Hebrides found that they were not welcome. Why was this situation not replicated across the Northern Channel, in Ireland? The problem of the Irish Reformation, why it failed, is a dense historiographical thicket, 'revisionists' against nationalist historians, which it would be wise not to penetrate towards the end of this substantial chapter. Enough perhaps to refer to the magisterial account of the subject in T. W. Moody, F. X. Martin, and J. F. Byrne (eds.), *A New History of Ireland*, 3. *Early Modern Ireland, 1534–1691* (2nd edn., Oxford, 1991).

Twentieth-century scholarship on the Reformation achieved a kind of closure in, first, the wide-ranging historiographical survey published in 1985 by A. G. Dickens and John M. Tonkin, *The Reformation in Historical Thought*. And then, in 1996, appeared from the Oxford University Press in New York *The Oxford Encyclopedia of the Reformation*: 4 volumes, 1,977 pages, 1,226 articles by 472 scholars in 24 countries. Combining, as it does, the theological and social–cultural approaches which have woven their texture throughout this chapter, it is unlikely that such a thing could have been published much before the 1990s, or will ever be repeated.

CHAPTER SEVEN
The long eighteenth century

JANE SHAW

Historians writing about the eighteenth-century Church of England at the turn of the twentieth century still largely laboured under the Victorians' assumption that the eighteenth-century church and its theology were worth little attention or, even, regard. Attempts to throw off this inheritance and see the eighteenth-century church in a more positive light were still double-edged, as the introduction to John Overton and Frederic Relton's 1906 history of the church from the accession of Queen Anne to the end of the eighteenth century suggests:

> The time is now past when the period from the death of Queen Anne down to the end of the eighteenth century, if not to the beginning of the Oxford movement, was regarded as practically a blank page in English church history. It has at least been recognised that a period which produced such clergymen as Joseph Butler and Daniel Waterland, William Law and Samuel Horsley, and such lay men as Edmund Burke and Samuel Johnson, William Wilberforce and William Stevens, must have been at any rate a period worth studying. It is true that a lover of the English church cannot study it without a blush. It is a period, for instance, of lethargy instead of activity, of worldliness instead of spirituality, of self-seeking instead of self-denial, of grossness instead of refinement. There was a grovelling instead of a noble conception of the nature and function of the Church as a Christian society, an ignoring instead of a conscientious and worthy carrying out of the plain system of the Church, work neglected instead of work well done.[1]

In this case, Overton was attempting to rewrite some of his own pessimistic conclusions in his earlier work, such as the well-known volume of 1878, written with Charles Abbey, *The English Church in the Eighteenth Century*, but the result is still ambivalent.

In a period when Anglicanism was the primary focus of ecclesiastical historians, little, if any, attention was paid to the history of nonconformity except

---

[1] John H. Overton and Frederic Relton, *The English Church from the Accession of George I to the end of the Eighteenth Century (1714–1800)* (London, 1906), p. 1.

insofar as it was seen to have an impact on Anglican attitudes after Toleration in 1689. Furthermore, ecclesiastical historians largely dismissed the theology of the period, still under the influence of Mark Pattison's famous contribution to *Essays and Reviews* (London, 1860), 'Tendencies in Religious Thought in England, 1688–1750' and Sir Leslie Stephen's agnostic *History of English Thought in the Eighteenth Century* (London, 1876) which reiterated the weakness of religious thought in the face of the Enlightenment challenge. Theologians were seen as having been no match for the emerging Enlightenment philosophy.

For historians writing at the beginning of the twenty-first century, the religious culture of eighteenth-century Britain is seen as having been thriving in many places, and certainly complex and interesting; while the Enlightenment—as an intellectual and cultural movement—is regarded as largely English in origin and strongly intertwined with religion. In short, over the last century an enormous sea change has occurred in how we think about the place of religion in eighteenth-century Britain. This chapter will attempt to sketch out this change, looking first at histories of the eighteenth-century Church of England, then turning to changing views of the Enlightenment's relationship to religious thought and practice in Britain, and finally examining the newer fields of study that have emerged, especially in the latter part of the twentieth century, and that have begun to shape our understanding of eighteenth-century British religious culture in new ways.

The eighteenth-century Church of England

Why were the Victorians so pessimistic about the eighteenth-century church and when was that pessimistic view first challenged? Victorian churchmen saw the eighteenth century as a period of decline for the church, playing little part in the lives of most people, staffed by inattentive and morally lax clergy who provided deeply boring worship. However, such a view of the eighteenth-century Church of England was in part motivated by a desire on the part of these churchmen to present their own revival movements—the Oxford Movement and the Evangelical revival—in a favourable light. The eighteenth century was a 'blank page' both for high churchmen, who looked back to the golden age of the Caroline divines and bemoaned the expulsion of the Non-jurors, and for evangelicals who disliked the reasonable or practical Christianity which was a hallmark of the era and led to the established Church's rejection of Wesley's revival. Victorian high churchmen and evangelicals, in their different ways, saw themselves living—providentially—at a time 'when the church once more rose to the height of her destiny' after a period in which 'the spirit of worldliness' had begun to infect the church and, as wealth had flowed into Britain, 'a new generation arose which knew not God in his great works' as one Tractarian apologist put it.[2]

That this attitude continued well into the twentieth century is illustrated by the work of Paul Moore and F. L. Cross who, in their joint American and English project of providing a book of documents illustrating the thought and practice of the Church of England, *Anglicanism* (London, 1935), chose to focus only on the period 1594–1691. This was a work that in some way launched the modern study of 'Anglicanism' as a phenomenon—which has, ever since, been largely promoted by American Episcopalians. Moore and Cross focused—as many studies before and afterwards have—on the seventeenth century because it was thought that it was then that the true spirit of Anglicanism developed. Moore wrote in his opening essay, 'The Spirit of Anglicanism':

> For the *terminus ad quem* the year 1691 has been chosen as dating the schismatic activity of the Non-Jurors, and as marking a notable break in English ecclesiastical history. As a result of that schism we see on the one side a succession of writers who in the main, though with some lack of balance, follow the true line of development from Hooker and Laud, but whose place in an exposition of Anglicanism might be challenged on the ground that they can hardly be called members of the National Church. On the other side the theology of those who continued within the Establishment becomes irrelevant to our purpose for another reason. The extrusion of so large a body of the more Catholic elements left the rest of the Church for several decades a prey to the rising tide of rationalism and deism, so that the apologetic literature of the orthodox took, perforce, a new turn.[3]

In this, Moore was not only expressing a rather romantic view of Anglicanism and the usual view of the eighteenth century, but also echoing the implicit sentiments of the Oxford Movement whose dislike of the interference of the state and whose rejection of the label 'Protestant' for the Church of England drew on the Non-jurors' work, though this was not always acknowledged in their own tracts.

However, in the first decades of the twentieth century, the prevailing picture of the eighteenth-century church was gradually challenged: J. Wickham Legg, for example, in his *English Church Life from the Restoration to the*

---

[2] William Palmer, *A Narrative of Events Connected with the Publication of the Tracts for the Times* (London, 1883), pp. 30, 31 and 19.

[3] Paul Elmer Moore, 'The Spirit of Anglicanism', in Paul Elmer Moore and Frank Leslie Cross, *Anglicanism: The Thought and Practice of the Church of England, Illustrated from the Religious Literature of the Seventeenth Century* (London, 1935), p. xix.

Tractarian Movement (London, 1914) looked at the piety of laypeople and the activities of the clergy. The most serious challenge to the Victorian view came in Norman Sykes's landmark work of 1934, *Church and State in England in the XVIIIth Century*, given as the Birkbeck Lectures at Cambridge in 1931–3, in which he noted that 'the history of the Hanoverian church has suffered especial severities at the hands of the disciples of the High Church revival.'[4] Sykes had begun to rehabilitate the eighteenth century with his biography *Edmund Gibson, Bishop of London 1669–1748: A Study of Politics and Religion in the Eighteenth Century* (London, 1926), one of quite a number of biographies, varying in quality, of Anglican bishops written in the middle of the century.[5] In his Birkbeck Lectures he sought to make a contribution to the 'complete history of the eighteenth-century Church', which he considered, as yet, unwritten. The strength of his work was in his use of archival and manuscript sources, by which he tackled head-on the assumption that the Hanoverian episcopate and clergy were lazy, worldly and self-seeking, looking at the work of the bishops and clergy through such materials as visitation records, diaries and letters. Sykes argued that the bishops and clergy were dutiful in fulfilling their parochial and pastoral duties. Acknowledging the existence of abuses such as pluralism and non-residence amongst some bishops, Sykes compared the records of eighteenth-century bishops with those of some of their predecessors, such as Lancelot Andrewes, so admired by the Tractarians, whom he showed to be pluralists on a greater scale; he noted too that bishops needed to be present in London for a large part of the year in order to discharge their duties in the Lords. He attempted to measure the achievements of the eighteenth-century clergy in accordance with the standards of their own day, noting the new pressures they faced: Toleration, urbanisation and industrialisation. He may be criticised for emphasising the organisational, practical and institutional, rather than spiritual, aspects of church life, but he would, perhaps, have defended this, for practical Christianity was the hallmark of the eighteenth-century church, 'testified in conduct and works'.[6]

While Sykes continued to write on the eighteenth-century church, most notably in a biography of William Wake (*William Wake: Archbishop of Canterbury, 1657–1737*, Cambridge 1957), and in his 1958 Ford Lectures at

---

[4] Norman Sykes, *Church and State in England in the XVIIIth Century* (Cambridge, 1934), p. 5.

[5] See, for example, E. Carpenter, *Thomas Sherlock, 1678–1761* (London and New York, 1936); id., *Thomas Tenison, Archbishop of Canterbury: His Life and Times* (London, 1948); A. Tindal Hart, *The Life and Times of John Sharp, Archbishop of York* (London, 1949); C. E. Whiting, *Nathaniel Lord Crewe, Bishop of Durham (1674–1721) and his Diocese* (London and New York, 1940).

[6] Sykes, *Church and State*, p. 425.

Oxford, *From Sheldon to Secker: Aspects of English Church History, 1660–1768* (Cambridge, 1959), his work had a rather limited impact in the middle decades of the twentieth century, despite his teaching career at the Universities of London and Cambridge (where he was Dixie Professor of Ecclesiastical History, before becoming Dean of Winchester in 1958). Several historians, including his student, G. V. Bennett, developed some of the political and ecclesiastical aspects of his research, writing about some eighteenth-century prelates and the relationship between church and state. The 1960s and 1970s therefore saw the publication of several books that melded political and ecclesiastical history: G. F. A. Best's *Temporal Pillars: Queen Anne's Bounty, the Ecclesiastical Commissioners and the Church of England* (Cambridge, 1964); Geoffrey Holmes's *The Trial of Doctor Sacheverell* (London, 1973) and G. V. Bennett's work on Francis Atterbury, Bishop of Rochester, *The Tory Crisis in Church and State, 1688–1730* (Oxford, 1975). These works did not, on the whole, develop Sykes's optimistic view of the eighteenth-century church; in fact, they often focused on the crises in church and state, especially in Queen Anne's reign, and were influenced by the keen interest in the development of party politics in the late seventeenth and early eighteenth century, then a flourishing area of research amongst British historians. For example, in examining the Sacheverell affair, in which a Tory Anglican parson was impeached by the Whigs following a seditious sermon he preached in St Paul's Cathedral on Guy Fawkes Day in 1709, Holmes suggested that this sequence of events was both a symptom of a political society deeply divided by party antagonisms and of 'the malaise which had stricken the Church of England by Sacheverell's day'.[7] Thus the emphasis in much of this work was on the ways in which the late seventeenth- and early eighteenth-century Church of England attempted to rest in an uneasy alliance between high churchmen and the 'Latitudinarians'—those who proposed a reasonable and practical Christianity compatible with the intellectual tenor of the day—and the moments of crisis when that uneasy alliance failed.

At the same time, there was a new influence on British history: Marxism. Historians such as Christopher Hill and E. P. Thompson began to look at history from 'the bottom up'. While their primary focus was not by any means the study of ecclesiastical history in the long eighteenth century, their work in advancing the study of social history had a lasting impact on this field. It broke open the almost exclusive focus on Anglicanism within British history, as Hill looked at the religious radicals of the civil war period and their

---

[7] Holmes, *The Trial of Doctor Sacheverell*, p. 1.

continued influence to the end of the seventeenth century, and Thompson examined the significance of Methodism in the making of the English working classes in the late eighteenth century, and it put the focus on the religious lives of ordinary women and men.[8] Less positively, religion was often seen as a retrograde force, but—paradoxically—as not much of a force at all in the eighteenth century in Britain.

It was against this Marxist historiography that J. C. D. Clark wrote his *English Society 1689–1832* (Cambridge, 1985) in which he argued that the Church of England remained a vital force in British politics and society throughout the long eighteenth century. He sought to show that the Marxists had, ironically, reinforced the Victorian view of the eighteenth century by denying the significance of religion—specifically Anglicanism—and both the Victorians and Marxists had therefore failed to understand the endurance of the *ancien régime* in Britain, maintained by a trinity of power: monarch, established Church and nobility. Over and against a historiography which had emphasised the significance of the revolution of 1688–9 as a turning point, the influence of Locke's philosophy and the development of Enlightenment notions of liberty, Clark argued that the old values of hierarchy, paternalism and deference remained deeply important in maintaining stability in eighteenth-century society, undergirded by the Anglican establishment, so that only with the repeal of the Test and Corporation Acts in 1828, which gave nonconformists the possibility of exercising formal power in politics, and the subsequent reform of Parliament, was the Anglican hegemony challenged and the *ancien régime*'s death-knell sounded. In short, England remained a 'confessional state' until 1832.

Clark's work has been much debated and, in some quarters much criticised, and it undoubtedly has weaknesses—for example, in focusing almost exclusively on the political élite and in paying scant attention to the means by which the practice of piety was the socially cohesive force that he assumes it was for the majority of the population. However, the impact of his work has been such that political historians of this period now find it hard to avoid a discussion of religion as a serious social and political force. This is indicated, for example, in Linda Colley's widely influential book, *Britons: Forging the Nation 1707–1837* (New Haven, NJ, and London, 1992), in which she emphasises the role of Protestantism in creating a new form of British identity in the eighteenth century, though her failure to

---

[8] See, for example, Christopher Hill, *The World Turned Upside Down: Radical Ideas during the English Revolution* (London, 1972), and E. P. Thompson, *The Making of the English Working Class* (London, 1963).

distinguish between different forms of Protestantism (including the rivalry between the Church of England and nonconformity, and sometimes between different forms of nonconformity) in the creation of that identity has garnered criticism.

While religion increasingly came to be seen as a significant factor in eighteenth-century British life by political historians writing in the 1980s, ecclesiastical historians had yet to provide (or at least publish) the real evidence for the state of the church and religious life at local level. Half a century after Norman Sykes's pioneering research on the eighteenth-century Church of England, the continuation of this archival work was finally taken up by a number of research students in the 1980s, and the fruits of this research were published throughout the 1990s, and continue to be published. A milestone volume in the initial publication of that research was *The Church of England c.1689–c.1833: From Toleration to Tractarianism* (Cambridge, 1993), edited by John Walsh, Colin Haydon and Stephen Taylor. This volume emphasised regional diversity and observed that such local variations could lead to both optimistic and pessimistic conclusions about the state of the eighteenth-century Church of England. In their introduction, Walsh, Haydon and Taylor noted especially the north–south divisions, and the town–country divisions, in shaping those variations.

Undoubtedly, local studies of the Church of England led to a more nuanced picture of the state of church life at every level of society. Mark Smith, in *Religion in Industrial Society* (Oxford, 1994), his study of Oldham and Saddleworth from 1740 to 1865, suggests that, contrary to many assumptions, in this industrial area the Church of England met the challenges of urbanisation and industrialisation with a hearty vigour. Jeremy Gregory, in his study of Canterbury, *Restoration, Reformation and Reform 1660–1828: Archbishops of Canterbury and their Diocese* (Oxford, 2000) looked especially at the pastoral role of the clergy and the ways in which they saw themselves continuing or even fulfilling Reformation ideals in their pastoral activities. Gregory maintains that, despite new difficulties such as Toleration, the Church in the diocese of Canterbury was remarkably successful at fashioning itself into an agent of religious and political stability after the Restoration. This picture is reiterated in research on other dioceses. W. M. Jacob in his study of parish life in Norfolk, *Lay People and Religion in the Early Eighteenth Century* (Cambridge, 1996), points to the effective teaching by the clergy through methods later adopted by the Methodists, suggests that there existed a flourishing lay piety, and remarks on the willingness of the laity to take responsibility for their churches in the form of gifts for the repair and improvement of parish churches.

By the end of the twentieth century, there existed a critical mass of local studies of the eighteenth-century Church of England,[9] such that a number of conclusions about the relative vitality of church life may be drawn: the clergy were, on the whole, pastorally effective in the face of new challenges; clergy were aware of the ignorance of some of their parishioners and were willing to develop and use new catechising methods to teach the orthodox (i.e. Anglican) faith. This was regarded as a vital tool by which people might be attracted away from Dissent, and its success, in certain dioceses, is measured by strong numbers for Confirmation. Nevertheless, the fact remained—and bishops especially were all too aware of this, though they varied in their responses to it—that toleration of Dissenters marked a turning point for the established Church. While in the past, some historians have regarded that turning point in terms of decline, it is perhaps better seen as the advent of real 'competition' amongst the churches. W. M. Jacob points to the ways in which, if the Church of England did 'decline' in influence in the mid- to late eighteenth century, it was in large part because of factors outside its own control and the competition it faced, not just from the nonconformists but also from other forms of entertainment and activity which were now more widely available, such as the theatre.

Not surprisingly, then, Sykes's optimistic picture does not necessarily hold true for the whole church. Some historians have found that in certain dioceses the picture is rather mixed. Donald Spaeth, in his study of the relationship between parson and parishioners in the diocese of Salisbury from 1660 to 1740, *The Church in an Age of Danger*, highlights the piety of parishioners and their keen involvement in church life in the early eighteenth century, while pointing to the ways in which the clergy themselves acted in a defensive manner and refused to give the laity the fuller participation in worship which they desired. So, for example, while in certain local situations, use of the church courts is a sign of effective pastoral care, in other contexts such as

---

[9] As well as those works mentioned, see for example: J. Albers, ' "Seeds of Contention": Society, Politics and the Church of England in Lancashire, 1689–1790', (Yale University Ph.D. thesis, 1988); M. Cross, 'The Church and Local Society in the Diocese of Ely, *c*.1630–*c*.1730' (University of Cambridge Ph.D. thesis, 1991); V. Barrie-Curien, *Clergé et pastorale en Angleterre au XVIIIe siècle: le diocese de Londres* (Paris, 1992); M. Snape, ' "Our Happy Reformation": Anglicanism and Society in a Northern Parish, 1689–1789' (University of Birmingham Ph.D. thesis, 1994); J. Jago, *Aspects of the Georgian Church: Visitation Studies of the Diocese of York, 1761–1776* (Cranbury, NJ, 1997); J. Chamberlain, *Accommodating High Churchmen: The Clergy of Sussex, 1700–1745* (Urbana, Ill., and Chicago, 1997). This is by no means an exhaustive list but suggests some of the areas and topics researched. For a much fuller list, see the select bibliography at the end of Jeremey Gregory and Jeffrey S. Chamberlain (eds.), *The National Church in Local Perspective: The Church of England and the Regions, 1660–1800* (Woodbridge, Va., 2003).

that delineated by Spaeth, it might indicate conflict between parson and parishioner. Spaeth also makes the perceptive observation that it is difficult to study popular religious observance after the Restoration: 'Clergymen were unable to understand non-observance as anything but dissent or irreligion, which they regarded as two sides of the same coin. It is hard for historians to avoid sharing their assumptions.'[10]

As in the case of the English Reformation, so with the eighteenth-century church: local variation is the key to understanding the complexity of the picture. Our understanding of the two periods is not, of course, unrelated. As Reformation historians have, in the last few decades, given us an increasingly more accurate picture of the ways in which Reformation thought and practice in sixteenth-century Britain did and did not make headway in different contexts and localities, so they have broken down a notion of a sixteenth- and early seventeenth-century Reformation 'Golden Age' against which the eighteenth-century church used to measure up so badly. As this archival evidence for local variation builds up, in the sixteenth, seventeenth and eighteenth centuries, Gregory's idea of a long Reformation, extending into the long eighteenth century, becomes increasingly appealing. Continued archival research is vital, and a recent collection of essays, edited by Jeremy Gregory and Jeffery S. Chamberlain, *The National Church in Local Perspective* (see n. 9 above) stands as a testament to that archival work. In their Introduction to this collection of essays, Gregory and Chamberlain note the influence of that volume about the Church of England in the long eighteenth century edited by Walsh, Haydon and Taylor, even though it was intended, on publication in 1993, only as an interim report on the state of research in this field. In publishing their own volume a decade later, they describe it as a further report on progress. As such a report, it stands as a testament to a field that is flourishing at the beginning of the twenty-first century.

Religion and the Enlightenment

The agnostic attitudes of several late Victorians, such as Leslie Stephen, overshadowed early twentieth-century British intellectual histories of the Enlightenment period. Their attitudes came to be reinforced by a prevailing view amongst intellectual historians that took the French model of the

---

[10] Donald A. Spaeth, *The Church in an Age of Danger: Parsons and Parishoners, 1660–1740* (Cambridge, 2000) p. 173.

Enlightenment as the norm. Thus, studies of the relationship between religion and the Enlightenment in the first half of the twentieth century worked with two presuppositions: first, that the Enlightenment posed a great challenge to religious belief, and that in that challenge lay the roots of secularisation and modernity; and secondly, that England did not really have an Enlightenment. 'The Enlightenment' as a movement was seen, initially, as French, followed by the German 'High Enlightenment'.

The 1930s saw the publication of several significant and influential intellectual histories of the Enlightenment, all by scholars outside the British Isles: Carl Becker's *The Heavenly City of the Eighteenth-Century Philosophers* (1932); Ernst Cassirer's *The Philosophy of the Enlightenment* (1932) and Paul Hazard's *La Crise de la conscience Européenne, 1680–1715* (1935). All of these works focused on French—and sometimes German—Enlightenment thinkers. The attitudes of the French *philosophes*, rightly seen by historians as antagonistic towards the Roman Catholic Church, tended to be thrown back onto any discussions of the English deists and radicals. Reason, newly emphasised and newly defined, was assumed to be in conflict with religion. This trend has continued in the historiography in the second half of the twentieth century, as indicated by the work of Peter Gay, in his *The Enlightenment, an Interpretation: The Rise of Modern Paganism* (1966) and subsequent works, which dominated the field in the 1970s.

While Becker's work questioned the notion of the Age of Reason, in general these writers saw the Enlightenment period as the great turning point in the history of ideas, the moment when human beings removed God from the centre of things and put themselves in God's place. The opening of Hazard's 1935 work epitomises this:

> Never was there a greater contrast, never a more sudden transition than this. An hierarchical system ensured by authority; life firmly based on dogmatic principle— such were the things held dear by the people of the seventeenth century; but these—controls, authorities, dogmas and the like—were the very things their immediate successors of the eighteenth century held in cordial detestation. The former were upholders of Christianity; the latter were its foes. The former believed in the laws of God; the latter in the laws of nature ... The most widely accepted notions, such as deriving proof of God's existence from universal consent, the historical basis of miracles, were openly called in question. The Divine was relegated to a vague and impenetrable heaven somewhere up in the skies. Man and man alone was the standard by which all things were measured. He was his own raison d'être. His interests were paramount.[11]

---

[11] Paul Hazard, *The European Mind: The Critical Years, 1680–1715* (Cleveland, OH, and New York, 1935) pp. xv, xvii.

This view was prevalent not just amongst historians but continued amongst theologians well into the mid-twentieth century. Paul Tillich wrote in 1959: 'Since the beginning of the eighteenth century God has been removed from the power field of man's activities. He has been put alongside the world without permission to interfere with it because every interference would disturb man's technical and business calculations.'[12]

There were, however, some exceptions to this attitude: Marjorie Hope Nicholson pursued the question of the impact of Descartes in England in the 1650s, in an important article published in 1929, and in 1930 she published her edition of the correspondence between the philosophers Anne Conway and Henry More, prompting an interest in the Cambridge Platonists of the mid-seventeenth century and their influence on the Latitudinarians of the eighteenth century in developing a reasonable religion which could stand up to both atheism and 'enthusiastic' religion. Rosalie Colie further developed some of these ideas, looking at both the Dutch Arminians and Cambridge Platonists, in her *Light and Enlightenment* (Cambridge, 1957).

A challenge to the Gallic view of the Enlightenment also came in 1954, when Ronald N. Stromberg published his *Religious Liberalism in Eighteenth-Century England*. The subjects of this study were the 'freethinkers', those who wished to make Christianity thoroughly 'rational', men like John Toland the deist, who argued against the supernatural and any form of metaphysical revelation at all, and those who questioned the Trinitarian nature of God and divinity of Christ. In this he observed that England led the way in 'freethinking' and, through Deism, Arianism and Socinianism, pioneered modes of thinking that would later spread to France and to America. The ideas of Franklin and Jefferson, Voltaire, Rousseau and Robespierre could all be traced back to the English deists, he argued. Nevertheless, Stromberg still saw this English thought in terms of a great challenge to the supremacy of the 'Christian epic' and—not surprisingly, given when he was writing—he worked with a view of the Church of England as too complacent and weak to meet adequately this intellectual attack.

Interest in the deists and freethinkers continued within intellectual history in the following decades but it was only in the 1990s that Justin Champion and Peter Harrison, among others, introduced an important new strand of thinking about the relationship between religion and the English Enlightenment. Against a historiography which had primarily seen the

---

[12] Paul Tillich, *Theology of Culture*, ed. Robert C. Kimball (Oxford, 1959), p. 25.

freethinkers as a wholesale threat to religion, Champion argued, in *The Pillars of Priestcraft Shaken: The Church of England and its Enemies* (Cambridge, 1992), that the freethinkers, especially the deists, in their attacks on priestcraft and corrupt religion did not necessarily seek to abolish or overthrow the national church but rather to reform Christianity and develop a civil theology. In suggesting this, Champion sought to break down the assumed division between religion and reason that had dominated scholarship for so long, and to show the ways in which reason was used in the service of religion. Working with similar ideas about the significance of religion within the English Enlightenment, Peter Harrison attempted to demonstrate, in his work *'Religion' and the Religions in the English Enlightenment* (Cambridge, 1990), how the English deists used reason to formulate pan-cultural notions of religion, and thus located the roots of the modern comparative study of religion in the English Enlightenment.

This recent understanding of the complex intertwining of religion and reason in late seventeenth- and early eighteenth-century thought has coincided with, and reinforced, a new emphasis on the *English* Enlightenment, on the English Enlightenment as decidedly *religious* in tone and position and, amongst some, the suggestion of a distinctly Anglican Enlightenment. A new emphasis on the significance and primacy of the English Enlightenment has, in part, emerged from historical scholarship that has attempted to be more precise about the varying national contexts of the Enlightenment, analysing it as a movement with different impulses and timing from country to country, as, for example, in Henry May's important work, *The Enlightenment in America* (New York and Oxford, 1976) and, subsequently, the essays edited by Roy Porter and M. Teich, *The Enlightenment in National Context* (Cambridge, 1981). Porter in one of the last major books he wrote before he died, *Enlightenment: Britain and the Creation of the Modern World* (London, 2000), argued a strong case for a distinctly English, or even British, Enlightenment—to which the French *philosophes* themselves looked (back) for inspiration—which was not necessarily an intellectually coherent movement, and decidedly not a monolithic movement, but rather, he suggested, a set of sensibilities which had practical outcomes and ultimately made Britain the birthplace of the modern. The variety of debates about religion in the long eighteenth century played a part in the formation of those Enlightenment sensibilities, and toleration was central to them. This move towards seeing a series of different Enlightenment impulses occurring across Europe has produced the important and original work of synthesis by Jonathan I. Israel, *Radical Enlightenment: Philosophy and the Making of Modernity 1650–1750*

(Oxford, 2001), in which both Britain and theology take their due place alongside other countries and other philosophical impulses in his analysis.

Several historians have argued that the impact of the deists and rationalist thinking in general in the eighteenth century in Britain has been exaggerated. This was certainly J. C. D. Clark's argument in positing that the old, hierarchical order of things lasted throughout the long eighteenth century. However, the emphasis can be shifted away from an exclusive focus on the deists without necessarily arriving at Clark's politically conservative conclusions. For example, it has been suggested that we should continue to study the dynamic interplay between religion and reason in the English Enlightenment, but beyond the rather narrow confines of the debates between Anglican clergy and the small group of deists and radical thinkers. B. W. Young turns instead to the 'sense of pervasive controversy *within* the clerical culture of early and mid-eighteenth-century England, as opposed to that between clergy and free-thinkers' in his *Religion and Enlightenment in Eighteenth-Century England: Theological Debate from Locke to Burke* (Oxford, 1998). He seeks to show that a whole series of religious apologists, from Daniel Waterland to William Law, and most especially perhaps Bishop William Warburton, helped form English Enlightenment ideas, but have been subsequently neglected. The most interesting intellectual debates of the century were not between free-thinkers and Anglicans but between different Anglicans. In his account, Young therefore provides a genuinely theological basis to the history of English Enlightenment philosophy, giving a new prominence to figures neglected from the nineteenth century onwards. Peter Nockles in *The Oxford Movement in Context: Anglican High Churchmanship, 1750–1857* (Cambridge, 1994) has also revived the fortunes of a number of high churchmen of the mid-to-late eighteenth century in whom he sees the origins of the Tractarian movement, thus revising one of the Tractarians' own myths about themselves.

B. W. Young is, to some extent, building on the work of J. G. A. Pocock who, in a series of articles and more recently in his two-volume work on the 'Enlightenments' of Edmund Gibbon, *Barbarism and Religion* (Cambridge, 1999), has suggested the possibility of an Anglican Enlightenment. Pocock argues against the notion of 'The Enlightenment', that is, a unified and universal intellectual movement, proposing instead—like Roy Porter—a series of enlightenments, of which the English Enlightenment was one. He argues too for the distinctly Protestant nature of that English Enlightenment, stressing the fact that Enlightenment in England was intimately bound up with the unique nature of the Church of England. Hence, he reads Gibbon's *Decline and Fall* as 'a great Enlightened history of Christian theology' arguing for its distinctly English character and suggesting that this 'did not necessitate the presence of [French] *philosophes*'.[13] This is a bold claim, perhaps not sustainable for the whole of *Decline and Fall*, but it is an important claim, not least for its suggested directions for future research.

The outcome of this scholarship as it has developed in the last decade or so has been to break down some of the barriers between intellectual and ecclesiastical history. Neither discipline can be so easily ghettoised when such a sweeping rethink of the relationship between (the) Enlightenment and religion has begun to prevail. Furthermore, the last two or three decades of the twentieth century witnessed a number of other trends in the historical profession and the humanities as a whole, such as the development of social and cultural history, the study of gender, ethnicity and popular culture, and a more inter-disciplinary approach overall, which has led and continues to lead historians to produce a more complex picture of religious events and beliefs in the eighteenth century. The final section of this chapter explores those trends.

Rethinking Enlightenment, rethinking secularisation: religion and culture

The focus of Enlightenment studies has, for most of the twentieth century, been ideas: the philosophies of the period. Cassirer's landmark work of 1932 saw the Enlightenment as a period defined by the lives of two philosophers: Leibniz (1646–1716) and Kant (1724–1804). Writing in the early 1930s, his stress was, not surprisingly, on the *rationality* of the Enlightenment. The Enlightenment, or, perhaps rather, enlightenments, have continued to garner attention for their impact on how we think about the self and how we think about the role of reason in negotiating and making sense of the world, not only from historians but from philosophers and theorists, each interpreting the Enlightenment(s) afresh for their generation. Theodor Adorno and Max Horkheimer wrote their *Dialectic of Enlightenment* (1947) in the aftermath of a Second World War that had dashed further to pieces Enlightenment visions of human progress and the hope of a common civilisation founded on reason. In their analysis of the dialectic of the Enlightenment they pointed to its paradoxes: in emphasising rationality, Enlightenment philosophers paved the way for the disenchantment of the world, but in exerting rationality as the only 'reasonable' means of understanding the world (sweeping aside such possibilities as divine revelation)

[13] J. G. A. Pocock, *Barbarism and Religion*, 1. *The Enlightenments of Edmund Gibbon, 1737–1764* (Cambridge, 1999), p. 8.

there was, ironically, an intolerance of all else and therefore there always lurked within the Enlightenment mentality the possibility of violence. Adorno and Horkheimer thus suggested that the Holocaust (and, for that matter, we might add earlier horrors such as the bloody events of the French Revolution and the First World War) was not perhaps so much a reaction against the Enlightenment as the outworking of its inherent paradoxes.

Adorno and Horkheimer's text had a very considerable impact. In the wake of it, some philosophers and political theorists attempted to rehabilitate a more positive view of what had traditionally been seen as Enlightenment values, especially the use of reason, most notably Jürgen Habermas in his work of 1962, *Structural Transformation of the Public Sphere*. But Adorno and Horkheimers's insights into the paradoxes of the Enlightenment continued to be influential, and a series of thinkers such as Michel Foucault, Gilles Deleuze, Michel de Certeau and Jean-François Lyotard, often labelled 'post-modern' or 'post-structuralist', and most of them writing in France in the 1960s, 70s and 80s, began to undo Enlightenment concepts of the self and of rationality, arguing, for example, that the apparently autonomous, thinking self, was rather a constructed subject, conditioned by a multitude of social, political, linguistic, psychic and cultural forces which hampered any form of authentic agency. While historians have had a rather complicated set of reactions to this body of post-structuralist work—and it is not the remit of this chapter to explore those reactions—there is no doubt that such theoretical work has been a deeply significant precursor to, and influence upon, an exploration of both the paradoxes and the 'underside' of the Enlightenment. Furthermore, that such theoretical work coincided with the development of social and cultural history, medical history, gender history and a deeper and greater attention to issues such as ethnicity, sexuality and class in historical studies, led to a great flurry of research into those characters and subjects which had been omitted from the usual stories that historians had been telling about the Enlightenment(s): women, black people, the 'irrational' elements of early scientific research, radical thinkers and—even, in certain quarters—religion.

The implications of the work of Adorno and Horkheimer, of the French post-structuralists and of all the Anglo-American scholars who followed in their wake was that the Enlightenment was not perhaps as 'rational' as it seemed, and, conversely, that those characters and events often written off as 'irrational' (or 'enthusiastic' or 'superstitious' to use the language of the day) may have been deeply engaged with those Enlightenment ideas and debates which were usually thought to be the preserve of the 'rational' élite. All of this has led, during the final two decades of the twentieth century, to a radical rewriting of the eighteenth century and, within that rewriting of the period, there has emerged a new understanding of aspects of eighteenth-century religious culture, some of them previously ignored.

A number of historians in recent years have looked at subjects that were previously considered to have been of no interest to Enlightenment thinkers, or at beliefs and practices which, it was assumed, had 'died out' in the eighteenth century because they were 'irrational'. Philip C. Almond's *Heaven and Hell in Enlightenment England* (Cambridge, 1994) demonstrates that people of the educated stratum of society held a range of views about life after death, the soul, heaven and hell. Thus Almond puts into question D. P. Walker's conclusions about the subject, indicated by the title of his *The Decline of Hell: Seventeenth-Century Discussions of Eternal Torment* (London, 1964). Several historians have pointed to the continued importance of providence as a means of interpreting not only the religious world but also the political scene, most recently William E. Burns in *An Age of Wonders: Prodigies, Politics and Providence in England 1657–1727* (Manchester, 2002). In my own work, I have explored the ways in which claims by a range of people that they had experienced miracles created debates about the possibility and plausibility of miracles amongst not only ordinary Anglican and nonconformist churchgoers and ministers, but also amongst scientists such as Robert Boyle, other gentleman scholars and Anglican bishops. As a consequence, a debate about miracles occurred in the late seventeenth and eighteenth centuries that was prompted by people's religious experiences, and pre-empted and foreshadowed the more famous philosophical debate on miracles in the early-to-mid eighteenth century. Literary scholars have also contributed to this range of work. Echoing Adorno and Horkheimer's focus on the paradoxes of the Enlightenment, Terry Castle, in *The Female Thermometer: Eighteenth-Century Culture and the Invention of the Uncanny* (Oxford, 1995), has explored the ways in which the rationality of the age paradoxically functioned to produce 'the impinging strangeness' of the eighteenth-century imagination—what Freud came to call the Uncanny. In a similar vein, E. J. Clery has suggested that it was the 'Age of Reason' that produced a great plethora of ghost stories, in *The Rise of Supernatural Fiction 1762–1800* (Cambridge, 1995).

Prophecy has also been a recently explored theme. Hillel Schwartz's study of the French Prophets, *The French Prophets: The History of a Millenarian Group in Eighteenth-Century England* (Berkeley, Calif., and London, 1980), arose out of a new interest, within social history, in the activities of 'ordinary' people. J. F. C. Harrison's *The Second Coming: Popular Millenarianism 1780–1850* (London, 1979) was written out of the same impulse to describe aspects of popular thought and culture. It brought to light a number of prophets, most notably Richard Brothers and Joanna Southcott, speaking and writing in the heady, radical days of the 1790s, who had a great impact in their time—Southcott, for example, had thousands of followers, including an astonishing number of Anglican clerics—but have been little studied. James Hopkins followed with a full-scale biography of Southcott, *A Woman to Deliver her People* (Austin, Tex., 1982). Iain McCalman published a work that wove together radical religion and politics in the 1790s, *Radical Underworld: Prophets, Revolutionaries and Pornographers in London, 1795–1840* (Oxford, 1993). New research is now being done on these prophets, their followers, their antecedents and successors, and their interpretation of the Bible, in The Prophecy Project, a research project directed by Christopher Rowland and Jane Shaw at Oxford.

The paradoxes of Enlightenment values have also been explored through the study of slavery and the slave trade in America and the British West Indies. This has led to research on the role of the churches, especially the Dissenting churches (most notably the Quakers and Baptists) as well as the work of the prominent evangelical Anglican, William Wilberforce, in campaigns against the slave trade, as, for example, in Claire Midgley's *Women Against Slavery: The British Campaigns 1780–1870* (London, 1992). The pioneering and widely influential work by the Harvard scholar, Henry Louis Gates, in publishing forgotten texts written by African-Americans, including slave narratives of the late eighteenth century, such as those by Olaudah Equiano and Mary Prince, for example, in *The Classic Slave Narratives* (New York, 1987), has reminded us of the centrality of Christianity as an emancipatory (as well as an oppressive) factor in the life of slaves. In literary form, the slave narratives took on the characteristics of the classic spiritual autobiography as produced by Protestants such as Bunyan in the late seventeenth century. Felicity Nussbaum, another literary critic, in *The Autobiographical Subject: Gender and Ideology in Eighteenth-Century England* (Baltimore, Md., 1989) has shown the endurance of the spiritual autobiography as a genre throughout the eighteenth century, and its influence on other forms of autobiography and writing about the self.

All of this work on the sheer religiosity and varieties of piety in the eighteenth century has helped put into question our notions of secularisation in the modern West. For a long time it has been assumed that as the enlightenment of the élite occurred, this had a 'trickle-down' effect, secularising the masses. Sir Keith Thomas argued in *Religion and the Decline of Magic* (Harmondsworth, 1971) that 'magic' and belief in the supernatural declined because of the intellectual changes in the scientific and philosophical

revolutions of the late seventeenth century; the resulting changes in the thinking of the intellectual élite in due course percolated down to affect the behaviour and beliefs of the people. Looking at things from the other end of the
eighteenth century, Owen Chadwick wrote, in his *The Secularisation of
the European Mind in the Nineteenth Century* (Cambridge, 1975), that
'Enlightenment was of the few. Secularisation is of the many.'[14] When historians did look at 'popular' religion, they tended to assume that its existence
was a sign of the endurance of older religious beliefs and practices, rather
than an indication of newly dynamic and changing forms of piety and 'lived
religion'. Hillel Schwartz's conclusion about the French prophets, for example, was that they were proof of both the enduring attractions of millennial
imagery and of the survival of certain forms of religion.

The increasing body of work on different forms of religious expression in
the eighteenth century both questions those assumptions and contributes to a
larger movement in the fields of history and sociology that challenges the
long-accepted tenets of the secularisation thesis. A recent conference at the
University of Amsterdam (April 2002), on alternative master narratives about
religion in the modern world, brought together many of the British, American
and European scholars engaged in research that implicitly or explicitly challenges or rewrites the secularisation thesis. One of the most significant books
in this scholarly movement is Callum Brown's *The Death of Christian
Britain: Understanding Secularisation 1800–2000* (London, 2001). Brown
argues against the usual view that secularisation has been a long and gradual
process beginning with the Enlightenment, suggesting rather that it was a sud-
den event in the 1960s. Furthermore, he proposes that the modern era in
Britain did not witness so much the secularisation as the *feminisation* of religion. In coming to this conclusion, he draws on the considerable body of
research on the contributions of women to religion in all its manifestations in
the eighteenth century, and the impact of ideas about gender (both 'feminin-
ity' and 'masculinity') on religious expression. Especially influential in this
body of work was Leonore Davidoff and Catherine Hall's work, *Family
Fortune: Men and Women of the English Middle Class, 1780–1850* (London,
1987). Davidoff and Hall indicated the ways in which, in industrial, middle-
class society, evangelical Christianity designated new and distinctly different
religious duties and roles for women and men, who were now perceived as
definitively different from each other, confined to their respective private and
public spheres. They also show how many women, despite the restrictions on

---

[14] Owen Chadwick, *The Secularisation of the European Mind in the Nineteenth Century* (1975; rev.
edn., Cambridge, 1990), p. 9.

their activities, exercised considerable informal power both in the churches and the household.

A further but rather different aspect of this rewriting of the religious sensibilities and activities of eighteenth-century Britain is a rethinking of the place of religion in the lives and thought of Enlightenment figures not normally interpreted in that light, or, conversely, of Enlightenment reason in the life and work of figures not previously analysed from such a perspective. Barbara Taylor's new biography of Mary Wollstonecraft as a thinker whose ideas were motivated by religion (*Mary Wollstonecraft and the Feminist Imagination*, Cambridge, 2003) and R. S. Westfall's 1980 biography of Isaac Newton, exploring his more speculative ideas about the nature of Christ and his interest in Arianism, illustrate the former trend. Indeed, recent work in the history of science by scholars such as Simon Schaeffer at Cambridge, explores the interest that scientists in this period showed in religion, wonders and much that might be described as 'irrational', while a very considerable body of work, by scholars such as Michael Hunter at London and many others, carefully delineates the role of Anglican clergymen in the work of the Royal Society and the clear connections between religious commitment and scientific research at many levels, clarifying and reiterating for us that a rift between religion and science cannot be seen in Enlightenment England. A prime example of the latter trend is Henry Rack's biography of John Wesley, *Reasonable Enthusiast* (London, 1989). The title indicates Rack's interpretation of Wesley. Rack shows him to be a man who was much influenced by Enlightenment thought, one who may have believed in witchcraft and divine healing but only did so after weighing up the evidence carefully according to Enlightenment principles. Phyllis Mack's ongoing research into the impact of Enlightenment ideas on both John Wesley and the Methodists at large will, when published, significantly broaden our picture of the relationship between the Enlightenment and religious practice.

Rack's book and Mack's research bring this chapter finally to the history of Methodists and 'old Dissenters', important aspects of the eighteenth-century religious picture. Both these areas of study have been freed from the narrow confines of denominational history in the twentieth century. Methodism has, of course, long been the subject of some key debates within the larger realm of political history. The French scholar Élie Halévy sought to explain why Britain had escaped a revolution in the wake of the French Revolution and when much of the rest of Europe experienced upheaval and turmoil. His answer, after examining Britain's political and economic institutions after the Napoleonic wars, was that the values of the evangelical revival gave meaning and purpose to the working classes such that revolution was avoided, and this was epitomised in the lives and piety of the hard-working lower classes attracted to Methodism. The publication of Halévy's two books, *The Birth of Methodism in England* (1906) and *England in 1815* (1913),[15] meant that early in the twentieth century the history of Methodism was released from a purely confessional or denominational approach, being integrated into the political and economic histories of late eighteenth- and early nineteenth-century England.

Debates about the place of Methodism in England were dominated for decades by Halévy's thesis. Perhaps the most significant development of that thesis came from the Marxist historians E. P. Thompson and Eric Hobsbawm. Hobsbawm criticised Halévy for seeing Methodism as too conservative and argued that in any case the thesis could not be tested adequately, since Britain lacked the necessary revolutionary fervour. E. P. Thompson to a large extent agreed with Halévy and expounded his thesis in his landmark work, *The Making of the English Working Classes* (Harmondsworth, 1963), emphasising the ways in which the Methodists helped to organise self-improvement efforts. This stimulated a number of works that examined the place of religion in advocating self-improvement and respectability amongst the working classes, most notably Thomas Laqueur's *Religion and Respectability: Sunday Schools and Working-Class Culture, 1780–1850* (Princeton, NJ, 1976).

Perhaps the greatest living scholar of British Methodism is John Walsh in Oxford. Not the least of his contributions has been in the supervision of doctoral students and the mentoring of students and scholars interested in Methodism from all around the world. This meant that the 1970s, 80s and 90s saw a steady output of excellent research in the history of Methodism and related topics. David Hempton's study, *Methodism and Politics in British Society 1750–1850* (London, 1984) is of particular note, and Hempton's later book, *The Religion of the People: Methodism and Popular Religion c.1750–1900* (London, 1996) provides a detailed account of key figures in the Methodist revival, the growth of Methodism and its appeal. In particular, this work places Methodism in the broader perspective of the transatlantic revivals, an essential move now that research has shown that the Church of England was functioning well pastorally in most dioceses, even in those areas where Methodism especially took hold. In the light of this reinterpretation of the eighteenth-century Church of England, the explanation that Methodism caught on because of a dead or dying Church of England no longer holds water. The appeal of the Methodist revival can only be understood adequately

---

[15] Élie Halévy, *La Naissance du méthodisme en Angleterre* (Paris, 1906; Eng. trans. Chicago and London, 1971), and *Angleterre en 1815* (Paris 1913; Eng. trans. London, 1949).

when placed in the wider transatlantic context and studied alongside and in relation to the comparable American religious revivals.

Deborah Valenze pointed to the importance of women preachers in cottage evangelism, especially in Primitive Methodism, in her *Prophetic Sons and Daughters: Female Preaching and Popular Religion* (Princeton, NJ, 1988). Phyllis Mack in an article in 1999 'Methodism and Motherhood',[16] suggested that John Wesley deliberately harnessed the labour and energy of women, knowing that his revival depended on that, thus revising an older historiographical tradition that saw any prominent activities of women in the Protestant churches as the result of women pushing their way in, over and against the wishes of a resistant male hierarchy. In the archives of the John Rylands Library in Manchester there are hundreds of boxes of manuscripts relating to the activities of female Methodist preachers in the late eighteenth and early nineteenth centuries, most as yet unexamined; fresh research into this archive could change the picture and scope of Methodist evangelism still further.

Research into the history of 'old Dissenters' was for some time confined to denominational histories. Michael Watts's two-volume work *The Dissenters* (Oxford, 1978, 1995) has now provided scholars with a significant work of reference and research. Interesting work has been done on rational Dissent, exploring the relationship between religion and Enlightenment in that context. Many of the themes and threads of this research have been usefully brought together by Knud Haakonssen in a volume entitled *Enlightenment and Religion: Rational Dissent in Eighteenth-Century Britain* (Cambridge, 1996). These essays explore such topics as the role of the Dissenting academy in fostering rational Dissent, the complexity of the engagement with Enlightenment ideas amongst Dissenters (a complexity often ignored by historians focusing on the Church of England in this period), figures such as Joseph Priestley, and the nexus of connections between the prophets of the 1790s and the radical politics of the period. There have also been significant studies of heterodox movements and thinkers, most notably Maurice Wiles's study of Arianism, *Archetypal Heresy: Arianism through the Centuries* (Oxford, 1996) in which, for the eighteenth century, the thought of William Whiston is especially considered, and the collection of essays edited by Roger Lund, *The Margins of Orthodoxy: Heterodox Writing and Cultural Response, 1660–1750* (Cambridge, 1995).

---

[16] Phyllis Mack, 'Methodism and Motherhood', in Jane Shaw and Alan Kreider (eds.), *Culture and the Nonconformist Tradition* (Cardiff, 1999), pp. 26–42.

In conclusion, our picture of eighteenth-century religious life has changed radically over the last century. This is in large part because of changing assumptions about the nature of Enlightenment and church life, careful and substantial archival work, and new impulses in the historical profession as a whole which have led to new subject areas being opened up for exploration. It may be, too, that the eighteenth century, which witnessed the birth of modernity, holds a particular fascination for our own age, which is witnessing the 'death' of modernity, and as we struggle with questions of faith and reason at this particular time, we look to the eighteenth century's own struggles with precisely those issues for insight.

CHAPTER EIGHT

Theology in the twentieth century

ROWAN WILLIAMS

At the beginning of the twentieth century, English theology was largely dominated by a set of issues generated ultimately by the diffusion of the critical
approach to the Bible. Echoes of the mid-Victorian crisis around *Essays and
Reviews* (1860) had not by any means died down; and most leading teachers
in the universities and beyond recognised the unavoidability of questions to
do with the evolution of religious understanding in different phases of scriptural composition, and the challenges to traditional Christology posed by new
approaches to the historical accuracy of the Gospels—particularly the Fourth
Gospel, source of most of the explicit scriptural witnesses to a 'high'
Christology (a clear identification of Jesus as embodying direct divine agency
or personality). In this respect at least, the theology of the Anglican Church
in particular—and Anglicanism was still the majority ecclesiastical presence
in academic theology—showed itself true to its heritage. Doctrinal issues had
only rather seldom been treated as matters of concern in their own right: in
the seventeenth and eighteenth centuries, writing about Trinitarian theology
had been stimulated by the need to defend the position of the established
Church as representing a primitive doctrinal consensus against the attacks of
those who refused to see clear evidences of credal orthodoxy in the earliest
centuries of the church. The encyclopaedic works of apologists like Bull and
Waterland, indispensable source books for generations to come, were essentially reactive confirmations of the credal stance of the Church of England
rather than analytical or exploratory reflections on the meaning of the credal
vocabulary, which could, for such writers, best be expounded in homiletic
form. Somewhat similarly, as the nineteenth century drew to a close, the felt
need was for a defence of a reasonably traditional piety (and morality) which
still allowed for intellectual honesty about the evident difficulties in basing
doctrine on the scriptural text. What was more rare was any attempt to state
a theological methodology or to try and clarify how traditional dogmatic
formulae had evolved, what pressures had shaped their vocabulary. These

characteristic omissions account for much in twentieth-century considerations of doctrine within English theology—though, as will become clear,
Scottish theology is less easy to sum up in such terms.

However, this does not mean that doctrinal reflection at the beginning of
the century lacked any systematic substrate. As has often been remarked, the
influence in Oxford of T. H. Green and other English Hegelians was very
powerful in religious circles. Several significant figures—Charles Gore,
Henry Scott Holland, J. R. Illingworth—had absorbed from Green a strong
reformist approach to social problems informed by convictions about the
social good that were based ultimately upon metaphysical assumptions. This,
combined with a gently evolutionist understanding of religious history, produced a very distinctive theological voice, pretty traditional in its devotional
register but open to biblical criticism and engaged in meliorist programmes in
society at large. The overlapping of Christian Socialism with residual
Hegelian philosophy had shaped the 1889 collection *Lux Mundi*, which had
been something of a watershed for Anglo-Catholic theological literature—
marking out Charles Gore, for example, as an incorrigible liberal in the eyes
of many. In the first decade of the twentieth century, this general trend, associated especially with Oxford, moved cautiously but perceptibly further away
from traditional doctrinal allegiances, eventually producing the 1911 symposium *Foundations*, written by members of the Oxford theological faculty,
mostly college chaplains. This collection included several challenges to the
miraculous elements in the biblical narrative—including the empty tomb—
on general philosophical principle, and what might be called an inductive
approach to doctrinal issues (dogmatic formulae being developed out of
reflection on historical experience). The Christological discussions of B. H.
Streeter and William Temple in particular argued for a form of 'kenotic' doctrine (that the second person of the Trinity in becoming incarnate had
assumed the limits of a historical human mind in respect of the knowledge of
worldly particulars), and were highly critical of patristic and scholastic formulations of Christology, Temple famously declaring that the *definitio* of the
Council of Chalcedon illustrated the 'bankruptcy' of Greek patristic thought.

Christological controversy in fact played a major part in the theological
debates of the period leading up to the First World War. William Sanday, Lady
Margaret Professor at Oxford, though less radical than the *Foundations*
group, shared with them a scepticism about miracle and about the classical
Christological formulae; he did, however, attempt to salvage some grounds
for theological construction in the historical self-consciousness of Jesus, and
later turned to the vocabulary of psychology to clarify this, arguing for the
location of divine–human unity in the psyche of Jesus within the 'subliminal

consciousness'. Bishop Frank Weston of Zanzibar, a gifted and idiosyncratic Anglo-Catholic, produced in 1907 an essay (*The One Christ*) which attempted to do justice to the limitations of the incarnate consciousness of Jesus without jeopardising full Chalcedonian orthodoxy. Another rather idiosyncratic Anglo-Catholic was John Neville Figgis, whose academic career had originally been in the history of political thought (where he made a highly distinguished contribution): apart from some extremely interesting work on church–state relations and the theology of authority in both secular and ecclesiastical contexts, work that shows the marks of his Cambridge masters, Acton and Maitland, as well as his wide reading in German political philosophy, he produced a sophisticated response to Sanday on miracles and creeds. Despite the occasional and fragmentary character of most of his later production, he is the most original and profound of the more conservative theologians of the period. He is also the first English religious writer to offer a serious critique of Nietzsche; and he stands far closer to the world of Baron von Hügel and George Tyrrell than practically any of his academic contemporaries. He was certainly *not* a Catholic Modernist, and some of his work is a riposte to Tyrrell; but he has the same concern to draw upon the sacramental and corporate mysticism of the Catholic Church so as to address the crises of the wider culture.

Equally out of the mainstream was Peter Taylor Forsyth, a Congregationalist educated in Scotland. Not a professional university academic, most of his published work represents direct preaching and teaching in church contexts, but it has had strong influence on a number of later twentieth-century thinkers. Influenced initially by Albrecht Ritschl, he became increasingly distanced from liberal theology, laying heavy emphasis upon revelation and judgment while still retaining the Ritschlian sense that doctrine was necessarily to do with transformations of behaviour. His version of kenotic Christology characteristically stressed the element of willing self-abandonment in the incarnation—not as a solution to the problems around the knowledge of the incarnate Christ but as a key to the nature of God's love, definitively revealed in the cross.

Forsyth is often spoken of as a 'prophetic' figure; and in the simplest sense of the word, he undoubtedly was so. His crisis-oriented and sometimes tragic vision seemed a good deal more plausible in the wake of the horrors of the Great War than the fairly untroubled Platonist and Hegelian idioms of pre-war theology, especially in the Anglican Church. The extent of the theological impact of the war is an intriguing question. It undoubtedly provoked a restlessness in ecclesiastical circles and a new eagerness for reform; but in strictly theological terms the main effect seems to have been a certain impetus

given to questions about suffering and providence. The passionate and raw
devotional poetry of Geoffrey Studdert-Kennedy, a celebrated forces chaplain
and, later, industrial missioner, frequently focused upon the issue of God's
suffering, God's direct involvement in human pain, and the hopeless inadequacy, as it seemed, of traditional language about divine impassibility. This
took time to find its way into more academic discourse, although both
Streeter and Temple were sympathetic to these concerns; but it was seen as
a significant enough matter to require attention from the (Anglican)
Archbishops' Doctrinal Commission in the mid-twenties. J. K. Mozley's little book of 1926 on the *Impassibility of God* was written originally for the
Commission, and provides a fine survey of the discussion—a discussion that
was to recur much later in the century.

Yet much immediate post-war theology showed remarkably little of the
war's effect. The famous Girton Conference of the Churchmen's Union (soon
to become the Modern Churchmen's Union) in 1921 on Christology illustrated both the survival of the *Foundations* style and the relative lack of connection between this and the social and intellectual questions of those years.
In many ways, it was the high water mark of Liberal Protestantism in Britain
in the first half of the century, and the statements emerging from it alarmed
many in the churches. But while the direct influence of theologians like
Streeter or Hastings Rashdall, author of a major study of the doctrine of the
atonement, waned in the twenties, many of the prevailing voices were still
recognisably carrying on something of the style of Green's Hegelianism.
William Temple was among the most prominent, producing in the twenties
and early thirties several books on the borderlands of theology and metaphysics, looking for the kinds of cosmic narratives of convergence and interdependence that had been typical of late Victorian and pre-war writing. From
the Free Church communities, notably the Presbyterians with their strong
Scottish connections, came a series of highly disciplined, serious and humane
theologians, whose work has a more pragmatic philosophical orientation. To
call them 'liberal' is not actually very illuminating; they are largely uncon-
cerned with the highly particular controversies over points of the Creed that
dominated much Anglican writing, and give the reader the sense of a rather
more relaxed intellectual world. Yet they tend to work from Christian experience and religious phenomenology towards doctrinal formulation rather than
the other way around, and to give a pivotal place to the moral dimension of
doctrine. The work of F. R. Tennant in fundamental theology had already
begun to give some definition to this. But the tone is authoritatively set by
John Oman's classic of 1917, *Grace and Personality*, which resolves the tension between the dependence required by religion and the autonomy required

by ethics (conceived in a strongly Kantian framework) by appeal to 'gracious personal relationship' as the means of revelation, offering us compelling insight but never overruling the processes of human motivation. There are many echoes of Forsyth, and some things in common with the doyen of Scottish systematicians, H. R. Mackintosh; the whole tenor of the work is reproduced many times in what might be called classical Free Church theologies in England (the books of the Baptist H. Wheeler Robinson are a case in point, and the philosophical theology of H. H. Farmer), and the brothers John and D. M. Baillie represent the continuance of a very similar style in Scotland through to the fifties. D. M. Baillie's *God was in Christ* (1948) is a fine example of this tradition; it is tempting to read it as a long footnote to Oman, and none the worse for that.

Only fairly slowly in the twenties and early thirties did the new trends from continental Europe begin to make any impression. O. C. Quick, author of some magisterial work on credal doctrine, showed little sign of interest in the wider European discussion, though he had written on the contrasts of Liberal Protestantism and Catholic Modernism; it is likely that he was more familiar than he looked with continental thinking, and his doctrinal exposition was serious and sophisticated, but he is not much in conversation with the non-Anglican intellectual world of the post-war years. Sanday too had written quite sympathetically, though not uncritically, about Harnack and his followers. But contact with the German faculties was not extensive in the years after the war. Intellectual xenophobia had been given a good deal of respectability by the tragedies of those years. E. C. Hoskyns at Cambridge (yet another maverick Anglo-Catholic, who had—unusually—studied in Berlin) was perhaps the first in England to see the immense importance of Barth, and his translation of Barth's Romans commentary appeared in 1933, before a somewhat baffled English theological public. But there had already been some attention to Barth in Scotland: John McConnachie of Dundee had published an essay in 1927 on Barth's thought, and followed it up with two monographs in 1931 and 1933. Some other younger Scottish theologians responded fairly sympathetically to Barth—and, once again, their influence on English Free Church theology was important in this connection. H. R. Mackintosh had also studied Barth, and published some comments in the mid-twenties; and his encounter with Barth had reinforced his journey away from the world of Ritschl and his pupils. It is interesting to see how in the twenties Barth's gradually increasing presence in the awareness of some (largely non-Anglican) British theologians provided a kind of rallying-point for those vaguely unhappy with too experientialist a method, those marked by Forsyth's concerns and by the bankruptcy of some kinds of liberalism in the wake of the war. The foundations were being laid for the far more thorough-going appropriation of Barth in Scottish theology after the Second World War.

Brunner's work was also read by some British theologians in the inter-war years, but its impact is far harder to trace. Curiously, one of those who initially found Brunner attractive was a young Anglican (a former Baptist, whose father was a friend of Wheeler Robinson) who was to make a very distinctive mark indeed in the period following the Second World War. Austin Farrer spent some months studying in Germany in 1931 and 1932, and his correspondence shows how positive an impact Brunner made—and how little he was at that time impressed by Barth. Farrer was already much influenced by the Aristotelian–Thomist tradition—though there is surprisingly little evidence that he had studied the French Thomists of the twenties and thirties in any depth. His commitment was initially to developing a viable and sophisticated natural theology, and he never found any variety of dialectical or existentialist theology at all sympathetic. The final point of this natural theology was a robust doctrine of divine freedom, with will and agency seen as the essentials of any analogy between the created and the uncreated subject. There are both parallels and immense gaps between this and Barth's thought: Farrer concludes his monumental essay of 1943, *Finite and Infinite*, by emphasising that natural theology can do no more than clarify the 'grammar' of divine action; only historical contingency can prompt the conviction that such action has occurred. This is not Barth; but neither is it the anthropocentrism that Barth repudiated.

The French Thomist revival had made some impact in English Roman Catholic circles by the mid-thirties, particularly among the English Dominicans and their associates; the work of Jacques Maritain had begun to be translated, and Etienne Gilson's expositions of St Thomas were being studied. On the whole, however, Maritain's influence fell chiefly within the sphere of aesthetic (and to a lesser extent political) theory. Gilson's restatement of Thomist natural theology, and his emphasis on the centrality in St Thomas of the concept of the '*act* of being', were well received in some Anglican circles as well, however, and E. L. Mascall emerged as a lucid and magisterial defender of this approach by the beginning of the forties. His 1943 treatise, *He Who Is*, was a very significant contribution to the ongoing debates on natural theology; but he was also to write a number of distinguished works on more strictly dogmatic subjects, making use of contemporary Roman Catholic work: *Christ, the Christian and the Church* (1946) has a good claim to be the most comprehensive and coherent Anglican essay on the interconnections between doctrine, liturgy and spirituality of the twentieth century. Its concern to integrate these superficially diverse interests bore obvious parallels to the aims of many post-Second World War Roman Catholic divines in Europe; and although Mascall does not engage all that closely with the French *nouvelle theologie* (which was for him too overtly in reaction against certain varieties of scholasticism), he helped a good deal in his later years, especially in the seventies, to familiarise British readers with Karl Rahner. This integrative passion is also evident in another Anglican writer, who produced only one really full-scale book, but a book of decisive and far-reaching influence: Gregory Dix's 1944 *The Shape of the Liturgy* was ostensibly a study of the origins of the eucharistic prayer, but in its pages of massive (if sometimes rather flawed) erudition and brilliant (if sometimes rather perverse) interpretation, the reader would also find an impressively coherent Christology and anthropology.

Mascall's espousal of Thomism is a reminder that the inter-war years were a period of great philosophical upheaval. The Idealist consensus of the turn of the century was long since gone, and nothing had really taken its place; but the advent of Logical Positivism as a powerful presence in the academy in the thirties was bringing home to some theologians at least that a theology without some credible philosophical grounding was more vulnerable than ever in an intellectual world fully prepared to write off the entire enterprise as empty. However, finding a philosophical ally was not easy. L. S. Thornton, like Figgis a member of the Anglican Community of the Resurrection, attempted in a series of solid and complex books, the first of them published in 1928, to effect a rapprochement with A. N. Whitehead's evolutionary metaphysics. The result has some things in common with the residual Hegelianism of Temple, but with a far more ambitious approach to building a detailed cosmological theory on Christian and theistic grounds. The appropriation of Whitehead in the form of 'Process Theology' lay well in the future (the late sixties), and Thornton was regarded as a good deal out of the mainstream in his own day. But his work remains as a strikingly bold venture. Like others who resisted the rising tides of Thomism and some approximation to Barthianism—such as Charles Raven—he also reminded the wider theological establishment of the need for some kind of dialogue with the largely alien world of scientific cosmology.

Barth's impact was increasingly felt in several diverse circles in the forties and fifties. In Scotland, T. F. Torrance was beginning to develop a systematic Barthian school—which by the sixties was also showing itself remarkably interested in just that scientific cosmology and epistemology that might have been supposed the natural partner of a more 'liberal' theology. Torrance's direct involvement in the monumental project of translating Barth's *Church Dogmatics* rendered incalculable service to English-language

theology more generally. The same could be said, though at a more modest
level, of the English Congregationalist, W. A. Whitehouse, who, from the late
thirties on, provided excellent expositions of Barth directed at students and
working pastors. As a Scottish Episcopalian, D. M. MacKinnon must be
regarded as in some respects a missionary to the south; his work at Oxford
and Cambridge (separated by an interval in Aberdeen) kept some of the
Barthian passions of his earliest work before the minds of new generations.
He was also, however, an unforgettable expositor of Kant and Plato, someone
who struggled to keep alive the interconnections of theology and the worlds
of politics and the arts, the mediator of a very great deal of continental
European theology and metaphysics to his students, and a Socratic presence
warning of the risks of 'easy speeches' in theology. He was among the first in
Britain to give serious attention to the work of Hans Urs von Balthasar in the
sixties; similarly, he was among the earliest to encourage British theologians
to tackle the complexities of the hermeneutical debates associated with
Gadamer, Habermas and Ricoeur. Throughout the post-Second World War
years, up to and beyond his retirement in the early eighties, he offered a kind
of marginal commentary on much British theological debate, informed by a
wider intellectual world and a fierce moral passion.

Meanwhile, most 'mainstream' academic theology in the late forties and
fifties appeared not very deeply interested in doctrinal or systematic questions. Discussions around the continuing challenge of positivist philosophy
attracted some attention; but this was a period when issues in New Testament
interpretation seemed to be at the heart of some of the liveliest debate. If
Edinburgh was a stronghold of Barthianism, the dominant presence at
Glasgow was Bultmann—Glasgow's Ronald Gregor Smith, whose premature
death in 1968 deprived Britain of a major creative mind, had begun to engage
deeply with the positive valuations of the secular found in the late Bonhoeffer,
as well as with the existentialism of Bultmann—and interest in his work was
growing elsewhere. The publication of Bishop John Robinson's *Honest to
God* in 1963 certainly helped to bring Bultmann's name more immediately
into the English theological arena—though the book unwittingly illustrates
the relative thinness of the resources which a constructive theologian in
England might be aware of at this point. Barth is hardly acknowledged, and
the contributions of the forties and fifties from the Thomist stable are evidently either forgotten or dismissed. The 1962 Cambridge symposium,
Soundings: Essays Concerning Christian Understanding, which preceded
and in some ways foreshadowed *Honest to God*, represented a fairly
widespread unease with what were considered doctrinal orthodoxies, but
the responses offered to this unease were cautious and sometimes

impressionistic. Further afield, however, Bultmann's existentialist concerns had a dramatically revitalising effect on some theological writing, especially in the USA. Another distinguished Scottish (Glasgow-trained) émigré, John Macquarrie, working in America until the late sixties, produced a number of essays on the issues raised by Bultmann, collaborated in the translation of Heidegger's *Sein und Zeit*, and completed the nearest thing for decades to a British systematics in the shape of the much-reprinted *Principles of Christian Theology*, a sustained statement of traditional dogmatic themes in a Heideggerian vocabulary.

Robinson had also introduced many readers to Tillich and Bonhoeffer (though translations of some of their work had been available for a few years); but their impact seems not at that time to have been as powerful as Bultmann's. At the end of the sixties and in the early seventies, there was much interest in the relation of theological assertion to history (Lessing's 'ugly ditch' between contingent historical events and credal belief was much invoked); and while Bultmann could resolve this by a very Lutheran appeal to the *theologia crucis*, the intrinsic and costly risk of self-commitment, British theologians were less eager to resolve it at all. A new interest in the sociology of knowledge (and in some cases a belated study of Durkheim and Troeltsch) encouraged some theologians towards a more radical relativism. Dennis Nineham, who had begun his career as a New Testament specialist and written an influential commentary on Mark in the sixties, pressed the question through the seventies in a number of essays and a book on *The Use and Abuse of the Bible* (1976).

But the mention of this work and its date might alert us to an unexpected phenomenon of that decade, in which two 'graph lines' appear to cross. The middle seventies saw the publication of the symposium, *The Myth of God Incarnate* (1977), arguing for a comprehensive rethinking of classical Christological language. Its authors in fact represented a wide spectrum of approaches—from the comparatively conservative work of Frances Young (already a much respected patristic expositor) and the cautious reformism of Maurice Wiles through to Nineham's negative assessment of the role of the gospel record as basic in Christology and Don Cupitt's Kierkegaardian insistence on the importance of keeping Jesus at a distance from God, to avoid idolatry. Central to the enterprise was the guiding hand of John Hick, an authoritative presence in the world of the philosophy of religion (especially after his 1966 book, *Evil and the God of Love*) who was increasingly interested in how to theologise about religious diversity. His intellectual development is one of the first signs of how the major changes in British society were affecting church and theology; earlier generations had not had other religious communities to concern themselves about as part of the daily and local scene. Hick continued to explore this area, producing a number of influential, accessible and impassioned books on the need for a theological perspective beyond religious particularism. Another weighty theological presence of the period, G. W. H. Lampe, a patrologist of immense attainment, added his voice to the chorus of pleas for theological reconstruction in his 1977 *God as Spirit*, a finely written apologia for dismantling most of the structure and vocabulary of classical Trinitarian theology, while retaining what he saw as the fundamental conviction about God as self-diffusing and self-bestowing 'spirit'.

So an observer at the time might have concluded that a broadly liberal and revisionist approach had triumphed at the highest professional levels of British (or at least English) theology. The truth was more complex. The year 1977 was another high water mark, after which the assumptions and conclusions of the authors of the *Myth* symposium began to shift or fade in the overall intellectual map. That broadly Christocentric (but not Chalcedonian), morally serious, doctrinally agnostic theism which represented a quite long tradition in English theological liberalism was sharply challenged on two fronts. The seventies had also seen a substantial increase in the translation of major theological works in German, and the writings of Jurgen Moltmann and Wolfhart Pannenberg became widely available. A number of younger theologians—mostly pupils or junior colleagues of Donald MacKinnon—began to take a strong interest in Barth and von Balthasar (the translation of Balthasar's longer works into English was initiated in the late seventies). In this light, the almost total lack of reference in works like the *Myth* to continental European work suggested some insularities to be overcome. But at the same time, different pressures from the 'left' of the liberal centre were evident. The sociology of knowledge can be a dangerous partner; the whole theological enterprise as classically conceived was challenged from several points of view in the light of various analyses of its ideological interest. Liberation theology, again becoming increasingly well known in Britain in the seventies, saw the academic system, liberal or conservative, as failing to realise the need for an emancipatory practice to accompany, even to ground, theological statement. A number of enterprises outside the academy developed models of such a method, notably John Vincent's Urban Theology Unit in Sheffield; the influence of this within the academic 'household' can be seen, for example, in the work of the New Testament scholar Christopher Rowland, who has written on apocalyptic in the context of political conflict. The (very) gradual entry of feminist concerns into British theological discourse again challenged both liberal and conservative strategies. And, in the early eighties, the presence of postmodernist theory began to make itself felt;

Don Cupitt, probably the most original and eloquent contributor to the *Myth*, moved rapidly from an early rather Kantian style, ethical and apophatic but still within the broad boundaries of classical theology, to the dialectical drama of his 1977 *Myth* essay, and then to the radically voluntarist and anti-realist scheme of *Taking Leave of God* in 1980; from this point onwards, the influence of European postmodernism becomes more and more powerful, as he engages with Derridean themes as well as important elements of the Nietzschean heritage. In his way as superb a stylist as Nietzsche himself, Cupitt has continued to define a position shared in full by few but with quite remarkable resonance for many in its simultaneously playful and intense appeals for a drastically new religious consciousness.

The older liberalism was not, then, an entirely easy territory to inhabit after around 1980, and the diversification of styles developed rapidly—also assisted to some extent by a growing familiarity in Britain with 'post-liberal' theologies from the USA, especially the work of Yale theologians like George Lindbeck and Hans Frei. By this time, the Roman Catholic presence in British theology had become more significant than anyone could have predicted a decade before. MacKinnon's successor at Cambridge, Nicholas Lash, pursued a distinctive course with studies of Newman, of Marxism, and of various accounts of religious experience; the influence of Rahner is evident early on, that of Wittgenstein increasingly to be seen as his work matures. In sharp contrast to John Hick, he has developed a detailed critique of any idea of 'pre-theological' (ideologically innocent) religious experience. The Scottish Dominican, Fergus Kerr, has shared some of his concerns; while retaining a relatively low profile among many theologians, he has in fact played a unique part in stimulating discussion of the impact of post-positivist philosophies—Wittgenstein (his book of 1986 on *Theology After Wittgenstein* is a very substantial work indeed), Heidegger, Derrida, even some American analytic philosophers like Davidson. Several lay Roman Catholic intellectuals made striking contributions to theological discussion in the late sixties and early seventies (Brian Wicker, the young Terry Eagleton before his disenchantment with the church), and they form part of the background to the emergence of a philosophically very sophisticated and culturally literate Catholic theology in the last decades of the twentieth century. Younger Catholic contributors in the eighties and nineties also represented something of the radical ideological critique of feminism and liberationism; several of the best minds in feminist theology—Angela West, Mary Grey, Elizabeth Stuart—were Roman Catholics. Gerard Loughlin and Gavin d'Costa likewise have worked on the frontiers of traditional dogmatics and the world of contemporary culture, producing work of real originality, strongly attuned to gender issues. D'Costa has also written clearly and authoritatively on questions of inter-religious dialogue, developing another alternative voice to that of John Hick, again one that is suspicious of any search for religious 'essences' to be abstracted from specific communities and practices.

However, the study of traditional systematics had established itself on the scene in some strength during the eighties. More German theological work became available in English; John Webster translated and interpreted Eberhard Jüngel with great clarity, and research on Moltmann flourished in several university departments. The prolific Alister McGrath produced some solid work on Luther and on German systematics, initiating a career of very professional and sophisticated popularisation and synthesis, issuing in several very highly regarded textbooks and survey volumes on systematics and doctrinal history. Colin Gunton at King's College, London, built up an impressive research tradition, while pursuing his own writing in systematics; this concentrates on the centrality of Trinitarian themes, showing an eclectic interest in philosophy, an impeccable literacy in European theology and an increasing concern with the theological ontology of the Greek Fathers and modern Orthodox theologians. These interests appear also in the work of Alan Torrance and Alastair McFadyen, highly creative younger writers who have stayed within the style and agenda of classical theology rather more than Loughlin or d'Costa. Research on Barth has by no means dried up. Several major theologians cut their teeth on themes in Barth—including Gunton himself, David Ford, whose thesis on Barth as narrative theologian was a definitive contribution, and Richard Roberts, who has written in some depth about the borderlands between theology and social science, as well as discussing (critically) many British and European divines of recent decades. The American Dan Hardy, who has spent his entire teaching career in the UK, has consistently brought the concerns of this kind of mainstream systematics into conversation with the philosophy of science and related areas, and has worked intensively on producing what British theology has historically not been very good at, a serious and critical ecclesiology.

The most determined critique of liberal methodology, however, has come from a theologian whose formation and interests have been very much at an angle to those of the Gunton–Hardy–Ford axis or axes. John Milbank's *Theology and Social Theory* (1990) offers a comprehensive re-reading of enormous tracts of intellectual history from antiquity to modernity, and argues that most post-thirteenth-century theology has definitively lost its way, by refusing to make claims for the comprehensiveness of the Christian narrative, that is, refusing the challenges of a properly theological ontology. The result is the pseudo-theologies of modern secularity, from Descartes through to modern sociology; and the greater part of Christian theology has colluded with this secularity. Milbank's strategy is to allow a Nietzschean or Derridean criticism to expose fully the ideological corruptions of modernity (including modern theology), to clear the space for an authentically theological and ecclesial vision: postmodernism harnessed to a strongly traditional but also radical project.

Few books of theology in the last couple of decades have attracted such a mixture of admiration and exasperation. But Milbank is not easily written off as a reactionary, and has drawn around him an exceptionally gifted group of slightly younger scholars, including Graham Ward (whose thesis was on Derrida and Barth) and Catherine Pickstock (who has written a groundbreaking book on liturgy). The group has adopted the designation 'Radical Orthodoxy' for their style, and their influence has been quite strongly felt in the USA as well as in Britain. Several who have not been directly identified with the group have sympathies and affiliations, as well as some questions—Loughlin and Kerr, for example, and Rowan Williams. The whole scheme has been criticised by those of Gunton's school for its negativity about most Protestant theology and its Platonist elements; by others like Roberts for its supposed sociological totalism; and by those who have attempted to preserve or revive something of the liberal tradition.

These include names such as those of Gareth Jones and Ian Markham; but a senior figure like Keith Ward might also be included. Ward's early work in the philosophy of religion developed into broader studies of both the future of religion and the rational grounding of various aspects of doctrinal language. He has pursued the dialogue with scientific theory and has evidently taken on board the inter-religious agenda, without quite following Hick's lead. Where exactly to locate John Bowker on this map is far from clear. His early work in religious studies, from the late sixties onwards, established his intellectual individuality (and wide learning), but he has never appeared as a 'revisionist' in respect of doctrine—so much was clear in his Wilde Lectures in Oxford in the early seventies (*The Sense of God*, Oxford 1973; 2nd edn. 1995). Subsequently, his interest in the theology and science frontier produced a number of shorter books that are hard to classify but might best be seen as an extraordinarily intelligent apologetic. David Brown of Durham, after publishing in 1985 a study, somewhat in the analytical manner, of Trinitarian doctrine which met with a rather mixed reception, has now completed two volumes, *Tradition and Imagination* (1999) and *Discipleship and Imagination* (2001), which expound with great sophistication and broad cultural reference a gently evolutionist approach to doctrinal questions and a fresh and intriguing hermeneutic of the reception of biblical narrative.

Despite the attrition of the older university departments (a number disappeared or were amalgamated into larger units during the eighties and nineties), the more recently augmented institutions of higher education proved surprisingly hospitable to theology—especially those with strong historic church connections (Liverpool Hope, St Mark and St John in Plymouth, Roehampton, Cheltenham and Gloucester, and others). These departments were in a sense obliged to respond more briskly to the student 'market'; hence the increase in courses on less traditional areas—ecology, art, gender issues; the proportion of women teaching in these institutions is probably rather larger than in the historic faculties. However, some women scholars have more than held their own in such faculties: Frances Young, who has continued to produce work of distinction in both patristics and systematics, as well as some exceptional writing in the area of what may loosely be called spirituality, is one of the most well known, but Janet Martin Soskice at Cambridge has established a solid international reputation, and Daphne Hampson at St Andrews has written one of the most sustained and provocative studies in feminist theology to appear in Britain (*Theology and Feminism*, 1990), as well as a major recent study in the history of confessional debates between Protestants and Catholics. She is one of the relatively few British theologians whom the label 'post-Christian' fits (a contrast to the situation in the USA). Sarah Coakley, though currently teaching at Harvard, should be mentioned as another very serious contributor in the feminist field, though she brings to bear her research on Troeltsch and a profound interest in and knowledge of patristic and medieval theology. On the borders of theology, ethics and religious phenomenology, Linda Woodhead of Lancaster has marked out a significant territory.

There are many growth points at present—not only in the popular new areas just outlined but in other and perhaps more demanding territories. Theology in Britain is still catching up with the revival in Hegel scholarship, and this is likely to produce more work in the near future. Andrew Shanks's books on Hegel and on 'civic theology', the possibilities of theological discourse outside the confessional structure, yet still in conversation with doctrinal and liturgical tradition, are as yet the only really serious appropriations of a Hegelian agenda on the British scene, but they are of remarkable power and originality. Work on Balthasar and other major Catholic writers has increased in volume, and interest shows little sign of falling off. Not unrelated to this, there has been a substantial growth in the serious study of spirituality, ranging from Denys Turner's groundbreaking work of 1995, *The Darkness of God*, to the beginnings of an engagement with Michel de Certeau in some of the work of Graham Ward, Rowan Williams, and one or two others. And the frontiers of religion and the arts (including now film as well as literature and the traditional visual arts) have been visited with increasing frequency, and with assistance from David Jasper's Glasgow-based research institute.

One of the things that this survey has perhaps brought out is that 'dogmatic' or 'systematic' theology in England and Wales (Scotland is another matter) has both suffered and benefited from its slightly tangential relation to what many would think of as mainstream academic theology. Because—especially in the earlier periods examined—it was often developed in the context of religious and ecclesial controversy, it could be impressionistic and under-resourced in terms of understanding of classical definitions and conventions. There can be an amateurish air to some English essays in doctrine in the twentieth century, a somewhat bewildered focusing on problems that a better acquaintance with the traditional vocabulary of patristic, scholastic or Reformation thought might have dissolved. But at the same time, this marginality has encouraged an interdisciplinary boldness and a willingness to find fresh idioms which a more rigorous theology could have missed; and even a theologian like Austin Farrer, who was anything but ignorant of classical theological debate, could, when discussing theological problems, use strikingly novel language precisely because he could not take for granted a knowledge of the detail of the tradition. It is in some ways the most problematic and vulnerable area of the curriculum, suspect in the eyes of some because of its obvious connections with the life of faith communities, and in the eyes of others because of the methodological uncertainties that surround it. Yet it is also the area where connections with public discourse can, surprisingly often, be made, and where otherwise apparently disconnected spheres of scholarship may be drawn into conversation. It need not be least among the princes of Judah as we survey the tribal territories that make up the typical landscape of modern theology and religious studies.

General Reading

Keith W. Clements, *Lovers of Discord: Twentieth-Century Theological Controversies in England* (London, 1988).
Anne-Kathrin Finke, *Karl Barth in Grossbritannien: Rezeption und Wirkungsgeschichte* (Neukirchener-Vluyn, 1995).
David Ford (ed.), *The Modern Theologians: An Introduction to Christian Theology in the Twentieth Century*, 2nd edn. (Oxford, 1997), especially chapters 13, 14 and 15.

H. R. Mackintosh, *Types of Modern Theology: Schleiermacher to Barth* (London, 1937).

John Macquarrie, *Twentieth-Century Religious Thought: The Frontiers of Philosophy and Theology, 1900–1960* (London, 1963).

Alec R. Vidler, *Twentieth-Century Defenders of the Faith* (London, 1965).

CHAPTER NINE
Philosophy of religion in the twentieth century

STEWART SUTHERLAND

I

The twentieth century differs from its predecessors in many ways. But in one respect it does not. It has a preceding history. This is as true of the interaction between philosophy and theology as it is of any other intellectual or indeed manual activity.

In Europe and North America, and certainly within Britain, much of the discussion of theological and religious issues by philosophers was shaped either implicitly or explicitly by the writings of Immanuel Kant, and with varying degrees of prominence, standing behind him, David Hume. Kant famously highlighted this in his introduction to the *Critique of Pure Reason*, with his tribute to the Hume who 'woke me from my dogmatic slumbers'.[1] Kant's use of language in that remark served notice of a reshaping of the debate between rationality and belief in all contexts, philosophical, scientific, moral and religious. He wrote of limiting knowledge in order to make room for belief, and this was read by some as opening the door to a form of religious apologetic. It is easy to be naïve in such matters, and Kant is not the place to start!

Kant's influence has been enormous, and we shall encounter it at many points within this chapter. This is particularly true of British philosophical thought in the twentieth century. One of the overt signs of this was the reassertion of empiricism as the dominant philosophical currency after a period in the engagement with various forms of idealism both in Germany

---

[1] Immanuel Kant, *The Critique of Pure Reason*, trans. N. Kemp Smith (London, 1961), p. 29.

and through its distinctive British variant in the writings of T. H. Green and others in the latter part of the nineteenth century.

This particular change in philosophical paradigms was not mirrored on mainland Europe which is one of the reasons why a chapter on the interaction between philosophy and theology in Britain in the twentieth century will pay less attention to German and French thought than it otherwise might. The story with regard to North America is however different, as what came to be categorised as 'Anglo-Saxon' approaches to philosophy came more correctly to be referred to as 'Anglo-American'.

It is appropriate to refer to David Hume once again. As the influence of the empiricism of John Stuart Mill was moderated by Green and others in the last quarter of the nineteenth century, so the influence of Hume reached its lowest point since Kant's complex and ingenious response to him. However, at the beginning of the twentieth century, a reassessment of Hume by Norman Kemp Smith in two seminal articles in *Mind*, followed by a major study of Hume almost four decades later, helped reinstate Hume to a position of influence through the redevelopment of the British empirical tradition.[2] Hume came to share with Locke the joint position of founders of British philosophy's most important contribution to European philosophy—the development of empiricism.

Kemp Smith's stress on the naturalism of Hume's thinking as a complement to his scepticism, was however overshadowed by the developments of a contrasting emphasis on the empirical tradition by Bertrand Russell and A. J. Ayer. The impact of this on the philosophy of religion and more broadly philosophical engagement with theology in twentieth-century Britain has been extensive. In this there is an important difference to be noted between the practice of philosophy and the practice of theology on these islands. In the case of the latter, the impact of Hume has been moderated by the fact that theology in Britain has engaged to a greater extent with continental responses to the agenda set by Kant, than has philosophy with most of its comparable German and French counterparts. The reasons for this, as well as the consequences, belong to a different study although they will occasionally impinge on the analysis offered in this chapter.

Philosophy and theology have been bound together in what might reasonably be compared to a form of marriage: sometimes the marriage is as if made in heaven, but often the cantankerous character of human frailty shows through. There is a relation of dependence of the one on the other, but whether

---

[2] N. Kemp Smith, *The Philosophy of David Hume* (London, 1941).

that relationship is mutual is disputed. In practice the dependence of theology on philosophy can be seen very clearly from the earliest days of the Christian tradition. There was, again in practice, early use of the concepts and categories of Greek philosophy in the exposition and exploration of the content and limits of the understanding of Christian belief. Indeed since then much of the articulation of Christian belief in succeeding cultures and generations has depended upon the adaptation of the philosophical categories of the age to this purpose. Sometimes the results of this are definitive for the development of theology in that age and well beyond—as was the case, for example, with the use made by Aquinas of the thought of Aristotle. Alternatively, Kant's attempt to develop his own thought from engagement with the fundamental questions of eighteenth-century metaphysics into a restatement of the Christian tradition in his *Religion Within the Limits of Reason Alone*,[3] was for most theologians a theological disaster. Interestingly, however, as we shall see, pale shadows of that attempt reappeared in the work of some briefly influential British philosophers of religion in the twentieth century, as well as having echoes in some post-Kantian German thought.

The relationship of dependence in the other direction would however be contested by many philosophers. This has been particularly the case in the forms of empiricism which have dominated twentieth-century British philosophy. Prior to that some philosophers for whom 'metaphysics' was a word with a meaning and role might well have argued that the completion of metaphysics by engagement with the questions of theology was an appropriate direction for philosophical thought. For the most part, however, this has not been the accepted view. This is clearly the case with Hume, whose posthumous *Dialogues Concerning Natural Religion*,[4] are increasingly understood as an argument to disengage, in particular, ethics and moral philosophy from religious or theological premises. There is, on this view of Hume's last work, a difference possibly from his earlier writings in which he suggested that the traditional claims of metaphysics and theology which could not pass the tests set by empirical methods should be 'committed to the flames'. This verbal extravagance is easily associated with the strictures on both metaphysical and theological claims in Ayer's *Language, Truth and Logic* which created a whole industry of responses by philosophers of religion in the second half of the twentieth century. Ayer wrote:

---

[3] Immanuel Kant, *Religion Within the Limits of Reason Alone*, trans. and introduction by T. M. Greene, H. H. Hudson and J. Silber, 2nd edn. (Chicago, 1960).
[4] D. Hume, *Dialogues Concerning Natural Religion*, ed. N. Kemp Smith (Oxford, 1947).

> And if 'god' is a metaphysical term, then it cannot even be probable that a god exists. For to say that 'God exists' is to make a metaphysical utterance which cannot be either true or false. And by the same criterion, no sentence which purports to describe the nature of a transcendent god can possess any literal significance . . .[5]

and so reset the agenda for much of the philosophy of religion for several decades in a way consonant with a particular interpretation of Hume and, by implication, his influence on Kant. The consequential climate in which philosophy of religion has existed is well characterised by H. H. Price in his most interesting essay, 'Faith and Belief': 'A clergyman, we think, ought to give up his job if he does not believe in God. It almost seems that a philosopher ought to give his up if he does.'[6] This climate, as well as the more specific philosophical claims with which it is associated, has dominated British (and much American) writing in this area for a significant part of the last century. Behind this stand the questions posed by Hume and Kant.

II

Within the Christian tradition, philosophy has had a dual role. As noted above, Aquinas's use of the philosophy of Aristotle in his exposition and explication of the central themes of Christian theology continues to have major influence today. Indeed in philosophical approaches to ethics, as well as in contemporary theology, Neo-Thomism is alive and well. In comparable ways, a thorough understanding of Rudolf Bultmann's hermeneutical methods requires an assessment of the influence of Martin Heidegger's thought. The impact of Kant on Friedrich Schleiermacher involved both influence and counter-reaction. However, each of these examples represents a central element of the interaction between philosophy and theology within the tradition—the power of philosophical thinking in structuring the questions of the age and also in providing, with varying degrees of success, the means of answering them. Especially within the second half of the twentieth century in Britain, the shaping of religious and theological questions by empiricism has not been clearly paralleled by the resources necessary to answer those questions.

    Within the tradition, the second main form of interaction between philosophy and theology has been in the use of philosophical thinking to develop natural theology. Once again we can appeal to the works of Aquinas—most

---

[5] A. J. Ayer, *Language, Truth and Logic*, 2nd edn. (London, 1946), p. 115.
[6] H. H. Price, 'Faith and Belief', in John Hick (ed.), *Faith and the Philosophers* (London, 1964).

obviously to the arguments for the existence of God, known as the Five Ways. Two of the most sustained and rigorous forms of this within the tradition are to be found in British writing of the twentieth century—F. R. Tennant's two-volume *Philosophical Theology*[7] and Richard Swinburne's *Coherence of Theism* and *The Existence of God*[8] to both of which I shall return in due course. That this should be one of the areas of significant contribution by British philosophers of religion in the twentieth century is wholly consonant with two factors in the history of British philosophy.

The first is that, as already implied, the development of empiricism has been the major British contribution to Western philosophy. In historical rather than any rank order, the contributions of Locke, Berkeley, Hume, John Stuart Mill, Bertrand Russell and A. J. Ayer are all important, though some will be more durable than others.

The second reason for this twentieth-century focus within British philosophy of religion on forms of natural theology derives from the importance of two strands within Anglican theology—the centrality both of the primacy of reason and the use of analogical thought in argument.[9] Within the philosophy of religion to the names of Locke and Berkeley must be added that of Bishop Butler as key figures engaged on study of the reconciliation of mainline Christian belief with the philosophical tenets of empiricism. In different ways Mill's posthumous *Three Essays on Religion*[10] were also an attempt to view theistic belief and its possibility from within the particular value system (utilitarianism) which was part of Mill's form of empiricism. Hume's treatment of forms of natural theology in *The Dialogues* has been the most influential and thorough of the sceptical treatments of theism to which twentieth-century writers responded, though at a popular level the anti-theist views of Bertrand Russell drew famous response in open radio debate between Russell and F. C. Copleston in 1948.

To the two traditional interactions between philosophy and theology noted above (respectively the influence of philosophical ideas in the explication of doctrine and in the construction of a natural theology) must be added three other themes which are the concern of this chapter. The first is the engagement between religious belief and moral belief, a matter of positive

---

[7] F. R. Tennant, *Philosophical Theology*, 2 vols. (Cambridge, 1928 and 1930).

[8] Richard Swinburne, *The Coherence of Theism* (Oxford, 1977) and *The Existence of God* (Oxford, 1979).

[9] For an analysis of the importance of one aspect of this, see Stewart Sutherland, 'The Presbyterian Inheritance of Hume and Reid', in R. H. Campbell and Andrew S. Skinner (eds.), *The Origins and Nature of the Scottish Enlightenment* (Edinburgh, 1982).

[10] J. S. Mill, *Three Essays on Religion* (London, 1874).

interaction in a number of writers such as John Oman, Basil Mitchell and Donald MacKinnon. The second is a series of complex questions about the nature of experience and whether there are distinctive forms of religious experience which have a special epistemological or revelatory role. Major contributions are to be found, amongst others, in the writings of H. D. Lewis, W. T. Stace and C. C. J. Webb. Two seminal twentieth-century works in this area which greatly influenced the British debate are William James's Edinburgh Gifford Lectures, *Varieties of Religious Experience*, and Rudolf Otto's *The Idea of the Holy*.[11]

A major preoccupation of those engaged in the philosophy of religion within the Anglo-Saxon tradition for at least four decades was the series of challenges set by A. J. Ayer's *Language, Truth and Logic*, particularly as targeted in the aggressive title of the first chapter—'The Elimination of Metaphysics'. The distinctive twist given to empiricism by Ayer was to apply the work of the Vienna School of Logical Positivism to empiricism. One consequence was the reformulation of the challenge to traditional Christian belief. The central issue was no longer to be epistemological ('How do I know, for example, that God loves us?'), but rather one of meaning ('What, if anything, does it mean to say that God loves us?'). The threat as well as the challenge of this particular form of empiricism dominated much twentieth-century philosophical writing in Britain and North America for three or four decades. Philosophy of religion was no exception. Influential British writers include John Hick, D. Z. Phillips, I. T. Ramsey, Anthony Flew and Ronald Hepburn.[12] Whether the debate, either in the formulation of the questions by Ayer, or in the responses offered to that, added a new dimension to the questions posed by Hume and Kant is a point for discussion below. The intensity of the engagement is not at issue.

There is one further area of philosophical discussion reshaped in the later stages of the twentieth century which will without doubt continue to be a source of major philosophical and theological preoccupation for some time to come, which ought to be mentioned here. This is the appropriate manner of and presuppositions of inter-religious dialogue. Major contributions to the formulation and exploration of the issues have been made by John Hick, Ninian Smart and Keith Ward. In fact this is the subject of the next chapter in

---

[11] William James, *Varieties of Religious Experience* (New York, 1902) and Rudolf Otto, *The Idea of the Holy* (New York, 1958).

[12] See, for example, John Hick, *The Philosophy of Religion* (New York, 1963); D. Z. Phillips, *The Concept of Prayer* (London, 1965), and *Faith and Philosophical Enquiry* (London, 1970); A. Flew and A. MacIntyre (eds.), *New Essays in Philosophical Theology* (London, 1955); R. W. Hepburn, *Christianity and Paradox* (London, 1958).

this volume, by Keith Ward, but the philosophical as well as historical and theological importance of the issue justifies this at least passing reference in the present chapter.

In the remainder of this chapter, I shall examine further the three main themes indicated above, discussion of the nature and significance of religious experience, the interaction between religious and moral beliefs, and the attempts in the twentieth century to deal with some of the links between religion and reason.

III

The seminal work in the shadow of which all others stand in the discussion of religious experience is William James's Gifford Lectures, delivered in Edinburgh at the very outset of the century (1901–2), *The Varieties of Religious Experience*. This work, subtitled 'A Study of Human Nature', may reasonably lay claim to be amongst the earliest, but more critically amongst the most important attempts to create a science of religions. James's analysis of the implications of this are worth quoting, for they remind us of a context which was much more explicit in the twentieth than in earlier centuries:

> The best man at this science might be the man who found it hardest to be personally devout.
>
> For this reason, the science of religion may not be an equivalent for living religions.
>
> The consequence is that the conclusions of the science of religion are as likely to be adverse as they are to be favourable to the claim that the essence of religion is true.

The development of the idea of a science of religion or religions belongs to another study, but it has a place here as one of the factors which defined the context of the interaction between philosophy and theology in the twentieth century.

The point of more specific relevance which we draw from James is that the empirical (or Anglo-Saxon) approach to these matters is an avenue which must be followed. And indeed it was, in a variety of ways which might be grouped under two different themes.

The first of these focused upon the fact that there were specific individual experiences to which religious believers attach particular importance. William James identified one particularly important group of these as 'mystical states of consciousness'. He argued that personal religious experience 'has its root and center' in these, while at the same time identifying the problem which many have with these: 'my own constitution shuts me out from their enjoyment almost entirely, and I can speak of them only at second hand'. He had no doubts about the reality of these states, but his blunt American pragmatism is as typical an expression of an essentially twentieth-century view of these matters as one is likely to encounter. But such dispassionately polite, indeed positively self-effacing, withdrawal from the ranks of this type of religious belief is hardly conceivable in earlier centuries. The religious enthusiasts who heard the original sermons of Jonathon Edwards would have been more likely to blame the absence of such depth of experience and emotion upon personal failing or indeed sin. Nor is it likely to be fruitful to search the writings of St Teresa or St John of the Cross for remarks of even remotely comparable tone.

Those who came after the change of context so clearly signposted by James lived in a different world—a world defined by the writings of Hume and Kant. Rudolf Otto, whose monumental *The Idea of the Holy* was first published in 1936, was no exception to this. Although working well outside the British empirical tradition, nonetheless he worked within the context set by Kant. His increasing focus upon the phenomenological exploration of the 'idea of the Holy' built upon the conclusions of his earlier writings (e.g. *Naturalism and Religion*, 1904) that reason cannot justify the claims of religion. Instead, he identified a distinctive group of feelings—those of the numinous—as lying at the core of religion and religious belief, and devoted much careful comment to the characterisation of them.

This, however, constituted a problem for the philosophical discussion of religion. One might in a Jamesian way accept that there are such experiences and feelings, and indeed accept that they are, as Otto and others have argued, unique. But what conclusion may be drawn from this other than that, as James implied, people are different? Such a view of the nature of religious experiences seems at odds with the importance attached to them by relevant believers. To talk in such detached terms about them seems *ipso facto* to misconstrue them.

John Oman's substantial *The Natural and the Supernatural* approaches these questions from a dual starting point; the first element is the extent to which the early scholarly experience of translating F. D. E. Schleiermacher's *On Religion* influenced his own philosophical position. At the centre of Schleiermacher's response to Kant is his proposition that religious consciousness and belief are based upon a 'feeling of absolute dependence' which is both the foundation of the sense of identity and of a consciousness of being in relation with God. Such themes were built by Oman into his own distinctive contribution to the area, drawing upon a form of empirical enquiry into the nature of human experience.

Oman did not seek the supernatural through the examination or evaluation of what is mysterious or uncanny in human experience. Rather he argued that the supernatural could be perceived and encountered through an enhanced perception of the full meaning of the natural, which if fully perceived belongs to the wider context which is the supernatural. Thus the focus of the discussion of religious experience moved from the analysis and evaluation of specific experiences of the unusual, or of an unusual character, to non-inferential or immediate forms of awareness of the natural world as containing meaning as it is grasped as part of a wider supernatural context. This second approach to the complex of issues which can be grouped under the heading of 'religious experience' thus accepted that there were distinctive modes of religious experience which gave access to perceptions of truths otherwise not available. One of the main problems associated with this is that the capacity to have such dimensions of experience seems too distributed or available in rather *ad hoc* ways.

The continuing and insistent challenge of the forms of empiricism developed by A. J. Ayer in *Language, Truth and Logic* led to a gradual distancing of philosophical discussion of these matters from the kind of extended and sometimes less than fully precise contributions of Oman and his successor at Westminster College Cambridge, H. H. Farmer.[13]

Two post-war thinkers, however, followed in the newer context comparable lines of enquiry and approach. H. D. Lewis agreed with both Oman and Farmer on the centrality of personal encounter, but did not accept the possibility of unmediated and direct experience of God.[14] His stress upon the transcendence, and therefore for him, mysteriousness of God precluded that.

John Hick, on the other hand, in some of his earliest writings, particularly *Faith and Knowledge*,[15] used an approach which is quite consistent with Oman's main thesis, to combat Ayer's challenges to the epistemological adequacy of Christian theistic belief. He did not accept the possibility of an immediate form of experience which non-inferentially would provide a platform for religious belief. However, in his analysis of religious experience, drawing in part on a most ingenious paper by John Wisdom, he characterised the interpretative and therefore epistemological role of religious experience as 'experiencing as'.[16]

---

[13] H. H. Farmer, *The World and God* (London, 1935).

[14] H. D. Lewis, *Our Experience of God* (London, 1959).

[15] John Hick, *Faith and Knowledge* (London, 1957).

[16] 'Gods', in John Wisdom, *Philosophy and Psychoanalysis* (Oxford, 1953).

There might seem to be a superficial comparison to be made with earlier writers in that Hick seems to be proposing a different or additional dimension to the way in which believers interpret or experience the empirical world. However, his primary intent was to use this analysis as the basis for the account of faith which he then expounded. Religious experience was not to be regarded as the means of solving the epistemological problem of how one knows that claims about God are true, by presupposing that religious experience provided an alternative route to establishing truths that could be known: rather, faith is analysed as distinct from knowledge rather than as an inferior prolegomenon to it. The price, however, is a problem about what to do about terms like 'assurance', let alone 'certainty', all of which have a place in the orthodox lexicon. On this view, regarded epistemologically, there is a decided ambiguity in the reading of the empirical world; at best, one 'experiences the world as' designed by a loving God rather than 'as' one of the many non-theistic alternatives would imply, much in the same way as, in the days before central heating, one could gaze into the fire and 'see' or 'picture' all sorts of 'designs'. Much was made by those who followed this approach of Wittgenstein's example of 'the duck/rabbit'—a doodle which could be interpreted as a picture of either a rabbit or a duck.[17]

One final point to be made in this section is that there were specific alternative analyses offered of some features of the world which tended to feature strongly in most writings on religious experience. Again, the starting point is Kant. In the *Critique of Practical Reason* he wrote: 'Two things fill the mind with ever new and increasing amazement and reverent awe ... the starry Heaven above me, and the Moral Law within me.' In the context of what can only be seen as a temperamental distancing from emotion, let alone religious emotion, in most of his earlier writings, this is a remarkable statement which has intrigued many since. It opens the door to the prospect of a rather different perspective upon the sense of wonder and awe which has played substantially different roles in, for example, the writings of Rudolf Otto and Hywel Lewis. The most interesting developments of the philosophical importance of the emotion of wonder is to be found in the wrings of Ronald Hepburn. His first central discussion of this occurs in *Christianity and Paradox*, and its appearance in 1959 just before the publication of Lewis's *Our Experience of God* allowed Lewis to insert a late comment. Lewis grasped the essential point, which is that Hepburn is offering a wholly secular interpretation of the range of experience to which Lewis and others mentioned in this chapter gave

---

[17] L. Wittgenstein, *Philosophical Investigations* (Oxford, 1953).

considerable religious significance: 'I suspect that in laying claim to the numinous as something of which religious persons have no monopoly, he is trying to salvage for atheism more than the case allows' (*Our Experience of God*, pp. 118–19). The difference between the two is significant, and cannot be pursued further, but exploration of it casts light on the ways in which the borderlands between philosophy and theology significantly changed in the twentieth century.

IV

In his published Bampton Lectures in America, *Faith and Reason*, Anthony Kenny wrote:

> I conclude, then, that belief in the existence of God as a basic belief is something which is justifiable and defensible only if traditional natural theology is a possible discipline, that is to say, if the traditional activity of offering evidence for the existence of God and arguments against disproofs of the existence of God can be successfully carried out.[18]

In the fourteenth or even the eighteenth century, such a comment would hardly justify utterance, let alone the dignity of the introductory 'I conclude'. The history of the practice of natural theology so defined, however, had so altered the standing of natural theology that its very existence as an intellectual discipline of rigour seemed to be at issue. This was not simply because of the slip down-market of its distant cousin 'apologetics'—the assembling of arguments in support of already accepted conclusions—but because of the increasing pressure of the influence of Kant, and in more local ways the influence of Ayer.

Hume and, in different and less sophisticated ways, Bertrand Russell practised natural theology, but to negative conclusions. Hume's *Dialogues* offered a number of counter-arguments to belief in God, of which two had particularly deadly effect. The first and more subtle was that any argument which attempts to justify the existence of a God who is creator and designer will depend upon drawing analogies between such a God and his creation. Indeed, the very arguments grow stronger as the comparisons grow closer. The contrary is also true: the more distant the comparison, the weaker the analogy, and the weaker the strength of the conclusion.

---

[18] A. Kenny, *Faith and Reason* (New York, 1983), p. 64.

If, to quote one of the most telling lines of the *Dialogues* (from Part V), 'the liker the better' the comparisons between God and his creatures, then the strength of the argument from design leads one inevitably towards anthropomorphism. One does not have to share Hume's Calvinistic upbringing to regard this as a *prima facie* major flaw in this form of natural theology.

The second main argument which Hume deploys is the most common and yet the most difficult of those consistently posed to theistic belief—the various versions of the problem of evil: 'Is God willing to prevent evil, but not able? Is he able but not willing? Is he both willing and able? Whence then is evil?' On such well-prepared grounds Kant argued, via a detailed analysis of the traditional proofs of the existence of God, that it was not simply a matter of the failure of the arguments; rather, the whole project was misconceived.

In such a context, the importance of Kenny's conclusion in the twentieth century is more easily appreciated. What is at issue is the very possibility of natural theology, rather than merely the cogency of specific arguments. This has been the central arena of discussion for much of the philosophy of religion of the last hundred years.

The two most substantial British responses to the Humean and, implicitly therefore as well as explicitly, to the Kantian charge, are to be found in the writings of two Fellows of the Academy, F. R. Tennant and Richard Swinburne. Each in his own way shows considerable philosophical sophistication, and each demonstrates the capacity to engage with the impact of the massive and growing development of the natural sciences through contributions also to the philosophy of science. Their respective formulations of conclusions show marked resonances, albeit that the one preceded the other by fifty years.

Tennant summarised his central claim as follows: '[There is] a theistic world-view commending itself as more reasonable than other interpretations or than the refusal to interpret, and congruent with the knowledge—i.e. the probability—which is the guide of life and science.'[19] Swinburne, in *The Existence of God*, wrote: 'The hypothesis of theism has greater explanatory power than the Humean hypothesis and is for that reason more probable.'[20] Tennant's carefully argued case includes a fivefold cumulative argument for the existence of God, and pays a due and proper regard to Darwinism as the main theoretical alternative to a theistic hypothesis. His explicit recognition of the fact that he is here dealing with probabilities rather than certainties

---

[19] Tennant, *Philosophical Theology*, vol. 2, p. 245.
[20] Swinburne, *The Coherence of Theism*, p. 141.

allowed him to give a very distinctive place to the importance of probability as the measure of success. This approach is part of the central emphasis of Swinburne's very substantial contribution to natural theology, developed as it is on the basis of a detailed analysis of inductive argument and the nature of explanation.

Each of these writers contributes in his own way to providing the sort of basis for the reinstatement of natural theology against the prevailing intellectual winds of the century, which Kenny stipulated as essential if belief in the existence of God is to be regarded in his terms as 'a basic belief'.

The strength of these respective natural theologies is considerable and the counter-arguments to Swinburne have produced a substantial literature. This has accompanied a repositioning of some of the traditional issues, which preoccupied Aquinas amongst others, in developments in the USA. The issues in question dealing with some of the central points of interaction between philosophy and theology concern the problems raised in the very title of another of Swinburne's books, *The Coherence of Theism*. Swinburne, Anthony Kenny and Keith Ward[21] have made leading contributions to this discussion in the United Kingdom, each moving the argument forward from ground explored by an earlier generation of British philosophers of religion such as Austin Farrer and E. L. Mascall.[22] The issues are not new—about, for example, what content can be given to terms such as omniscience, omnipotence, and whether the God of Christian theism is in any sense a temporal being—but they need to be reassessed in each generation.

Kenny is right, however, to insist that justified and defensible belief in such matters does ultimately depend upon the possibility of natural theology, and the questions which pose most difficulty for that project are still those defined by Hume and Kant. There are those who believe, including Stewart Sutherland,[23] that the most central of these, collectively simplified under the heading 'the problem of evil', do constitute grounds for the withholding of belief in traditional theism. These counter-arguments however, contribute to rather than undermine the project of natural theology as such.

One of the most difficult arguments to evaluate in this context is what has been described as a 'moral objection' to Christian belief. A crucial reason for this has been one of the dominant approaches to the analysis of moral beliefs

---

[21] See A. Kenny, *The God of the Philosophers* (Oxford, 1979); Keith Ward, *The Concept of God* (Oxford, 1974), and *Rational Theology and the Creativity of God* (Oxford, 1982).

[22] A. Farrer, *Finite and Infinite* (London, 1943), and E. L. Mascall, *He Who Is* (London, 1943).

[23] Stewart Sutherland, *Atheism and the Rejection of God* (Oxford, 1977), and *God, Jesus and Belief* (Oxford, 1984).

in twentieth-century philosophy that Alasdair MacIntyre traces to earlier roots, and in so doing simultaneously links the fates of moral and theological argument:

> For the most part and increasingly, moral and theological truth ceased to be recognised as objects of substantive enquiry and instead were relegated to the realm of privatised belief . . . questions of truth in morality and theology—as distinct from the psychological or social scientific study of morals and religion—have become matter for private allegiances, not to be accorded such formal badges of academic recognition.[24]

This thought provides a convenient bridge to the final main theme of this chapter, the relationship between moral and religious beliefs.

V

There have been a number of standard approaches to the discussion of the relationship between moral and religious beliefs. These have often drawn upon the formulation of a basic question posed by Plato in the *Euthyphro*: 'Is that which is holy loved by the gods because it is holy, or is it holy because it is loved by the gods?' (10a). The central issue is thus defined as a question of whether statements such as 'God is good' and 'What is good is what is approved by God' are analytically true, that is, true by definition. If they are, then the problem of evil is transformed. On this view, a God who is omniscient and omnipotent cannot logically be the source of evil because that God is by definition good. In that case a human perception of an apparent case of God being responsible for an evil that has befallen human beings can at best be a misperception by fallible human beings of what, if we thought 'rightly', would be perceived in some other way.

Hume's approach, however, followed in general terms by Mill, is to view the claim that God is good as an empirical rather than an analytic claim. In such a context, the judgment that God is good requires justification in the light of the empirical facts—thus leading to the need for traditional theistic belief to develop a theodicy, or justification of the ways of God to man.

Hume took the view that the justification was not forthcoming, but this was simply part of his larger project to separate moral beliefs from religious beliefs, and so to remove the dangers of mistakes in religion being visited on

---

[24] Alasdair MacIntyre, *Three Rival Versions of Moral Enquiry* (London, 1990), p. 217.

wider society. Kant took a rather different approach and in his *Religion Within the Limits of Reason Alone* used as one of his tests of the acceptability of specific religious beliefs the criterion of whether they met the standards of otherwise derived moral beliefs.

Not least for the reasons lying behind Kenny's insistence upon the importance of natural theology for traditional theistic belief, most serious philosophers of religion have felt the need to tackle the questions of theodicy and its possibility.

In the twentieth century, approaches to the relationship between moral and religious beliefs in the English-speaking philosophical world have on the whole built on these foundations. Significant discussions of and attempts to respond to the problems of evil have been offered by, amongst others, Austin Farrer in *Love Almighty and Ills Unlimited* (London, 1962), Richard Swinburne in *The Existence of God*, Basil Mitchell in *The Justification of Religious Belief* (London, 1973) and perhaps pre-eminently by John Hick in *Evil and the God of Love* (London, 1977). In this chapter I have argued that in the end the proposed solutions, whether tentative or bold, are ultimately flawed and that therefore a radically different approach to traditional theism is required.[25]

A starting point for the redrawing of the contours of these issues was offered by Donald MacKinnon in his Gifford Lectures, *The Problem of Metaphysics*. One of the distinctive lines of enquiry which he explored was the extent to which the concept of tragedy had a part to play in the articulation of Christian theology. In what he accepts is perhaps an over-harsh comment if universalised, he refers to some approaches to theodicy as follows:

> It is often said that, where the Christian religion is concerned, those who accept its claim and seek to practise it, have moved beyond tragedy. Yet, one could claim that where the treatment of 'the problem of evil' is concerned, we reach an area in which in very various ways, theologians have allowed apologetic eagerness to lead them to suppose they had reached solutions, when in fact they had hardly begun effectively to articulate their problems.[26]

This line of enquiry needs further articulation in the twenty-first century, drawing, as MacKinnon did, on the significant scholarship of the twentieth-century classicists who continued, perhaps against the stream, to keep the work of Aeschylus, Sophocles and Euripides alive in the theatre as well as the tutorial.

---

[25] See Sutherland, *Atheism and the Rejection of God* and *God, Jesus and Belief.*
[26] Donald MacKinnon, *The Problem of Metaphysics* (Cambridge, 1974), p. 127.

Its particular significance for the present survey is that it sharpened very precisely the question set in Plato's *Euthyphro*. To invoke the questions of Sophocles or Ivan Karamazov about the apparent behaviour of God or the gods, is to insist that the claims made by theologians about the God of Christianity are subject to the bar of moral acceptability. Hume had grasped this, as had Kant. In the twentieth century, for all sorts of reasons, including of course heightened public awareness of massive human suffering, this issue came to the forefront of many minds in the evaluation of traditional Christian theism.

Following Wittgenstein, Roy Holland put one view of the matter thus:

> God is not a member of a moral community or of any community . . . To credit the one true God with having a moral reason for doing anything is to conceive Him in the manner of Greek popular religion as a being among beings instead of the absolute being who is Creator of the world. When 'God' is conceived as a one among many he becomes subjectable to moral judgement.[27]

If I am right to leave this as one of the central unresolved questions of the interaction between philosophy and theology in the twentieth century, then I am right also to point to the derivation of the shape of these arguments in Hume and Kant. There are those who would contest this emphasis and who would point to the significant growth of an interesting alliance between reformed thought and Neo-Thomism led by a number of very influential American thinkers. There are doubtless others who will be surprised at the absence of detailed discussion of a theme which preoccupied many British and North American writers for a number of decades—the question provoked by Ayer's *Language, Truth and Logic*, of whether religious and theological claims are meaningful at all. There were interesting discussions provoked by this, the earliest including collections edited by Basil Mitchell, and Anthony Flew and Alasdair MacIntyre.[28]

It is doubtless a foolhardy conclusion to offer, but despite the genuine specific insights provoked into the nature of language uses, the main intellectual issues which underlay this debate about the impact of empiricism and the Kantian response to it on theological discourse had already been defined by Hume and Kant.

A respect for empirical reality informs much of MacKinnon's writings, and arguably the following comment points to a future fruitful direction for the interaction of philosophy and theology:

---

[27] R. F. Holland, *Against Empiricism* (Oxford, 1980), p. 238.

[28] Flew and MacIntyre, *New Essays in Philosophical Theology*; B. Mitchell, *Faith and Logic* (London, 1959).

It is when one allows one's attention to fasten upon the sorts of exploration of the human reality [sc. found in Oedipus or Shakespeare's Lear] ... that we come to recognise the paradox that, while in one way a proper respect for the irreducibility of the tragic inhibits ambitious metaphysical construction, in another the sort of commentary on human life which one finds in the tragedies here reviewed and the parables analysed, makes one in the end discontented with any sort of naturalism. It is as if we are constrained in pondering the extremities of human life to acknowledge the transcendent as the only alternative to the kind of trivialisation which would empty of significance the sorts of experience with which we have been concerned.[29]

---

[29] MacKinnon, *The Problem of Metaphysics*, p. 145.

CHAPTER TEN
The study of religions

KEITH WARD

Defining religion

It would be difficult to say exactly when the study of religions, as opposed to theology, began in the English-speaking world. The first academic appointment in the field in America was that of William Fairfield to be the professor of comparative theology at Harvard in 1873. By the late nineteenth century there were posts in comparative theology at Princeton Theological Seminary, Cornell, Harvard, Chicago and Brown Universities. These were all designated as theological posts, and were naturally held by Christian theologians. In Britain one of the first scholars to study world religions was Friedrich Max Müller, who edited the fifty-volume series, *Sacred Books of the East*, and who in 1873 wrote an *Introduction to the Science of Religion*. Eric Sharpe has described this as 'the foundation document' of comparative religion.[1] Müller was a vitally important figure in the compilation and translation of Sanskrit texts, and his post at Oxford was in comparative philology. The first post in comparative religion in Britain was that of Joseph Estlin Carpenter in 1876, at Manchester College, then a Unitarian college in London, until it moved to Oxford in 1889. It was not until 1967 that the first department of religious studies was founded at Lancaster, and developed under the leadership of Ninian Smart, who became the doyen of the subject in Britain until his death in 2001. By that time most universities in Britain had at least some courses relevant to the study of religions. Although in the 1980s there was marked contraction in the number of university posts in the subject, it has undoubtedly become an established academic subject, whether in conjunction with the study of theology or standing on its own.

---

[1] E. J. Sharpe, *Comparative Religion: A History* (London, 1986), p. xi.

The first full British university post-holder to study religion as a wholly non-theological discipline was E. B. Tylor, appointed to the Readership in Anthropology at Oxford University in 1884. Tylor aimed to produce a naturalistic explanation of religion, which would make no appeal to the supernatural or to revelation, and yet which would explain the causes and origins of religious belief. He suggested what he called a minimal definition of religion as 'belief in spiritual beings'.[2] This simple definition might be criticised in a number of ways. Perhaps it emphasises the dimension of intellectual belief or doctrine too much. Perhaps the expression 'spiritual beings' seems rather restrictive for the many sorts of supernatural reality that religions can embrace.

What Tylor did not stress is that religions typically offer a set of social practices for coming to know and participate in the power of the spiritual, for disciplining the mind and shaping the will. They often originate in personal visions, shaped and reshaped over many years by many minds and cultures. These visions, in diverse particular forms, are evoked in each new generation as types of personal experience which make the tradition a living source of spiritual power. Religion is not just a matter of individual intellectual belief. It also embodies social practices which encourage personal experiences of immense emotional power. These are aspects to which Tylor's minimal definition fails to draw attention.

Other proposed definitions of religion range from that of the sociologist M. E. Spiro—'a culturally patterned interaction with culturally postulated superhuman beings'[3]—to that of Max Müller—'perception of the Infinite insofar as it is able to influence the moral character of man'.[4] At one end of the spectrum, to speak of the postulation of superhuman beings seems to imply a rather negative view of religions, as inventing anthropomorphic superhuman heroes, perhaps to explain why the sun rises or the rain falls. At the other end, religion seems to disappear into the miasma of 'the Infinite', wherein all distinctions are merged into one all-enveloping Romantic conceptual fog.

Specific definitions of religion clearly express the inclinations of their propagators. Nevertheless, both 'superhuman beings' and 'the Infinite' refer to a supernatural reality, a reality which is other and in some sense greater

---

[2] E. B. Tylor, *Primitive Culture* (London, 1873), p. 424.

[3] M. E. Spiro, *Religion: Problems of Definition and Explanation,* in M. Banton (ed.), *Anthropological Approaches to the Study of Religion* (London, 1965), p. 96.

[4] Max Müller, *Natural Religion* (London, 1889), p. 188.

than publicly observable material objects, and which exists objectively, that is, independently of human beings.

It is sometimes held that there is no need to define religion at all, or that it is even misleading to do so. Wittgenstein's analogy of 'family resemblances' is often appealed to in this respect. People may be members of the same family, though they have no one thing in common, but may resemble each other in a number of different ways—some have the same big noses, some big ears, some blue eyes, but none of them looks just like the others. So we might call something a 'religion' if it has a sufficient number of resemblances to other things we call 'religions', even though we cannot get one definite feature which is found in every case.

This is not in fact a refusal to define religion, however. It is a definition in terms of a set of central features, which is extendable if further resemblances become important. What we want to know is why we should want to group these sets of resemblances together under some one term, 'religion'. In the case of families, the crucial factor is genetic relationship, or upbringing within a particular social group. We want to speak of 'families' because we want to establish special duties of care, or formulate rules of inheritance and responsibility. Is there any such factor in the case of religion? Is there any reason for grouping things together as 'religions'? And is there any reason for picking out specific sorts of resemblance as relevant to this?

To speak of a religion is to pick out some area of human practice and concern, which we can either associate ourselves with or dissociate ourselves from. We might say, 'Yes, that is the sort of thing I do or approve of', or 'I would not do that sort of thing in a million years'. It is rather like picking out 'classical music' as marking a range of interests that I either have or do not care for. So what are the practices or interests that we might want to put together under the heading of religion?

Ninian Smart has suggested that there are seven main 'dimensions' of religion, seven general descriptive categories under which one can list religious activities.[5] These are: myth or narrative, doctrine, ritual, ethics, social institutions, experience, and the material dimension (buildings, art-works and so on). If one is seeking to describe the phenomenon of religion, these, he suggests, are some categories one can use to get a reasonably adequate description. It might be misleading to focus too much on one dimension, such as doctrines or sets of beliefs. No doubt all religions have some doctrines, but for some the dimension of doctrine will be much less important

---

[5] Ninian Smart, *The World Religions*, 2nd edn. (Cambridge, 1998), Introduction.

than for others. Some Christian groups would define themselves almost entirely in terms of doctrines, by which they differ from other groups. But others, like the Society of Friends, do not have a firm emphasis on set and agreed beliefs, though they will have some agreed beliefs—like an emphasis on the 'Inner Light'. Of much greater importance for Quakers is agreement on the ethical principle of pacifism. For some groups, the performance of correct ritual might be more important, while others will have as little ritual as possible.

It is possible to think of different descriptive categories. Eric Sharpe suggests four 'functional modes'—existential, intellectual, institutional and ethical.[6] Or one might think of religion as having the three main aspects of belief (including both myths and doctrines), practices (ethics, institutions and ritual, and the places in which rituals take place), and experiences. The exact categories do not matter, as long as one sees that religions are diverse, and have different dimensions, and that it may be helpful to describe them under a number of different headings, or from a number of points of view.

There is something, however, which unites these dimensions or categories. We are not interested in any kind of narrative, any kind of worldview, or any kind of experience. What seems to unite these dimensions is that they all relate directly or indirectly to some description of supernatural reality or realities, to some way of maintaining a relationship with it (or them) which is conducive to human good and avoids human harm, and to some way of eliciting typical types of experiences in the context of such a relationship. Those are the interests which the word 'religion' picks out.

In recent years, however, many scholars, both in anthropology and in social and cultural studies, have queried whether 'religion' is an appropriate or even an identifiable subject of study. Wilfred Cantwell Smith, in *The Meaning and End of Religion*, argued that the concept of religion is recent, Western and unstable, and that the term should be dropped.[7] Trying to turn religion into an object of study, he says, turns a matter of living faith into a set of abstract, 'frozen' doctrines, as though there were a number of 'religions', each with a fixed essence. He recommends that we should separate the many cumulative traditions, which are always in flux, always changing, from the lived experience of faith, of personal relation to the Transcendent.

Others argue that it is artificial to separate religion from the general cultural life of a society. We may speak of the beliefs and practices of various cultures, and the way they change in response to new environmental and

---

[6] E. J. Sharpe, *Understanding Religion* (London, 1983), p. 95.
[7] W. C. Smith, *The Meaning and End of Religion* (New York, 1962), p. 194.

economic pressures and opportunities. Religion should be subsumed under cultural studies, since it falsifies the situation entirely to see it as a matter of static sets of doctrines which can be abstracted from their cultural and social setting. So one could study specific cultures at specific times, but it would not be helpful to study an abstract entity called 'religion'.

It can indeed be misleading to see religions as separate and distinct entities, defined by lists of doctrines. Even to see Christianity, which is unusually creed-based, like this is misleading, if it leads one to neglect its very diverse social embodiments and its historically changing forms. Yet Cantwell Smith himself states that the cumulative traditions are the ground for individual faith in Transcendence. In using the concept of 'transcendence', he is focusing attention on a supernatural reality and on the possibility of personal experience of it. For 'the Transcendent' is that which is beyond and greater than the immanent or the everyday. Thereby he is in fact picking out precisely what is central to religion—as distinct from music, morality or social custom.

There are practices intended to relate humans appropriately to such a transcendent or supernatural reality (or realities), and presumably there are some alleged apprehensions of it (or them) by at least some human beings. So it is possible to speak of a distinctive area of human belief, practice and experience, in which humans seek to relate to a supernatural order of being, in ways intended to attain human goods or avoid human harms. One can call such beliefs, practices and experiences 'religious', and they can become the objects of reflective and analytical study. The study of religions may no doubt be part of cultural studies—though it will also be concerned with questions of rationality and truth that cultural studies often sets aside. But it is primarily a study of those beliefs, practices and experiences in which humans consider themselves to have a potentially fulfilling relation to an objective transcendent reality. There does not seem to be anything particularly 'Western', elitist or essentialist about such a study. Nor does the study of religion require or commit the scholar to any presuppositions about what he or she should believe or practise.

Patterns of religion

In the course of human history, there have been many differing ways of conceiving of supernatural reality. In many indigenous religions, a host of good and bad spirits is said to exist, causing fertility, victory in war, plagues, earthquakes and death. Holy men, and sometimes women, are thought to be able to communicate with these spirits, and to influence them to help produce human good or avoid human harm. In the earliest city-states of which we possess records, pantheons of gods and goddesses, who are often said to have descended from more ultimate primal powers of being, represent various aspects of human activity, from war to music, or become patrons of particular rulers and cities, or symbolise the powers which are expressed in natural forces like the sun or the stars, but which have their own hidden reality.

After the eighth to sixth centuries BCE, at the beginning of what Karl Jaspers called 'the Axial Age' (800–200 BCE), a number of religious teachers, whose names have been recorded and remembered, founded some of the great religious traditions which still exist in the world. The major prophets of Israel and Judah founded a great tradition of the worship of one God of justice and mercy, which was in time to give rise to the Semitic faiths of Judaism, Christianity and Islam. Mahavira and Gautama founded the Indian traditions of renunciation and the pursuit of a liberated state of wisdom, compassion and bliss. The many Indian traditions which now comprise Hinduism reconfigured their own diverse teachings around these central themes of renunciation and liberation, and interpreted the gods as personalisations of the one ultimate reality, Brahman, of which all things are parts. Confucius and Lao Tzu founded the East Asian traditions which are concerned with the harmony of nature and the discernment of the 'Way of Heaven' in social and political life. And in the fourth century BCE, Plato and Aristotle devised philosophical systems which, while not themselves religions, were to shape the character of the Semitic traditions in fundamental ways.

These four great streams of thought have developed, divided and interacted ever since, and they could be said to express an almost universal human concern with a supernatural reality, conceived either as a personal God to whom humans can relate in worship, as a liberated state to which humans have access, as an immanent moral order which underlies the observable cosmos, or as the supreme Good which draws all things to itself by desire.

Those who speak of perceptions of the infinite are speaking of apprehension of a supreme spiritual being. Those who are indifferent to anthropomorphic gods, and who aim at liberation from suffering through meditation, believe in spiritual beings. They could be the Enlightened ones of Buddhism, or the Tirthankaras of Jainism, but in both cases they are beings who have attained spiritual states, other and greater than the mundane states of ordinary sense-awareness. Those who seek to follow the Way of Heaven are seeking to follow a moral order which is built into the universe as its transcendent dimension. One might prefer to speak of a spiritual dimension to reality, rather than of a spiritual being, yet insofar as these views are religious, they affirm an objective spiritual aspect of being. And those who seek awareness of an objective Good, regard it as a spiritual existent, even if they are apt to say, as Plato did, that it is 'beyond being itself'.

Anthropological approaches

It must be said, however, that Tylor did not have quite such sophisticated notions in mind. He coined the word 'animism' to denote a belief that all living things, and perhaps the forces of nature too, are animated by quasi-personal powers or 'souls'. This he apparently saw as a theoretical hypothesis to account for their behaviour, and as an essentially primitive and mistaken one.

His major work, *Primitive Culture* (2 vols., London, 1871) proceeds on three great methodological principles. First, he is a linear evolutionist, holding that religious beliefs develop from simpler and more elementary forms. They are not, as many theologians held at that time, degradations from some primeval revelation which only Judaism and Christianity have preserved. Second, he is a comparativist, trying to see religious belief and practice as arising from common roots in human nature, and as displaying similar features in every culture, which suggest one sort of basic explanation appropriate to its many particular forms. Third, he is a naturalist, trying to explain the genesis of religious beliefs without any reference to the supposed supernatural reality to which they point. Whatever the defects of these principles, Tylor has the distinction of being the first scholar seriously to consider in detail some of the major phenomena of religion throughout the world, from a non-theological point of view.

It was, however, Sir James Frazer who caught and who has held the public imagination with his great work, *The Golden Bough*. Frazer, one of the first Academicians, was a Fellow of Trinity College, Cambridge for almost all his working life, and he developed the work of Tylor in a way that was to influence modern literature—especially through D. H. Lawrence, Ezra Pound and T. S. Eliot—as much as it influenced the study of religions itself. Frazer declined the first Chair of Comparative Religion in Britain, at Manchester University, and it was established in 1904 with the Pali scholar T. W. Rhys Davids as its first incumbent. Frazer remained at Cambridge, and *The Golden Bough* was first published in 1890 in two volumes. It then grew to twelve volumes, though in 1922 a one-volume abridgement by Frazer himself was issued, which is what most people now read.

He begins with an apparently simple question: what accounts for the rule of succession to the priesthood of Diana in the sacred grove by the Lake of Nemi? In an amazingly imaginative way, the answer to this question leads him into almost every myth of classical times, every folk-tale in literature, and every record of tribal practice gathered from missionaries and businessmen throughout the far-flung corners of the world. In the end (and, one suspects, in the beginning) he propounds one theory to explain all this mass of data, and show the origins of religious belief in the early history of the human race.

Thus the study of religions began with the attempt to give a naturalist, evolutionist and comparativist account of religious beliefs and practices, which would show them to be natural and inevitable stages in the historical progress towards civilisation which has now rendered them obsolete. Frazer saw the earliest stage of human thought as concerned with magic, the simple quasi-scientific idea that things can be made to happen either by doing something similar (causing rain by sprinkling water), or by performing some rite on an object that has been contiguous with the real object of concern (sticking pins into a doll clothed with material taken from an enemy). Homeopathic and contagious magic, he thinks, are the results of an elementary association of ideas. The link with David Hume's account of causality is clear. For Hume causal relations are based on two main associations of ideas, similarity and contiguity. Frazer is taking these two elementary ideas, and conjecturing that they find a primitive expression in the magical practices of early humans. They assume a regular order in nature, but one based on false beliefs about the nature of the causal connections in nature. Magic is 'the bastard sister of science'; a good effort, but it does not work.

Religion, which Frazer defines as 'an attempt to propitiate or conciliate spirits',[8] succeeds magic, as a hypothesis that there must be spirits behind the events of nature, and if one cannot control them, at least one might seek to appease and placate them by prayer and sacrifice. This is an intellectual advance on magic, but a moral regression, since it leads to unworthy human self-abasement: '[man's] old free bearing is exchanged for an attitude of lowliest prostration.'[9] The final stage of human intellectual progress is, of course, science, when we at last discover the true causal connections between things, and both magic and religion lost their utility.

The Golden Bough is a magnificent work, but few if any anthropologists would now accept its basic hypothesis. Is religion really a primitive attempt to explain the world? Edward Evans-Pritchard, a later Academician, who was Professor of Social Anthropology at Oxford from 1946 to 1970, calls this an 'intellectualist' view of religion. It treats early humans as though they were already experimental scientists, and as though their rituals were the

[8] James Frazer, *The Golden Bough*, abridged ed. (London, 1922), p. 60.
[9] Ibid., p. 70.

consequence of (mistaken) explanatory causal hypotheses. What is missing is any serious account of human sentiments and feelings in the practice of religion, and any recognition of the important social role that religion plays, or of its relation to culture and society.

Are the practices of religion ways of getting the gods to do what one wants? Or, when that fails, are they attempts to placate or propitiate spiritual beings? This seems a very Utilitarian account of religion. Frazer says: 'If [the savage] resists on occasion the sexual instinct, it is from no high idealism, no ethereal aspiration after moral purity, but for the sake of some ulterior yet perfectly definite and concrete object.'[10] How on earth does Frazer, who never actually met a savage, know that? May there not be some genuine spark of reverence, devotion and gratitude in the attitude of worshippers of the gods, however 'primitive'? And why should religion be defined as 'propitiation or conciliation', terms which imply that the gods are angry, and need placating? Whatever one's personal view of the matter, it seems clear, first, that Frazer had no way of knowing what primitive humans actually thought on these matters, and second, that his account is highly emotive. Religion, for him, is based on fear and utility, not on reverence and moral endeavour. It is based on the calculation of personal advantage, and not on the search for moral ideals. Well, it may be so. But how does Frazer know that? And may there not be, in the first origins of religion, the same sorts of diversity as there are in its adherents now?

Does magic precede religion, as a more elementary form of explanation? And do the natural sciences provide the only ways of knowledge, so that we can be sure there are no spirits and no God? These are highly contentious questions, and Frazer's answers to them have not been widely accepted. As Edward Evans-Pritchard puts it rather bluntly, 'No one accepts Frazer's theory of stages today.'[11] Even a primal animism—to use Tylor's term—seems simpler, more elementary than the rather complex hypothesis that nature is ordered by general causal laws, which magic, on Frazer's account, requires. More importantly, anthropologists have become much more sceptical of being able to trace the first origins of religion at all. The data are just too meagre.

There are still those who remain convinced that all religious beliefs are founded on a mistake. But it does seem rather odd to insist that the study of religions can only properly be undertaken by those who hold such a dogma. An understanding of the study of religions which requires of its students

---

[10] Ibid., p. 167.
[11] E. Evans-Pritchard, *Theories of Primitive Religion* (Oxford, 1965), p. 28.

religious unbelief and commitment to purely naturalistic explanation is just as ideological as the confessional theology which it sometimes attempted to replace.

Most anthropologists would now seek not to make prejudgments about the truth or falsity of the beliefs of those whom they investigate, but try to give accurate accounts of religious beliefs and practices. Evans-Pritchard's own studies of Nuer religion provide an outstanding example of this more open approach. Attention is paid to what the Nuer themselves say, and assessments of truth and rationality are left to philosophers.

Even his work, however, has come under criticism for what is sometimes felt to be his assimilation of Nuer concepts, like that of Kwoth, to monotheistic ideas of God. Perhaps Evans-Pritchard was too sympathetic, a sympathy which took the form of making their ideas more like his own than they really were. It might even be doubted that 'religious' ideas can be differentiated from others, so that one should simply speak of beliefs and practices, without trying to sort out religious ones in particular. One must here simply record a disagreement which still persists within anthropology. There are those who think that every culture is a distinctive form of life which must be studied in its particularity without comparisons which might mislead or distort. And there are those who think that there are universal human needs, dispositions and desires, and that one can discern beneath the diversity of cultural forms certain universal elements, some of which it is useful to call 'religious'.

The comparativist project did no doubt exaggerate the extent to which one could look for a 'universal science of religion', or of 'mythology'. And it did overestimate the chances of explaining such universal elements in simple psychological or social terms, which would account for their genesis, and preferably show their illusory and socially constructed character. But since human beings are genetically similar, and are, according to most biologists, descended from just one pair of ancestors, it would be odd if they did not share certain basic characteristics. And it does seem to be a characteristic of almost all human societies that some humans believe themselves able to communicate with a world of gods or spirits or transcendent entities. All human languages are translatable, with enough patience, and it seems unduly pessimistic to insist on the incommensurability of cultural practices in a world in which a determined individual can fairly easily be a member of two or more such cultures at the same time. The extreme thesis of cultural relativism is sometimes defeated by a plane journey, and the very enterprise of anthropology presupposes that alien cultures can be understood.

It is precisely the attempt to understand that has led the anthropological study of religion to change enormously since Frazer's day. Even in 1937, when Radcliffe-Brown was appointed to the first Chair of Social Anthropology at Oxford, he criticised the 'conjectural history' which marked the work of previous ethnologists. Instead of armchair reconstructions of what might well have happened, what was needed, he believed, was participant observation. The student of religion should participate in the life of a religious group, and record in as neutral a way as possible, without raising questions of truth and falsity, what is said and done.

Yet such observations need to be organised and systematised in some way. Radcliffe-Brown was a proponent of the then new discipline of sociology, which sought to see customs in their total context of meaning and significance, and contemporary structure. One cannot understand religion outside its particular social context. But comparative religious study is possible by comparing total social structures, and the function of religion within them.

Moreover, as Talcott Parsons was later to point out, understanding a culture may well require an effort of empathetic understanding, which interprets meaning of webs of significance. It is not, despite the hopes of some sociologists, a 'hard' scientific discipline, in the sense of measuring observable quantities and devising general laws of nature which can be experimentally observed by any competent observer. It is a work of human understanding, requiring judgment and interpretative skill. It deals with how things are seen and understood by persons in their own experience, and not simply with public and observable facts. Anthropologists like Mary Douglas[12] have shown how such sympathetic understanding can shed light on apparently non-rational customs and beliefs, and reveal deep and enduring human concerns. In such an approach, one seeks imaginatively to enter into the world of the other, and allow that encounter to react back upon one's own prior understanding of reality. Such 'interpretative' or imaginative anthropology, while resisted by those who regard all religious views as basically false, moves anthropology away from quasi-scientific explanations of aberrant behaviour towards appreciation and understanding of differing forms of human life and experience.

The phenomenological approach

Whether or not the social study of religion can properly be called scientific, the change of stance from the conjectural history of the early anthropologists

---

[12] See Mary Douglas, *Purity and Danger* (London, 1966).

to what Radcliffe-Brown called comparative sociology was associated with another major change in emphasis from Frazer's interpretation of primitive religion as primitive philosophy. Among British Academicians, R. R. Marett provides an early example of such a change.

Marett was a philosopher, and an amateur anthropologist, but he did advance an idea which was to become of some interest. He advocated a 'pre-animistic' stage of religion, for which feelings of awe and wonder were primary, rather than the rather intellectual postulation of ghosts or spirits of which Tylor spoke. He thus stressed feeling, sentiment or emotion more than theory as the central core of religion. In this he reflected the much earlier views of Schleiermacher, who in his *Speeches On Religion* of 1799 saw religion as 'a sense and taste for the infinite'. He also built on the insistence of fellow Academician Andrew Lang that at the core of religion there is 'an unanalysable sensus numinis',[13] which is a primal and distinctive religious feeling.

Feeling, in this context, should not be viewed as something purely subjective and without cognitive content. Feeling is a subjective response to something objectively apprehended. For Schleiermacher, Lang and Marett, feelings provide a distinctive mode of access to forms of reality not directly accessible to the senses. They are apprehensions, not just moods. What they apprehend is not some additional object, but a reality which is *sui generis*, sensed in and through knowledge of finite objects. Rudolf Otto called it the sense of the 'numinous', of a 'wholly other' which is both uncanny and intoxicating, the *mysterium tremendum et fascinans*.[14] Otto held that this is the core of all religion, and in this he followed Marett and Lang, though that fact is not often recognised. Religion is not primarily a matter of speculation and inference. It is a matter of a distinctive mode of apprehension, a sense of 'holy power', which is pre-moral and pre-rational, though it may later be moralised and rationalised.

Religion is much more a matter of passion and emotion, of commitment to ways of encountering experience and maintaining important values. It has not the objective, dispassionate approach of science, but the engaged, passionate defence of crucial experiences and evaluations.

The student of religion may wish to remain agnostic about whether any such feelings put one in touch with an objective supernatural reality, but the claim that they do is widespread in religions. Ranging from a sense of the presence of God, to possession by spirits, and the experience of liberation

---

[13] Andrew Lang, *The Making of Religion* (London, 1898).
[14] Rudolf Otto, *The Idea of the Holy*, trans. John Harvey (Oxford, 1923).

from the wheel of suffering, claims to experience in a distinctive way a being or state of superhuman, and perhaps of ultimate, value are central to most religious traditions. Such claims may be those of rare individuals, called shamans, mystics or prophets, but ordinary believers usually desire, and often partly share, such forms of experience. A study of the forms of religious experience, experience of the supernatural, is an important part of the study of religion.

Such a study is one form of what is sometimes called the 'phenomenology of religion'. Influenced by the work of the philosopher Edmund Husserl (1859–1938), the term 'phenomenology' carries with it a great deal of theoretical freight. It has been used in at least three rather different senses. In one sense it asks only for an accurate, value-neutral description of observable religious phenomena, an account of religious beliefs and practices which sets aside ('brackets') questions of truth and falsity, and works to no theological or ideological agenda. It is the attempt to describe phenomena 'as they appear', without any presuppositions, and without any framework of already existing theoretical beliefs.

In a second sense, more dependent on the philosophy of Husserl, it is an attempt to arrive at an understanding of the 'essence' of the phenomena being described. By 'eidetic intuition', one might discern the essential and universal forms which underlie all the contingencies of historical phenomena. One classifies and relates phenomena in 'ideal types', recording the essence of appearances, though without making any judgment as to their ultimate truth or falsity. Gerardus Van Der Leeuw introduced this approach in his *Phenomenology of Religion* (published in English as *Religion in Essence and Manifestation*, London, 1933), and held that the key phenomenological ideas around which religions are based are the ideas of 'Power, Will and Form', which define the Object of religious faith. The basic religious experience, for Van Der Leeuw, is that of a strange, 'Wholly Other' Power, which obtrudes into life and is met with astonishment and awe.

A third, related but different sense stresses the element of empathy (*Einfühlung*), even self-surrendering love that is needed to attend to the religious experiences of others, as they appear to them. One seeks to enter into the experiences of others and live them from the inside, as it were. This requires an appreciation for religious feeling, and a participative understanding of the lives of others, and results in an engaged, particularised, relation to other cultures and persons which is far removed from any neutral or value-free enquiry.

These three senses of phenomenology overlap and are often blended, so that it can be unclear whether the researcher is attending only to appearances, searching for essences, or seeking to have deeply empathetic experiences. In Husserl's case, it would seem that he wanted all three, but it is not hard to see that deep tensions may exist between them.

What must immediately strike one about Van Der Leeuw's account, as with the similar account of Rudolf Otto, is how very prescriptive it is. He may be aiming at pure objectivity, but he does not hesitate to say that 'all religion is the religion of deliverance', that its fundamental aim is 'power for living', and that it is rooted in a particular type of experience of the 'Wholly Other'.

The phenomenological method is quite different from that of the speculative anthropologist, though similar to that of the interpretative anthropologist, in seeking empathy with religious experience, in seeking to describe it as the experiencer would, and in refusing to give 'scientific' explanations for how religious beliefs occur. But is it just coincidence that both Otto's and Van Der Leeuw's accounts end up sounding very like a liberal form of Christianity, which centres on a life-giving encounter with a Wholly Other numinous object?

It could be that Van Der Leeuw is correct in uncovering an essence to religion, by empathetic description of its appearances in consciousness. On the other hand, it might well be thought that simply describing appearances cannot possibly lead to a detection of essences, because such detection must drive beneath the appearances to some level at which they are united or categorised theoretically. Theoretical classification undermines the attempt simply to describe what appears without any presuppositions. Perhaps 'pure description' is impossible. If we classify certain phenomena as 'religious' in our terms, we may well be importing general categories of description which are alien to religious traditions themselves.

The phenomenologist tries not to make judgments on the truth or falsity of what is being investigated. The crucial question is whether the phenomena of religion can be understood neutrally, or whether classifications of them will not already imply some standpoint relevant to their truth or falsity. It is very difficult to describe the significance religious phenomena have for believers without making some evaluation of that significance. The very act of categorisation may already express evaluations. If one compares Frazer's way of listing the phenomena, the various forms and categories of religion, with Van Der Leeuw's way, they look very different. Frazer is clear that these are all primitive mistakes and delusions. Van Der Leeuw sees them as ways of pointing to 'the Infinite', even eventually to a fulfilment in Christian revelation. Can these ways of seeing be abstracted from pure description, or do all illuminating descriptions have to incorporate evaluations, judgments, and a way of seeing, however sensitively expressed?

Just as it is difficult to separate evaluation from pure description, so it is difficult to attempt a study of religious experiences without some element of personal involvement and reaction. When Freud treated the subject of religion, he assumed that it arose from unresolved psychological tensions which had built up in early childhood, and expressed obsessional neurosis or wish-fulfilment. Jung had a much more positive attitude to personal religious experiences, linking them to attempts to face up to repressed aspects of personality and achieve integration and balance. Neither of these founding figures of schools of psychoanalysis gives a value-neutral account of religious experiences. They explicitly give recommendations about how one is to deal with such experiences, and about which, if any, of them are to be encouraged. Both discourage the view that experience gives apprehension of objectively existing supernatural realities, limiting their enquiries to events, conscious or unconscious, in the human mind. To accept their diagnoses is probably to change one's view of religion, and is almost certainly incompatible with adherence to any orthodox religious tradition.

There have been attempts to list religious experiences without this sort of value-imbued analysis and comment. The best known is probably that of William James, whose *The Varieties of Religious Experience* (New York, 1902), remains a classic in the field. He, too, however, distinguishes between healthy and unhealthy religious states, and proposes a thesis about what sort of reality religious experiences put one in contact with. James isolated a particularly important class of experience which is called 'mystical', having the properties of being ineffable, noetic, transient and passive. He held that mystical experiences give direct knowledge of a supernatural reality, that they form a sort of 'common core' in all the world's religious traditions, that they are the real foundation of religious belief, but that they can be interpreted in various ways, depending on the belief-systems of the cultures in which they occur.

R. C. Zaehner's *Mysticism Sacred and Profane* (Oxford, 1957), on the other hand, argued that there is not one common sort of mystical experience. He identified three different types of mysticism—'panenhenic' (oneness with nature), 'monistic' (interior unity), and the mysticism of loving union. These are not reducible to some common type, and Zaehner argued that the third, Christian, type of experience is the highest type of experience. Zaehner was the second holder of the Chair in Eastern Religions and Ethics, which H. N Spalding had initially endowed at Oxford in 1936. The first incumbent of the Chair, Sarvepalli Radhakrishnan, had upheld a 'common core' doctrine of religious experience, though he saw the non-dualism of Sankara as the most adequate exposition of the view. Zaehner, however, wished to reject the idea of one common core altogether.

More recently, Steven Katz has argued,[15] even more radically, that mystical experiences are much more diverse and very different from one another in character because presupposed beliefs and dogmas dictate the sorts of experience believers will have. So experiences cannot be the source of religious beliefs at all.

Disputes about the character and importance of religious experience continue, but Zaehner's was one of the last attempts to frame a general theory of religion from a study of experience. One major problem of a psychological approach is that it is extremely difficult to get reliable reports of inner experiences. Religious phenomena are just too varied for there to be one core religious feeling shared by all of them. How can we even know what inner feelings people are having, or how can we compare one private feeling with another? Even if one does so, it is unclear what can be done with them apart from listing correlations between sorts of experience and brain or behavioural activity.

Those who have been influenced by behaviourism, or by the philosophy of Wittgenstein, tend to be sceptical of any reports of inner experience, and to regard them as parasitic upon the existence of prior beliefs which derive either from theory or from public experience. At one time there may have been a hope that one could categorise sorts of inner religious experience, but such investigations have usually proved disappointing.

It is as though one attempted to analyse, not music, but the inner experiences of listening to music. So, in religion, one might analyse various structures of belief or ritual practices. But to try to dissect the experiences of participants is to enter a world of undefined subjectivity, not capable of exact categorisation except in the most general terms (as 'unitive' or 'numinous', for example).

Perhaps the mistake is to think that one can give a quasi-scientific description of inner experiences. Yet the capacity to have such experiences may be an important part of learning to appreciate, to have participant knowledge of, religious beliefs and practices. Whereas the naturalistic study of religion requires a certain distancing from religious belief, a more empathetic study might presuppose the ability to know what it feels like to have such a belief. Participation in rituals, and engagement in the creative interpretation of beliefs, at least in an imaginative sense, may be a condition for understanding religion. One would expect this to be true, if religion indeed claims to mediate relationship with supernatural reality. Just as it would be absurd to study

---

[15] Steven T. Katz, 'Language, Epistemology, and Mysticism', in id. (ed.), *Mysticism and Philosophical Analysis* (New York, 1978).

music without some attempt to increase appreciation of music and to develop the skills of musicianship, so it might be absurd to study religion without some attempt to increase appreciation of prayer, meditation and worship, and to develop the skills needed to interpret religious texts and to understand one's life from a religious viewpoint. The difficulty is that such a programme would fall outside a strictly scientific programme in experimental psychology.

Social theories of religion

A similar dilemma exists for the anthropologists' method of participant-observation. For how can one be a participant and a critical theorist at the same time? Is the most one can hope for a 'pretending to participate', or an acting-as-if one were participating? One may not be able to observe or share, or know whether one was sharing, inner feelings and experiences. One may not wish to do so—would one really wish to share the feelings of an Aztec priest, sacrificing children on the altar? What anthropologists can do, however, is to observe the behaviour in which feelings are expressed. In that sense, while not really being a participant, the anthropologist of religion can closely observe and record the behaviour of the religious. And that might be a better way of understanding religion than a Frazerian attempt to reconstruct the thought processes of primitive men. So the focus of interest to a great extent shifted to the study of ritual and religious behaviour.

Already in phenomenology there was a move from considering inner experience in its inherent quality towards considering its function in empowering human lives. Since questions of truth were systematically set aside, the most natural question became, 'Is this experience healthy or pathological? Is it good for the experiencer or not?' So, when the focus moved to behaviour, the primary interest was not on questions of truth—which does not seem an appropriate property of actions—but on questions of function or efficacy. Behavioural or social theories of religion tend to be functionalist theories, which interpret religious behaviour in terms of its role in social life.

To Emile Durkheim must go the honour of establishing the first truly social theory of religion. For Durkheim, the function of religion is to create and sustain a strong sense of tribal unity, by focusing devotion on a sacred power, which is in fact the group mind itself. Society is the higher power to which individuals must subordinate their desires, and society is figured under the symbols of totems, spirits or gods.

Whereas for Frazer religion was false and obsolete, for Durkheim, religion is necessary for society, and Durkheim insists that he maintains the essential truth of religion. Yet the truth he sees is not the truth any believer sees, and most believers would be, and are, appalled at the thought that the object of their worship is society itself, however symbolically expressed. In general, the many French attempts to invent a new, more rational, religion have all foundered on the unfortunate fact that once people see a religion is being invented for its utility alone, they can no longer think it to be true, and so it is no longer useful. Durkheimian accounts of religion are self-undermining, since religion can only be useful if it is believed to be true.

It is noteworthy that Durkheim's is one of the few definitions of religion which does not mention belief in spiritual beings or in supernatural powers at all. He describes religion as 'a unified system of beliefs and practices relative to sacred things, things set apart and forbidden, which unite into one single moral community all those who believe in them'.[16] His lack of reference to the supernatural is no doubt due to the fact that he thought what underlay such setting apart was not at all supernatural, though it was super-individual. He thought that things were set apart because they were felt to contain or transmit a sort of sacred power, energy or force which was both dangerous and inspiring, and which was focused in particular things. This power was, in the end, he thought, the power of the social mind, capable of raising individual minds to a higher level, though also of destroying their individuality. He sees analogues to this 'totemic principle' in the *wakan* of the Sioux, or in the *mana* of Melanesia. Thus it is what I have called supernatural, as far as believers in it are concerned. But Durkheim thinks that it does not possess independent supernatural existence.

He does think religion is true, as a social construction which has an essential function in subordinating the individual to the group, and in 'raising the individual to a higher level of life'. But it is not true in the sense of referring to objective entities, spirits or personal beings which exist whether or not human beings exist. A Durkheimian might say that the question of objective reference can be bracketed out, or set on one side, and one would still be able to talk about the function of religion, the role it plays in social life. It seems very odd, however, to ignore almost completely what believers themselves might actually think and say. One does not have to accept the truth of what they say to register the fact that they do think sacred things are those associated with some supernatural reality, whether a god or a more indistinct power like *mana*.

---

[16] Emile Durkheim, *Les Formes élémentaires de la vie religieuse* (Paris, 1912); Eng. trans. J. N. Swain, *The Elementary Forms of the Religious Life* (London, 1963), p. 47.

Durkheim is quite prepared to construe what they say as referring in fact to the power of social pressure. That could be called 'supernatural' in the sense that it is other and greater than any material objects. But it has no objective reality, in the sense that it exists even if human beings do not. Believers do refer to something, according to Durkheim, but it is not, as they think, objective. It is a real, but natural and social (and therefore at best intersubjective), power. But there is a problem about who is in the best position to say what believers are actually referring to. Durkheim may see them as referring to a social reality that enables individuals to rise to a new level of self-sacrificing moral life. But might it possibly be that religion, while indeed having that function, pursues it by trying to relate human lives in helpful ways to the more than either natural or social powers which are believed to bound and circumscribe human existence? If believers came to think that they were really giving their devotion to the 'social mind' of their group, they might well give up their religious beliefs. Awareness of the function Durkheim assigns to religion is usually incompatible with holding religious beliefs. That is the paradox upon which Durkheim is impaled when he holds religion to be both necessary and socially constructed.

Of course one can think of a belief as socially constructed, yet as also intended to have an objective reference. The ideas of science are precisely like that. Such social constructions, however, must be believed to have real objective reference. In the case of religion, there is no way of independently verifying the existence of the object of belief. Religious belief is condemned always to be contested, and anthropologists and sociologists must be content to record that fact. If they go further, and attempt to explain how and why religious beliefs and practices arise in purely naturalistic terms, they are in danger of destroying the very beliefs they are trying to explain.

Reasons and religious belief

Explanation deals with causes, and with general causal laws, whereas the justification of belief appeals to reasons and validating evidence. These are quite different logical categories, and there are few who have the confidence, or temerity, to say that one can be satisfactorily reduced to the other. In the case of religious beliefs, some may hold that there are no good reasons for holding such beliefs, and no validating evidence to support them. If that is the case, then it may be appropriate to seek causal explanations for why such non-rational beliefs occur. But even those who believe that religion is irrational have to concede that there are many apparently intelligent people who find it reasonable, at least in some of its forms. As a matter of fact in the history of philosophy the vast majority of the best-known 'classical' philosophers have accepted the existence of God as the very foundation of a rational view of the world. It is precisely the philosophers often known as 'Rationalists' who are the most active in setting out reasons for believing in God.

It is simply not obvious to every rational person that religion is unreasonable. If that is so, then there is an important place for examining the sorts of reasons religious believers have for their beliefs, and it is arrogant and demeaning to assume that their beliefs are so odd that they require causal explanations, probably in terms of some malfunctioning of cognitive faculties. Even a Durkheimian explanation in terms of social function and utility methodologically ignores the sorts of reasons believers give. While believers may be pleased if their views help social cohesion and give urgency and absoluteness to morality, they will not be pleased if informed that these are the reasons why they believe what they do. If morality is thought to be absolute, it will not be out of any sense of social unity—few things are more productive of social conflict than adherence to an absolute morality.

The sorts of explanations that have been given for religious belief range from a Frazerian view that religious beliefs are false hypotheses for explaining why events happen as they do, to a Durkheimian view that religions are means of assuring social harmony, or, in a Marxian version, of oppressing or consoling the weak and reinforcing or justifying the principles of the strong. Or religious beliefs could be the result of obsessional neuroses, or compensations for a failure to obtain fame or money by other socially available routes. Very few such putative explanations are friendly to religious belief, for the simple reason that if religious belief were accounted for by someone's apprehension of a god or spiritual reality, there would be little need for further explanation.

It would always be of interest to explore any psychological correlations that may exist between religious beliefs and personality types, or between particular beliefs and particular social systems or socio-economic positions in such systems. But one would not expect such correlations to provide an adequate explanation of the origin and maintenance of religious beliefs. By far the best explanation of the growth of a belief would be that it evokes and sustains genuine apprehensions of a reality which is either irresistible in its appeal or overwhelming in its power.

At that point, however, one moves beyond the social sciences, even beyond the psychological study of the conscious states which might be involved in such experiences, to an investigation of the claims to spiritual apprehension which are made, their coherence and plausibility. One moves to the study of rationality and truth, and this is the area of philosophy and theology.

Philosophy will attempt to investigate religious claims as fully and yet as critically as possible, raising all possible objections, assessing various arguments as dispassionately as possible, and perhaps proposing a 'best theory', in awareness that it will not be universally agreed. Philosophy will not, as a discipline, be committed to any position in advance, even though individual philosophers will inevitably begin with a set of beliefs, which may or may not change as they pursue their studies. It will not accept a set of revealed truths as given, and so will be free to consider many claims to revelation among its other objects of study.

Theology has often been construed as a confessional discipline, which is committed to one religious position. It is clearly possible, however, to have a comparative theology (and this is where the study of religions began) which takes as its data, so far as is possible, the whole religious history of humanity. Ecumenical Christian theology already exists, which supports the exploration of Christian faith from many perspectives. Why, then, should a fully ecumenical, global theology not exist, which supports the exploration of faith from the whole range of human religious perspectives? Admittedly there are some religious traditions, like Buddhism or Jainism, which do not have theologies, insofar as they have little interest in God. Yet if one takes *theos* in a broad sense, to denote a supremely valuable state, process or being, then the rational investigation of the nature and possibility of such a state is certainly part of the Buddhist and Jain traditions. Nevertheless, some might prefer the term 'comparative religion', despite its unfashionableness, precisely because it circumvents this slight awkwardness. Whatever the preferred title, Mircea Eliade, who was at Chicago from 1956 till 1986, who inaugurated the *History of Religions Journal* in 1961, and who edited the magisterial *Encyclopedia of Religion*, was perhaps the best-known exponent of such an approach to the study of religions.

The distinction between comparative philosophy of religion and comparative theology of religion can be vanishingly small, and may consist largely in the fact that theology is more concerned with history, with religious organisation and ritual, and with religious practice than philosophy tends to be. In addition, comparative theology may suggest a sympathy with and appreciation for the religious aspirations and experiences of humanity, which is not necessary to a rigorously analytical philosophical approach. Such appreciation need not, however, be confined to one religious tradition. There is no reason why, as a discipline, theology should not concern itself with beliefs about the supernatural from wherever they arise, paying special attention to the rationality, coherence and plausibility of those beliefs. Indeed, in the late nineteenth and early twentieth centuries a number of British philosophers, like founding Academician Edward Caird, took religion in a broad sense to be central to the construction of an Idealist philosophy.[17] Though that school of thought seems to have passed away, it remains true that a generally philosophical and comparative theology is an important part of the study of religions, complementing the aspects of phenomenology and social studies, and of historical and literary analysis, which are also involved.

The problem of religious diversity

The study of religions does not have to be comparative, but where it is, there is a tendency to speak of traditions, not as just embodying 'true' or 'false' claims, but as systems of symbols for a rather generally conceived idea of 'the Transcendent'. This is because one might not wish to regard all religious experience as illusory, which would imply that a great number of the most devout, morally committed and reflective humans (as well as many charlatans) were grossly deluded. Nevertheless, the incompatibilities between their particular accounts of the object or objects they experience are so great that they cannot all be literally true. If one does not make an exception of one tradition, the most obvious hypothesis is that their specific accounts are imaginative symbols which take their form from local cultures, though there is some underlying reality to which they point which is a genuinely objective reality. This will obviously have to be very vaguely conceived, if it is to underlie all specific forms.

It is at this stage that some would doubt whether one can find any such underlying reality at all. John Hick finds it in what he calls 'the Real', of which, he says, we know nothing at all.[18] But if that is true, then we do not even know that it is real, or one Real, or good or bad, or the cause of all things or not. But any attempt to be less vague seems to leave one with something that not all religious believers would agree about. Suppose, for instance, one talks of 'One Supremely Valuable Absolute Reality'. That would be widely agreed, but many Buddhists would protest that it is exactly such a thing that they reject when they say that all things are empty of inherent existence. Even they might agree to speak of one supremely valuable state of consciousness,

---

[17] See Edward Caird, *The Evolution of Religion* (Oxford, 1902).
[18] John Hick, *An Interpretation of Religion* (London, 1989), ch. 14, section 4.

which it is the object of meditation to attain. But it is not a cause, and not a substantial Being like a personal God. One could say that they really are in contact with an absolute reality, though they do not recognise it as such. But then one is saying that they are mistaken in their description of the object of their belief. They may in fact point to the reality of the Absolute, but they do not think they do or mean to do so. Then one is privileging some account of the religious object, saying that some traditions have a more correct account than others.

It looks as if the most one can say is that religious narratives are concerned with superhuman (more valuable or powerful than human) beings or states, but they really do have differing ideas of such states or beings. They cannot all be correct. They cannot even all be more or less equally roughly correct. Some must be wrong, even if none is absolutely right. As a matter of fact, it might be more accurate to say that religious positions spread out to fill every possible space in the array of modes of relationship between the Transcendent and the physical cosmos, than that they all agree.

Nevertheless there is a general descriptive core which fits many ideas of the Transcendent. In many traditions there is said to be a supreme reality that embodies perfection, and that perfection includes such characteristics as wisdom, freedom, compassion and bliss. Virtually all theistic faiths, and the renouncing traditions of Buddhism and Jainism, would affirm that there is such a reality, whether it is God or the state of finally liberated souls. The goal of the religious life is accessing that reality, and in general the goal is to be achieved by overcoming egoism, hatred, greed and ignorance.

One does not have to go as far as John Hick in denying all knowledge of the Real *an sich*, but it seems reasonable to assent to his 'pluralistic hypothesis' that 'the great post-axial faiths constitute different ways of experiencing, conceiving and living in relation to an ultimate divine Reality, which transcends all our varied visions of it'.[19] This does not commit one to saying that all these ways are of equal truth or efficacy. Nor does it commit one to saying that just one of them has all-important truths adequately formulated. It is quite possible to say that in many religious ways people are justified in believing what they do on the basis of their experience and of the plausibility of the tradition as they see it. Presumably some set of propositions expressing religious truths is the most adequate, but we may not know what it is, or even have formulated it yet. Since religious traditions live mainly by images and metaphors which spring from the originative experiences and teachings of major religious figures, the question of theoretical truth may be less important

---

[19] Hick, *An Interpretation of Religion*, pp. 235–6.

in practice than the personal efficacy of the images in leading one from ego-ism towards union with the Reality of compassion and bliss. So one may con-sistently be committed to one tradition of images as efficacious and illuminating, while allowing that other traditions may be so for other people, and that it is not known for certain which set of truths, if any of those known to us, is most adequate.

The study of religions

One way in which the study of religions can proceed is to seek to deepen and extend the religious imagination by practical encounters with a range of reli-gious traditions, their devotional practices and ways of seeing the world. This is participative understanding, and requires a more personal involvement than the less engaged 'participant observation' of many anthropologists. It requires an initial sympathy for religion, a capacity for religious feeling, and a deter-mination to extend one's experience beyond the boundaries of one's own tradition.

I believe this to be an important part of the study of religions, but it can-not be required of those who see religion as some sort of social construct or even as a symptom of psychological dislocation. It cannot be a precondition of the careful study of ancient texts, or of formulated beliefs, or of the history of religious institutions. Like religion itself, the study of religions needs to be a multi-disciplinary study. What has been peculiar about it is that it has partly been the province of scholars who dislike and oppose religion, who regard it as an aberration to be reductively understood so as to denude it of appeal. It is also, however, the province of those who share a religious sensibility, whether this takes the form of commitment to one revealed tradition, or of a more general appreciation of many cultural, symbolic and conceptual forms. And it is the province of those who are simply fascinated by a widespread and often exotic part of human cultural history. This means that religious studies will always be diverse both in its methods of scholarship and in the goals and objectives of its exponents. Its coherence lies in the fact that it is the explo-ration of human beliefs and practices in relation to Transcendence. As such, it offers an almost unique scope for inter-disciplinary work focused on one area of human life in all its diverse aspects. And it offers an understanding of the fascinatingly diverse attempts of humans to formulate a view of their place in the cosmos, their destiny within it, and the ways to achieve a goal which would be a wholly worthwhile object of human endeavour.

Index